Renaissance &
Reformation
Almanac

Renaissance & Reformation Almanac

Volume 1

PEGGY SAARI &
AARON SAARI, EDITORS

Julie Carnagie, Project Editor

U·X·L

A part of Gale, Cengage Learning

GALE
CENGAGE Learning·

Detroit • New York • San Francisco • New Haven, Conn • Waterville, Maine • London

GALE
CENGAGE Learning

Renaissance and Reformation: Almanac

Peggy Saari and Aaron Saari

Project Editor
Julie L. Carnagie

Permissions
Kimberly Davis

Imaging and Multimedia
Robert Duncan, Kelly A. Quin

Product Design
Pamela A. Galbreath

Composition
Evi Seoud

Manufacturing
Rita Wimberly

REF
940.2
REN
V.1

11/13

LIBRARY OF CONGRESS CATALOGING-IN-PUBLICATION DATA

Saari, Peggy.
    Renaissance and Reformation. Almanac / Peggy Saari and Aaron Saari ; Julie L. Carnagie, editor.
        p. cm.
    Includes bibliographical references and index.
        ISBN 0-7876-5467-1 (set hardcover : alk. paper)
    1. Renaissance–Juvenile literature. 2. Reformation–Juvenile literature. I. Saari, Aaron Maurice. II. Carnagie, Julie. III. Title.
    CB359 .S23 2002
    940.2'1–dc21
                                                    2002006152

Vol. 1. 0-7876-5468-X; Vol. 2. 0-7876-5469-8; Set 0-7876-5467-1

Printed in Mexico
3 4 5 6 7 8 15 14 13 12 11

Contents

Volume 1

Volume 2

Reader's Guide

Renaissance and Reformation: Almanac provides a wide range of historical information on the period in European history between the mid-1300s and the early 1600s. The two-volume set explores both the Italian and Northern Renaissance as well as the Protestant and Catholic Reformations. Arranged in fourteen subject chapters, *Renaissance and Reformation: Almanac* includes topics such as the rise of European monarchies, Martin Luther and his role in the Protestant Reformation, Italian and Northern Renaissance culture, science during the Renaissance, education and training, women in Renaissance society, and daily life.

Additional Features

Renaissance and Reformation: Almanac includes numerous sidebars, some focusing on people associated with the Renaissance and Reformation era, others taking a closer look at pivotal events. More than one hundred black-and-white illustrations enliven the text, while cross-references are made to people or events discussed in other chapters. Both volumes contain a timeline, a glossary, research and activity ideas, a bibliography, and a cumulative index providing access to the subjects discussed in *Renaissance and Reformation: Almanac*.

Comments and suggestions

We welcome your comments on this work as well as your suggestions for topics to be featured in future editions of *Renaissance and Reformation: Almanac*. Please write: Editors, *Renaissance and Reformation: Almanac*, U•X•L, 27500 Drake Rd., Farmington Hills, MI 48331-3535; call toll-free: 1-800-877-4253; fax: 248-699-8097; or send e-mail via www.gale.com.

Introduction

Renaissance and Reformation: Almanac presents an overview of the most significant revolution in Western history. Beginning with the Italian Renaissance in the mid-1300s and lasting until the end of the Protestant and Catholic Reformations in the early 1600s, this revolution essentially turned the European world upside down. By the close of the seventeenth century, unprecedented changes had taken place in politics, religion, science, economics, education, the arts, and society throughout Europe. Scholars and teachers are still intrigued by this historical period, but the twenty-first century student might wonder, "Why should I want to read about the Renaissance and Reformation? How could anything that happened hundreds of years ago possibly be relevant to my life?" The answer to the first question is that it was a fascinating time, filled with dramatic events, interesting people, and great achievements. The answer to the second question is that we can understand more about the world today by studying this era, which historians consider the beginning of the modern age.

The Renaissance produced many innovations that are now ordinary facts of modern life. Among them was the printing press, which facilitated mass communication and became the first step in advanced information technology. Of even greater importance was the scientific revolution led by astronomers who used the newly perfected telescope to make observations of celestial bodies. Their discoveries paved the way for present-day knowledge about the universe. Renaissance scientists pioneered modern medicine, introducing chemical-based drugs and acquiring new knowledge about human anatomy. Navigators and explorers led the way for European settlement of the Americas, expanding the borders of the Western world to the other side of the globe. The Renaissance brought the rise of the middle class and the emergence of feminist thinking, which became hallmarks of Western society. Economic innovations included capitalism and global banking, which are now the basis of the world economy. The Protestant Reformation led to the founding of the Protestant faiths that still exist today, and the Catholic Reformation established Catholic Church policies that remained in place for more than four hundred years. Finally, the human-centered view of the world promoted by Italian humanists established individualism and secularism as dominant themes in modern Western culture.

The Renaissance and Reformation also set in motion political and social tensions that had a profound impact during the modern era. European settlement of the Americas ultimately resulted in the destruction of native cultures. The first worldwide war took place in Europe in the seventeenth century, setting the stage for conflicts that involved all the major world powers in the twentieth century. Anti-Semitism steadily increased, as did the expansion of the African slave trade: two developments that had tragic consequences in the nineteenth and twentieth centuries. And throughout the three hundred years of the Renaissance and Reformation period, Europeans in the West and Muslims in the East became increasingly bitter enemies. The result was a widening gap between East and West that has continued into the present day.

Renaissance and Reformation: Almanac traces all of these developments, and more, with the goal of establishing a direct link between our twenty-first century world and the not-so-distant past.

Timeline of Events

c. 300 Jews arrive in Spain.

395 The Roman Empire is split into the West Roman Empire and the East Roman (Byzantine) Empire.

711 Moors invade Spain.

late 700s–c. 1000 Feudalism is established in Europe.

800 Emperor Charlemagne claims to revive ancient Roman Empire.

1076 Pope Gregory VII excommunicates Holy Roman Emperor Henry IV.

1096 Christians launch the Crusades against the Muslims.

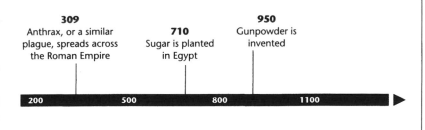

309
Anthrax, or a similar plague, spreads across the Roman Empire

710
Sugar is planted in Egypt

950
Gunpowder is invented

200   500   800   1100

1233 Pope Gregory IX establishes the medieval Inquisition.

1291 The Crusades end when the Muslims defeat the Christians.

1300 Pope Boniface issues *Unam Sanctam,* declaring all people to be subjects of the pope.

1305 The Papacy is moved to Avignon, France, beginning the Babylonian Captivity.

1327 Italian poet Petrarch begins writing *Canzoniere,* a series of love lyrics in which he departs from the medieval convention of seeing a woman as a spiritual symbol and depicts Laura as a real person.

1337 France and England begin the Hundred Years' War over control of the French throne.

1347–50 The Black Death, or bubonic plague, sweeps Europe.

1376 The Babylonian Captivity ends with the return of the papacy to Rome.

1378 The Great Schism in the Roman Catholic Church begins with the election of Pope Urban VI.

1396 Greek scholar Manuel Chrysoloras comes to Florence, Italy, to teach Greek.

1402 Mongol warrior Timur Lenk (Tamerlane) conquers the Ottoman Empire.

1414 The Council of Constance is convened to discuss problems within the Roman Catholic Church.

1415 Czechoslovakian priest Jan Hus is executed by the Council of Constance because of his criticism of the Catholic Church.

c. 1417 Italian architect Filippo Brunelleschi invents linear perspective, a system derived from mathematics in

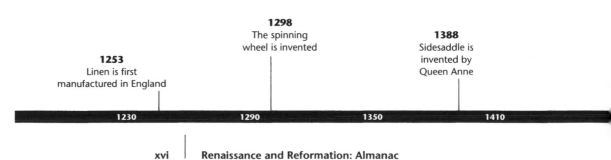

1253
Linen is first
manufactured in England

1298
The spinning
wheel is invented

1388
Sidesaddle is
invented by
Queen Anne

1230   1290   1350   1410

which all elements of a composition are measured and arranged from a single point of view, or perspective.

1418   The Council of Constance ends the Great Schism.

1420   Florentine artist Massaccio is the first to use linear perspective in painting.

1420   Filippo Brunelleschi begins work on the dome of the Florence Cathedral.

1421   Sultan Mehmed II restores the Ottoman Empire.

1423   Italian educator Vittorino da Feltre establishes a humanist school.

1440   Italian scholar Lorenzo Valla questions the legitimacy of the pope.

1450   Francesco I Sforza starts an eighty-year dynasty in Milan.

1451   Italian scholar Isotta Nogarola writes "On the Equal and Unequal Sin of Eve and Adam," which is considered the first piece of feminist writing.

1453   Constantinople falls to the Ottoman Turks.

1454   German printer Johannes Gutenberg perfects movable type.

1455   The houses of York and Lancaster begin the War of the Roses in England.

1458   Margaret of Navarre's *Heptaméron* is published and becomes an important work of the Renaissance period.

1461   Wanting to be separate from the continents of Asia and Africa, and thus the Muslims, Pope Pius II introduces the idea of Europe as separate continent.

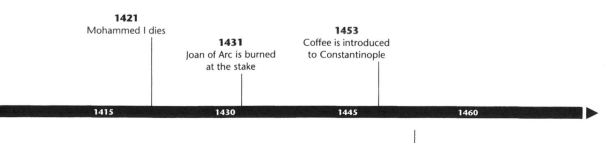

1421
Mohammed I dies

1431
Joan of Arc is burned at the stake

1453
Coffee is introduced to Constantinople

1415   1430   1445   1460

1469 Italian merchant Lorenzo de' Medici takes control of Florence and becomes famous for his contributions to countless artists.

1474 Catholic monarchs Ferdinand II and Isabella I begin the Spanish Inquisition to enforce Christianity as the sole religion of Spain.

1485 The War of Roses ends and the Tudor dynasty begins in England

1490s German artist Albrecht Dürer raises woodcut to the level of high art.

1492 Ferdinand II and Isabella I issue the Edict of Expulsion, ordering all Jews to leave Spain.

1492 Italian navigator Christopher Columbus makes his first voyage to the New World.

1494 Pope Alexander VI issues the Treaty of Tordesillas that gives Portugal authority over Brazil.

1494 Italian preacher Girolamo Savonarola influences a new pro-French government in Florence.

1494 King Charles VIII of France invades Italy, initiating the Italian Wars with Spain.

1495 Italian painter Leonardo da Vinci begins *The Last Supper,* in which he experimented with oil-based paint, which is more easily blended.

1495 Alexander VI organizes the Holy League, an alliance between the Papal States, the Holy Roman Empire, Spain, Venice, and Milan against France.

1497 Italian navigator John Cabot begins his search for the Northwest Passage, a water route to the Indies.

1457
Donatello moves
to Florence

1467
Turkish forces
enter
Herzegovina

1475
World's first coffee
house opens

1455   1465   1475   1485

1498 Girolamo Savonarola is executed for heresy, or the violation of church laws.

1498 Italian sculptor Michelangelo starts the *Pietà,* his first important commission.

1498 Albrecht Dürer introduces humanism, a human-centered intellectual movement based on the revival of classical culture, into northern European art.

c. 1500 The *Querelle des femmes* movement begins. It refers to the literary debate over the nature and status of women.

c. 1500 Germany replaces Italy as the center of European banking.

1503 Leonardo begins work on the *Mona Lisa,* one of the most famous portraits in the Western world.

1511 Italian artist Raphael paints *School of Athens,* considered to be one of his greatest achievements.

1512 Michelangelo completes the decoration of the Sistine Chapel ceiling at the Vatican in Rome.

1513 Italian diplomat Niccolò Machiavelli writes *The Prince,* in which he proclaimed his controversial political philosophy.

1516 Dutch humanist Desiderius Erasmus publishes *Praise of Folly,* a satire of the Roman Catholic Church and its clergy. That same year Erasmus published his translation of the New Testament of the Bible, the first published Greek text.

1516 English humanist Thomas More publishes his greatest work *Utopia.* Modeled on Plato's *Republic, Utopia* describes an imaginary land that is free of grand displays of wealth, greed, and violence.

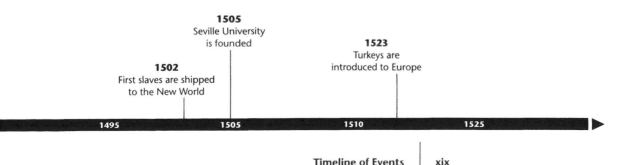

1505
Seville University
is founded

1523
Turkeys are
introduced to Europe

1502
First slaves are shipped
to the New World

1495   1505   1510   1525

1517 German priest Martin Luther posts his *Ninety-Five Theses,* initiating the Protestant Reformation.

1519 King Charles I of Spain is elected Holy Roman Emperor Charles V, leading to the spread of the Spanish empire east from Spain to include the kingdoms of Germany, Hungary, Bohemia, Naples, and Sicily. The empire also extends south and west to include possessions in North Africa and the Americas.

1520 King Francis I of France and King Henry VIII of England meet at the Field of the Cloth of Gold in order to form an alliance against Holy Roman Emperor Charles V.

1520s Swiss-born physician Theophrastus Paracelsus pioneers the use of chemicals to treat disease.

1520 Paris *collèges* adopt classical Latin and Greek studies.

1521 At the Diet of Worms, Charles V declares Martin Luther an "outlaw of the church."

1521 The Ottoman Empire begins to reach it height when the sultan Süleyman I defeats Hungary in the Battle of Mohács.

1523 Swiss priest Huldrych Zwingli issues "Sixty-Seven Articles," or proposed reforms, which become the basis for the Reformation in Switzerland.

1524–26 The German Peasants' Revolt challenges the rule of Catholic noblemen.

1525 French king Francis I is captured by the Spanish at the Battle of Pavia.

1526 The Diet of Speyer permits German princes to determine which religion is practiced in their regions.

1527 Armies of Holy Roman Emperor Charles V sack Rome.

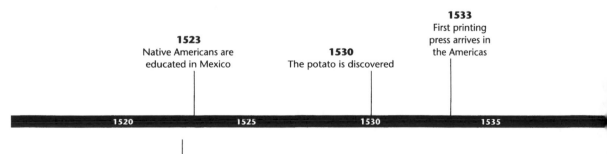

1523
Native Americans are educated in Mexico

1530
The potato is discovered

1533
First printing press arrives in the Americas

| 1520 | 1525 | 1530 | 1535 |

1527 King Gustav I Vasa begins establishing Lutheranism in Sweden.

1528 French diplomat Baldassare Castiglione publishes *Book of the Courtier.* The book is an immediate success, and quickly becomes a guide to etiquette for both the bourgeoisie and the aristocracy in Europe.

1534 King Henry VIII is declared supreme head of the Church of England, completing the break between England and the Roman Catholic Church.

1534 French author François Rabelais begins publishing his most popular work, *Gargantua and Pantagruel.*

1535 Thomas More is beheaded by Henry VIII after refusing to acknowledge the Act of Supremacy that made Henry supreme head of the Church of England.

1536 French-born Protestant reformer John Calvin writes the first edition of *Institutes of the Christian Religion,* which outlines his beliefs and gains him attention as an important religious leader.

1536 Ottoman sultan Süleyman I forms an alliance with France.

1540 Spanish priest Ignatius of Loyola founds the Society of Jesus (Jesuits). His Jesuit order eventually becomes the single most powerful weapon of the Catholic Reformation.

1543 *On the Revolution of Celestial Spheres* by Polish astronomer Nicolaus Copernicus is published. The book gives important information about the orbits of the planets and begins a revolution in human thought by serving as the cornerstone of modern astronomy.

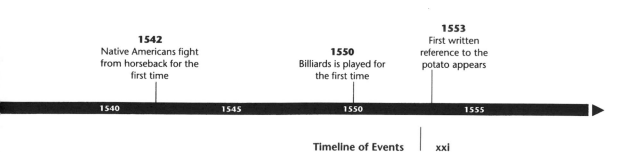

1542
Native Americans fight from horseback for the first time

1550
Billiards is played for the first time

1553
First written reference to the potato appears

1540   1545   1550   1555

1543 Belgian anatomist Andreas Vesalius publishes *On the Fabric of the Human Body,* one of the most important contributions to human anatomy.

1545 Pope Paul III convenes the Council of Trent, a meeting to discuss reforming the Roman Catholic Church from within.

1547 Michelangelo directs construction of the new Saint Peter's Basilica in Rome.

1547 Charles V defeats German Protestant princes at the Battle of Mühlberg. Charles hopes his victory will stop the spread of Protestantism throughout the Holy Roman Empire.

1548 Ignatius of Loyola publishes *Spiritual Exercises.* This short but influential book outlines a thirty-day regimen, or systematic plan, of prayer and acts of self-denial and punishment, with the understanding that devotion to God must be central.

1550s Italian architect Andrea Palladio popularizes the villa.

1550s Italian composer Giovanni Pierluigi da Palestrina creates the oratorio, a lengthy religious choral work that features recitatives, arias, and choruses without action or scenery.

1553 Queen Mary I restores Catholicism in England and begins persecuting Protestants after ascending to the English throne.

1555 John Calvin organizes an evangelical government in Geneva, Switzerland.

1555 French astrologer Nostradamus begins publishing *Centuries,* his best-selling book of predictions.

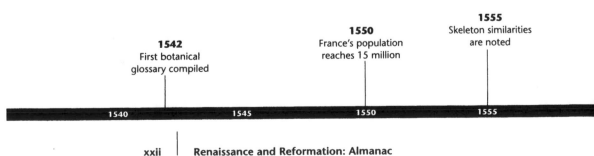

1542
First botanical
glossary compiled

1550
France's population
reaches 15 million

1555
Skeleton similarities
are noted

1540   1545   1550   1555

1555   Italian artist Sofonisba Anguissola paints *The Chess Game*. This painting is meant to demonstrate female excellence at an intellectual game.

1556   Charles V abdicates the throne after building one of the largest empires in history.

1558   Elizabeth I begins her forty-five-year reign as queen of England and Ireland.

1559   The Italian Wars end with the Treaty of Cateau-Cambrésis.

1560   Catherine de Médicis is named regent of France after the death of her husband King Henry II.

1560s King Philip II of Spain begins building the Escorial, an enormous complex of buildings north of Madrid.

1562   The French Wars of Religion begin.

1562   Teresa de Ávila founds the Reformed Discalced Carmelite Order.

1563   The Council of Trent adjourns and issues *Canons and Decrees of the Council of Trent,* a statement that upholds Catholic doctrine, or religious rules, but shows more tolerance of opposition.

1563   German artist Pieter Bruegel paints *Tower of Babel,* one of his most famous works.

1566   Revolt against Spanish rule begins in the Netherlands.

1567   Philip II introduces the Spanish Inquisition in the Netherlands.

1570   Flemish mapmaker Abraham Ortel publishes the first world atlas.

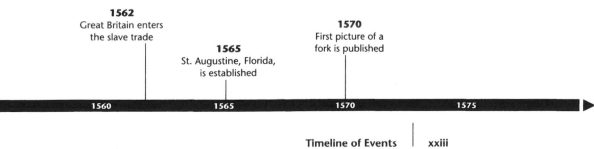

1562
Great Britain enters the slave trade

1565
St. Augustine, Florida, is established

1570
First picture of a fork is published

1560   1565   1570   1575

1571 The European Christian alliance defeats the Ottoman fleet at the Battle of Lepanto, ending Ottoman control of the Mediterranean Sea.

1572 Catholics kill Huguenots in the Saint Bartholomew's Day Massacre in Paris.

1572 Danish astronomer Tycho Brahe introduces the term "nova" for an exploding star.

1580 French author Michel de Montaigne publishes *Essays*. The work created a new literary genre (form), the essay, in which he used self-portrayal as a mirror of humanity in general.

1580–1640 Witchcraft trials reach peak in Europe.

1582 Pope Gregory XIII issues the Gregorian calendar.

1587 Elizabeth I orders the execution of Mary, Queen of Scots after a conspiracy to assassinate Elizabeth is discovered.

1588 Spanish Armada is defeated by the English fleet, marking the high point of Elizabeth's reign.

1592 English playwright William Shakespeare begins his career in London.

1595 The Edict of Nantes grants religious and civil liberties to Huguenots.

1605 Spanish author Miguel de Cervantes publishes the first part of *Don Quixote*, one of the great masterpieces of world literature.

1606 Foremost English playwright Ben Jonson's dramatic genius is fully revealed for the first time in *Volpone, or the Fox*, a satiric comedy that contains the playwright's harshest and most unrelenting criticism of human vice.

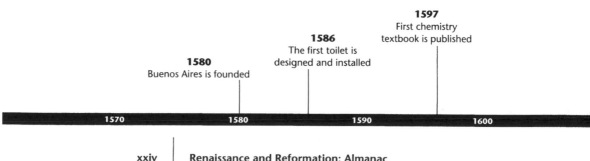

1580
Buenos Aires is founded

1586
The first toilet is designed and installed

1597
First chemistry textbook is published

1570   1580   1590   1600

1607   Italian composer Claudio Monteverdi publishes his first opera, *La favola d'Orfeo.*

1609   English scientist Thomas Harriot makes the first recorded use of the telescope.

1609   German astronomer Johannes Kepler publishes his first two laws of planetary motion.

1609   Philip II begins expelling Moriscos (Jews) from Spain.

1610   Italian astronomer Galileo publishes *The Starry Messenger.*

1611   *The Life of Teresa of Jesus* is published.

1611   King James I of England approves a new English translation of the Bible.

1614   Scottish mathematician John Napier discovers logarithms.

1616   Galileo is ordered to cease promoting new science.

1616   Italian painter Artemisia Gentileschi becomes the first woman to be admitted to the Florentine Academy of Art.

1618   Johannes Kepler publishes his third law of planetary motion.

1618   Thirty Years' War begins; it becomes the first armed conflict involving all major world powers.

1620   English philosopher Francis Bacon publishes *New Method.*

1621   English mathematician William Oughtred makes the first slide rule.

1624   Peter Paul Rubens paints his famous *Self-portrait.*

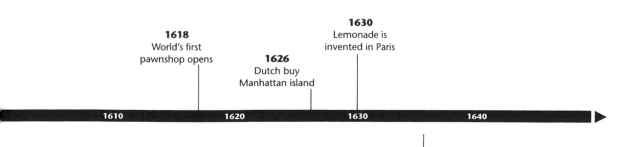

1618
World's first
pawnshop opens

1626
Dutch buy
Manhattan island

1630
Lemonade is
invented in Paris

1610   1620   1630   1640

1628	English anatomist William Harvey announces the discovery of the circulatory system.
1630s	French noblewoman Madame de Rambouillet presides over one of the first salons.
1642	English Civil War begins.
1648	Thirty Years' War ends with the Peace of Westphalia.
1648	English Civil War ends.
1651	Leonardo's *Treatise on Painting* is published.
1666	Margaret Cavendish publishes *The Description of a New World Called the Blazing World,* considered to be one of the first works of science fiction.

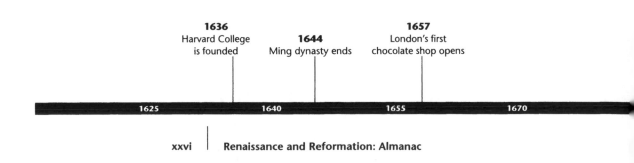

1636
Harvard College
is founded

1644
Ming dynasty ends

1657
London's first
chocolate shop opens

1625   1640   1655   1670

Words to Know

A

Abbey: A church connected with a monastery.

Abbot: A head of a monastery.

Abbess: A head of a convent.

Abdicate: To step down from the throne.

Absolution: Forgiveness of sins pronounced by a priest.

Absolutism: The concentration of all power in the hands of one ruler.

Adultery: Having sexual relations with someone who is not the person's husband or wife.

Agriculture: The growing of crops for food and other products.

Alchemy: The medieval science devoted to changing common metals into gold and silver.

Algebra: A form of arithmetic in which letters represent numbers.

Allegory: A story featuring characters with symbolic significance.

Altarpiece: A work of art that decorates an altar of a church.

Anatomy: The study of the structure of the body.

Annulment: An order that declares a marriage invalid.

Anti-Semitism: Prejudice against Jews.

Apprentice: One who learns a craft, trade, or profession from a master.

Aristocracy: The upper social class.

Armor: A protective suit made of iron worn by a soldier in battle.

Artillery: Various types of weapons.

Astrolabe: A device used to observe and calculate the distance of celestial bodies.

Astrology: The study of the heavens to predict future events.

Astronomy: The study of celestial bodies, such as planets, stars, the Sun, and the Moon.

Atheist: One who does not believe in God.

Augsburg Confession: An official statement of Lutheran churches prepared in 1530.

Auto da fé: Act of faith; public expression of commitment to Christianity required of supposed heretics during the Inquisition.

Autopsy: The dissection and examination of a corpse to determine the cause of death.

Axiom: A statement accepted as being true.

B

Babylonian Captivity: The name given to the period from 1307 to 1376 when the Roman Catholic pope lived in Avignon, France.

Baptism: A Christian ceremony in which a person is blessed with water and admitted to the Christian faith.

Barbarism: A lack of refinement or culture.

Baroque: The term used to describe the music, art, literature, and philosophy of the seventeenth century; exuberant, sensuous, expressive, and dynamic style.

Battle of Lepanto (1571): A sea battle in which the European Christian naval alliance defeated the fleet of the Ottoman Empire.

Battle of Mohács (1526): A conflict in which the Ottoman Empire conquered much of Hungary.

Battle of Mühlberg (1547): A conflict in which Holy Roman Emperor Charles V defeated the Schmalkaldic League.

Battle of Pavia: A conflict during the Italian Wars, in which Spain defeated France; resulted in the Treaty of Madrid (1526), requiring France to give up claims to Italy, Burgundy, Flanders, and Artois.

Battle of Preveza (1538): A sea battle in which the Ottoman navy defeated the Genoan fleet and gained control of the eastern Mediterranean Sea.

Bewitch: To cast a spell over someone or something.

Bible: The Christian holy book.

Biology: The study of living organisms and their processes.

Bishop: The head of a church district.

Black Death: A severe epidemic of the bubonic plague that started in Europe and Asia in the fourteenth century.

Blasphemy: An expression of contempt toward God.

Bleeding: The procedure of draining blood from the body to cure disease.

Bourgeoisie: The middle class.

Brethren of the Common Life: The Protestant organization that founded humanist schools.

Bull: An order issued by a pope.

C

Cadaver: A dead body used for study purposes.

Canon: Church law or degree; clergyman at a cathedral.

Canonized: Named as a saint, or a person declared holy by the Roman Catholic Church.

Canton: A province or state.

Cardinal: A Roman Catholic Church official ranking directly below the pope.

Carnival: A celebration of a holy day.

Cartography: The study of maps and map-making.

Cartoon: A preparatory design or drawing for a fresco.

Castle: The residence of a lord and his knights, family, servants, and other attendants; eventually the center for a village and local government.

Catechism: A book of religious instructions in the form of questions and answers.

Cathedral: A large Christian house of worship.

Catholic Reformation: The reform movement within the Roman Catholic Church of the sixteenth and seventeenth centuries; also called the Counter Reformation.

Cavalry: Soldiers who ride horses in battle.

Censored: Suppressed or prohibited, as by the church.

Chamber music: Music composed for performance in a private room or small auditorium, usually with one performer for each part.

Chancellor: A chief secretary or administrator.

Chivalric code: A complex system of honor observed by knights during the Middle Ages.

Christ: The name for Jesus of Nazareth, founder of Christianity.

Christendom: The kingdom of Christ; name given to Europe by the Christian church.

Christianity: The religion founded by Jesus of Nazareth, who was also called the Christ.

City-state: A geographic region under the governmental control of a central city.

Classical period: The ancient Greek and Roman world, especially its literature, art, architecture, and philosophy.

Clergy: Church officials, including bishops, priests, and monks.

Cloister: Walkways with an arched open side supported by columns; also a term for an enclosed monastery or convent.

Coat of arms: An emblem signifying noble rank.

Commedia dell' arte: A type of comedy performed by professional acting companies that improvise plots depending on the materials at hand and the talents of the actors.

Commune: A district governed by a group of leaders called a corporation.

Communion: A Christian religious ceremony in which bread and wine represent the body and blood of Jesus of Nazareth (Christ).

Concordat of Bologna (1516): The agreement in which the Catholic Church in France came under direct control of the king.

Confession: An admission of sins to a priest; statement of belief forming the basis of a religious faith or denomination.

Confirmation: The act of conferring the gift of the Holy Spirit.

Confraternity: A society devoted to a charitable or religious cause.

Conscription: The requirement of all men above a certain age to serve in the military.

Constitution: A document that specifies the laws of a state and the rights of its citizens.

Consubstantiation: The concept that bread and wine in the Christian communion service are only symbolic of the body and blood of Christ, not transformed into the actual body and blood.

Convent: A house for women who are dedicated to religious life; also called a nunnery.

Conversion: The act of leaving one religion to accept another.

Converso: The Spanish word for a Jew who converted to Christianity.

Coup d'etat: A violent overthrow of a government.

Courtier: A member of a court; a gentleman.

Courtly love: Part of the chivalric code according to which a knight undertakes a quest (religious journey) or a tournament (game of combat) dedicated to a special lady.

Creed: A statement of religious beliefs.

Crucifix: A carved image of Christ crucified on a cross.

Crusades (1096–1291): A series of wars waged by Christians against Muslims in an effort to recapture the city of Jerusalem in the Holy Land; also wars against other non-Christians and Christians who challenged the church.

Curate: A clergyman in charge of a parish.

D

Democracy: A government based on the will of the majority of people.

Dialectic: Conversation based on discussion and reasoning.

Dialogue: A written work in which two or more speakers discuss a topic.

Diet: A meeting of representatives from states and districts in the Holy Roman Empire.

Diet of Augsburg (1530): A meeting in which Protestants and Catholics tried unsuccessfully to reach a compromise.

Diet of Nuremberg (1532): A meeting in which Protestant princes forced Emperor Charles V to continue toleration of Lutheranism indefinitely.

Diet of Speyer (1526): A meeting in which it was decided that each prince was responsible for settling religious issues in his own territory "until a general council of the whole Church could be summoned."

Diet at Speyer (1529): A meeting in which the 1526 Diet of Speyer decision was revoked; some Lutheran reformers protested, thus gaining the name "Protestants."

Diet of Worms (1521): A meeting in which Martin Luther refused to recant his beliefs and was declared an outlaw of the church by Emperor Charles V.

Diocese: A territorial district of a bishop.

Diplomat: A political negotiator or representative of a government.

Disciple: One who spreads the doctrines of a religious leader; one of the twelve followers of Jesus of Nazareth (Christ).

Disputation: A formal debate.

Divine right: The concept that a ruler is chosen directly by God.

Doctrine: Official church teachings.

Doge: The duke of Venice, Italy.

Dowry: Money, goods, or the estate that a woman brings to her husband in marriage.

Ducat: A gold coin used in various European countries.

Duel: A form of combat with weapons, usually pistols, between two persons in the presence of witnesses.

Dynasty: Rulers from the same family who hold political power for many generations.

E

East Roman Empire: In the Middle Ages, the countries of eastern Europe; based in Byzantium (now Istanbul, Turkey) and formed after the split of the Roman Empire in A.D. 395; also known as the Byzantine Empire.

East-West Schism (1052): The splitting of the Christian church into the Eastern Orthodox Church at Constantinople and the Roman Catholic Church in Rome.

Easter: The commemoration of Christ's resurrection, or rising from the dead.

Eclipse: The total or partial obscuring of one celestial body by another, as in the eclipse of the Sun by the Moon.

Edict of Worms: The statement issued by Emperor Charles V at the Diet of Worms in 1521; it condemned Lutheranism in all parts of the Holy Roman Empire.

The Elect: A few people chosen by God to receive salvation and to lead others who are not chosen for salvation.

Elector: A German prince entitled to vote for the Holy Roman Emperor.

Elegy: A poem expressing sorrow.

Epic: A literary work, usually a poem, in which the main character undertakes a long journey.

Epidemic: A widespread outbreak of disease.

Etiquette: Rules for proper manners.

Evangelism: A personal commitment to the teachings of Jesus of Nazareth (Christ).

Excommunicate: The act of being expelled from membership in a church.

Exile: Forcibly sending a person away from his or her native country or state.

F

Fable: A story with animal characters that teaches a moral lesson.

Facade: The outer front wall of a building.

Factions: Opposing sides in a conflict.

Faith: The acceptance of truth without question; also a profession of religious belief.

Farce: Literary or theatrical work based on exaggerated humor.

Fasting: Abstaining from food.

Feudalism: The social and political system of the Middle Ages, under which rulers granted land to lords in exchange for loyalty.

Fief: Territory granted to a nobleman by a king or emperor under feudalism.

First Helvetic Confession (1536): A statement of Protestant reform goals.

Florin: A coin made in Florence, Italy; later used by various European countries.

Free will: Exercise of individual choice independent of the will of God.

French Wars of Religion (1562–98): Series of conflicts between Catholics and Huguenots (Protestants) in France.

Fresco: A wall painting made by applying paint over a thin layer of damp lime plaster.

Friar: A man who belongs to a religious order that takes a vow of poverty.

G

Galaxy: A very large group of stars.

Galley: A ship propelled by oars.

Genre: A form of literature.

Geography: The study of the physical and cultural features of the Earth's surface.

Geometry: The branch of mathematics that deals with points, lines, angles, surfaces, and solids.

German Peasants' War (1524–26): Rebellion staged by peasants against Catholic princes in Germany.

Gospel: The word of God delivered by Jesus of Nazareth (Christ).

Grammar school: An elementary school; in the Renaissance, called Latin grammar school because students were required to learn Latin as the basis of the humanist curriculum.

Great Schism (1378–1418): The name given to a period of time when there were two Roman Catholic popes, one in Rome and one in Avignon, France.

Guild: An association of craftsmen, merchants, and professionals that trained apprentices and set standards of production or business operation.

H

Habit: The garment worn by a nun.

Hanseatic League: A trading network formed in the Middle Ages among cities around the Baltic Sea and the North Sea.

Heliocentric: Sun-centered.

Heresy: Violation of church laws.

Heretic: One who violates or opposes the teachings of the church.

Hermit: A member of a religious order who retires from society and lives in solitude.

Holy Roman Empire: A revival of the ancient Roman Empire; established by Otto the Great in A.D. 962.

Holy Spirit: The third person of the Christian Trinity (God the Father, the Son, and the Holy Spirit).

House: A family of rulers.

Huguenots: French Protestants.

Humanism: A human-centered literary and intellectual movement based on the revival of classical culture that started the Renaissance.

Humanistic studies: Five academic subjects consisting of grammar (rules for the use of a language), rhetoric (art of effective speaking and writing), moral philosophy (study of human conduct and values), poetry, and history.

Hundred Years' War (1337–1453): A series of intermittent conflicts between England and France over the French throne.

I

Idolatry: The worship of images, or false gods.

Incarnate: The spirit in bodily form.

Index of Prohibited Books: A list of books banned by the Roman Catholic Church.

Indulgence: The Roman Catholic Church practice of granting a partial pardon of sins in exchange for money.

Infantry: Soldiers trained to fight in the front line of battle.

Inquisition: An official court established by the Roman Catholic Church in 1233 for the purpose of hunting down and punishing heretics; during the Renaissance, it continued under the Spanish Inquisition (1492) and Roman Inquisition (1542).

Investiture struggle: An eleventh-century conflict between popes and rulers over the right to appoint bishops.

Islam: A religion founded by the prophet Muhammad.

Italian Wars (1494–1559): A conflict between France and Spain over control of Italy.

J

Janissaries: An elite army of the Ottoman Empire, composed of war captives and Christian youths forced into service.

Journeyman: The stage of apprenticeship during which one travels from job to job working in the shop of a master craftsman.

Joust: Combat on horseback between two knights with lances.

K

Kabbalah: Also cabala; system of Jewish religious and mystical thought.

Knight: A professional warrior who rode on horseback in combat; also known as a vassal, or one who pledged his loyalty to a lord and a king.

L

Laity: Unordained church members.

Lance: A long polelike weapon with a sharpened steel point.

Lent: The forty week days prior to Easter, the celebration of Christ's rising from the dead; a time devoted to prayer, penance, and reflection.

Limbo: A place where the unbaptized remain after death.

Linear perspective: A system derived from mathematics in which all elements of a composition are measured and arranged according to a single point (perspective).

Liturgy: Rites and texts used in a worship service.

Logarithms: A system of numbers with points that move on two lines of numbers, one point on increasing arithmetic value and the other moves on decreasing geometric values.

Loggia: An open, roofed porchlike structure with arches that overlooks a courtyard.

Logic: A system of thought based on reason.

Lord: One who was granted a large estate by a king in exchange for loyalty.

M

Madrigal: A song based on a poem or sacred text.

Magic: The use of spells or charms believed to have supernatural powers over natural forces; black magic is the use of evil spirits for destructive purposes; white magic is beneficial use of magic.

Magistrate: A government official similar to a judge; a mayor.

Marburg Colloquy (1529): Gathering of Protestant theologians who met to create a common creed (statement of beliefs) as a united front against Catholics.

Martyr: A person who voluntarily suffers death for a religious cause.

Masque: Court entertainment featuring masked actors, elaborate costumes, music, and dance.

Mass: The Roman Catholic worship service in which communion is taken.

Medical practitioner: An unlicensed healer who treats illness and disease.

Medieval: A term for the Middle Ages.

Mercenary: A hired soldier.

Mercury: A silver-colored, poisonous metallic element.

Metallurgy: The study and use of metals.

Metaphysics: The study of the nature of reality and existence.

Meteorology: The science that deals with the study of weather patterns.

Middle Ages: A period in European history that began after the downfall of the West Roman Empire in the fourth and fifth centuries and continued into the fifteenth century; once called the Dark Ages.

Midwife: One who assists in childbirth.

Mistress: A woman who has a continuing sexual relationship with a married man and is not his wife.

Monarchs: Kings and queens who have sole ruling power.

Monastery: A house for monks, members of a religious order.

Monk: A man who is a member of a religious order and lives in a monastery.

Monopoly: Exclusive control or possession of a trade or business.

Moors: Muslim Arab and Berber conquerors of Spain.

Morisco: The Spanish word for a Muslim who converted to Christianity.

Mortal sin: An act of wrongdoing that causes spiritual death.

Mosque: A Muslim house of worship.

Muslim: A follower of the Islamic religion.

Mysticism: Religion based on intense spiritual experiences.

N

Natural history: An ancient and medieval term for the study of nature.

New Testament: The second part of the Bible, the Christian holy book.

New World: The European term for the Americas.

Nobility: Members of the upper social class.

Novella: A form of short fictitious story originating in Italy.

Nun: A woman who is a member of a religious order and lives in a convent.

O

Occult: An aspect of religion that relies on magic and mythology.

Old Testament: The first part of the Bible, the Christian holy book.

Opera: A musical work that combines choruses in complex harmony, solo ensembles, arias, dances, and independent instrumental pieces.

Oratorio: A lengthy religious choral work that features singing that resembles speaking in the form of arias and choruses without action or scenery.

Oratory: Public speaking.

Orbit: The path of a heavenly body such as a planet.

P

Pagan: A person who has no religious beliefs or worships more than one god.

Papacy: The office of the pope.

Papal: Relating to a pope or the Roman Catholic Church.

Papal State: The territory owned by the Roman Catholic Church and governed by the pope.

Parish: A local church community.

Parliament: The main governing body of Britain.

Patron: A financial supporter.

Peace of Westphalia (1648): An agreement that ended the Thirty Years' War; by it, Catholic and Protestant states were given equal status within the Holy Roman Empire.

Penance: An act performed to seek forgiveness of sins.

Persecution: Harassment for religious beliefs.

Philosophy: The search for a general understanding of values and reality through speculative thinking.

Physics: The science that deals with energy and matter and their interactions.

Piety: Dutifulness in religion.

Pilgrimage: A religious journey.

Plague: A widespread communicable disease.

Planetary motion: The movement of planets around the Sun.

Pope: The supreme head of the Roman Catholic Church.

Predestination: The belief that the fate of all humans is determined by a divine force.

Prince: A political and military leader; Renaissance ruler.

Prior: The head of a monastery.

Protestantism: Christian religion established by reformers who separated from the Roman Catholic Church.

Protestant Reformation: The reform movement that established a Christian religion separate from the Roman Catholic Church.

Purgatory: A place between heaven and hell.

Q

Quadrant: A device in the shape of a quarter circle that measures angles up to 90 degrees and is used for determining altitudes.

Quest: A religious journey.

R

Regent: One who rules in place of a minor or an absent monarch.

Relief: A carving or sculpture with detail raised above the surface.

Renaissance: The transition period in European history from medieval to modern times, marked by a revival of classical culture, which brought innovations in the arts and literature and initiated modern science.

Rhetoric: Art of effective speaking and writing.

Roman Catholic Church: Christian religion based in Rome, Italy, and headed by a pope.

S

Sack of Rome (1527): Destruction of parts of Rome by armies of Emperor Charles V.

Sacraments: Rites of the Catholic Church: communion, baptism, confirmation, penance, anointing of the sick, marriage, and holy offices.

Sacrilege: The violation of anything considered sacred to God.

Saint: A person who is declared holy by the Catholic Church.

Salic law: A law stating that a male could be the only legitimate heir to the throne.

Salon: A gathering of nobles for discussion of literature and ideas.

Salvation: The forgiveness of sins.

Satire: Criticism through the use of humor.

Schmalkaldic League: A military alliance of German Protestant princes formed in 1531.

Scholasticism: Medieval scholarly method that combined Christian teachings with Greek philosophy.

Scriptures: The text of the Bible, the Christian holy book.

Sect: A small religious group.

Secular: Nonreligious; worldly.

Seignor: An owner of a large estate; also called a lord.

Seignorialism: European social system inherited from the Roman practice of forcing poor people to be dependent on a large landowner called a seignor or lord.

Serf: A peasant who was loyal to a lord and worked on land under the system of feudalism.

Sextant: An instrument used for measuring angular distances.

Simony: The selling of offices in the Roman Catholic Church.

Smallpox: A contagious disease caused by a virus that produces severe skin sores.

Soul: Eternal spirit.

Spanish Armada: The fleet of heavily armored ships built by Spain to defeat England.

Sultan: Arabian king.

Swiss Brethren: A Protestant group who believe in adult baptism; also called Anabaptists.

Swiss Confederation: An alliance of cantons (states) in Switzerland.

Synagogue: Jewish house of worship.

T

Tapestry: A large embroidered wall hanging.

Telescope: A tube-shaped instrument with a lens or mirror used for viewing distant objects.

Theologian: A scholar who studies and teaches religion.

Thirty Years' War (1618–48): A social, religious, and political conflict involving all major world powers; known as the first "world war."

Tithe: Contribution of one-tenth of a church member's income to the church.

Topography: The study of natural and man-made features of a place.

Tournament: A game in which knights engaged in combat with lances on horseback.

Tragedy: A drama that portrays the rise and fall of an honorable man.

Transubstantiation: The belief that bread and wine actually become the body and blood of Christ.

Treatise: A written study of a topic or issue.

Treaty of Cateau-Cambrésis (1559): The peace agreement between France and Spain that ended the Italian Wars, giving Spain control of Italy.

Trigonometry: The branch of mathematics dealing with the study of triangles.

Triptych: A three-panel artwork.

Troubadours: French and Italian poet-musicians.

U

Universe: The totality of the world, including the Earth and the heavens.

V

Vassal: A knight; nobleman soldier who pledged loyalty to a lord.

Vatican: The palace of the pope.

Vestimentary laws: Laws relating to the clothes, or vestments, worn by clergymen.

Villa: A country house; a popular architectural style during the Renaissance.

Vulgate: The official Latin version of the Bible.

W

War of the Roses (1455–85): Conflict between the houses of York and Lancaster in England that resulted in the founding of the House of Tudor.

West Roman Empire: Countries of western Europe; based in Rome, Italy, and formed after the split of the Roman Empire in A.D. 395.

Witchcraft: The practice of communicating with supernatural spirits to bring about certain events or results.

Y

Year of Jubilee: A special spiritual celebration held every twenty-five years by the Catholic Church.

Research and Activity Ideas

The following list of research and activity ideas is intended to offer suggestions for complementing English, social studies, and history curricula; to trigger additional ideas for enhancing learning; and to suggest cross-disciplinary projects for library and classroom use.

Activity 1: Living history: Life in the Renaissance

Assignment: Your social studies class has been selected to create a "living history" presentation on life in the Renaissance. The presentation will be featured in a school program that will be attended by fellow students, parents, and members of the community. You will determine the format of your presentation, but you are expected to make it informative, involve all members of the class, and engage the imagination of the audience.

Preparation: The first task is to hold a class discussion and plan your presentation. One possibility is to assign specific roles, such as kings, queens, dukes, duchesses, courtiers, peasants, slaves, merchants, clergymen, scholars, scientists, patrons, *salonnières,* artists, writers, playwrights, and musicians. Once you have assigned roles, gather information about the lives of the people you will portray. Focus on food, clothing, housing, community and family life, work, recreation, religion, education, and other relevant topics. Each class member might do individual research for his or her role, or teams of students could conduct general research on two or three topics. Using *Renaissance and Reformation: Almanac* as a starting point, find information at the library and on Internet Web sites. Search for sources such as historians' accounts and documents from the period. Try to find little-known or especially interesting facts.

Presentation: After you have gathered information, prepare a fifty-minute group presentation. Use various strategies to dramatize your roles: wear Renaissance-style clothing, give speeches, act out skits, read excerpts from documents of the period, play recordings of Renaissance music, and exhibit color photocopies of artworks. Explore other possibilities to draw upon the knowledge and talents of each class member.

Activity 2: Renaissance science fair

Assignment: Your class has completed a unit on the history of science and is now planning a science fair that will highlight the Renaissance period. You have invited another class in your school to attend the fair. The assignment is to plan and stage the fair, which will feature five- to ten-minute individual presentations and ten- to fifteen-minute group presentations on aspects of Renaissance science.

Preparation: In planning the fair, it is necessary to do some preliminary research. The teacher has distributed a list of general topics such as astronomy, mathematics, geography, navigation, medicine, technology, and scientific instruments. Hold a class meeting in which you assign teams of three or four students to research a topic. Using *Renaissance and Reformation: Almanac*

Chapter 10 as a starting point, find additional information at the library and on Internet Web sites. After the teams have completed their research, hold another class meeting to make assignments for individual and group presentations. Individual presentations might focus on a particular scientist, invention, or scientific experiment; group presentations might cover the methods and discoveries in a specific field. The goal should be to give a comprehensive overview of science in the Renaissance period.

Presentation: After you have made assignments, prepare your presentations. Concentrate on engaging the audience's interest with such techniques as demonstrating an experiment and distributing photocopies of scientists' portraits, diagrams of theories, and illustrations of instruments. Think of other techniques that draw upon the knowledge and talents of individual and group presenters.

Activity 3: Renaissance and Reformation literature

Assignment: Your English class is completing a unit on Renaissance and Reformation literature. The teacher has distributed a list of topics for independent projects that will enable class members to learn more about a particular writer. Your project will involve preparing a paper that (1) presents biographical information about the writer, (2) explains the writer's significance to the Renaissance or Reformation, and (3) interprets a brief excerpt from an example of the writer's work. You will present your paper as an oral report to the class.

Preparation: The first step is to choose a subject for your paper. Then you will need to conduct research on (1) the writer's life, (2) his or her significance to the Renaissance or Reformation, and (3) locate one of the writer's works. Using *Renaissance and Reformation: Almanac* as a starting point, find additional material in the library and on Internet Web sites. After deciding on an example of the writer's work, choose a one-page excerpt (250–300 words). Once you have completed your research, write a paper at least five pages in length (excluding the excerpt of the writer's work).

Presentation: Your teacher has requested that, after you have completed your paper, you make a photocopy of it for each person in the class. You will then present a five-minute oral report, summarizing the results of your research. At the end of the report you might also lead a brief discussion of the writer and his or her work.

A Changing Europe

The Renaissance began in Italy in the latter half of the four-teenth century, when a group of scholars called humanists set out to revive the Greek-based culture of ancient Rome (an era known as the classical period). They took the name "hu-manist" because they focused on the importance of the indi-vidual human spirit and concentrated on secular (nonreli-gious) subjects. They set out to initiate a new age, which they called a renaissance, a term that comes from the French word for "rebirth." The Renaissance took place during the latter part of the Middle Ages (also called the medieval period), the thou-sand-year era that followed the downfall of the West Roman Empire in the fourth and fifth centuries. Based in Rome, the West Roman Empire consisted of countries that are now in Western Europe. The Roman Empire had been permanently split into the West and East Empires in A.D. 395. The East Roman Empire, also known as the Byzantine Empire, was based in Byzantium and consisted of present-day Eastern Euro-pean countries and Turkey. Historians usually divide the Mid-dle Ages into three phases: Early Middle Ages (c. A.D 400–1100; often called the Dark Ages), High Middle Ages (1100–1300), and Late Middle Ages (1300–c. 1500). The Renaissance covered most of the Late Middle Ages and represented a break with the earlier medieval periods. Historians have not determined an exact date for the end of the Renaissance, though most agree that it reached a peak at the end of the fifteenth century. In some parts of Europe, achievements associated with the Renaissance continued into the first half of the 1600s.

Leaders of the Renaissance believed that classical art, science, philosophy, and literature had been lost during the "dark ages" that followed the fall of the West Roman Empire. They held that the ideals represented by the ancient arts and sciences were waiting to be rediscovered, and Italians in particular considered themselves the true heirs to Roman achievement. For this reason, it was natural that the cultural revival should begin in Italy, where the ruins of ancient civilization provided an ever-present reminder of the past. By the fifteenth century scholars and traders were taking the Italian Renaissance into other parts of Europe, where the era was known as the northern Renaissance. These separate movements are now regarded as a single Renaissance.

The humanists introduced radically new ideas. Throughout the Middle Ages, art, literature, and scholarly activities were related solely to the Catholic Church (a Christian faith based in Rome, Italy, and led by the pope). The church taught that the only purpose of human existence on Earth was to glorify God in preparation for life after death in heaven (the Christian concept of the place where the righteous go after they die). Human achievement therefore had no importance except as a reflection of God's work. Yet by the 1300s people were ready for change: Europe was in the midst of political, religious, and social turmoil that was overthrowing old traditions. Consequently, humanist ideals were embraced with enthusiasm. The Renaissance began as a literary movement, but by the time it reached a peak in the fifteenth and sixteenth centuries, a transformation was taking place in all areas of public and private life—philosophy, science, the arts, architecture, music, politics, social customs, and popular culture. Humanism also contributed to the rise of the Reformation, a widespread religious reform movement that began in the sixteenth century and resulted in the founding of Protestantism as a Christian faith separate from the Catholic Church. The Renaissance and Reformation period is regarded as the beginning of the modern age—the time in Western (non-Asian) history when people rejected familiar traditions and found new ways to express their experience of the world.

Achievements of the Renaissance

The Renaissance started in northern Italy, where numerous city-states (geographic regions under the control of central cities) developed independently of the larger kingdoms in the rest of Europe. These small states—including Florence, Rome, Venice,

The Roman Forum. Ruins such these led Italians to consider themselves the true heirs to Roman achievement, and encouraged the development of the Renaissance period. *Reproduced by permission of Popperfoto/Archive Photos, Inc.*

Milan, and the combined city-state of Naples and Sicily—became prosperous through trade and banking. Wealthy businessmen and bankers wanted to celebrate their own achievements. They became patrons (financial supporters) of artists and architects who designed magnificent buildings and created beautiful paintings and sculptures that glorified the patrons' commercial success. Bankers and merchants also supported scholars, poets, and musicians. The most influential patrons were the Medicis, a prominent banking family in Florence. As a result of the Medicis' support of important artists, Florence became the center of the early Italian Renaissance. (See "Florence" in Chapter 2.)

One way patrons promoted creativity was to sponsor competitions. In many cases, the losers of these contests went on to greater fame than the winners. An example was the Florentine sculptor and goldsmith (one who makes items from gold) Filippo Brunelleschi (pronounced broo-nail-LAYS-kee;1377–1446). In 1401 he was defeated by the Florentine sculptor

Lorenzo Ghiberti (pronounced gee-BEHR-tee; c. 1378–1455) in a competition to design bronze doors for the Baptistery, a church in Florence. Brunelleschi then made several trips to Rome to take measurements of ruined ancient buildings. He was one of many fifteenth- and sixteenth-century Italian artists who created the classical style of architecture, which was based on such features of ancient Roman buildings as domes, columns, arches, and vaults. In 1420 Brunelleschi began building the immense dome of the cathedral in Florence, a classically influenced structure that became the first great monument of the Renaissance (see "Architecture" in Chapter 8).

Wealthy merchants also began collecting classical texts that had been forgotten during the Dark Ages. They supported humanist scholars who searched for ancient manuscripts in Catholic monasteries (houses for men who were devoted to the religious life), where monks called scribes had copied the texts during the Middle Ages. The manuscripts were placed in great libraries where they could be studied by other European scholars. With the revival of classical texts came a new way of looking at the world. During the medieval period, most intellectuals who studied ancient works had focused on ways to combine Greek and Roman achievements with Christian teachings. Church leaders taught that life on Earth was merely a preparation for the afterlife and they frowned upon the recognition of individual talent. Human creation or learning for its own sake, as exemplified by the Greeks

and Romans, therefore had no value and was even considered sinful. For this reason, many of the great works of the Middle Ages were created anonymously; one example is the gargoyles (rain spouts in the form of grotesque human or animal figures) that sit, often hidden from view, atop medieval cathedrals in western Europe.

In contrast, Renaissance artists and thinkers studied classical works for the purpose of imitating them. Like the ancient Greeks and Romans, they valued the earthly life, glorified human nature, and celebrated individual achievement. One of the most important developments of the Renaissance occurred in the latter half of the fifteenth century, when humanists began searching for ancient texts that would increase current knowledge about the natural world. Among the rediscovered works were *Geography*, a book by the Egyptian astronomer Ptolemy (second century A.D.), and studies of human physiology and anatomy by Greek physician Galen (A.D. 129–c. 199). Renaissance thinkers also attempted to refine ancient knowledge of astronomy, leading the way to a scientific revolution in later centuries.

Innovations in culture, society, and politics

As an expression of their optimism, Renaissance scholars defined a new field of study called the "humanities," which initially included language and literature, art, history, rhetoric (public speaking), and philosophy. Above all, humanists believed in the human potential to become well versed in many areas. This idea produced the concept of the "Renaissance man," an individual whose talents span a variety of subjects. Artists such as Michelangelo (1475–1564) absorbed a broad range of subjects and came upon a new way to view the world. One important discovery was perspective, the technique used by painters to create the illusion of depth—to show distances and the relative sizes of various three-dimensional objects—on a flat canvas (a cloth used for paintings).

Renaissance ideas also influenced personal behavior and social customs. An example of Renaissance attitudes is *The Book of the Courtier,* written by the Italian diplomat (political negotiator) Baldassare Castiglione (pronounced kass-teel-YOH-nay; 1478–1529) in the early 1500s. The book is a collection of conversations set in Urbino, a state in the mountains of northern Italy, that outline the qualities of the ideal Renaissance courtier, or gentleman. In contrast to the knight, who was given rules for behavior in the chivalric code, the Renaissance courtier was expected to be a well-rounded man who had knowledge of the arts, the classics, and politics. Although he was expected to be talented in many areas, however, he was cautioned against showing off his abilities. Castiglione also described feminine virtues such as delicacy, sweetness, and chastity (not having sexual intercourse), which implied that women should be passive and unassertive. In spite of these restrictive

 ## The Renaissance Man

Humanists believed in the human potential to become accomplished in many areas. This idea led to the concept of the "Renaissance man," a person who pursued success in many different fields. For instance, the Italian artist Michelangelo was not only an accomplished painter and sculptor but also a skilled architect and poet. The architect and goldsmith Brunelleschi was noted for his great churches, but he was also an engineer who invented an ingenious plan for flooding Lucca, Florence's rival city, by changing the course of a river. Italian artist Piero della Francesca enhanced his craft by studying mathematics and anatomy (the structure of the human body). The great Italian artist Leonardo da Vinci was one of the finest examples of a Renaissance man: in addition to his considerable skills as a painter, Leonardo also was a writer, an inventor, an architect, an engineer, a mathematician, a musician, and a philosopher.

social rules, Renaissance women were offered greater opportunities—the ability to become scholars and artists, for example—than at any time since the Roman Empire.

Renaissance ideals changed attitudes toward government. Under feudalism, the system in place through much of the Middle Ages, kings and noblemen were the unquestioned rulers who had gained the right to rule because they controlled the land. During the Renaissance, the ancient Greek and Roman concept of citizenship—the need for the people to be involved in public service and government—was revived. As a consequence, forms of government based on representative rule by the people took hold in cities like Florence and Venice. Republics were often short-lived and plagued by bloody rivalries. One such feud caused turmoil in northern Italy throughout much of the Renaissance period. Encouraged by the humanistic optimism of the Renaissance, a new middle-class party, the Guelphs (pronounced gwelfs), vied for power with the Ghibellines (pronounced GIB-eh-leens), members of the old noble class. The cities controlled by one of these parties were continually at war with cities loyal to the opposite side. When power shifted from one group to the other in a given area, the policy of the victorious party was to exile (forcibly send away) all members of the opposition and burn their houses to the ground. During the Renaissance, Italy was filled with exiles waiting for the chance to return home and seek revenge on their enemies.

Cultural and political advances also brought technological innovations. In the 1450s the German inventor Johannes Gutenberg (c.1390–1468) perfected the printing press, which is recognized as one of the most important advances of the time. A mechanism by which small metal pieces engraved with single characters (letters) could be arranged to form words and sentences, the first press was used in Germany to print the Bible (the holy book of Christianity). Soon presses began to spring up all over Europe, and the impact was enormous. Literacy (the ability to read) grew rapidly and knowledge spread as, for the first time, literature became available and affordable to many people. With the aid of printing, ideas born in Italy during the late 1300s spread northward to France, England, Spain, the Netherlands, Scandinavia, and eastern Europe during the fifteenth and sixteenth centuries.

Renaissance produces influential works

The European Renaissance produced many artists, thinkers, writers, and scientists who made major contributions to the culture and society of the time, setting the stage for the modern era. Even brief descriptions of representative figures reflect the magnitude of Renaissance achievements. Although humanist scholars introduced the concept of cultural rebirth, the works of great artists provided visual evidence that the Renaissance was taking place. Therefore, this overview will begin with artists, then move on to humanist thinkers, writers, and scientists.

Artists depict past, make innovations

The first visual artist to break with the medieval past was the Florentine painter Giotto (pronounced JOH-toh; c. 1266–1337), whose paintings demonstrate an early sense of perspective and real space. According to a story, a fly in one of Giotto's paintings looked so real that a viewer tried to brush it away. Raphael (1483–1520) celebrated classical ideals in his *School of Athens* (1513), a work commissioned by the pope to portray the philosophers of ancient Greece. Another school of painting is characterized by Sandro Botticelli (pronounced boht-tee-CHEL-ee; born Alessandro di Mariano Filipepi, 1445– 1510), whose *Birth of Venus* and *Primavera* explore more passionate aspects of the classical past.

The most accomplished artist of the time, however, was Michelangelo. Raised in the hills near Florence, Michelangelo is known for frescoes (using paint on freshly spread plaster) depicting great biblical events; these works can be seen today on the ceiling of the Sistine Chapel in Rome. A sculptor by training, Michelangelo also created many of the most remarkable statues of the period. His *David* celebrates not only the human form but also the pride and confidence of small independent states like Florence that were often under threat from larger neighbors. When the Spanish besieged Florence in the middle 1500s, Florentine officials commissioned Michelangelo to build an inner wall around the city. He constructed the wall, and though the outer defense fell to the Spaniards, the inner fortification still stands as proof of Michelangelo's skill as an engineer and architect. However the most enduring monument to Michelangelo's genius stands not in Florence but in Rome. The artist completed the dome of Saint Peter's Church (also called Saint Peter's Basilica), which was built to celebrate the revival of the ancient city (see "Rome and the Papal States" in Chapter 2).

Johannes Gutenberg's printing press is considered one of the most important technological innovations of the Renaissance. *©Underwood & Underwood/Corbis. Reproduced by permission of the Corbis Corporation.*

Italian painter Leonardo da Vinci (1452–1519), while less well known than Michelangelo at the time, is now regarded as an artistic genius. Two of his works, *Last Supper* (1495–97) and *Mona Lisa* (1503–06), are among the most famous and most studied paintings in the world. The most accomplished northern Renaissance artists worked in Flanders, a region in northern Belgium. There, they perfected the medium of oil on canvas, a technique that enabled Flemish artists to represent scenes with great clarity. The van Eyck (pronounced vahn IKE) brothers, Hubert (c. 1370–1426) and Jan (before 1395–1441), along with Pieter Brueghel the Elder (pronounced BROY-gehl; c.1525–1569), are noted for their attention to fine detail. Rembrandt (1606–1669) is recognized for his haunting use of light and shadow.

Humanists promote change The Italian humanist scholar Petrarch (pronounced PEE-trark; 1304–1374) was the first great writer of the Renaissance as well as one of the earliest promoters of a cultural "rebirth." A student and teacher of classical literature, he achieved fame for his Latin writings. He is known today for a series of love sonnets that he dedicated to an idealized woman named Laura. Petrarch is now considered the first modern man.

A central figure in the northern Renaissance was the Dutch humanist Desiderius Erasmus (c. 1466–1536). Unlike Italian Renaissance thinkers, Erasmus applied his study not only to classical civilization but also to early Christianity. He felt that medieval Christian scholars had corrupted the faith, making doctrines, or church teachings, too abstract and complicated, moving Christianity away from its original intent. He produced his own translation of the New Testament (the second part of the Bible), and his book *In Praise of Folly* (1509) is a scalding criticism of the clergy (church officials), scholars, and philosophers of his day.

Another notable northern Renaissance figure was Thomas More

(1478–1535). An English statesman and advisor to King Henry VIII (1491–1547; ruled 1509–47), More shared his friend Erasmus's frustration with human shortcomings. More's *Utopia*, published in 1516, criticized the times by envisioning an ideal society in which police would be unnecessary, politicians would be honest, and money would cease to exist. A Roman Catholic, More was executed for refusing to sanction Henry VIII's divorce (see "England" in Chapter 3).

Niccoló Machiavelli (pronounced mahk-yah-VEL-lee; 1469– 1527), a Florentine historian, wrote what might be the most important work of the period, *The Prince* (c. 1513). In his book Machiavelli outlined the requirements of an effective ruler. Rather than seeing politics in terms of morality, *The Prince* suggests that a successful ruler must disregard such virtues as honesty, justice, and compassion if these qualities stand in the way of political goals. According to Machiavelli, the end justifies the means. In other words, the final result is more important than the methods used to achieve that result. This attitude seems contrary to the humanistic values expressed by other Renaissance philosophers. Nevertheless, Machiavelli arrived at his conclusions using both classical sources and critical reasoning, two prominent aspects of Renaissance ideals.

Shakespeare and novelists explore human nature English Renaissance literature—and perhaps all literature of the modern age—culminated in the

Petrarch

The Italian poet Petrarch was a scholar of classical antiquity who became one of the most important promoters of humanism. Often called the first modern man, Petrarch observed the world and analyzed his own thoughts and feelings with a new awareness of human experience. According to a famous story, in 1336 Petrarch had a profound experience when he climbed Mount Ventoux in Provence (a region in southern France). Upon reaching the summit he opened his copy of St. Augustine's *Confessions,* a book written around A.D. 400 by the famous theologian and church leader. Petrarch always carried *Confessions* with him, and on that day he read that men admire mountains and rivers and seas and stars, yet neglect themselves. This insight was important because at that time in history the life of the individual did not have any special significance. Painfully aware of the fleeting nature of existence, Petrarch embarked on a mission to bridge the ages and to save the works of classical authors. He attained vast knowledge of ancient texts, subjecting them to critical evaluation and prizing them as an expression of the living human spirit. Today he is credited with starting the Renaissance in Europe.

Petrarch is best known for *Canzoniere,* or *Rerum vulgarum fragmenta,* (Fragments of common things), a series of 366 poems that he dedicated to a young woman he called Laura. Petrarch fell in love with her in 1327, but she did not return his love. Laura's true identity is not known; however, there is no doubt of her existence or of the intensity of the poet's passion for her, which endured long after she died of the plague. From 1327 until the end of his life. Petrarch composed and revised the poems inspired by Laura. His work became a model for other Italian poets and influenced all European literature for more than three centuries.

career of English playwright William Shakespeare (1564–1616). An actor by trade, Shakespeare embodied in his plays many of the ideals of both Italian and northern Renaissance artists. In addition to refining the English language, Shakespeare used such classical sources as *Parallel Lives,* biographies of distinguished Greeks and Romans written by the Greek writer Plutarch (pronounced PLOO-tark; c. A.D. 46–c. 119), to create plots and characters that are still popular today. Shakespeare's examination of human nature, his celebration of human potential, his criticism of people's shortcomings, and his understanding of individual personalities place his plays and poems among the greatest artistic achievements of all time.

Other great writers of the Renaissance include Spanish novelist Miguel de Cervantes Saavedra, usually known as Cervantes (pronounced sehr-VAHN-tees; 1547–1616), and François Rabelais (pronounced rah-bleh; c. 1483–1553) of France. In 1605 Cervantes published his famous book *Don Quixote*, a tale that gently pokes fun at medieval codes of conduct. Rabelais is best known for such works as *Pantagruel* (1532) and *Gargantua* (1534), which satirize (criticize with humor) contemporary events and beliefs.

Scientists redefine nature During the Renaissance scientific thinkers attempted to redefine ancient knowledge about the natural world. Foremost among them were Italian artist and architect Leonardo da Vinci, Polish astronomer Nicolaus Copernicus (1473–1543), Italian astronomer Galileo (1564–1642), Danish astronomer Tycho Brahe (1546–1601), and German astronomer Johannes Kepler (1571–1630). Leonardo developed metallurgical techniques (use of metals) that enabled him to make great statues, and his study of anatomy increased the accuracy of his drawings of human figures.

Copernicus posed a revolutionary theory in *De revolutionibus* (1543), a work in which he placed the Sun at the center of the universe and described the planets as revolving in a semicircular path around it. This view contradicted the church-approved Ptolemaic theory, which stated that the Earth is the center of the universe. In 1609 Galileo invented an accurate telescope through which he was able to observe the heavens and confirm Copernicus's findings. In 1632 he wrote *Sopra I due massioni sistiemi del mundo* ("Dialogue concerning the two chief world systems"), which supported Copernicus's Sun-centered view of the universe. The following year he was summoned before the Inquisition (official church court) and found guilty of heresy, or violation of church laws. He was placed under house arrest in Siena, a city-state in central Italy, for the remainder of his life.

Brahe gave an accurate estimate of planetary motion (movement of the planets around the Sun), thus refuting the theory of Greek philosopher Aristotle (384–322 B.C.), who stated that the planets revolve within crystal spheres. Kepler was the first astronomer to suggest that planets revolve in an elliptical (oval-shaped) orbit. Ideas about botany (study of plants), zoology (study of animals), magic (use of supernatural powers), alchemy (methods for changing common metals into gold), and astrology (study of the heavens to predict future events) were also developed during the Renaissance.

Influences on the Renaissance

The Renaissance was influenced by several events that took place in the Early and High Middle Ages. The most important was the collapse of feudalism, an economic and social system that began developing in the ninth century. Feudalism left Europe divided into hundreds of separate states, each with its own customs and

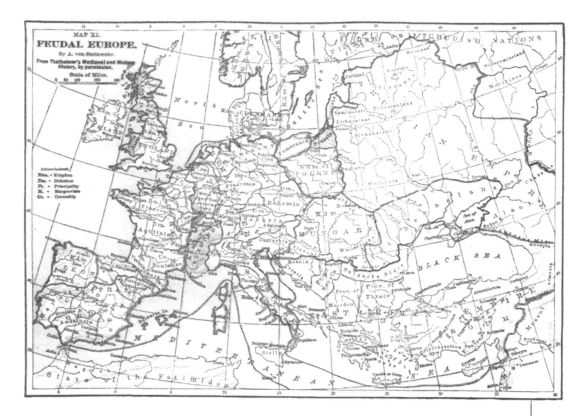

A map of how Europe was politically divided during the era of feudalism. *Reproduced by permission of The Granger Collection.*

laws. This situation severely weakened the Holy Roman Empire, which had placed northern and central Europe under the rule of a single emperor since the tenth century. Many states were seeking independence, while others had left the empire and formed their own governments. The result was continuing conflict and war throughout Europe. The Roman Catholic Church was also going into decline. The pope (supreme head of the Roman Catholic Church) approved the appointment of Holy Roman Emperors, and the church had dominated religious and secular life in Europe for hundreds of years. During the thirteenth and fourteenth centuries, however, the power of the church had been challenged by the rulers of the states. Similarly, the nobility was being threatened by a middle class that developed along with the rise of cities, as capitalism (an economy driven by private ownership and competition) expanded trade among the European states and into Asia. The new middle class was replacing noblemen, who were once at the top of the social ladder, as the most significant force in business, society, and politics. At the same time, peasants were staging revolts, casting off the chains of servitude that had kept them in bondage for centuries. During the Middle Ages, Europeans also were trying to prevent an invasion by the Ottoman Empire, a vast kingdom headed by Muslims (followers of the Islam religion), on the eastern border of the Holy Roman Empire. All of these factors contributed to ongoing turmoil throughout Europe; at the same time they created the environment that produced the revolution triggered by the Renaissance.

Feudalism

Feudalism was a social and economic system that developed during the ninth and tenth centuries in Europe and, later, in parts of Asia. (The term "feudalism" comes from the medieval Latin word *feudum,* meaning "fee.") Under feudalism there were distinct social classes whose power came from the amount of land they controlled. At the top were kings, who owned the land. Beneath them were lords (noblemen) and clergymen (church officials), who were granted land by the king. Below the lords were vassals (knights), who held smaller amounts of land awarded to them by lords. At the bottom were serfs (peasants), who farmed the land but had no ownership rights. These classes were dependent on one another through a complex system of pledging loyalty in exchange for goods and services. In the eleventh century, cities began to emerge as commercial centers, bringing about

the eventual collapse of feudalism in Europe. Lords were no longer able to maintain their estates when serfs moved to cities and found other jobs. At the same time a new middle class, composed of merchants and bankers, was forming and threatening the power of lords.

Based on seignorialism The beginning of feudalism can be traced to the decline of the West Roman Empire, when Germanic tribes established short-lived kingdoms on former Roman territory. Among these tribes were the Franks, whose leader Clovis (pronounced CLOH-vees; c. 466–511; ruled 481–511) founded the first significant kingdom. He united the Franks and conquered other Germanic groups to create a strong state that occupied much of the territory in present-day France. After Clovis accepted Christianity, he received support from the pope; that support guaranteed Clovis absolute power. Clovis's rule established the Merovingian (pronounced mehr-eh-VIN-jee-ehn) Age, named after Meroveus, his family's founder. Clovis's state was organized in the usual Germanic fashion. In an effort to secure power, conquering Germanic tribes adapted their own laws and customs to the legal and cultural traditions of the Roman state. One of these customs was seignorialism (pronounced san-YOR-ee-al-ism), the Roman practice of forcing poor people to be dependent on a lord (seignor), who controlled a large estate known as a manor. This system established the practice of serfdom, under which a peasant, or serf (the term is derived from the Latin *servus,* for "slave"), was confined to his lord's manor. In true servitude, serfs worked to support the lord, living in poverty and receiving hardly any benefits from their own labor.

The Merovingian Age ended in 751 when a Frankish king, Pépin III (pronounced PEH-pehn; c. 714–768; ruled 751–68), overthrew the last Merovingian king. Pépin then received the crown with the pope's blessing. Pépin's successor was Charlemagne (pronounced SHAR-leh-main; 742–814; ruled 800–14). His family's reign was called the Carolingian Empire. Charlemagne, whose name comes from the Latin *Carolus magnus,* or "Charles the Great," expanded Frankish territory, pushing its boundaries south to present-day Spain, north into Saxony (territory that is now in Germany), and southeast as far as the border of the Byzantine Empire in southern Italy. Upon being crowned Roman emperor by Pope Leo III (d. 816; reigned 795–816) in 800, Charlemagne consolidated his rule and claimed to revive the ancient Roman Empire. His theory was that the Roman Empire had merely been suspended, not ended, by the defeat of the last Roman emperor in 476. Although Charlemagne could not read or write, he was a brilliant soldier, administrator, and ruler. He introduced an organized government, supported education, and encouraged the spread of Christianity. Charlemagne initiated a great cultural and artistic period that scholars have named the "Carolingian Renaissance."

After Charlemagne's death in 814 the Carolingian kingdom was divided and the empire soon collapsed.

Developed by Carolingians In addition to their cultural achievements, the Carolingians developed feudalism. Based on seignorialism, feudalism was a system in which rulers exchanged land for loyalty. This arrangement originally developed with the use of armored cavalry—warriors who wore protective armor, carried weapons, and rode horses while fighting battles. These soldiers became known as knights. Supporting large numbers of knights involved considerable work and expense because their horses and equipment required constant maintenance. Consequently, large tracts of land called fiefs (pronounced feefs) were established as permanent bases for knights. Fiefs were administered by lords, who swore loyalty to a king. Knights in turn swore their loyalty to a lord. Serfs, the vast majority of the population, farmed the land and turned over most of their harvest to the lords. Because churches, monasteries, and other religious establishments also were considered fiefs, religious officials became known as "knights of Christ."

Lords provided services to a king in exchange for use of a fief, which always remained the property of the king. Lords supplied the king with knights in time of war. They also paid taxes to the king in the form of crops and other products that they collected from the serfs. The relationship between the serf and the lord was essentially the same as that be-

Knights, like the one pictured here, were an important part of the feudalist system in Europe. *Engraving by Albrecht Dürer. Reproduced by permission of AP/Wide World Photos.*

Feudalism first spread from France to Spain, and then to Italy. It later expanded into Germany and eastern Europe. The English king William I (also know as William the Conqueror; c. 1028–1087; ruled 1066–87) made it the common practice in England after 1066. From England, feudalism extended into the frontier areas of eastern Europe and was partially adopted in Scandinavian countries (present-day Denmark, Norway, and Sweden).

The castle as center of community

Another important feature of feudalism was the castle, which was the basis of the Renaissance palace. The castle was primarily the residence of the lord, but it eventually functioned as a treasury (place where valuable items are kept), armory (storage facility for weapons), and center of local government. Lords first built castles in order to defend their fiefs. The original castles were little more than hills surrounded by ditches and topped with wooden forts. These forts were known as motte and bailey castles. "Motte" was the original term for a "moat," a deep ditch that surrounded a castle to provide protection from invaders. The bailey was a hill constructed with the dirt that had been removed in digging the motte. Usually located at the fringes of a territory, a castle could be built quickly and was cheap enough to abandon in a hurry. Eventually castles were massive, elaborate structures built of stone. The medieval castle took on special significance as both the residence of a lord

tween the lord and the king. In return for providing the lord with a steady supply of agricultural goods, peasants were allowed to grow their own food on small plots of land and to sell any excess crops. They were guaranteed protection by the lord in case of invasion. Churchmen paid their dues to the king in the form of prayer and spiritual strength. They enhanced the power of the king through their direct contact with God, so they were considered valuable allies by rulers.

and as a king's primary military base. Lords wanted to live in luxury, so castles were generally grand affairs equipped with the latest technology of the day. As they were designed to be the center of action during war, however, they also served a practical purpose. In addition to providing living quarters for the lord, who was the wealthiest person in the area, the castle contained rooms for his family, staff, servants, and a number of knights. Although knights were granted lands of their own, they usually stayed with their lord for a set number of months every year to be on alert in the event of invasion.

Castles were generally self-sufficient, offering services for meeting daily needs and fighting battles. For instance, most castles had a blacksmith (one who makes objects from iron, such as horseshoes) because a lord caught without his own blacksmith in time of war was destined to lose. Castles became the focal point for villages that eventually grew up around them. All castles had great dining halls that were used primarily by the lord and his knights. However, lords opened their houses to the peasantry on special occasions such as Christmas. The castle also had to be large enough to provide temporary housing for peasants when the land was invaded. Castles were expensive, and the decline of feudalism made it difficult for lords to maintain their sprawling estates. The introduction of gunpowder in the fourteenth century made the castle outmoded as a military fortress because even the thickest

 Chivalric Code and Courtly Love

Two traditions arising from feudalism were the chivalric code and courtly love. The chivalric code was a set of rules, or a code of honor, that encouraged a knight to perfect his skill with a sword and a lance (a long polelike weapon with a sharpened steel point) in combat and to practice simple dignity in daily life. According to the chivalric code, a knight was expected to honor the king, be loyal to his lord, fight bravely, and respect human life—even that of his enemies. The code also involved the church giving its blessing to knights in elaborate rituals with a strong religious element.

Courtly love was another chivalric ritual, in which a knight chose a special lady to whom he would dedicate a quest (religious journey) or a tournament (game in which knights engaged in combat with lances on horseback). Courtly love was best documented in such stories as the English legend of King Arthur and the Knights of the Round Table, as well as the songs of French and Italian troubadours (poet-musicians), which were tributes to the beauty and purity of noblewomen. The chivalric code and courtly love had a strong influence on social customs, art, literature, and music during the Renaissance.

stone walls could be penetrated by bullets and cannonballs fired from powerful new weapons. During the Renaissance castles became palaces for kings, popes, emperors, noblemen, and merchants who promoted culture and gracious living. Many well-preserved medieval castles still stand today throughout Europe as lasting reminders of feudalism.

Decline caused by capitalism Feudalism began to decline in the eleventh century with the rise of capitalism, an economy based on investing money and earning profit from business ventures. This development was significant because feudalism was an agriculture-based economy that depended on the exchange of goods and services, not money. Along with capitalism came cities, which were built as hubs in a network of trade routes throughout Europe. The cities replaced fiefs as economic, government, and population centers. The growth of a new economy posed another threat to the feudal system: serfs started escaping to urban areas in search of work. Freedom was granted to any serf who lived in a city and managed to avoid being captured by his lord for one year and one day. The labor force that had once supported the feudal system gradually disappeared and a middle class emerged.

The new middle class, consisting of merchants and bankers, eventually replaced the feudal nobility. Bankers and entrepreneurs (business owners) employed workers, supervised the production of goods, sought new markets, financed wars, and controlled a web of complex financial operations. Freed from the rigid social restrictions of the feudal era, more people had time to think about such things as philosophy and the nature of man. An inquiring spirit stimulated the age of exploration that culminated during the Renaissance (see "The age of European exploration" in Chapter 3). Powerful monarchies, such as those in England and France, responded to these changes by modernizing their governments and replacing the feudal system with centralized rule. In other words, power was no longer held by lords who controlled local communities, but rather by officials in a city that was the center of government for a large area.

The Holy Roman Empire

The Holy Roman Empire, founded in 962, was a continuation of the revived Roman Empire that had been started by Charlemagne in the previous century. It was an effort to unite territory that is now Germany and Italy under a single ruler, the Holy Roman Emperor. From the beginning, however, the empire was beset by numerous problems, which caused continuing conflicts and wars. Emperors, kings, popes, and noblemen competed over land, seeking to expand their territories and gain more power. When feudalism began to decline in the eleventh century, the empire was further weakened by the rise of the middle class and by increasing social unrest. States began withdrawing and forming their own governments, and by the mid-seventeenth century the Holy Roman Empire existed in name only.

Founded by Otto After the fall of the Carolingian Empire, Europe was divided into hundreds of fiefs. Many lords had acquired considerable power, yet their economic control diminished as they continued to divide their lands to win the loyalty of other lords. Consequently, rivalries often led to destructive wars that further weakened the ability of the states to fight outside invaders such as the Vikings, Arabs, and Magyars (people from the region that is now Hungary). Europe then entered a period of economic and cultural decline. Conditions began to improve during the tenth century, however, as rulers in Saxony and Franconia (two of the five main districts of medieval Germany) succeeded in maintaining stability. A Saxon king, Otto I (the Great; 912–973; ruled 936–73), created the Holy Roman Empire when he was crowned in Rome by Pope John XII (c. 937–964; reigned 955–64) in 962. When Otto took the throne, the Holy Roman Empire consisted roughly of territory encompassing Germany, Italy, and parts of what is now France. Over the centuries the empire was expanded by other emperors. Otto reigned until his death in 973. Although less impressive than the Carolingian state, Otto's empire ushered in a period of relative stability that promoted a significant cultural revival.

The Holy Roman Empire received its name from the Bible, which was the basis of Christians' understanding of the world. The first part of the Bible is the Old Testament, which was derived from the Torah, the Jewish holy book. In the Old Testament the Hebrew prophet (wise man) Daniel predicted that four kingdoms would exist before the appearance of a messiah: these were the Babylonian, Persian, Grecian, and Roman empires. The ancient Roman Empire was considered the last empire of the world, at the end of which the Last Judgment (the judgment of human beings by God before the end of the world) was to take place. Christians therefore saw the Holy Roman Empire as a continuation of the last empire on Earth.

Emperors' power weakened The Holy Roman Empire was based on the claim that the emperor was God's representative on Earth in state affairs, just as the pope was God's representative on Earth in spiritual matters. Although the emperor was considered the supreme earthly ruler of Christendom (the kingdom of Christ; the name given by the church to what is now Europe), most emperors were never able to maintain their control over all the kings in the huge empire. By the beginning of the Renaissance, the Holy Roman Emperor had no power in France, southern Italy, Denmark, Poland, and Hungary. Emperors ruled in name only in England, Sweden, and Spain. The emperor's power in northern Italy and Germany was sometimes nonexistent, sometimes real. Countries such as Hungary were headed by the emperor or an imperial prince (a nobleman who was the emperor's representative), but they remained outside the empire. Others, including Flanders (now in Belgium and France), Pomerania (now in Russia and Poland), and Schleswig and Holstein (a region in western Germany), were part of the empire but were ruled by foreign princes who were granted fiefs by the emperor and took part in the election of emperors.

Problems in the Holy Roman Empire can be traced back to the reign of Otto I. Upon taking the throne, he moved the seat of the empire into German territory and maintained connections with the church. This decision created a complicated situation because the capital of the empire was in Germany, but the church was based in Rome. After Otto's death, German kings frequently served as Holy Roman Emperors. Eventually, when a king was elected by German princes, he automatically expected to be crowned emperor by the pope. Even though kings and Holy Roman Emperors were supposed to be elected, these positions gradually became hereditary (passed on from father to son). From time to time German princes were able to exercise their authority in deciding who would become king, but final approval always rested with the pope. After 1045 a king who was not yet crowned emperors was known as king of the Romans, a title that gave him the right to the throne of the Holy Roman Empire. German kings did not always become emperors, however, because the popes sometimes exercised their right to select emperors and chose leaders other than German kings, especially when an election was in dispute.

Middle class poses threat Unifying the Holy Roman Empire was made even more difficult because the emperor was the ruler of both Germany and Italy. Continuing warfare in Italy and the weakness of monarchs in other kingdoms increased the power of German princes, particularly in the kingdoms of Bavaria, Saxony, Swabia, Franconia, Thuringia, and Upper and Lower Lorraine. In 1338, at diets (meetings of church officials and representatives of states) in the German cities of Rhense and Frankfurt, the German princes proclaimed that their appointed electors (voting representatives) had the right to choose the emperor without the intervention of the pope. In 1356 Holy Roman Emperor Charles IV (1316–1378; ruled 1355–78) issued an official declaration called the Golden Bull, which supported the princes' decision and regulated the election procedure. Emperors continued to be crowned by the pope in Rome, however, until after the coronation of Charles V (Charles I of Spain; 1500–1558; king 1516–56, emperor 1519–56). Thereafter they were crowned at Frankfurt. After 1438 all emperors, except for Francis I of Lorraine (1708–1765; ruled 1745–65), came from the house of Habsburg (also Hapsburg), a powerful German family dynasty.

Holy Roman Emperors also were confronted with conflicts between noblemen and merchants. As trade and commerce continued to flourish, German merchants gained increasing wealth and power. They were opposed by the princes, who were still claiming the rights that had been granted to them under feudalism. Partly as a defense against the princes, the merchants had formed a

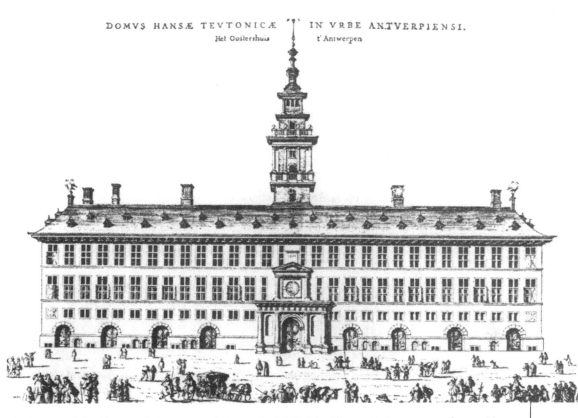

DOMVS HANSÆ TEVTONICÆ ⁙ IN VRBE ANTVERPIENSI.
Het Oostershuis   t'Antwerpen

The house of the Hanseatic League at Antwerp in 1563. The Hanseatic League was formed by merchants as a partial defense against princes. *Reproduced by permission of The Granger Collection.*

network of trading associations known as the Hanseatic League. They established cities, called Hansa cities, that served as trading centers. Since the Holy Roman Emperors were already having problems with unruly princes, they tended to side with the merchants. In an effort to increase their power base, the emperors declared the Hansa to be free cities that came under the direct control of the emperor and were given voting rights in the diet. This change was a significant step toward expanding the influence of the middle class and weakening the status of noblemen.

Empire shrinks Another problem with the Holy Roman Empire was that emperors put more effort into maintaining a dynasty than into governing the empire. This situation arose because the emperor's throne was usually given to the king who had the most land and wealth. Over time, as kingships became hereditary and kings accumulated vast estates, the throne was held by emperors from just a few families. Most prominent were the Luxembourgs (Henry VII, Charles IV, Wenceslaus, and Sigismund) and the Habsburgs. These emperors were more interested in expanding family territories than in unifying the empire. The problem reached a crisis during the reign of Habsburg emperor Maximilian I (1459–1519; ruled 1493–1519), who also was king of the German nation. The princes became alarmed when Maximilian I seemed to be placing the Habsburgs' interests above the welfare of the empire. He had become involved in the war between Italy and France, which could have resulted in expansion of Habsburg territory into Burgundy (see "Italian Wars dominate Renaissance" in Chapter 2). In 1495 the princes established a supreme court of justice to impose Roman law throughout the empire. Five years later they forced Maximilian I to place administration of the empire in the hands of an imperial council, which would control all external and internal affairs.

These measures simply slowed the disintegration of the Holy Roman Empire. In the sixteenth century, the empire shrank until it was concentrated primarily in Austria. Most of the states were seeking independence, a trend that was encouraged by the Protestant Reformation. The German princes accepted Protestantism, while the emperors remained Roman Catholic. The result was the Thirty Years War (1618–48), in which the Holy Roman Emperors joined Spain against the Protestant princes, who were allied mainly with Sweden and France. The struggle ended in 1648 with the Peace of Westphalia, a treaty that recognized the sovereignty (right to self-rule) of all the states in the Holy Roman Empire. The only limita-

tion was that the princes could not form alliances against the empire or the emperor. The states still belonged to the Holy Roman Empire, and the emperors remained powerful monarchs in their home regions. (The Holy Roman Empire continued until 1806, when Francis II of Austria renounced the title of emperor.)

The Roman Catholic Church

The Roman Catholic Church was the dominant institution in Europe during the Middle Ages. The pope and other church officials were involved in all aspects of life—social, political, and economic as well as religious. Yet the authority of the church, and especially the pope, was constantly being challenged by kings and noblemen, who did not want any interference in their affairs. The church was also plagued by corruption and internal squabbling, which caused numerous problems and crises. In the sixteenth century the power of the church was threatened by a reform movement that soon spread throughout Europe and produced widespread social and political change.

Pope's authority challenged The Catholic Church is headed by the pope, who is appointed by a sacred college (representative group) of cardinals. (Cardinals are officials ranking directly below the pope; they are appointed by the pope himself.) The pope is considered a direct successor of Saint Peter, a disciple, or follower, whom Jesus of Nazareth had named the true spiritual leader of Christianity. The pope is therefore the vicar, or representative, of Christ on Earth, as well as the lawgiver and judge for followers of the Catholic faith. During the Middle Ages the pope was a powerful figure because the church controlled not only Europe but also most of the Middle East (the region now extending from Libya to Afghanistan) and parts of North Africa. Since the ninth century, however, the eastern and western divisions of the church had disagreed over the right of the pope to rule all Catholics. (The eastern division included territory that is now Eastern Europe, the Middle East, and North Africa; the western division encompassed present-day Western Europe and Poland and Hungary, which are now in Eastern Europe.) Finally, in 1054, the eastern division established the Orthodox Eastern Church at Constantinople and refused to recognize the legitimacy of the pope. Headed by leaders called patriarchs, the Orthodox Eastern Church continued to observe all other Catholic teachings. The western branch in Rome was called the Roman Catholic Church and retained its authority over western Europe.

The church had been greatly affected by the fall of the Carolingian Empire, which brought corruption, greed, growing secularism, and a general spiritual uneasiness. This decline was reversed in 910 with the creation of the Cluniac monastic order (a group of Catholic men called monks at Cluny, France, who were devoted to the religious life), one of the momentous events of the Middle Ages. The Cluniac order beautified the liturgy (texts used in worship services) and built schools. They revitalized the entire church, initiating reforms that continued for centuries. Inspired by the Cluniac movement, popes tried to create an institution that had spiritual authority over secular rulers. As God's representative on Earth, a pope made it difficult for a secular leader to oppose church meddling in state affairs. Popes such as Gregory VII (c. 1020–1085; reigned 1073–85) initiated the concept known as "fullness of power," which gave them control over both church and state. A pope could therefore undermine secular law by declaring canon (church) law to be above the law of the land. Popes favored particular rulers, launched crusades (holy wars), took sides in political conflicts, and promoted secular laws that were advantageous to the church. The Roman Catholic Church controlled vast amounts of property throughout Europe, including its own fiefs and estates that were used for monasteries and cathedrals (large houses of worship). It also carved out its own territories, known as the Papal States. At various times the Papal States included the coast of France on the Mediterranean Sea, near the city of Avignon, and a large area of central Italy.

Kings in Germany and other states were not willing to give up any of their power to popes. Their resistance became known as the Investiture Struggle, which reached its height when Holy Roman Emperor Henry IV (1050–1106; ruled 1084–1105) challenged the authority of Gregory VII.

Henry insisted on the royal right of investiture, a king's right to name bishops (heads of church districts). This power would have made the emperor equal to the pope and weakened church control over government affairs. In 1076 Gregory excommunicated, or expelled Henry from the church, and the emperor lost the support of his nobles. Henry traveled to Italy the following year and received forgiveness from Gregory. The struggle between popes and emperors continued, however, after Henry regained support from his nobles and successfully overthrew Gregory.

The Crusades Another important event of the Middle Ages was the Crusades, a series of religious wars launched by the popes against the Muslims. Starting in 1096 and lasting until 1291, the Crusades united Europeans as "knights of Christ" against a common "pagan" enemy. (A pagan is a person who has no religious beliefs or worships more than one god.) The Christians were trying to recapture the Holy Land (called Palestine at the time; the territory is now in parts of Israel, Jordan, and Egypt), which they considered sacred because it was the place where Jesus of Nazareth founded Christianity. In 1071 Muslim Turks had seized Jerusalem—the center of the Holy Land and a city considered sacred to Jews, Muslims, and Christians—when they conquered the Byzantine Empire. Although the First Crusade provided some victories and enabled the Europeans to establish kingdoms called Crusader States in Muslim territory

around the Mediterranean Sea, they were finally driven out by the Muslims in a battle at Acre (in what is now Israel) in 1291. In spite of this loss, the Crusades actually strengthened the European economy by opening new markets for trade in the Near East (the countries of southwest Asia and northeast Africa around the Mediterranean Sea). Europeans came into contact with Eastern culture, which had a significant impact on the Renaissance. Scholars brought ancient texts from the Middle East back to Europe that were later used as models for literary and philosophical works.

The Inquisition The Roman Catholic Church reached the peak of its power as a secular force during the High Middle Ages. Pope Innocent III (c. 1160–1216; reigned 1198–1216) triumphantly oversaw the Fourth Lateran Council of 1215, which formulated church laws. Fearing rebellion against these laws, Innocent had launched a bloody crusade against the Albigensian religious movement in southern France in 1208. The Albigenses (pronounced al-beh-JEN-sees) were a Christian sect (small religious group) that had attracted an increasing number of followers during the late twelfth century. Living a strict life independent from the church, they held a complex system of religious beliefs. For instance, they claimed the existence of good (God) and evil (the Evil One) as equal forces, a view that violated Catholic teachings. The pope proclaimed them heretics, those who rebel against or violate church laws, and attempted to bring

Europe Expanded by Crusades

One of the most important events of the Middle Ages was the Crusades, a series of religious wars waged by Christians against the Muslims from 1096 until 1291. (The Crusades also included wars against other non-Christians and against heretics, or Christians who challenged the church.) The Christians were trying to recapture the city of Jerusalem in the Holy Land, which they considered sacred because it was the site of the crucifixion of Jesus of Nazareth. Muslim Turks had seized Jerusalem in 1071, when they conquered the Byzantine Empire, the center of the Orthodox Eastern Church. In 1095 the Byzantines appealed to Pope Urban II for help against the Turks. By this time western Europeans had a great fear of the "Turkish menace," so when Urban announced the First Crusade in Clermont-Ferrand, France, he received an enthusiastic response.

The First Crusade (1096–99) resulted in the successful Christian conquest of Muslim territory. The Crusaders established feudal states in the Near East around the Mediterranean Sea, expanding European culture and religion outside their own borders and learning about other cultures. The Christians were finally defeated at the end of the Ninth Crusade (1271–91) when the last Christian stronghold, the city of Acre in present-day Israel, fell to the Muslims. The remaining Crusaders withdrew from the region. In spite of this defeat, Europe emerged with a stronger economy: it had acquired new markets in Asia, and its political power remained undiminished. The Crusades had also brought Europeans into contact with Eastern (non-European) cultures, thus contributing to the development of the Renaissance two hundred years later.

them under the control of the church. The Albigensian Crusade soon developed into a series of political wars, however, producing no significant religious results by the time the campaign ended in 1229.

In 1233 Innocent's successor, Gregory IX (c. 1170–1241; reigned 1227–41), issued an official pronouncement called a bull that established a tribunal, or formal court, in Albigensian centers in France. The tribunal was given the power to seek out and punish heretics. This event marked the beginning of the Inquisition, which permitted the Roman Catholic Church to wield its power throughout southern France, northern Italy, and Germany for the remainder of the Middle Ages. (Called the medieval Inquisition, this tribunal was separate from the Spanish Inquisition, which was established in 1478; see "Spain" section, Chapter 3). The Inquisition was highly successful, and the Albigensians were completely eliminated in the 1330s. Inquisitors (heads of tribunal proceedings) expanded their search for heretics to other parts of Europe. They targeted anyone who did not seem to be following Christian teachings, such as Jews, Muslims, and other "pagans." The inquisitors punished supposed heretics if they did not accept Christianity according to terms specified by the church. Careful preservation of records promoted the effectiveness of the court, preventing any suspect from escaping punishment. In fact, on the basis of trial records some people were apprehended years later, far from the scene of their original trials.

Heretics punished for sins The Inquisition was supposed to be conducted in cooperation with bishops, but in practice it was usually controlled by the pope. Dominicans (members of a religious order founded by Saint Dominic in 1215) and Franciscans (members the Order of Friars of Minor, founded by Saint Francis of Assisi in 1209) were generally chosen as inquisitors. Given sole responsibility for seeking out heretics, an inquisitor was a privileged person—always male—who answered only to the pope. He was surrounded by numerous assistants: delegates who asked preliminary questions and heard witnesses; familiars who acted as personal guards; and agents, notaries (secretaries), counselors, and servants.

After arriving in a town, the inquisitor let it be known that, for a certain period of time, he would receive testimony, or sworn statements, from witnesses who accused people of being heretics. He would then hear confessions from the accused. He sent out summonses, or court orders, to suspects who had not appeared in court voluntarily. Accused persons were not permitted to question their accusers, but they were permitted to draw up a list of any enemies who might gain from their conviction. Evidence from such enemies was not to be admitted in court. The inquisitor was assisted by a council, and in theory he was to reach his verdict in consultation with the council and the bishop. In reality the verdicts, or court decisions, were often made by the inquisitor alone. The use of torture (infliction of physical injury) was permitted by Pope Innocent IV (d. 1254; reigned 1243–54) in his bull *Ad extirpanda* (1252) as a means of obtaining a confession.

The inquisitor was confronted with a challenging task because he had to determine the state of a person's religious faith on the basis of a vague definition of heresy. Inquisitors dealt with a complex range of supposed heretics, from those who were merely suspected of guilt to those who refused to admit error. Suspects who refused to admit they had committed sins were quickly handed over to state authorities for execution. Yet all those who came under even the slightest suspicion were given some type of punishment, since letting them escape without penalty was considered an insult to God.

The list of offenses included anticlericalism (opposition to church rule), association with heretics, moral offenses (violation of the concept of correct behavior), sorcery (use of power gained from evil spirits), and witchcraft (use of sorcery or magic). It was rare for an accused heretic to escape some form of punishment, even if he or she claimed to be innocent. Sentences were pronounced at an *auto-da-fé* ("act of faith"; pronounced awh-toh deh FAY), a public exhibition that all local residents were urged to attend. Punishments included prison terms, confiscation of goods, pilgrimages (religious journeys), and lesser penances (acts performed to seek forgiveness of sins). Although burning at the stake was thought to be fitting punishment for heretics who did not confess their sins, execution by fire was not widely practiced during the medieval Inquisition.

Crisis in the papacy Although the Inquisition gave the Roman Catholic Church absolute power over the lives of ordinary people, the church itself was engaged in bitter conflicts that eventually weakened its authority in Europe. In 1294 church leaders were embroiled in a crisis over the selection of a pope. For eighteen months, since the death of Pope Nicholas IV (1227–1292; reigned 1288–92), the sacred college of cardinals had been divided into two opposing sides and could not reach an agreement. Neither side would recognize the legitimacy of the other. A schism (division) of the church seemed inevitable. Then Pietro da Morrone (c. 1209–1296), an elderly Benedictine (member of a religious order founded by Saint Benedict), wrote the college a letter promising severe divine judgment if a pope was not elected soon. Terrified of God's

wrath, the dean of the college called for Morone to be elected pope. The cardinals agreed and quickly approved the decision. Morone became Pope Celestine V (reigned 1294).

As a Benedictine, Celestine had been a hermit, a member of a religious order who retires from society and lives in solitude. He soon found that his new responsibilities did not allow the quiet, reflective life he had been leading before his election. He refused to move to the loud, congested city of Rome, where the papacy had traditionally been centered. Instead, he had a special wooden cell built at the papal castle located in Naples, Italy, so he could escape the constant attention of cardinals, bishops, and other church officials. Celestine became so depressed about his new life that he asked for advice from Benedetto Caetani (pronounced kah-ay-TAH-nee; c. 1235 or 1240–1303), a respected member of the church and one of the cardinals who had elected him. Caetani, who had aspirations of his own, suggested that Celestine resign. On December 13, 1294, after only fifteen weeks as pope, Celestine stepped down.

On December 23 the college of cardinals met once again in Naples and elected Caetani the new pope. Taking the name of Boniface VIII (pronounced BAHN-ih-fus), he returned the center of the papacy to Rome. Like Gregory VII and Innocent III before him, Boniface focused on expanding his secular authority. In 1296 he found himself in a conflict with King Philip IV (1268–1314; ruled 1285–1314) of

France and King Edward I (1239–1307; ruled 1272–1307) of England. Both kings had begun taxing clergymen in order to finance the Hundred Years' War, a conflict between England and France over the French throne. This taxation had been started without the permission of Boniface. Outraged, the pope issued a statement, known as the *Clericus laicos,* which forbade the taxation of clergy members without the permission of the papacy. The penalty for defying the order would be excommunication (forced to leave) from the church. Threats of excommunication had been used several times by Gregory VII and Innocent III to persuade monarchs to change their countries' political policies to those of the church. By the Late Middle Ages, however, such threats carried less weight. Philip and Edward both refused to give in to Boniface's demands. The pope attempted to strike a compromise, but he was forced to back down when Philip stopped all French money collected for the papacy from leaving his kingdom and being sent to Rome.

The "evil" pope

In 1300 thousands of religious pilgrims flocked to Rome for a great church event called the jubilee celebration. The jubilee celebration was normally held every twenty-five years by order of the pope, and it was a time of solemnity and prayer. The church usually received quite a bit of money in donations. Feeling more confident in his authority, Boniface issued another decree, this one known as *Unam Sanctam.* The order stated that all human beings, regardless of religion or country,

were subjects of the pope and Rome. Philip was outraged by this claim. With the support of his nobles, Philip publicly accused Boniface of crimes such as committing murder, practicing black magic (use of supernatural evil forces), and keeping a demon, or evil spirit, as his personal pet. Boniface was soon seen as an evil pope attempting to overthrow a legitimate king.

In 1303 Philip sent armed French soldiers to confront Boniface at his private home in Agnan, Italy. The soldiers ransacked the house, stealing everything of value. They attempted to force Boniface to return to France in order to stand trial. After three days, the pope was rescued from the soldiers. The ordeal proved to be too much for the aging Boniface, however. A few weeks later he died, overcome with humiliation and shock.

Papacy moved to France

A new pope was soon elected. This time Bertrand de Got (pronounced deh GOH; c. 1260–1314), a Frenchman, was elevated to the highest post in the church and took the name Clement V (reigned 1304–14). King Philip and Clement, probably because they were fellow countrymen, had a good relationship. In 1307 Clement moved the headquarters of the papacy once again, this time to the city of Avignon in France, a Papal State in his native country. The papacy remained in Avignon for seventy years. Since the city had not been equipped to house the papacy in the manner that popes had enjoyed in Rome, massive building projects commenced. Yet the papacy ran into considerable problems by moving the center of religious authority. Popes had to raise money in order to fund the troops that were necessary to reclaim control over central Italy, where opposition to the move was sometimes violent. Other Papal States lost money because of the move, and the various popes who served during this time were forced to find ways to return the lost revenue.

The massive financial pressure required the Avignon popes to rely on a practice known as simony, or the selling of church offices. Any nobleman who had enough money could become a bishop. For instance, Pope Clement VI (c. 1290–1352; reigned 1342–52) was once heard saying that he would make a donkey bishop if the donkey had enough money. The financial worries of the church began to take a heavy toll on the spiritual authority of the papacy. One pope, John XXII (c. 1235–1334; reigned 1316–34), did try to raise money in ways that did not damage the respectability of the church, but he had limited success. The spiritual authority of the church had already been severely weakened. Furthermore, Rome was still regarded as the rightful home of the papacy. With the pope centered in Avignon, it was widely believed that church interests were controlled by the French monarchy.

Petrarch wrote extensively about conditions in the church at this time. He declared Avignon to be the "Babylon of the West," referring to the story of the Jewish exile in Babylonia (an ancient country in Asia, located between the Tigris and Euphrates Rivers) in the Old Testament. According to Petrarch, Catholics were being held captive in Avignon just as the Jews were held against their will by the Babylonians. Many prominent Catholics, such as England's King Edward III (1312–1377; ruled 1327–77), shared this opinion and questioned the motives of the church.

In spite of the controversy, a number of the popes who served in Avignon were among the most talented in the long history of the papacy. And regardless of what many believed, not all of them were controlled by the French monarchy. During the "Babylonian captivity" there were several attempts to move the papacy back to Rome, but internal arguments always prevented it from happening. Finally, in 1376, Pope Gregory XI (1329–1378; reigned 1370–78) returned the papacy to Rome, but only because of mounting pressure from important Catholics. Avignon had been the center of Roman Catholic worship for seventy years, the same length of time as the original Babylonian captivity. Upon returning to Rome, Gregory was horrified to discover extensive corruption in the Italian church. He made plans to return to Avignon, but he died before he could carry them out. Mob rioting forced the sacred college of cardinals to elect an Italian pope, Urban VI (c. 1318–1389; reigned 1378–89).

The Great Schism Pope Urban was determined to end the corrupt practices and extreme wealth of the cardinals. Fearing Urban's reform efforts, the French cardinals declared that his election was invalid because of the pressure put on the college by the mobs. In 1378 they elected as the new pope Robert of Geneva (1342–1394), who became Clement VII (reigned 1378–94). He had been a cardinal from the French-speaking city of Geneva, a city in southwestern Switzerland that was surrounded by French territory. The cardinals returned to Avignon with Clement, who was called an antipope because Urban was still the pope in Rome. Clement intended to establish Avignon as the center of papal authority once again. Urban refused to recognize the legitimacy of the new pope and excommunicated Clement and the French cardinals. Urban then appointed new cardinals to replace those who had been banished. For thirty-seven years, the rival camps in Rome and Avignon each elected new popes and hurled accusations of heresy at one another. This dispute is known as the Great Schism (also called the Schism of the West).

The Roman Catholic Church was now deeply divided as each camp claimed to be the rightful heir to Saint Peter and the legitimate authority for Catholicism. All of western Europe was divided as well. With Catholicism as the only form of Christianity, a choice had to be made by monarchs of Catholic countries: Would they support the popes of Avignon or Rome? France recognized the popes of Avignon, as did Scotland, the Italian island of Sicily, and Portugal. England, still involved in the Hundred Years' War with France, support-

ed the popes of Rome. The papacy in Rome also was recognized in parts of the Holy Roman Empire, northern and central Italy, and Ireland. Loyalty to the two camps was dependent on the individual interests and needs of a country, often changing when these interests were met by one side and not by the other.

During this turmoil Catholics across western Europe began to discuss questions concerning the fate of the individual soul. Many wondered if they would be saved from damnation (being sent to hell after death) if they were represented by a false priest and a false pope. As time dragged on and it seemed that a compromise would never be reached, some Catholics suggested that a general council of church leaders should meet to provide a solution. Yet the popes at Avignon and Rome would not agree to be judged by followers from the other side. In 1409 the situation became even more complicated when a group of five hundred high-ranking bishops, called prelates, met in a council at Pisa, Italy. The prelates decided that both popes should be removed and a new one should be elected. The popes of Avignon and Rome would not accept this solution, and for a while there were three popes claiming to be the legitimate ruler of the Roman Catholic Church.

Sigismund of Luxembourg (1368–1437) was the king of Hungary and several other lands as well as the Holy Roman Emperor (ruled 1433–37). He wanted the papacy to be controlled by a council, not by a pope

The Babylonian Captivity

When the papacy was moved to Avignon, France, by Pope Clement V in 1307, many Roman Catholics protested because they felt that the rightful spiritual center was Rome. When the Italian poet and scholar Petrarch called Avignon the "Babylon of the West," he was referring to the Babylonian captivity of the Jewish people as described in the Old Testament in the Book of Jeremiah, Chapter 20, verse 4. In 586 B.C. the city of Jerusalem, which was the capital of the Jewish empire, fell to the Babylonians. An unknown number of Jews—some estimates place the total in the thousands—were deported, or forcibly sent, to Babylonia. Those who were sent away were picked because of their affluence and intelligence. It is unknown how many Jews remained in Jerusalem. The deportations were meant to separate the Jewish people as a whole; the deported Jews, however, kept close ties with those who remained in Jerusalem. In 538 B.C. Cyrus the Great (c. 585–529 B.C.) took over the Babylonian Empire. He began new relationships with the Jews and decreed that Jerusalem would once again be the center of Jewish worship. In 516 B.C., seventy years after the Babylonian invasion, a new temple, or Jewish house of worship, was built in Jerusalem, officially ending the captivity of the Jews and signifying their return as a united people.

who made his own decisions. This idea had been suggested years earlier but had not been accepted by church officials. Sigismund hoped to get enough backing to accomplish his goals. In 1414 he called a number of important churchmen to the Swiss town of Constance for a meeting. The council met until 1417, when it was decided that all of the existing popes should be removed and a new one elected. Pope Martin V (1368–1431; reigned 1417–31) was then named the only rightful leader of the Roman Catholic faith. The other three popes did not want to step down, but none of them had enough support to stay in power. The Great Schism came to an end with the Council of Constance. The question remained, however, whether future popes would be required to meet with councils before making decisions about church policy.

The Hussite Revolt Although the Great Schism had ended, the Council of Constance resulted in another serious challenge to the stability of the church. Among those who attended the council was Jan Hus (c. 1372–1415), a Czechoslovakian priest who had been invited by Sigismund. In 1410 Hus had been excommunicated from the church. One of his crimes was criticizing the church's practice of selling indulgences, which were partial pardons of sins in exchange for money. When Hus was invited to the Council of Constance, he was told that no harm would come to him. Nevertheless, many officials were still angry about his daring to challenge the church. Shortly after arriving in October 1414, Hus was arrested and imprisoned. He was kept in prison until June 1415, at which time he was finally given an opportunity to go before the council. When he tried to explain his views, he was shouted down. Hus was heard to say that he expected more piety and order among the council members. He withstood weeks of pressure to recant, or take back, what he had said. A month to the day after his original meeting with the council, Hus was once again given a chance to withdraw his criticism of the church. He refused. He was then stripped of his clerical robes and forced to wear a paper crown painted with three demons and the words "We commit thy soul to the Devil." Hus was led to the town square, where he was burned alive. The members of the council claimed that fire was the only way to cleanse Hus's soul.

After Hus's execution, nobles in Bohemia (located in present-day Czechoslovakia) sent an angry letter to the council and Sigismund, protesting the actions against Hus. Sigismund angrily replied that he would eliminate all followers of Hus, who were called Hussites. Sigismund and Pope Martin began a crusade against the Hussites, who then retaliated by blaming Sigismund for the death of a Czech hero. Rebellion and chaos soon spread throughout Bohemia and Mor-

avia (now territory in the Czech Republic), leading to the Hussite Revolt (also called the Hussite Wars).

The Hussite Revolt lasted from 1420 until 1434. The Hussites issued their demands to Sigismund and Martin in the Four Articles of Prague (1420). They called for freedom of preaching, limits to property holding by the church, and civil punishment of mortal sin (a sin causing spiritual death), among other religious reforms. The Hussites were led by Bohemian nobleman Jan Žižka (c. 1346–1424), who headed their military efforts even after he was blinded in battle. In 1431 the Council of Basel was called for the purpose of drafting an agreement between the church and the Hussites. The war continued, however, as the Hussites argued among themselves; eventually they split into two factions, or opposing sides. Despite this division, Sigismund was unable to achieve victory.

The two Hussite camps continued fighting, with the side known as the Ultraquist Hussites finally winning out in 1434 and ending the hostilities. During peace talks the Ultraquist Hussites demanded that Bohemia and Moravia be granted independence from Germany. They also wanted their own religious practices to be recognized by the Roman Catholic Church. The Council of Basel, not wanting to lose its influence, agreed to these demands. In 1436 the Ultraquist Hussites signed the Compact of Jihlava (also Iglau), in which they agreed to accept Sigismund as king of Bohemia. As a result, Bohemia became independent from Germany; Moravia came

Jan Hus Attacks Indulgences

Among those who attended the Council of Constance in 1414 was Jan Hus, a Czechoslovakian priest who had been invited by Sigismund of Luxembourg, king of Hungary. Four years earlier Hus had been excommunicated from the Roman Catholic Church. One of his crimes was criticizing the church's practice of selling indulgences, partial pardons of sins in exchange for money. Hus believed that people who purchased indulgences should suffer the full penalty of their actions and should not be allowed to buy God's forgiveness. He claimed that a truly penitent, or sorrowful, soul would be cleansed in purgatory; indulgences were therefore not only useless but also wrong. Hus's view angered many church leaders and state officials, who often split the money raised by the selling of indulgences. This practice had been especially important during the Great Schism, when various popes were competing for support from monarchs. The monarchs frequently depended on the money to fund their wars or to help finance their kingdoms.

Hus continued to be outspoken in his demands for church reform, and he made many powerful enemies. After being excommunicated in 1410, he retired to the Czech countryside to write. Hus had the support and protection of King Wenceslaus of Bavaria. While in the countryside, Hus composed his most famous work, *De ecclesia*, in which he claimed that Scriptures (text of the Bible), not the pope, had supreme authority over the church. He also wrote that the pope was not a perfect being who was always correct, and that the state had the right and duty to supervise the church. As a result of his outspokenness, Hus is regarded as one of the forefathers of the Protestant Reformation.

under the rule of Bohemia. The Council of Basel was the last influential religious meeting of the medieval period.

Social and political change

Problems in the Holy Roman Empire and the Roman Catholic Church brought political and social unrest in Europe throughout the thirteenth century, the period that led into the Renaissance. During this time King John of England (1167–1216; ruled 1199–1216) began his reign. Eventually he yielded to pressure from unhappy lords, who objected to his misuse of power, and issued the Magna Carta in 1215. A document of great historical importance, the Magna Carta subjected the monarch to the law, paving the way for democracy (government based on the will of the people) movements in the eighteenth century. In contrast, French kings built a strong state by imposing their authority on feudal lords.

Germany was unable to consolidate its territories into a centralized state. During the late twelfth century, unity seemed possible under King Frederick I (also called Frederick of Barbarossa; c. 1123–1190; ruled 1155–90). Nevertheless, the emperor was more interested in foreign conquest and generally neglected his country. His grandson, Frederick II (1194–1250; ruled 1220–50), who also ruled Sicily (an island south of Italy in the Mediterranean Sea), was one of the most fascinating figures of the medieval period. Frederick II presided over his court with a dazzling intellectual brilliance but, like Frederick I, he ignored German affairs. After the death of Frederick II in 1250, Germany found itself in a political struggle with the papacy, or office of the pope, that lasted for centuries.

In Italy, numerous city-states were involved in the conflict between the papacy and Holy Roman Emperors. Therefore, Italy remained politically unstable; the exception was Venice, which became a sea power. The Iberian Peninsula (now Spain and Portugal) was still under the control of the Moors (Arab and Berber tribes). The new kingdoms of eastern and central Europe were struggling to win acceptance from western European states. In central Europe, however, the Habsburg dynasty gained prominence when Rudolf I (1218–1291; ruled 1273–91) became the king of Germany and the uncrowned emperor of Austria.

Culture flourishes Despite the turmoil, the High Middle Ages were a time of intellectual and literary achievement. Scholars studied Greek philosophy, Arabic science, and Christian theology (religious philosophy) in an effort to understand a complicated world. They attempted to combine faith—acceptance of truth without question—with reason, a struggle that created a complex blend of thought. For example, the French philosopher and priest Peter Abelard (1079–1142) concluded that reason could be the basis of religious belief, while his opponent, French church official Saint Bernard of Clairvaux (1090–1153), approached faith as a purely spiritual experience. English bishop Saint Anselm of Canterbury (1033–1109) developed the famous proof for the existence of God that states that God must exist because people can formulate the "concept" of God. The crowning accomplishment of the thirteenth century was the *Summa theologica*, a work by the Italian theologian (a scholar who formulates religious theories) Saint Thomas Aquinas (1226–1274). This work united Christian theology with the philosophy of Aristotle.

The Black Death

The most devastating event of the High Middle Ages was the Black Death, or plague, a deadly and highly contagious disease that ravaged Europe throughout the fourteenth century. Entire villages were wiped out, and cultural and social progress came to a standstill. At that time medical knowledge was limited, so people did not understand what was causing the

Saint Thomas Aquinas

The Italian philosopher Saint Thomas Aquinas was one of the foremost thinkers of the Middle Ages. He is recognized as the leading theologian of the Roman Catholic Church; he is also one of the principal saints (people who are declared holy) of the church. Saint Thomas resolved the central question facing Christians in the thirteenth century: how to approach the work of the ancient Greek philosopher Aristotle.

Specifically, theologians were trying to decide how to utilize Aristotle's view of the nature of God, man, and the universe. For example, Aristotle considered God to be the prime mover of the universe, who exists outside of time and place. He also believed that humans share a single intellect into which souls are absorbed after death, and that all human love is based on self-interest. These ideas caused problems for Christians, who believed that God created the world freely and at a particular point in time. They also thought that God cares about humans, and that a person who loves God rather than himself or herself will be rewarded with eternal life after death.

Christian thinkers, known as scholastics, resolved this dilemma by concluding that there could be no serious conflict between philosophy and theology, or between Aristotle and Christianity. Since for them Christianity could not be wrong and since Aristotle was an esteemed ancient authority, they wanted to bring Aristotle and Christianity into agreement. The foremost scholastic was Saint Thomas. In his *Summa theologica* (1267–73) he created a system that remained basically Christian while incorporating significant aspects of Aristotle's philosophy. Many modern historians view this system, which is sometimes called the Thomist synthesis, as the most important achievement of medieval thought. (Synthesis is the weaving together of diverse elements.) Saint Thomas's system formed the basis of modern philosophy and theology.

plague. In some parts of Europe the Black Death continued into the eighteenth century.

First use of biological warfare

The plague apparently originated near Delhi in northern India in the 1330s. It spread to southern Asia by 1346, and to the cities of Kaffa and Constantinople by the end of the following year. The Black Death was introduced in Europe as the result of the first known incident of biological warfare (use of living organisms, such as disease germs, as weapons against an enemy). In 1343 Tatars (also known as Tartars; a nomadic tribe from east central Asia) flung dead bodies infected with the plague over the walls of an Italian trading post at Kaffa, in the Crimean region of southern Russia. The Tatars hoped that fear of the disease would drive Italian merchants from the western edges of the Mongol Empire (a vast territory in China and east Asia), which was losing much of its power as a result of the European presence in the region. The retreating Italians then carried the plague to the ports of Genoa and Venice in northern Italy, Messina in Sicily, and Marseilles in southern France. As more people became infected and continued to travel, the epidemic spread to Spain, northern France, and England in 1348. By the following year the plague had attacked Scandinavia and north-central Europe. Northern Russia first felt its effects in 1352, after the epidemic had declined in western Europe. China suffered the full impact of the disease between 1352 and 1369.

The plague came to be called the "Black Death" because it produced open sores on the body that turned black. The disease took such a toll on populated areas that by 1350 at least one-fourth of Europe's inhabitants had died from it. The devastating epidemic returned in the latter part of the fourteenth century. Half of Florence's ninety thousand people perished; some two-thirds of the population of Siena, Italy, and Hamburg, Germany, died. By 1400 the death toll in Europe had reached more than one-third of the total population. People did not know how to prevent the disease, so large sections of Europe and Asia were almost entirely wiped out.

Low food supply

Poor health and malnutrition also made Europeans susceptible to the plague. Prior to 1350, the agricultural market had been attempting, with great difficulty, to feed an ever-increasing population. Areas with large numbers of inhabitants had a hard time keeping up with the high demand for food. Compounding the problem was the fact that many farmers had begun growing highly profitable nonfood crops such as textile fibers, so there was less food available. The shortage reached a peak in 1346, thus making people more vulnerable to disease. With large numbers of people starving, it became necessary to transport foods such as cereals, which were immediately infested by rats, to areas where food was especially scarce. Foods therefore arrived infected with the plague, which struck most savagely at undernourished and weak people. Most of the victims were children, the elderly, laborers, and the poor. Mature adults and wealthy people survived to a greater extent.

The fact that more adults survived the plague helps to explain Europe's fairly swift recovery from the catastrophic death rate. Cities suffered the worst losses in population, yet most soon returned to business as usual. Since many of the plague victims were laborers, in the later fourteenth century there was a desperate need for workers. As a result, wage rates increased. The agricultural areas of Europe suffered more lasting economic effects: central Germany lost at

Causes of Black Death

The Black Death was caused by a bacillus (disease-producing bacterium) that lives in a flea. The unsanitary conditions of the Middle Ages permitted bacillus-carrying fleas to infest and infect black rats, which then bit humans. The bite of the flea produces buboes, or lumps the size of chestnuts, usually in the groin and the armpit. This type of infection is known as the bubonic plague. Healthy people could recover from bubonic plague. Since the disease spread so quickly after 1347, in what is known as a pandemic (widespread) plague, there had to be another form. This form was the pneumonic plague, or plague complicated by pneumonia (infection of the lungs), which scattered a highly contagious form of bacillus. When people who had the pneumonic plague sneezed, coughed, or bled externally, small microbes carrying the disease were released into the air. Healthy people who inhaled the infected air would then catch the disease. This type of bacterial transferal helped spread the disease across Europe. Other strains of plague probably existed, and the population was weakened by diseases such as typhus, which is spread by body lice and is characterized by a high fever, delirium, and a dark red rash. The plague was also spread by influenza, or flu, a highly contagious virus caused by unknown factors and characterized by high fever, body aches, and inflamed nasal tissue.

The main culprit, however, was the black rat, which was the host for the plague flea. The plague was not entirely eradicated (eliminated) until Europeans got rid of black rats by introducing the brown rat in the 1700s. The ferocious brown rat did not carry the plague flea and was a natural enemy of the black rat. Eventually brown rats wiped out black rats, contributing to the decline of the plague after the eighteenth century.

least half of its agricultural settlements after 1352, and numerous French villages disappeared. Many English villages similarly were abandoned.

Europe experienced great physical and mental anguish as whole families passed away. Only large trenches could accommodate the corpses; twelve thousand bodies filled eleven such pits in Erfurt, Germany, in 1350. Across Europe, superstition grew and wild rumors about the nature of the disease were started. Some believed the disease was God's punishment for sins. The intellectual class crumbled as no cure for the disease became clear. Roving bands of religious penitents (people who were repenting their sins) traveled from town to town, where they would publicly whip themselves for sins they believed had caused the disease. Their exposed blood released microbes infected with disease into the air, thus spreading the plague even more widely. Anti-Semitism, or prejudice against Jews, raged in central Europe in 1348 and 1349 because many accused Jewish people of causing the plague by poisoning wells. (Medieval Christians were fearful of Jews, whom they mistakenly blamed for crucifying Jesus of Nazareth.)

Positive results of Black Death

The Black Death resulted in two lasting benefits: better medical literature and programs of public sanitation. Medical science in the Middle Ages was heavily influenced by astrology, yet more than seventy medical writings of the late fourteenth century provided practical and sensible advice about the contagious nature of the plague. These works recommended better surgery, more autopsies (examination of corpses to determine the cause of death), and improved health practices. In addition, certain city governments, especially at the ports of southern Europe, imposed programs to prevent contagion (transmission of a disease by direct or indirect contact) and improve sanitation. The Italian cities of Florence and Venice established commissions for public health in 1348, and in the same year Pistoia issued regulations on burial, clothing, and food to counter the spread of plague. Later legislation recommended that those infected with the disease be isolated. Beginning in 1374, Milan, Italy, isolated plague victims until their death or re-

covery. Ragusa, Italy, isolated such persons for thirty days after 1377. In 1383 the French city of Marseilles extended the period of isolation to forty days in a *quarantaine,* the origin of the modern term "quarantine." The plague continued to attack Europe in varying cycles until 1666, when it left England, and into the 1720s when it ceased in France.

Peasant uprisings

As the Black Death continued to claim lives, civil unrest in rural and urban areas became more widespread. In 1358 peasants in northern France rebelled after being worn down by the plague, starvation, economic depression, and the violence of the Hundred Years' War with England. So many of the male peasants were named Jacques that the rebellion became known as the "Jacquerie" (pronounced JOCK-ehr-ee). The peasants struck out against the nobles for two weeks. The conflicts were exceptionally brutal and savage. When the nobility regained control, they squashed the rebellion with equal brutality. Other violent uprisings took place in Flanders, Italy, the Netherlands, the Iberian Peninsula, and England.

In the English Peasants' War of 1381, a serious attempt was made to eliminate the remaining elements of serfdom. At the time, many nobles blamed Oxford professor John Wycliffe (1330–1384) for encouraging the revolt. Wycliffe was a religious reformer who challenged the authority of the church. He also questioned how the church obtained its vast wealth. Followers of Wycliffe, called Lollards, insisted on using his English translation of the Bible, which had previously been written only in Latin. The Lollards also questioned the injustices inflicted by both the church and state. At one point in the 1381 rebellion, another uprising erupted in London. Called the Wat Tyler Revolt, this uprising was named for one of its leaders, Wat (Walter) Tyler (d. 1381). Rebels marched around the city carrying the severed head of the archbishop of Canterbury. Like the "Jacquerie" rebellion, this revolt was also put down with extreme violence.

Although employment levels increased at the end of the 1300s and into the 1400s, the European economy had suffered greatly during the height the plague. People from towns that were destroyed by the epidemic would wander to other villages and towns to find work. The Black Death had disrupted trade in much of Europe, resulting in higher than usual unemployment rates. Some guilds (associations of merchants and craftsmen established during the Middle Ages) placed severe restrictions on employment to protect their monopolies, the exclusive control or possession of a trade or business. In some areas, the only way to own and operate a shop was by inheritance. Those who had owned a business or had been in a trade guild before the plague did not experience as much economic hardship as those who had

 Black Death and Immunity to AIDS

Twentieth-century scientists found that descendants of survivors of the Black Death have apparently inherited a resistance to HIV (human immunodeficiency virus), which causes AIDS (acquired immunodeficiency syndrome). Often compared to the Black Death, the AIDS epidemic is the most lethal disease in modern history.

The discovery was made in 1998 by molecular biologists (scientists who study the cells of living organisms) at the National Cancer Institute, a U.S. government medical research agency. In a published report the researchers announced that a rare genetic mutation (change in genes) made certain fourteenth-century white Europeans immune to the plague. The mutation was passed down to these people's ancestors who, seven hundred years later, are now immune to HIV infection. According to the study, slightly more than 10 percent of white northern Europeans carry one or two copies of the mutation. It has not been found in East Asians, Africans, and Native Americans whose ancestors were not exposed to the Black Death.

not. Tensions among the social classes increased. Struggles for power, conflicts between guilds, and petty disagreements often resulted in outbreaks of violence. Cities such as Nuremberg, Germany, and Florence, Italy, were sites of civil unrest.

The Ottoman Empire

Adding to the instability of Europe was the threat of invasion by the Ottoman Empire, which bordered Poland and Hungary on the eastern edge of the Holy Roman Empire. This vast kingdom was formed in Asia and North Africa in the 1300s, when the Byzantine Empire was conquered by the Ottoman Turks, who were Muslims from Turkey. For centuries Europeans had feared that they would be overtaken by the Muslims. Not only did Europeans consider Muslims to be pagans, but they also thought the inhabitants of Asia and North Africa were racially and culturally inferior to themselves. Now that the Muslims occupied territory close to Europe, invasion was a real possibility. Throughout the Renaissance, European states were thus involved in ongoing efforts to prevent the Muslims from moving into Europe. Nevertheless, the Renaissance was also heavily influenced by Ottoman culture. In fact, European scholars had been visiting cultural centers in the East since the Crusades.

Osmanli start empire

The history of the Ottoman Empire began when Turkish warrior tribes called the Oghuz moved from central Asia into Asia Minor. Asia Minor (modern-day Turkey) is a large peninsula, or finger of land, that forms western Asia and is bordered by the Black Sea, the Aegean Sea, and the Mediterranean Sea. After accepting Islam in the tenth century, the Oghuz gathered around the Seljuk (Seljuq) family and started expanding their territories. In 1037 they conquered Persia (present-day Iran) and founded the Seljuk empire, which eventually included Syria (a country at the east end of the Mediterranean Sea), Iraq (a country between Turkey and Iran), and Palestine (present-day Israel and surrounding territories). The Seljuks were weakened by squabbles among their own tribes, however, and were defeated by the Mongols (tribes from Mongolia, a region in East Asia) in 1243. This crisis resulted in the rise of Turkish principalities (states ruled by princes) in Anatolia, the western part of Turkey. Among the ruling families of these principalities were the Osmanli.

Historians have found it difficult to separate fact from fiction in stories about the Osmanli. According to legend, they were a noble Oghuz family dedicated to waging a *jihad* (holy war; pronounced jeh-HAHD) against Christians, who had invaded the region during the Crusades. Yet some scholars believe the Osmanli made up this story to strengthen their power. Even Osman (1258–c. 1326), the first sultan (king) of the Osmanli, was a somewhat shadowy figure. Osman inherited the position of war chieftain from his father around 1300, then set out to expand his kingdom in western Anatolia. The conquest of western Turkey was completed by Osman's oldest son, Orhan I (also spelled Orkhan; c. 1288–1360; ruled 1326–62), who followed him to the throne. In 1327 Orhan chose the city of Bursa, in northwest Turkey on the shore of the Sea of Marmara, as his capital. Bursa remained the seat of the Ottoman Empire until 1402, when it was invaded by the Tatars.

The reign of Orhan is significant because he tried to consolidate Ottoman rule. He was still fighting other Turkish tribes so he needed to build a strong state. Orhan I formed a permanent army and organized a legal system. He also introduced such well-known Ottoman institutions as the *divan* (council of state) and *vezir* (also spelled vizier; high executive office). The Ottoman state was now ready to invade Europe. Nevertheless, the first Turkish military presence in Europe came about not through Ottoman invasion but as a result of actions by the Byzantine emperor John VI (also known as John Cantacuzene; 1292–1383; ruled 1347–54). John VI, while possessing virtually all of the power, was actually co-ruler for those years with the rightful emperor, John V (also known as John Paleologus; 1332–1391; ruled 1341–91), who was too young to rule. In 1346 John VI formed an alliance with the Ottomans by arranging for his daughter Theodora to marry Orhan. The Ottomans then provided John VI with military assistance, and in 1353 Orhan was given a base on the Gallipoli peninsula (a strip of land in Europe between the Dardanelles and the Saros Gulf). Turkish presence was now established in Europe.

Ottomans move into Europe

Orhan was succeeded as sultan by his son, Murad I (c. 1326–1389; ruled c. 1360–89). Murad I had his three brothers executed, thus starting the Ottoman custom of eliminating any competition for the throne. From 1361 until 1387 he continued his father's policies. During this time he expanded Ottoman territory in Europe with victories at the Byzantine cities of Edirne, Turkey; Serrai, Greece; Sofia, Bulgaria; Niš, Serbia; and Salonika, Greece. In 1371 Murad moved the capital of the Ottoman Empire to Edirne, deeper into Christian territory. He created the famous Janissaries (*Yeniçeri,* meaning "new army" in Turkish), an army composed of non-Turks, which eventually developed into a powerful military and political force. While extending his rule in Europe, Murad also overpowered the remaining Turkish principalities in Anatolia. He completed his conquest of southern Europe at the battle of Kosovo, a region in southern Serbia, in 1389.

After the battle of Kosovo, Murad was assassinated by a Serbian officer who had claimed to be an ally. Murad's oldest son Bayezid I (pronounced by-yeh-ZEHD; c. 1360–1403; ruled 1389–1402) immediately took control. He secured Ottoman territory in Europe and subdued the remaining independent Turkish principalities in Anatolia. Western European leaders realized that Bayezid I posed a serious threat to Europe, so they formed an alliance against the Ottomans. In 1396, Pope Boniface IX (1355–1404; reigned 1389–1404) proclaimed a crusade. European and Ottoman armies met at the town of Nicopolis (now in Bulgaria), where the Europeans were crushed by Bayezid's superior forces. Although the Ottomans seemed unconquerable, they were defeated by the Mongols at Ankara, Turkey, in 1402. Led by the fierce warrior Timur Lenk (also known as Timur the Lame, or Tamerlane; 1336–1406), the Mongols gave back all the Anatolian principalities that had been taken by Bayezid.

Empire revived

In spite of this devastating blow, the Ottoman Empire did not vanish. The Mongols were not organized as a state, so they could not hold onto political power. Thus, when Timur died in 1405, Bayezid I's sons and several leaders from other families resumed their struggle for the throne. The struggle ended in 1413, when Bayezid I's son Mehmed I (also known as Mehmet I or Muhammad I; d.1421) defeated his last opponent. Ruling until 1421, Mehmed restored the Ottoman Empire. He was followed by his oldest son, Murad II (1404–1451; ruled 1421–51), who fought off the Europeans during most of his reign. The Italian city-state of Venice challenged Ottoman power in the Aegean Sea, and Hungary threatened Turkish territories in southeast Europe. The Ottomans took Salonika from the Venetians, but had to face revolts in Albania (a country on the west side of the Caspian Sea) and in Anatolia. The Anatolian revolt was led by the Karamanoglu, inhabitants of a Turkish region called Karamania, who were longtime enemies of the Turks. After defeating the Karamanoglu in 1437, the Ottomans were attacked by János Hunyadi (c. 1385–1456), the Hungarian warrior hero and duke of Transylvania. Hunyadi was attempting to liberate the Balkans (the name for countries occupying the Balkan Peninsula) from Turkish rule. Although the Karamanoglu and Hungarians rose again, the Ottomans regained total control in 1448.

Mehmed II consolidates rule

When Murad died, his son Mehmed II (also known as Mehmet II or Muhammad II; 1432–1481; ruled 1444–46 and 1451–81) became sultan. Mehmed was called "the Conqueror" because, in 1453, he seized Constantinople, the seat of the former Byzantine Empire. Mehmed then moved the Ottoman capital to Constantinople. A more important accomplishment, however, was that he consolidated Ottoman power, especially in the newly conquered areas. Mehmed extended his rule to Bosnia and Herzegovina in the Balkans, and in 1461 he took Trebizond, the Greek empire, which was the last state in the Byzantine Empire. Several years later he incorporated Karamania into an Ottoman province. In 1473 the Ottomans won a war against Azerbeijan (then a state in northwest Iran; now East Azerbeijan and West Azerbeijan), and in 1478 the coast of Dalmatia (a region along the Adriatic Sea) came under Ottoman control. Mehmed II passed many reforms, establishing a political and social structure that lasted for centuries. He centralized the government, strengthened the Janissary army, and encouraged legal and religious education. He also introduced a unified legal system and established the tradition of training captured Christian children as civil servants (government workers). In addition, he introduced a comprehensive system of taxation, which also affected the people in conquered territories. They lived in communities called *millets* and enjoyed many liberties, including religious freedom.

Mehmed was followed by Bayezid II (c. 1447–1512; ruled 1481–1512), who had to contend with the Egyptian Mamluks in southern Anatolia. The Mamluks were descended from the slave army of Saladin, the twelfth-century warrior-sultan of Egypt and Syria. They had ruled Egypt for centuries. The greatest threat to Bayezid II's rule, however, was the Safavid empire in Persia. It was founded by Esmā'īl I (pronounced is-mah-EEL; 1497–1524), the first Shah of Iran, in 1501 (ruled 1501–24). The Safavids became enemies of the Ottomans, primarily because the Safavids, who were Shiites (pronounced SHEE-ites; members of a branch of the Islam religion), viewed the Ottoman Muslims as heretics. The Shiites believed that the prophet Muhammad, the founder of the Islam religion, designated his brother Ali as the only rightful leader of the Islamic state. Therefore they thought the Ottoman government was unlawful. Bayezid's son Selim I (1467–1520; ruled 1512–20) started his reign by defeating the Safavids at Chālirān, in eastern Anatolia, in 1514. Two years later he conquered the Mamluks at Aleppo, Syria. When Selim took Cairo in 1517, he extended Ottoman power to the Arabian peninsula.

The Ottoman Empire reached its height under the great sultan Süleyman I. *Reproduced by permission of Hulton Archive.*

Süleyman I: greatest sultan

The Ottoman Empire reached its height under the great sultan Süleyman I (c. 1494–1566; ruled 1520–66). Called "the Magnificent," Süleyman continued Ottoman conquest. He moved against Hungary, initiating a conflict with the Habsburg rulers of Austria. Süleyman took Belgrade, Serbia, in 1521. He then defeated the Hungarian king, Louis II (1506–1526; ruled 1516–26) at Mohács, Hungary, in 1526. He even attacked Vienna, Austria, in 1528 and forced Austria to pay tribute (an amount of money in exchange for protection) sixteen years later. Süleyman's understanding of European politics contributed to Ottoman successes in Europe. For instance, he was able to advance his goals by making alliances with certain European powers such as France, and by playing rival European states against one another. Among Süleyman's greatest accomplishments was making the Ottoman Empire into a mighty sea power. In 1538 the Ottoman navy defeated Andrea Doria (1466–1560), the great admiral from the Italian city-state of Genoa, in a battle at Preveza, Greece. The Ottomans now had control of the Mediterranean, from Egypt to Algeria. Süleyman died during the siege of Szigetvár, Hungary.

Ottomans in decline

After Süleyman's death the Ottoman Empire went into decline. One reason was that the role of the sultan had been weakened. For instance, Murad IV (ruled 1623–40) was the last ruler to command his army in battle. The Janissaries had also gained enough influence to remove some sultans from the throne and to have others murdered. Another reason for the decline was that powerful military families protected their own interests, often ignoring the central government, the *Bâbiâli* (called the *Sublime Porte* in French). In 1571 the Ottoman navy was defeated by Holy Roman fleets under the command of the Spanish-born general John of Austria (1545–1578) at Lepanto (now Návpaktos), a seaport in Greece on the strait (thin strip of land)

between the Gulfs of Corinth and Patras. Ottoman control of the Mediterranean had come to an end. Finally, the Safavid ruler 'Abbās I (1571–1629; ruled 1588–1629) conquered Baghdad. After concluding a peace treaty with the Safavids in 1639, the Ottomans tried to seize territory in Hungary. For the remainder of the seventeenth century the Ottoman Empire continued its decline in a power struggle with the Habsburgs in Austria. In 1699 Turkey signed the Treaty of Karlowitz, renouncing Hungary and ending the possibility of Ottoman military conquests in the region.

European wars

Although Europeans had a great fear of the Muslims, they were being equally threatened by their own political instability when the Renaissance began in the mid-1300s. The downfall of feudalism and the decline of the Holy Roman Empire had fractured Europe into hundreds of independent states. The result was that the states remained separate from one another and had their own laws. Although borders were continually changing, the states were crowded together on the world's smallest continent. Being close neighbors enabled Europeans to spread new ideas and enjoy prosperity from a thriving economy. Nevertheless, they were constantly embroiled in disputes over control of territory, which then erupted into prolonged wars.

Throughout the Renaissance, Italy was torn apart by the Italian Wars.

For sixty-five years France and Spain formed complex and shifting alliances—at one time or another each side was supported by Roman Catholic popes, Holy Roman Emperors, and leaders of various Italian states. The Italian Wars resulted in the Italian Renaissance being taken to France by French armies returning from battle in Italy. (See "Italian Wars dominate the Renaissance" in Chapter 2.) Elsewhere in Europe the major conflicts were the Hundred Years' War (1337–1453) and the War of the Roses (1455–85). The Hundred Years' War was not actually a single war that lasted a hundred years. Instead, it was a series of conflicts mixed with periods of peace that involved the Plantagenets (pronounced plan-TAJ-eh-nets) in England and the Capetians (pronounced keh-PEE-shehns) in France. The wars were triggered by English claims to French territory and ended with the defeat of England by France. The War of the Roses was fought in England by two rival houses (royal families), York and Lancaster, who each claimed to have the right to the English throne. Each house used the image of a rose to represent itself—a red rose for Lancaster and a white rose for York. For this reason the conflict is known as the War of the Roses. The war ended in 1485 with a Lancaster victory. A new royal house, the Tudors, was established and Tudor monarchs played an important role in the English Renaissance.

The idea of Europe

One result of the Renaissance was the idea of Europe as a continent.

Pope Pius II, called the humanist pope, was the first to make official use of the term "Europa." *Reproduced by permission of Hulton Archive.*

This was a response to the increasing Muslim threat as well as an effort to promote unity. Europeans wanted to create the concept of Europe as being separate from the continents of Asia and Africa. (Europe is actually the western part of the continent of Asia. Europe is separated from Asia by the Ural Mountains and the Ural River.) Throughout the Middle Ages, popes and emperors had called their kingdom "Christendom" to differentiate it from Muslim kingdoms in the East. However, as the Holy Roman Empire and the

Roman Catholic Church went into decline and independent states began emerging, humanists gradually replaced the name Christendom with the more secular term "Europa" (Europe).

Pius II introduces term "Europa"

Historians have found that Pius II (1405–1464; reigned 1458–64), called the humanist pope, was the first to make official use of the term "Europa." He recognized that the emerging states were diminishing the power of the church and making Christians more vulnerable to a Muslim invasion. In 1461 Pius wrote a letter to Ottoman Sultan Mehmed II. The letter stated that if Mehmed accepted baptism (the ceremony that initiates a person into the Christian faith), he would be recognized by all of the Christian world, which Pius II called "Europa." In addition, Pius coined the adjective *Europeos* (Europeans), making the word equivalent to Christians.

Pope Pius and other humanists considered Europeans superior to the inhabitants of Asia and Africa, and they wanted to promote this image. The idea of European superiority was spread during the fifteenth and sixteenth centuries, when Spain, Portugal, France, England, and the Netherlands sent explorers to the New World (North and South America). Maps depicting Europe as a separate continent also began appearing on the title pages of geography books. Europe was featured as a mighty military and scientific power in the first atlas (map of the world), *Theatrum orbis terrarum* ("Theater of the world"; 1570), by the Flemish map maker Abraham Ortel (called Ortelius; 1527–1598). After 1600 European scholars were calling Europe the *Republica literaris* ("Republic of letters") in an effort to create the image of an intellectually sophisticated culture. Nevertheless, the term Europe was not widely adopted until the eighteenth century.

A Divided Italy: Home of the Renaissance

2

The Renaissance is known today as a single cultural and intellectual movement. It actually began in Italy as the Italian Renaissance, however, and then spread to the rest of Europe, where it was called the northern Renaissance. The Italian Renaissance was started in the mid-1300s by a group of scholars called humanists. Led by the Italian poet Petrarch (pronounced PEE-trark; 1304–1374), they set out to revive the Greek-based culture of ancient Rome (an era known as the classical period). They called themselves "humanists" because they wanted to focus on human achievement, which was exemplified by the arts, science, philosophy, and literature of the classical period (see "Humanism sparks Renaissance" in Chapter 8). The humanists felt that Greek and Roman contributions to European culture had been lost during the "dark ages," the period after the fall of the West Roman Empire in the fourth and fifth centuries. Not content simply to look back to past accomplishments, the humanists used classical works as models to write philosophy and literature that reflected their own times. Moreover, they expressed a newfound hope in the future. They stressed the value of daily life and contended that the individual is capable of doing great things. The humanists' ideas were controversial, though, because they concentrated on secular (nonreligious) subjects, which previously had not been approved by the powerful Roman Catholic Church (a Christian faith based in Rome, Italy).

Because of the dramatic social and political upheaval occurring throughout Europe at the time, society was eager for change. As a result, humanist ideals were embraced with enthusiasm. Feudalism was collapsing, the Roman Catholic Church was weakened, and the Holy Roman Empire could not maintain unity among the hundreds of European states that had emerged during the Middle Ages. As old traditions disappeared, people began looking for different ways to express their experience of the world. Beginning in the fifteenth century and continuing into the seventeenth century in many parts of Europe, the Renaissance completely transformed all aspects of life—the economy, the arts, literature, philosophy, education, social customs, and political institutions. Humanist ideals strongly influenced the Protestant Reformation, a religious reform movement against the Roman Catholic Church that swept Europe in the sixteenth century. The Renaissance also led to discoveries about the natural world that formed the basis of modern science.

Renaissance spreads from Italy

The history of Italy during the Renaissance is extremely complex. Like the other states in Europe, Italy was not unified under a single ruler. In fact, most people at the time had never heard the term *Adela* (Italy), and the united nation of Italy was not created until 1861. In the fourteenth century the Italian peninsula was made up of independent city-states that consisted of main cities with several other cities, towns, and rural areas clustered around them. City-states in the north, with the exception of Venice, were part of the Holy Roman Empire. The city-states were either republics or duchies. The republics were governed by oligarchies, a form of government in which power is exercised by a small group of people from prominent families. The duchies were ruled by noblemen called dukes who belonged to powerful families. Some city-states were subjected to intense rivalries among numerous families, while others had relative internal stability. All of the city-states had a merchant class that made huge profits from an extensive trade network based in Italy. The city-states had taken advantage of the fact that they were located between thriving ports around the Adriatic Sea and along the eastern end of the Mediterranean Sea. Italians, therefore, dominated European trade, banking, and cloth manufacturing. Wealthy Italian noblemen and merchants became active patrons, or financial supporters, of the arts in order to glorify their own success. Although their motives for supporting artists were largely personal, they played a major role in promoting the Renaissance, both in Italy and elsewhere in Europe.

Innovations in painting, sculpture, architecture, poetry, philosophy, and music flourished in all of the city-states, especially in the north, which was the most prosperous part of Italy. As the Renaissance moved southward down the Italian peninsula and, beginning in the fifteenth century, northward into Europe, Italy increased in stature as the center of intellectual and artistic creation. Renaissance ideas were spread by Italian artists and scholars who visited other European states and, conversely, by artists and scholars who came to study in Italy and returned home with new concepts. The Italian Renaissance was also taken to other places by merchants and traders. Scholars often accompanied trade caravans and brought back classical texts. Renaissance ideas were even spread by warfare. When foreign soldiers came to Italy to fight in the numerous wars that took place throughout the Renaissance period, they took Italian culture home with them. Another important factor in the expansion of the Italian Renaissance: Rome was once again the home of the papacy, or the office of the pope, who is the supreme head of the Roman Catholic Church. The papacy was permanently returned to Rome after the Great Schism, a period in the thirteenth and fourteenth centuries when there were popes in both Rome and Avignon, France (see "Babylonian captivity and the Great Schism" later in this chapter). Italy therefore held special significance for Roman Catholic Europeans, who made religious pilgrimages to the

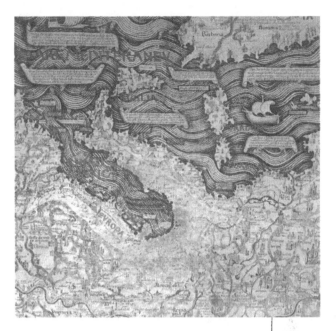

Fifteenth-century map of Italy and the Mediterranean Region. Beginning in the fifteenth century, Italy increased in stature as the center of intellectual and artistic creation as the Renaissance moved northward into Europe. ©Archivo Iconografico, S.A./Corbis. Reproduced by permission.

city. In addition, many popes actively supported the Renaissance.

The Italian Renaissance nevertheless had a dark side: Popes and emperors, kings and queens, noblemen and noblewomen, merchants and traders drained the resources of their communities. They funded elaborate building projects, financed extravagant courts, and organized armies—all with the purpose of enhancing their personal glory. They engaged in bribery, deception, and murder to advance their own ambitions. They ruthlessly competed for better profits, greater trading advantages, more territory, and increased political power. In fact, Renaissance Italy has often been described as a boiling cauldron of greed and corruption.

Italian Wars dominate Renaissance

The Italian Renaissance took place against a backdrop of almost constant warfare and political instability. The major event of the period was a series of conflicts called the Italian Wars (1494–1559), which initially resulted from a dispute between France and Spain over control of Italy. Then the wars escalated into an attempt by the Habsburgs (a royal family based in Austria) to expand their territory through their status as the family of Holy Roman emperors. For sixty-five years France and Spain formed complex and shifting alliances—at one time or another each side was supported by Roman Catholic popes, Holy Roman emperors, and leaders of various Italian states—in numerous wars that took place on Italian soil. Consequently, the Italian states had complicated and tumultuous individual histories.

The Italian Wars began when King Charles VIII of France (1470–1498; ruled 1493–98) invaded Italy in 1494. Charles VIII sent his armies into Italy because he claimed that both Naples and Sicily belonged to France. The French invasion was welcomed and even encouraged by some Italian political leaders, but for other Italians it signified the opening of a new and unhappy period in Italian history. The political turmoil and bloody warfare ended with Spain gaining control of Italy. Many scholars consider the termination of the Italian Wars in 1559 to be the conclusion of the Renaissance period.

First phase: The Angevin and Argonese dispute

The dispute over whether France or Spain had the right to rule Naples and Sicily had been going on since the thirteenth century. In 1266 Charles I (Charles of Anjou; 1226–1285; ruled 1266–85), the youngest brother of King Louis IX of France (1214–1270; ruled 1226–70), took the thrones of the two kingdoms. The reign of Charles I and his family, the Anjous, was called the Angevin (pronounced AHN-jeh-vehn) dynasty. Charles I lost control of Sicily in 1306 at the end of a twenty-year conflict called the War of the Sicilian Vespers (see "War of the Sicilian Vespers" section later in this chapter). In the previous century Sicily was placed under the rule of the Spanish king, Peter of Aragon (Peter III; 1239–1285; ruled 1276–85), a member of a royal family in the Aragon region of Spain. Peter and his successors were called the Argonese.

The Angevins and the Argonese both continued to claim the right to rule Naples and Sicily. In 1489 Charles VIII was offered the crown of Naples by Pope Innocent VIII (1432–1492; reigned 1484–92). This acquisition gave Charles VIII the opportunity to move into Italy. His plans to launch an invasion were later encouraged by such Italian leaders as Girolama Savonarola (see "Florence" section later in this chapter), who wanted the French to protect them from enemies in nearby states. The most persuasive appeal came from the duke of Milan, Ludovico Sforza, a member of the powerful family that controlled politics in Milan (see "Milan" section later in this chapter). Sforza feared that an alliance between Florence and Naples would isolate Milan and leave it vulnerable to attack by Venice, which was expanding its empire in northern Italy. In September 1494 Charles VIII marched his army of eighteen thousand cavalry (soldiers mounted on horses) and twenty-two thousand infantry (soldiers on foot) across the Alps.

French driven out of Italy By the end of the year, the French had entered Rome. With the exception of a bloody battle fought at Rapallo, a seaport near Genoa in northwest Italy, the campaign was a success. The French were welcomed in Milan and in Ferrara, another city-state in northern Italy. Florence fell with no resistance, and, after parading his army through the city streets, Charles VIII went on to Siena and Rome in central Italy. By the end of February 1495, Charles VIII had entered Naples and laid claim to what he called "my kingdom." At first he was welcomed into Naples, but his policies toward the Neapolitan nobility soon alienated them, and his soldiers' open contempt for the Italian people aroused intense hostility. Outside Naples, Pope Alexander VI (also known as Rodrigo Borgia; see "Rome

King Charles VIII of France was responsible for starting the Italian Wars when he invaded Italy in 1494. *Reproduced by permission of Archive Photos, Inc.*

and the Papal States" section later in this chapter) formed an alliance against the French called the Holy League. The members included the Papal States (territory under the direct rule of the pope in central Italy), the Holy Roman Empire, Spain, Venice, and Milan. Milan had turned against the French and entered into an agreement with Charles VIII's enemies. In an attempt to confuse Charles VIII and his ambassador, Philippe de Comines (c. 1447–c. 1511), the Holy League announced that it had been formed to protect Italy against the Ottoman Turks, a vast kingdom founded by Muslims, followers of the Islam religion, located along the eastern border of Hungary (see "Ottoman Empire" in Chapter 1).

The French were not fooled, however, and in May 1495 Charles left Naples. Accompanied by half of his conquering army, he moved northward out of Italy. On the Taro River at Fornovo in northern Italy, the French fought an indecisive battle with an allied army commanded by Francesco Gonzaga, a member of the noble family that ruled the city-state of Mantua (see "Mantua" section later in this chapter). The French continued their retreat from Italy, and by October they were back in France. The other part of the French army, which had remained in Naples, was driven out by a Neapolitan force that had been strengthened by Spanish troops. Historians credit the retreating French troops with taking Italian Renaissance ideas back to France with them.

Second phase: France versus the Habsburgs

The rule of the House of Aragon was now restored in southern Italy. Although Charles VIII promised to return to Italy, he died in 1498, and his successors were left to carry on the next part of the long French involvement in Italian affairs. The second phase of the Italian Wars began during the reign of Louis XII of France (1462–1515; ruled 1498–1515), but the most intense conflict took place while his successor, Francis I (1494–1547; ruled 1515–47), was on the throne. At the beginning of his reign, Francis had concluded an alliance with England and Venice against the Holy League. His first military efforts were successful. In 1516, after a victory at Marignano (now Melegnano), a commune in the Lombardy province of northern Italy, Francis negotiated satisfactory peace terms with all of his opponents. The peace did not last long, however, and in 1522 the French were once again at war, this time against the Holy Roman Empire. The empire was now under the rule of emperors who came from the Habsburg family in Austria and Spain. The Habsburgs were trying to expand their own territory into northern Italy (see "Empire shrinks" in Chapter 1).

The imperial forces—the emperor's army—were led by Holy Roman Emperor Charles V (King Charles I of Spain; 1500–1558; king 1516–56, emperor 1519–56), who was descended from both the Spanish and the Austrian Habsburgs. Although Francis had tried to gain the support of King Henry VIII of England (1491–1547; ruled 1509–47) against Charles V, Henry instead signed an alliance with the emperor. At first the war went badly for the French, who were driven from their bases in Milan, Genoa, and elsewhere in northern Italy. However, in October 1524, Francis crossed the Alps with a new army consisting of thirty thousand French, Italian, Swiss, and German soldiers. At that time Milan was weakened by the Black Death, an epidemic, or widespread outbreak of disease, that had been sweeping Europe since the 1340s (see "Black Death" in Chapter 1). The city was speedily recaptured, and the victorious French army marched on Pavia, a strongly fortified town on the banks of the Ticino River, south of Milan. It was apparent later that the march on Pavia was a mistake, for it gave the imperial army, which was based at Lodi near Milan, an opportunity to reorganize and bring in additional troops from Germany. If Francis had marched first on Lodi, he might have destroyed the last imperial force in northern Italy. Expecting that Pavia could easily be taken by a massive assault, however, he was convinced that his army's superior artillery (various types of weapons) would make the operation relatively simple.

The Battle of Pavia The French completely surrounded Pavia by the end of October 1524 and began a long artillery bombardment during the first week in November. This bombardment was followed by two costly infantry assaults that failed because of the skill and toughness of the Pavians. The governor, Antonio de Leyva, had not only strengthened the fortifications of the city, but had also organized all the able-bodied men into a well-trained militia (citizens' army). Combining the militia with his regular force of six thousand men, de Leyva had enough soldiers to withstand the French attacks. Francis's forces began a long siege on Pavia, believing that famine, disease, and the harsh winter weather would help

them accomplish their goal. As the weeks passed, it appeared that Francis was correct. The winter was unusually severe, and the Pavians suffered not only from shortage of food but also from lack of fuel. Finally, it became necessary to demolish churches and houses within the city to provide wood for fires to keep the Italian soldiers of Pavia from freezing to death. The French, on the outside of the city, had an abundance of supplies, and their camp has been described as an immense market in which a pleasure fair was constantly going on.

France defeated While the siege continued, the emperor was assisted by a Frenchman, Charles de Bourbon-Montpensier (pronounced buhr-BOHN mohn-pahn-syay; 1490–1527), duke of Bourbon. The duke had lost favor with Francis, so he shifted his support to the Holy Roman Empire. He helped Charles V collect the money and organize the men necessary for the rebuilding of imperial forces. By the end of January the army, now consisting of more than twenty thousand soldiers, left Lodi to confront the French at Pavia. The imperial forces were commanded by the Spanish general Fernando de Ávalos (pronounced ABH-ahl-ohs; 1490–1525), the marquis of Pescara. (Marquis is a noble rank below duke.) The army reached the outskirts of Pavia early in February. Francis did not fear the sight of a new imperial army because he believed in his own strength and knew that defeat of Bourbon's men would leave France in control of the whole of Italy north of Rome.

The Battle of Pavia in Lombardy, Italy, between the forces of Francis I of France and the Holy Roman Emperor Charles V. This may have been the first battle in which hand firearms led to victory. *Reproduced by permission of Hulton Archive.*

The battle began on February 24 with an imperial attack, but the emperor's soldiers were swiftly thrown into confusion by the superior artillery fire of the French. Then Francis, in his eagerness to engage the enemy, led a disastrous charge. The French cavalry, pursuing a Spanish infantry force equipped with hand firearms, was suddenly met with a hail of bullets from the Spanish and was almost annihilated. Then an attack by soldiers inside the garrison (fortified building where soldiers stay) threw the French into complete disarray. The

French withdrew from the field, leaving thousands of dead and wounded. Francis was injured several times and finally taken prisoner toward the end of the battle. The Italian states were now at the mercy of Charles V. Charles V sent Francis to Madrid, Spain, where he was put in prison and required to sign the Treaty of Madrid in 1526.

Italy comes under control of Spain
Under the terms of the treaty, Francis abandoned all French claims to Italy,

gave up Burgundy (a region of France on the northern border of Italy), and renounced his rights to Flanders (a region in the Low Countries) and Artois (a region in northern France). He was permitted to return to France, but within a short time he broke the treaty, which he claimed he was forced to sign. He then organized the League of Cognac (1526), which was joined by England, the Papal States, Venice, and Florence. In 1527 Francis invaded Italy a second time, but once again he lost the war. He signed the Treaty of Cambrai (1529), which was the same as the Treaty of Madrid, except that Burgundy was returned to France. Francis abided by the terms of the Cambrai agreement until 1535, when the throne of Milan was left open by the death of the duke of Milan, Francesco Sforza (see "Milan" section later in this chapter). After yet another war (1542–44), Francis renounced his claims to Italy for the third time. He died in 1547. The French invaded Italy again (1556–57), but they were defeated by Charles's forces. With the Treaty of Cateau-Cambrésis (1559), Italy came under the control of Spain until 1706. The Italian Wars reduced France to a secondary position in European affairs.

The major city-states

At the height of the Renaissance, in the fifteenth and sixteenth centuries, there were five main Italian city-states in three distinct geographic regions: Florence, Milan, and Venice in northern Italy; Rome and the Papal States in central Italy (Rome and the Papal States were considered a single state because they were under the control of the pope.); and the combined state of Naples and Sicily in southern Italy.

Florence

Located along the Arno River in north central Italy, the city of Florence was a major center for Italian Renaissance culture. A hub of banking, commerce, and textile manufacturing, Florence was one of the five major Italian powers. In 1434, as the Renaissance was underway, Florentine politics was dominated by the Medici (pronounced MED-ee-chee) family, who were wealthy and influential bankers and merchants. By 1494 the Medicis had been expelled from Florence and the city came under the power of Girolama Savonarola (pronounced sah-voh-nah-RO-lah; 1452–1498), a Roman Catholic friar (member of a religious order) and preacher. After the death of Savonarola in 1498, the city was ruled by a group of wealthy men, each representing a powerful Florentine family. In 1512 the Medicis returned as the *signori* (pronounced seen-YOR-ee; lords) of Florence, but they were expelled again in 1527. Florence experienced extreme turmoil during its last years as a republic before the Medici family made their final return, in 1530, and became dukes of Florence. By 1569 they were grand dukes of Tuscany, a region in north central Italy, with Florence as its capital. At that time Tuscany was divided into Arezzo, Florence, Grosetto,

Livorno, Lucca, Massa-Carrara, Pisa, Pistoia, and Siena. Although Tuscany was under a republican government, the Medicis were the supreme rulers. They reigned for the next three hundred years.

The Medicis were active patrons of the arts, and for two centuries artistic and intellectual life flourished in Florence. The cultural revival funded by the Medicis attracted some of the greatest Italian artists of the time, including painters Michelangelo (1475–1564), Leonardo da Vinci (1452–1519), and Raphael (1483–1520) as well as sculptor Donatello (c. 1386–1466). Poets and scholars were also active in Florence, and a university, the Academia della Crusca, was founded in 1582.

Florence before the Medicis Florence had been the site of settlements since prehistoric times. All of these early communities were destroyed by wars, but in the time of Roman leader Julius Caesar (100–44 B.C.), Florence was a walled city under Roman rule. Even during that period Florence was an important commercial center, though it was subjected to numerous sieges and occupations by invaders. Despite these attacks, the city survived to become an important educational center for Roman Catholic bishops (officials in charge of church districts). In 1081 Matilda, countess of Tuscany (1046– 1115; ruled 1055–1115), the leader of Florence, sided with the church in a disagreement between the pope and the king of France. Matilda's action earned Florence a reputation of being friendly to the Catholic Church. The city became a self-ruling commune (municipal corporation) in the twelfth century. In the thirteenth century Florence was split into two factions (opposing sides) in the conflict between Holy Roman emperors and Roman Catholic popes over control of Italy. The faction called the Guelphs (pronounced gwelfs) supported the pope, and the faction called the Ghibellines (pronounced GIB-eh-leens) backed the Holy Roman Emperor. By the end of the thirteenth century the Guelphs had secured power, but they then began fighting among themselves and split into factions called the Blacks and the Whites. The poet Dante (1265– 1321), whose work later influenced Renaissance literature, was banished from Florence as a White Guelph in 1302. The growth of Florence was temporarily halted in 1348, when 60 percent of the city's population died in the Black Death. Florence became a city-state in the fifteenth century.

During the Renaissance, Florence was involved in conflicts with neighboring city-states over rights to trade routes. Having access to seaports, rivers, and roads was important to merchants and traders who needed to ship their goods to customers in distant places. Rulers of city-states, therefore, wanted to seize land that gave them better access to trade routes. At the start of the fifteenth century, Florence nearly fell to Gian Galeazzo Visconti of Milan (see "Milan" section later in this chapter). His unexpected and early death in

1402 gave the Florentine army a chance to reorganize their forces. In 1406 they succeeded in capturing Pisa, thus gaining a port on the Arno River that was only fifty miles off the coast of Italy. Since the Arno flows through the heart of Florence, it provided the region even greater potential for business and trade. Florence went to war again with Milan from 1409 until 1411 and again in 1421. From 1429 until 1433, Florence battled with the nearby republic of Lucca, an important silk-producing region. Milan eventually joined Lucca in this conflict, which almost destroyed Florence.

Complex political system Florence had a complex political system. By the first part of the thirteenth century, guilds were involved in the city government. Similar to modern-day labor unions, guilds were associations formed by people involved in the same line of work. Florence had twenty-one major and minor guilds. Major guilds were divided into seven categories: wool manufacturers, silk manufacturers, bankers, physicians, judges, apothecaries (similar to modern-day pharmacists), and furriers (people who sold, sewed, and treated fur clothes). Minor guilds were for shopkeepers and blacksmiths. Thousands of workers did not have a guild for their trade, however. Some were not allowed to be in a guild because they were too poor.

In 1283 members of guilds had formed an organization and made changes to the constitution (the document that specifies a state's laws) of Florence. The city-state was now a re-public, and governing power was taken away from the noblemen (members of the upper social class) and given to the guildsmen. Noblemen were lords who had been granted large tracts of land called fiefs (pronounced feefs) by a king under feudalism, a social and economic system that developed in Europe in the Early Middle Ages (see "Feudalism" in Chapter 1). The lords were given control of their fiefs in exchange for vowing loyalty to the king, and they passed their fiefs on to their sons, who in turn exercised absolute power. Even after the fall of feudalism and the rise of republicanism, noble families were able to gain political positions because of their prominence and wealth. However, according to the new constitution, noblemen were no longer allowed to run for political office.

Yet the guilds were soon exercising the same kind of control that had once been wielded by noblemen. Although members of both major and minor guilds could be candidates for office, the major guilds held the most power. To be eligible for office, one had to pass the test of the *accoppiatori* the group that decided who was allowed to compete for political positions. Usually they chose only 10 to 15 percent of the guild members. The *accoppiatori*, then put the names of those who had been selected into a bag. Offices thus were not filled by voting but instead by random chance. Moreover, only a few people were actually involved in the government and there was also extensive corruption. Powerful families that were able to pay off the *accoppiatori* often ran Florentine politics.

Florence under the Medicis Florence's city council, the Signoria, was run by a complicated system. Certain members would serve longer terms than others, depending on which department they were involved in. The main purpose of the Signoria was to introduce legislation, or laws. If the legislation was passed by a two-thirds majority of the council, it would move to the legislative bodies. The legislative bodies were the Council of the People and the Council of the Commune. Each council consisted of around three hundred men. These councils could reject or accept the proposed legislation, but otherwise they had little power. When the Medicis took over Florentine politics for the first time, in 1434, the councils were replaced by the Council of One Hundred and the Council of Seventy. The government was changed a few more times, as the Medici family came in and out of power, with different councils replacing the old ones. By the time the Medicis returned in 1530, the entire constitution had been withdrawn and Alessandro de' Medici (1510–1537; ruled 1531–37) was named "duke of the republic of Florence." The Signoria was replaced by the Magistrato Supremo (supreme magistrate), which shared power with the duke. The legislative bodies were replaced by the Council of Two Hundred and the Senate of Forty-Eight. Appointment to these councils was for life.

Rise to power In the early fourteenth century a number of powerful and influential families were all striving to gain control of Florence. The most prominent were the Medicis, who had gained wealth and social influence from banking, trade, and cloth manufacturing. The patrician, or male head, of the family was Cosimo de' Medici (called the Elder;1389–1464). He first came to political prominence when he opposed the war with Milan and Lucca. The war was supported by the Albizzis (pronounced al-BEET-tsees), the dominant family in Florence at the time. The Albizzis and their allies exiled Cosimo and the other leaders of the Medici clan. In 1434 a new Signoria was chosen, and this group asked Cosimo de' Medici to return to the city. Cosimo's enemies were exiled and he was acknowledged as the leading citizen of Florence. The Albizzis plotted to overthrow the government, but the plan ultimately failed. The entire Albizzi family, along with their supporters, were exiled from the city. This event started the Medicis' three-hundred-year reign in Florence.

Cosimo de' Medici made sure that Florence was ruled with a steady hand. Having become wealthy through the cooperation of others, he knew that a government had to be made up of many different people. He established advisory councils and often asked for advice, kept taxes low, and respected the republican form of government. He served as Standard Bearer of Justice, the highest office at the time, for six months. The government councils often met at his palace, and in

Medicis Support Renaissance

Cosimo de' Medici was instrumental in promoting the arts in Florence, which became the center of the Italian Renaissance. Educated at a strict monastic (religious) school, Cosimo learned Arabic, French, Greek, Hebrew, and Latin. As he grew into adulthood he found politics and business to be too simple. While he excelled in all of his endeavors, young Cosimo found that philosophy was the only subject that truly challenged him. He frequently attended meetings of humanist thinkers throughout Florence. He also developed a keen interest in art and architecture, both of which he felt were ideal ways to honor his family. He gave large amounts of money to many artists and architects. He erected the Medici Palace in the heart of the city and funded the construction of many elaborate cathedrals and other buildings. Cosimo became known as the "father of the state."

Cosimo's grandson, Lorenzo, called "Magnificent Lorenzo," carried on the Medici tradition of supporting the arts and learning in Florence. To the family collection of antiquities—classical medals, jewels, and vases—Lorenzo added expensive and celebrated pieces of his own. He also expanded the extensive Medici private library, with his acquisitions including a number of Greek manuscripts. Lorenzo supervised the reestablishment of the University of Pisa, involving himself in every aspect of the enterprise from the appointment of faculty to questions of student discipline. Turning his attention to architecture, he started modestly by contributing to the rebuilding of the convent of Le Murate in Florence in 1471 and continuing to fund his family's patronage of their neighborhood church of San Lorenzo. In 1474 he acquired a rural estate on a beautiful site at Poggio a Caiano near Pistoia; at that time he may already have begun planning the great villa, a model of the advanced Renaissance style that he started to construct a decade later with his architect Giuliano da Sangallo (c. 1445–1516). Lorenzo also started writing poetry at this time. He enjoyed discussions with the philosopher Marsilio Ficino (1433–1499), and he came to appreciate the friendship and learning of Angelo Poliziano (1454–1494), one of the greatest philologists (a person who specializes in literary study or classical scholarship) of his day. Lorenzo had a genuine interest in intellectual activities, but he also assured that his reputation as a patron and practitioner of the arts consolidated his authority in Florence and beyond.

times of trouble he made huge personal loans to the city. He also gave money to other prominent Florentine citizens, thus making them obligated to him. The owner of a number of local textile mills, Medici was the largest employer of Florentine workers, and he seldom let council members forget that fact.

Medici knew that the only way to gain political power was through money. As a result, he took on a number of business partners. He would allow these partners to make their own decisions only if they had invested enough money in the business. Nevertheless, Medici demanded that he himself own at least 50 percent of any business so he could take control if it started to fail. The Medici family loaned money all across Europe and to the papacy. Even when dealing with the church, Cosimo insisted that he be given the same amount of control as in his other partnerships. The Medici family spread their influence even further by owning banks throughout Europe.

Cosimo's son Piero (1416–1469; ruled 1464–69) continued the Medici dynasty after the death of his father in 1464. Piero lacked Cosimo's political skills, and he often suffered from poor health. Yet he was an intelligent banker and a supporter of the arts. Like his father, he was a patron of artists and architects. His wife, Lucretia, was a respected Florentine poet. She helped Piero spread the family's wealth to talented artists, and together they had five well-educated children. Although Piero reigned for only five years, he passed his legacy on to his more able son, Lorenzo.

The Magnificent Lorenzo Lorenzo de' Medici (1449–1492; ruled 1478–92) continued the patronage of the arts that was started by his father and grandfather. A complex and intelligent man known as "Magnificent

Lorenzo," he became famous for his contributions to countless artists. Expanding the already spectacular Medici library, he periodically held poetry readings and stage performances. Like his grandfather, Lorenzo attempted to protect the financial interests of Florence. In 1471, when Pope Paul II (1417–1471; reigned 1464–71) was succeeded by Pope Sixtus IV (1414–1484; reigned 1471–84), Lorenzo met a worthy political enemy. The Papal States and Florence were both interested in the fertile alum (a vital metal use in dyeing cloth) mines located in Volterra, an area in the Pisa province. Lorenzo had invaded Volterra and gained control of the region. When Sixtus became pope, he vowed to destroy Lorenzo.

The Medici family had traditionally maintained friendly relations with the papacy, and for years they had served as the official bankers of the Roman Catholic Church. When Sixtus took the papal throne, however, relations between the church and the Medicis became tense. A rival Florentine banking family, the Pazzis, had replaced the Medicis as the papal bankers. The Pazzis began formulating a plot to assassinate Lorenzo and his brother Giuliano. The pope blessed this plot, and on April 26, 1478, Giuliano was stabbed to death. An attempt was also made on Lorenzo's life, but he escaped with only a wounded shoulder. The Pazzis family failed to gain the support of the people, and the plotters were given the punishment of death. Some were hanged from the windows of the town hall and others were murdered by angry mobs. Angered by the failure of the plot, Sixtus excommunicated, or expelled, Lorenzo from the church and invaded Tuscany, the region with Florence at its center. Milan joined the Papal States in the invasion, which lasted for two years. During this time, Florence suffered greatly. Lorenzo risked his own life by going on a secret mission to speak with the leader of Naples, Ferrante I (see "Naples and Sicily" section later in this chapter). Ferrante was an often cruel man, and many feared that he would kill Lorenzo. Instead, Lorenzo convinced Ferrante that war with Florence was not in the best interest of Naples. Sixtus was forced to agree to a peace with Florence.

Fall, return, fall, return After surviving the assassination plot and the subsequent war, Lorenzo de' Medici continued to be a dominant force in Florentine politics. He helped form the Council of the Seventy, the reformed legislative body, and became a lifetime member. Lorenzo also invested his own fortune in business and banking ventures in Florence, a move that made quite a bit of money for both the Medicis and the city. By the end of his life, however, risky financial moves had cost the family a substantial portion of their wealth. Some of his personal loans had turned out to be unwise, and by 1492, the year of his death, a number of Medici banks had already closed.

In 1494 the French invaded Italy in the first phase of the Italian Wars (see "Italian Wars dominate Renaissance" section previously in this

Lorenzo de' Medici was a complex and intelligent man who became famous for his contributions to many artists during the Renaissance period. *Reproduced by permission of Archive Photos, Inc.*

chapter) and the Medici family was forced to shut down its bank in Rome. Finally, the home bank in Florence also closed its doors. The Medicis managed to hold onto enough wealth to support themselves, and family members continued to hold prominent positions in the city. Lorenzo's second son, Giovanni (1475–1521), became a cardinal, a high-ranking church official, at the age of thirteen and was later named Pope Leo X (reigned 1513–21). Lorenzo was succeeded by his oldest son, Piero (1471–1503; ruled 1492–94), who turned out to be a terrible ruler. He was blamed for the loss of territory to the French, and in 1494 the Medicis were exiled from Florence.

After the exile of the Medici family, the pro-French council under Savonarola came to power. He set out to rid Florence of vice and corruption, which he claimed had been promoted by the Medicis, and promised to restore spiritual and moral values. During the Italian Wars, Savonarola supported the French invasion of Italy. He hoped that King Charles VIII of France would lead the way in establishing a democratic government (rule by the will of the people). Savonarola also attacked the sinfulness of the court of Pope Alexander VI (also known as Rodrigo Borgia; see "Rome and the Papal States" section later in this chapter), who excommunicated him from the church for disobeying orders to stop preaching. The policies of Savonarola and his followers were not popular with the people of Florence, so they soon fell out of favor. Savonarola and two disciples were arrested . After being subjected to torture, Savonarola confessed to being a false prophet (one who falsely claims to be able to foretell future events). He and the other two men were hanged in 1498.

In 1512 Lorenzo's youngest son, Giuliano de' Medici, duke of Nemours (1479–1516; duke 1515–16), returned to Florence. With the support of Holy Roman Emperor Maximilian I (1459–1519; ruled 1493–1519), he restored his family to power. The Medicis remained in Florence until 1527, when they left peaceably after the fall of Rome to Holy Roman Emperor Charles V (see "German Fury" section later in this chapter). For two more years, Florence existed as a republic. In 1529 pro-Medici forces invaded Florence and once again took control. Three years later Florence became a duchy under Charles V, but it remained an important part of Italian commercial and cultural life. In 1537 Cosimo I de' Medici (1519–1574; ruled 1537–74), one of the most important members of the family, became duke of Florence. He devoted his life to the complicated maneuvering that was still an integral part of city politics. Cosimo manipulated guilds whose members he controlled and brought in outsiders who owed him allegiance. Cosimo had considerable success. In 1557 Florence conquered Siena, fulfilling a longtime ambition of Florentine rulers to seize the city, and in 1569 Cosimo became the grand duke of Tuscany. Under his leadership, culture and arts once again thrived in Florence.

Cosimo was succeeded by his son Francesco (1541–1587; ruled 1574–87), who presided over the decline of the Medici family. He allowed the Spanish and Austrian branches of the Habsburg royal family to virtually control Florence while he pursued his interest in alchemy (a medieval science devoted to turning common metals into gold) and other nonpolitical activities. Nevertheless, the city remained a center of intellectual and artistic life throughout the Renaissance in Europe.

Milan

At the time of the Italian Renaissance, Milan was a duchy that consisted of the capital city of Milan and other, less influential cities. Located in the far northern region of Italy, along the border of present-day Switzerland, Milan had been one of Italy's largest and wealthiest cities since the late Roman Empire. The city occupied a strategic position at the crossroads of major routes between the Italian peninsula and northern Europe. Although Milan was surrounded by a fertile agricultural area, the economy was based mainly on commercial trade. The city was known for luxury goods, especially cloths such as silk, satin, and velvet. It was also a center for the production of weapons and armor. The other cities in the duchy of Milan also had commercial specialties, but none had reached the size or the success of the capital. Merchants in the area conducted active and sophisticated trading relationships with most of the European states and with kingdoms along the eastern coast of the Mediterranean Sea.

Each town and region within the Milanese state had a strong sense of local patriotism. In rural areas, which were not yet touched by the cultural and political advances of the cities, feudalism continued to dominate throughout the Renaissance. In urban areas, the medieval tradition of communal republicanism, in which a group of community leaders formed a governing body, continued even after Milan came under the rule of a duke. The result was that each region had its own form of government. The nobles who controlled the countryside estates were often members of the dominant political groups of nearby cities, giving the nobles considerable influence. Like most Italian city-states, Milan therefore had a complicated political history that was dominated by a few powerful families. The foremost families were the Viscontis (pronounced vees-KOHN-tees), who controlled Milan at the beginning of the Renaissance, and the Sforzas (pronounced SFORT-sahs), who held power during the remainder of the period. Both the Viscontis and the Sforzas were patrons of the arts.

One of the many challenges confronting the rulers of Milan was the ongoing turmoil caused by the Italian Wars, a series of conflicts in which France and Spain fought over control of Italy (see "Italian Wars dominate Renaissance" section previously in this chapter). King Charles VIII of France started the wars in 1494 when he invaded Italy and attempted to assert his claim to the throne of Naples, in southern Italy. To reach Naples, he had to march his forces through northern Italy, but he did not have enough support. Charles left after fighting a major battle in Milanese territory in 1495. Four years later, however, his successor, French king Louis XII, returned to Italy and began the second phase of the Italian Wars. Louis easily captured Milan and declared himself the rightful ruler. From 1494 until 1559 Milan became a prize to be fought and bargained over by the kings of France, the Holy

Roman emperors, and Spain. The emperors were members of the House of Habsburg, a royal family based in Austria that had expanded Habsburg rule to Spain. Spain and the Holy Roman Empire were therefore allies during the Italian Wars.

Viscontis seize power When the Renaissance began in the mid-1300s, the duchy of Milan was controlled by the Visconti family. They came from the powerful Lombard family of Milan, which belonged to a political faction called the Ghibellines. The Ghibellines supported the Holy Roman emperor in a conflict between the Holy Roman Empire and the Roman Catholic Church over control of Italy. Supporters of the church were called Guelphs. The Viscontis had dominated political life in Milan since the twelfth century. They were given the title of viscount (pronounced VIE-count; a title of nobility), from which they took the their name. The Viscontis moved in and out of power in Milan for 136 years.

In 1277 Ottone Visconti (c. 1207–1295; ruled 1262–95), the archbishop, or head church official, of Milan, was named lord of the city. He had overthrown the opposing Della Torre family, leaders of the popular party. Ottone wanted to maintain his family's claim to the lordship, so in 1287 he had his grandnephew, Matteo I Visconti (1250–1322; ruled 1310–22), elected as captain of the people. Matteo was exiled from Milan by the Della Torres from 1302 until 1310. With the assistance of German king and Holy Roman Emperor Henry VII (c. 1275–1313; king 1308–13; emperor 1312–13), Matteo returned to the city and was named imperial vicar (deputy of the emperor). He gained control over all Lombard cities, but he was forced to retire in 1322 by opposition from the Guelphs. Matteo I's son, Galeazzo I Visconti (c. 1277–1328; ruled 1322–28), was named lord of the city. Galeazzo continued the struggle against the popes and the Guelphs.

Viscontis expand Milan Galeazzo was followed by his own son, Azzo Visconti (1302–1339; ruled 1328–39), who unified the state, made peace with Pope Clement V (1260–1314; reigned 1304–14), and expanded Milanese territory. When Azzo died, his two uncles, Giovanni Visconti (1290–1354; ruled 1349–54) and Lucchino Visconti (1292–1349; ruled 1339–49), were named dukes of Milan. Lucchino ruled alone and conquered territory in Piedmont, Tuscany, and the Ticino canton (county) of Switzerland. The other Italian city-states became alarmed at the growing power of Milan and formed alliances against the Viscontis. When Lucchino died in 1349, Giovanni took over the government and continued his brother's policies, annexing the seaport republic of Genoa in 1353. Giovanni was also the archbishop of Milan and a friend of the humanist scholar Petrarch. Upon Giovanni's death in 1354, Milanese territory was divided among his three nephews, Matteo II Visconti (1319–1355), Galeazzo II Visconti (1321–1378), and Bernarbò Visconti (1323–1385). Matteo II died after being poisoned, probably by his brothers, who divided his possessions. Galeazzo II established a court at Pavia and became a patron of Petrarch. He also built a castle and founded the University of Pavia. Bernarbò jointly ruled Milan with Galeazzo II's son, Gian Galeazzo Visconti (1351–1402; ruled 1378–85). Bernarbò pursued his ambitions for more land and power. He was constantly at war with the pope, Venice, Florence, and Savoy (a region in southeastern France). Bernarbò finally was arrested by Gian Galeazzo, who had him put in prison. Some scholars speculate that Gian Galeazzo had Bernarbò put to death in 1385.

Gian Galeazzo promotes arts As the sole heir of Visconti holdings, Gian Galeazzo became master of northern and central Italy in 1385. He was an ambitious man who wanted to rule the whole of Italy. He allied his family with France by marrying Isabella, the daughter of the French king, John II (1319–1364; ruled 1350–64). Gian Galeazzo's daughter by a second marriage, Valentina (1366–1408), married Louis, duc d'Orléans (1372–1407) in 1387. (Valentina became the grandmother of King Louis XII of France who, a century later, claimed he had a right to take over Milan in the Italian Wars; see "Sforzas establish reign" section later in this chapter.) During the first few years of his reign Gian Galeazzo brought political stability to the city-state, reforming and centralizing the government and promoting

the arts and industry. He ordered construction to begin on the elaborate cathedral of Milan, a gigantic, multi-spired building that still stands today. Another magnificent building commissioned by Gian Galeazzo was the Certosa di Pavia, a richly ornamented monastery church in Pavia, which is considered one of the architectural masterpieces of the Renaissance.

Gian Galeazzo also focused on expanding his kingdom and conquered the Italian city-states of Bologna, Perugia, Pisa, Siena, and Verona. His main goal, however, was to overtake the republic of Florence. To strengthen his position, in 1495 he purchased the title of duke of Milan from uncrowned Holy Roman Emperor Wenceslas (1361–1419), who was also king of Germany and Bohemia (now part of Czechoslovakia). In 1401 Gian Galeazzo defeated the forces of King Rupert of Germany (1352–1410; ruled 1400–10), who wanted to be Holy Roman Emperor. Rupert had invaded Italy and tried to return it to the empire. The following year, when Florence was about to fall to Visconti forces, Gian Galeazzo died of the plague. Gian Galeazzo's two sons, Giovanni Maria Visconti (1388–1412; ruled 1402–12) and Filippo Maria (1392–1447; ruled 1412–47), were unable to keep the expanded kingdom together. Giovanni Maria lost several Lombard cities and was finally assassinated. This problem reflected the general situation in Italy: States formed and broke alliances with one another on a regular basis. Warfare constantly broke out, usually under the leader-

During the first years of his reign Gian Galeazzo ordered the construction of the cathedral in Milan, Italy. *Reproduced by permission of Hulton Archive.*

ship of generals with little or no loyalty to their leaders.

Filippo Maria is last Visconti ruler
Filippo Maria was the last Visconti ruler of Milan. He died in 1447 without a legitimate heir (child born in a legal marriage). His only acknowledged child was a daughter, Bianca Maria (1425–1468), who had been born to his mistress (a woman who was not his wife), a Milanese noblewoman. Bianca

Maria had been raised as a noble-woman and was recognized as Filippo's heir at an early age. While he was still alive, Filippo attempted to use her as a bargaining tool, promising her hand in marriage to various political leaders. These attempts failed, however, and he was forced to arrange Bianca's marriage to the condottiere (pronounced kahn-deh-TYER-ee; commander) of the Milan armies, Francesco I Sforza (1401–1466; ruled 1450–66).

Francesco I was the illegitimate son of Muzio Attendolo Sforza (1369–1424), a farmer in the Romagna region of northern Italy who became a noted condottiere and took the name Sforza (the Italian word for "forcer"). Muzio headed a band of skilled mercenaries, or hired soldiers, whom he led in battle for several Italian city-states, including Naples. He was killed while serving Queen Joanna II in her attempt to hold onto the throne of Naples (see "Naples and Sicily" section later in this chapter). Francesco I took over command of his father's mercenaries and soon gained prominence as one of the most powerful condottieri of the time.

After Fillipo's death, the Visconti family castle was attacked by Milanese republicans (those who advocate representative government), who felt betrayed by him. They established the Ambrosian Republic in an attempt to return to the communal form of government, a tradition established in the Middle Ages that placed the city under the rule of representatives from the community. The government was not supported by the Milanese people,

however, and the republic collapsed when the economy began to fail.

Sforzas establish reign In 1450 Francesco I Sforza took his powerful army—along with his connections to the Visconti family—into Milan and declared himself master of the republic. He was then named duke of Milan. Welcomed by most of the population and supported by the Medicis of Florence (see "Florence" section previously in this chapter), he set out to return Milan to its former glory. Francesco I thus began the eighty-five-year Sforza reign in Milan. During that time the Sforzas developed one of Europe's most effective governments and one of its earliest permanent armies. Using their extensive personal power, they ruled through force and skillful political maneuvering. Their methods were similar to those used by the Medicis in Florence, except that the Sforzas were warriors, whereas the Medicis were bankers. Although the Sforzas promoted their own interests, they did beautify Milan and, as generous patrons of the arts, they presided over the city's "golden era" during the Renaissance.

Francesco I leaves legacy After Francesco I Sforza took over as duke of Milan he expanded the government, built new and elaborate buildings, created a number of civil positions, and strengthened his army. He was not only an effective military leader but also a shrewd diplomat, or political negotiator. He promoted political stability by entering into alliances with

Valuable Alliances

When Francesco I Sforza became duke of Milan he began the practice of establishing connections that would benefit his family. One of his sons, Ascanio Maria Sforza (1455–1505), became a cardinal, a high-ranking official, of the Roman Catholic Church and was instrumental in the election of Rodrigo Borgia as Pope Alexander VI. Francesco's illegitimate daughter, Caterina Sforza (c. 1463– 1509), married Gerolamo Riario, lord of the cities of Imola and Forlì and a nephew of Pope Sixtus IV. When Gerolamo was murdered in 1488, Caterina ruled Imola and Forlì until she lost the cities to Cesare Borgia in 1499. She then married Giovanni de' Medici, duke of Florence, with whom she had a son, Giovanni della Bande Nere. Giovanni became a well-known condottiere in the Italian Wars. Francesco's granddaughter, Bianca Maria Sforza, married Holy Roman Emperor Maximilian I. His grandson, Gian Galeazzo, married Isabella, the granddaughter of King Ferdinand I of Spain.

the Medicis, the king of Naples, and the kings of France. The alliance with Florence brought Sforza the funding needed for his expensive projects. To secure political connections with other states, Sforza married off family members. For instance, he assured friendly relations with France by arranging the marriage of his oldest son, Galeazzo Maria (1444–1476; ruled 1466–76), to Bona of Savoy, a member of the French royal family. Sforza's greatest diplomatic achievement, which he accomplished with the help of Cosimo de' Medici, was the Peace of Lodi in 1454. This important agreement was signed by all the major and most of the minor states of Italy. The Peace of Lodi ended a century of constant warfare and political sparring among the various states. The treaty provided a balance of power and lasted until 1494, when the French invaded Italy during the Italian Wars.

When Francesco I died in 1466, Galeazzo Maria Sforza became duke of Milan. Galeazzo was well educated and actively supported the arts. Among the artists hired by Galeazzo was the Italian architect and painter Donato Bramante (1444–1514), who designed the Church of Santa Maria presso San Santino, which still stands today. Although Galeazzo financed the work of many Renaissance artists, he was a corrupt and cruel leader who had many enemies. In 1476 he was assassinated by republican rebels in a failed attempt to start an uprising. Galeazzo's wife, Bona of Savoy, acted as regent (one who rules in place of a minor) for their son Gian Galeazzo Sforza (1469–1494), who was next in line to become duke of Milan. In 1480, however, Galeazzo's younger brother, Ludovico Sforza (c. 1451–1508; ruled 1494–99), seized control of Milan and prevented Bona of Savoy from ruling in place of her son. Gian Galeazzo then became a virtual prisoner and Ludovico took over the role of duke, though he could not officially claim the title while Gian Galeazzo was still living.

Ludovico is great Renaissance prince
Ludovico became one of the wealthiest and most powerful princes of the Italian Renaissance. With his wife, Beatrice d'Este, whom he married in 1491, he presided over a splendid court that was renowned throughout Europe. Among the many artists, poets, and musicians who gathered in Milan were the painter Leonardo da Vinci and the architect Donato Bramante. Noblemen and common people alike were proud of the grand spectacles hosted by Ludovico and Beatrice, yet scholars have pointed out that the citizens of Milan paid high taxes in order to fund these events. Soon Gian Galeazzo, the rightful duke of Milan, and his wife Isabella became resentful of the extravagant life enjoyed by Ludovico and Beatrice. Gian Galeazzo and Isabella left Milan to establish their own court at Pavia. Isabella then appealed to her grandfather, King Ferdinand I (1423–1494; ruled 1458–94) of Spain, for assistance in restoring the duchy of Milan to her husband. In 1492 Ferdinand ordered Ludovico to give the duchy to Isabella and Gian Galeazzo, but Ludovico refused to comply.

When Gian Galeazzo died in 1494, Ludovico paid Holy Roman Emperor Maximilian I an enormous amount of money to install him as the duke of Milan. Maximilian further sealed the connection with Milan by marrying Gian Galeazzo's sister, Bianca Maria. In an effort to prevent Spanish takeover of Milan, Ludovico then

 Beatrice d'Este

Beatrice d'Este (1475–1497) was born into one of the most respected families in Europe. She and her sister, Isabella, split their time between Ferrara, Italy, where their father, Ercole d'Este I (1433–1505) was duke, and Naples, Italy, where their grandmother was a member of the royal court. When it came time for husbands to be chosen for the sisters, it appeared that Beatrice would have the more influential marriage. In 1491, at the age of sixteen, she married Ludovico il Moro (the Moor), the acting duke of Milan, who had seized control from his nephew, Gian Galeazzo Sforza, the rightful heir to the title. Together Beatrice and Ludovico established a brilliant court in Milan, which attracted the greatest artists, poets, and scholars of the Renaissance. In 1494 Ludovico paid Holy Roman Emperor Maximilian I a huge sum of money to declare Ludovico and his heirs dukes of Milan. Beatrice died in January 1497 while giving birth to their first child. Ludovico, who had never been known for his ability to save money, spent an extravagant amount on her burial. He burned thousands of candles in her honor and had her corpse wrapped in gold. Soon afterward he was driven from Milan. Ludovico was captured by the French in 1500. He died while imprisoned in a French castle in 1508.

formed an alliance with Charles VIII of France, who wanted to seize the kingdom of Naples from Ferdinand.

(Ferdinand died later in 1494.) Milan remained safe during Charles VIII's invasion, which started the Italian Wars in 1494 and threw the city-states into chaos. During the second phase of the wars, however, in 1499, Milan was seized by King Louis XII of France, who said he had a right to the territory because he was a great-grandson of Gian Galeazzo Visconti. In 1500, with the aid of Swiss mercenaries, Ludovico tried to retake his land, but he was defeated in a battle at Novara. He was captured and taken to France, where he was put in prison. One time he disguised himself as a Swiss soldier and tried to escape, but he was recaptured. He died in prison in 1508.

Francesco II ends Sforza reign In 1512 the Swiss, as members of the Holy League alliance against France, stormed Milan and installed Ludovico's son, Massimiliano Sforza (1493–1530; ruled 1512–15) as duke of Milan. Although Massimiliano was duke, the Swiss actually controlled Milan until 1515, when they were defeated by the French at Marignano. After surrendering the city to the French king, Francis I, Massimiliano retired to France. Holy Roman Emperor Maximilian I named Massimiliano's brother, Francesco II Sforza (1495–1535; ruled 1521–1525, 1529–1535), as the next duke of Milan. The city was still occupied by the French, but Francesco took over the duchy in 1521 after France was defeated by the army of Holy Roman Emperor Charles V at Bicocca. Francesco lost his title four years later, however, when the Spanish imperial general Fernando de Ávalos, marquis of Pescara, accused him of plotting against Charles. The following year Francesco joined the League of Cognac, an alliance against the emperor that was formed by King Francis I. Other members included England, the Papal States, Venice, and Florence. Soon thereafter Francesco was forced to surrender Milan when the emperor's troops invaded the city. After the Treaty of Cambrai in 1529 Francesco II became duke and ruled Milan until he died six years later. Francesco had no heirs, so for the next twenty-four years France and Spain fought over the right to control Milan. Spain finally emerged victorious after the Treaty of Cateau-Cambrésis (1559), which awarded Italy to Spain and reduced France to a minor European power. Milan then became part of the Habsburg Empire, which was held by the Spanish crown until 1706. The duchy of Milan, under Spanish control until 1714, remained fairly prosperous.

Venice

Venice was one of the most important cities of Renaissance Italy and perhaps the most beautiful. A prosperous sea empire and merchant republic, it was the only Italian city-state to remain independent while others were being invaded and occupied. Throughout the High Middle Ages (1100–1300), various factions struggled over control of the government, but the republic was stable during the Renaissance. By the thirteenth century Venice was the main trade link between Europe and Asia. Re-

Venice: A Floating City

Venice, which is considered one of the most beautiful cities in the world, has a unique structure. Located in a lagoon, it sits on 118 small islands linked by about 150 canals that are crossed by 400 bridges. The canals are lined with hundreds of elaborate churches and palaces clustered around impressive squares. The main traffic thoroughfare is the Grand Canal, which is shaped like a reversed "S." During the Renaissance, Venetians traveled about the city in gondolas, long narrow flat-bottomed boats with a high bow and stern. Gondolas were propelled with long poles by sailors called gondoliers. A distinctive feature of Venice, gondolas are now used primarily for tourists.

Wealthy traders made Venice a center of architecture and culture in the High Middle Ages, but the city achieved the height of its glory during the Renaissance. Great architects like Jacopo Sansovino (1486–1570) and Andrea Palladio (1508–1580) helped create the illusion that churches and palaces were floating on water. (The buildings were constructed on piles, or long slender columns, anchored in the ground). Ablaze with color and light, the buildings were filled with art treasures. Venice was the home of the Venetian school of painting, whose members included Titian (c. 1488–1576), Tintoretto (c. 1518–1594), Giovanni Bellini (c. 1430–1516) and Veronese (1528–1588).

sponding to threats by Muslim Turks in the East, Venice expanded its land empire by conquering cities in Italy. During the Renaissance, when Venice reached the height of its power, life in the republic was relatively calm in comparison to the volatile situations in other Italian city-states. While Venice was the aggressor in numerous conflicts involving the city-states and European states, it seemed blessed by internal peace and commercial success. As the sixteenth century progressed, however, Venice lost much of its importance because trade became more concentrated in the Atlantic Ocean. Despite this decline, Venice's commercial prosperity helped to sup-

port a great number of Renaissance artists. Venetians were constantly constructing new churches, thus providing employment for architects, builders, and artists.

Doge-led republic formed Venice is situated on 118 islands in a lagoon, or shallow body of water, at the extreme northern end of the Adriatic Sea. It was founded after the fall of the West Roman Empire and named for the Veneti, itinerant (traveling) fishermen and salt workers who lived in the region during ancient times. Settlement of the site of Venice began in A.D. 452, when inhabitants of Aquileia, Padua

Government Assures Stability

The republic of Venice was different from the other Italian city-states because it maintained its independence while the other states were constantly being invaded and occupied. Venice was also relatively free of internal political strife. The main reason was its distinctive government, which was headed by an elected duke known as a doge. The doge was elected for life by the male members of the wealthiest Venetian families through an elaborate approval process that involved nine different committees. The purpose was to make sure that one family did not dominate the position generation after generation. Once elected, the doge became a person of great public importance, but his position was basically ceremonial. He was responsible for assuring that the government ran smoothly, but he had no real authority. The doge's power was limited because he had to consult with a series of state councils (groups representing cities in the republic of Venice) before making any policy decisions. Above the state councils was the Great Council. Comprised of all Venice's noblemen, the Great Council was in charge of electing officials, such as the doge, and making laws. Unlike other Italian states, Venice did not sell titles of nobility. After the seventeenth century, no new families were recognized as nobles of Venice. This policy meant that the Great Council was ruled by the members of about one hundred eighty families.

The doge was assisted by the ducal council, which was made up of six councilors and three chief judicial magistrates. The ducal council headed the meetings of the Great Council and the Venetian Senate.

(Padova), and other northern Italian cities fled from Lombard invaders and occupied islands in the lagoon, between the mouths of the Po and Piave rivers. Although the islands were under the control of the Byzantine Empire (the eastern part of the former Roman Empire), the refugees started their own government. Headed by tribunes (officials who protect citizens against unlawful actions of magistrates) from each of twelve main islands, the government remained essentially independent until the islands became part of the newly created Exar-chate of Ravenna in 584. The center of political power then shifted to Rialto, one of the islands, in 641 when the Byzantine city of Oderzo, located on the mainland, fell to the Lombards.

In 697 Venice was organized as a republic headed by a doge (duke) who was to be elected by the people. The first doge, Orso, was put in office by anti-Byzantine military leaders in 727. He was followed by a series of Byzantine officials until about 751, when the Exarchate of Ravenna was dissolved. The political situation in

The Senate was responsible for making laws, managing the financial affairs of the state, deciding what foreign policy would be, and electing ambassadors. By the fifteenth century, the Senate was comprised of one hundred twenty members, as well as an additional forty who served in the *Quarantia* (Forty). The *Quarantia* was like a court meant to prevent Senate members from abusing their power. It was headed by three *capi* from the Council of Ten, a group of ten men chosen from the wealthiest and most influential families in Venice.

The Council of Ten was created in 1310 after a group of nobles attempted to organize a revolution against the government. The original purpose of the council was to investigate the treasonable activity of these revolutionaries, as well as others who wished to overthrow the government. In time, the council began to deal with policy matters, such as state security. When the Senate did not have time to meet, or the issue was so important that the city could not wait for the three hundred men to decide what to do, the council would hold meetings. The Council of Ten had the same powers as the Great Council, and it could pass laws without the consent of the Senate. The three *capi* each took turns assisting the Senate for one month at a time. In the late 1400s the Council of Ten became an important part of Venetian government. The council used a frightening secret police force to acquire even more power, eventually reducing the doge to a mere figurehead (leader with no authority). By the seventeenth century the council was viewed as a group of tyrannical rulers.

Venice remained unstable for more than a century as noble families, pro- and anti-Byzantine groups, and Roman Catholic Church officials struggled for control of the government. Although the doge was supposed to be elected, the office was often held by members of family factions (opposing groups) who gained power through force or influence. Despite political unrest, Venetians were united against the threat of foreign invaders. They managed to fight off attacks by Saracens in 836 and the Hungarians in 900. In 991 Venice signed a commercial treaty with the Saracens (nomadic, or wandering, groups of people from the deserts between Syria and Arabia), establishing a European trade link in the East.

Byzantine trade rights granted Venetians soon became quite wealthy and began assembling one of the strongest navies in the world. Economic prosperity not only brought political stability but also created a merchant ruling class that limited the power of the doge. In 1032 people regained the right to elect the doge, but it was limited to residents of Rialto and a select group of nobles. During the eleventh century the papacy and the Holy Roman Empire were engaged in a struggle over control of European territories. Although Pope Gregory VII (c. 1020–1085; reigned 1073–85) wanted support from Venice, the doge refused to take sides in the conflict. Doges continued to maintain neutrality while safeguarding Venetian trade connections in the Adriatic.

During the mid-eleventh century Venice's commercial routes in the southern part of the Mediterranean Sea were threatened by Norman expansion under military leader Robert Guiscard (c. 1015–1085). Normans lived in the Normandy region of northwest France and were descendants of Scandinavian conquerors who invaded France in the ninth century. Guiscard had taken over Apulia and Calabria in southeast Italy, and in 1059 he was named duke of those regions by Pope Nicholas II (c. 980–1061; reigned 1059–61). In 1071 he drove Byzantine forces out of Italy, then captured part of Sicily from the Saracens. He went on to take Palermo, Salerno, and Rome. To assure their freedom on the Mediterranean, the Venetians moved against the Normans. These actions benefited the Byzantine Empire, which was also at risk of being invaded by the Normans. As a gesture of gratitude, in 1082 Byzantine Emperor Alexius I (1048–1118; ruled 1081–1118) gave Venice full trading rights, with no customs dues (fees paid for goods taken from one country to be sold in another), throughout the Byzantine Empire. This agreement began Venetian commercial activity in the East.

However, relations with the Byzantine Empire began to disintegrate because Venetian traders offended the Byzantines with their arrogance and aggressive business practices. Soon the Venetians and the Byzantines hated one another. Alexius therefore began to encourage the Italian republics of Genoa and Pisa to compete with Venice. Angered by this development, which would limit their access to Byzantine markets, the Venetians destroyed Genoan and Pisan trading facilities in Byzantium. In 1171 Alexius tried to keep order by arresting all Venetian residents in Constantinople and outlying territories and confiscating their goods. Although efforts were made to improve relations in 1187 and again in 1198, the Venetians remained bitter toward the Byzantines.

Trade link between Europe and Asia
At the end of the eleventh century, the Roman Catholic Church, in league with leaders of the European states, had launched the Crusades (1096–1291), a series of holy wars against Muslims in the Middle East (see "Crusades" in Chapter 1). The Christians wanted to retake the Holy Land (called Palestine at the time; the territory is now in parts of Israel, Jordan, and Egypt), which had been captured by the Muslims in the seventh century. The Europeans soon realized they could make huge profits from trade

with new markets in the East. They set up kingdoms called Crusader States in conquered Muslim territory around the Mediterranean Sea, then gave trading privileges to merchants. In 1204 the Venetian doge, Enrico Dandolo (c. 1107–1205; ruled 1192–1205) led the Fourth Crusade (1202–04) and captured Constantinople. Venetian Crusaders later seized territory along the Ionian, Aegean, and Mediterranean Seas and claimed the island of Crete in the eastern Mediterranean.

Venice was now the main link for trade between Europe and Asia. Surpassing the other prosperous commercial city-states of Naples and Genoa in trade volume, Venice produced such items as glass, saddles, soap, textiles (cloth), books, metal work, and other luxury goods. From the East they brought back teas, spices, and silk, among other items. The republic was also a major ship-building center. The arsenal (building where military equipment is manufactured and stored), founded in 1104, came to be known as one of the wonders of the world at the time. Venetians celebrated their alliance with the sea in an elaborate "marriage" ceremony between the doge and the Adriatic, which took place on a great gold-painted gondola called the *Bucentaur*. The Venetian spirit was exemplified by the merchant-traveler Marco Polo (c. 1254–c. 1324) who, in 1275, began a twenty-year visit in China.

Venetian empire expanded Venice continued to dominate European

 Marco Polo

In 1275 the Venetian merchant-traveler Marco Polo journeyed to China, where he stayed for nearly twenty years. As a favored guest of Kublai Khan (1215–1294), the Mongol emperor of China, Polo traveled throughout Asia, visiting places never before seen by a European. He later wrote a book about his experiences, stimulating European interest in trade with China. During the Renaissance, Polo's book was the main Western source of information about the East. (The work had various titles, including *The Book of Marvels*, *The Book of Marco Polo*, and *The Travels of Marco Polo*.)

trade with the East during the fourteenth and fifteenth centuries, reaching the height of its power in the 1400s. In 1380 Venice defeated Genoa, a rival Italian port city, in the War of Chioggia (1379–80) at Chiogga, a small island at the southern end of the Lagoon of Venice. Venice was now known as the "queen of the Adriatic." Yet the Venetians faced a threat from the Ottoman Empire, a vast kingdom ruled by Muslim Turks, which was overtaking the Byzantine Empire (see "Ottoman Empire" in Chapter 1). From 1361 until 1387 Sultan (king) Murad I (c. 1326–1389; ruled c. 1360–89) expanded Ottoman territory in Europe with victories at the Byzantine cities of Edirne, Turkey; Serrai, Greece; Sofia, Bulgaria; Niš, Serbia; and Salonika, Greece. In 1371 Murad moved the capital of the Ottoman Empire to Edirne. He completed his conquest of southern Europe at the battle of Kosovo, a region in southern Serbia, in 1389.

For a time Venice tried to maintain friendly relations with the Turks in order to protect trade routes in the Byzantine Empire. Finally, in the 1420s Venice challenged Ottoman power in the Aegean Sea, but the Ottomans took Salonika from the Venetians. The Venetians realized they could no longer utilize their sea routes in the empire. To make up for the loss in sea trade, they focused on acquiring secure routes on the mainland. In 1420 Venice took over Istria, a peninsula in present-day Slovenia and Croatia. In 1423 Doge Francesco Foscari (c. 1373–1457; ruled 1423–1457) initiated a series of wars against neighboring northern Italian city-states, particularly Milan. From 1426 until 1457, the cities of Verona, Vicenza, Padua, and Belluno were added to the Venetian empire. Venice established a strong army to help in these territorial acquisitions, and soon its land army was as mighty as its navy.

Venetian aggression caused resentment among the other city-states. In 1454 Francesco I Sforza, the duke of Milan, with the help of Cosimo de' Medici, the duke of Florence, drafted the Peace of Lodi, a treaty designed to end the wars. On the basis of this agreement the Italian League was established the following year to provide a balance of power among Venice, Milan, Florence, Naples, and the Papal States. Despite signing the Peace of Lodi, Venice continued to push for territorial expansion. Its image was badly damaged when, in 1481, the city attempted to overtake Ferrara, a duchy ruled by the powerful Este family. The conflict over Ferrara ended in 1484, when Venice conquered the Polesine region and triggered even more intense opposition from the other Italian states.

Venetian empire declines The Venetian empire began to decline in the early 1500s. Venice's expansion in Italy was halted during the second phase of the Italian Wars, a conflict between France and Spain over control of Italy (see "Italian Wars dominate Renaissance" section previously in this chapter). In 1508 Holy Roman Emperor Maximilian I formed the League of Cambrai, which consisted of the Holy Roman Empire, the Papal States, Spain, and France. Mantua and Ferrara were also allowed to join because these city-states had lost possessions to Venice. The League claimed it was protecting Italy against an Ottoman invasion, but the actual goal was to take back territory Venice had conquered and divide it among the allies. Nevertheless, the four main Cambrai allies—Spain, France, the Papal States, and the Holy Roman Empire—could not work together because each wanted to claim the territory for itself. Venice was defeated by the French in 1509 at Agnadello, an area east of Milan that France had given to Venice a few years earlier. As a result of this victory, Maximilian took Verona, Vicenza, and Padua. Ferdinand V of Spain regained Apulia and the port of Brindisi in southern Italy. Nevertheless, the Venetian republic was not completely destroyed, and the League of Cambrai collapsed in 1510.

In 1515 Venice joined its former enemy, France, in an alliance with England against the Holy League. The Holy League consisted of Spain, the Holy Roman Empire, the Papal States, and Milan. The Holy Roman Empire was closely identified with Spain. The empire was under the rule of the Habsburgs, a royal family with branches in Austria and Spain whose members had held the post of emperor since 1438. In addition, Spanish Habsburgs controlled Lombardy, and Austrian Habsburgs held the region to the north of Venice. The Habsburgs wanted to expand their territory in northern Italy. Consequently, Venice was doomed not only by allying itself with France but also by being hemmed in by the Habsburgs in the north. French king Francis I was finally defeated at the Battle of Pavia in 1526. Holy Roman Emperor Charles V (who was descended from both the Spanish and Austrian Habsburg lines) arrested Francis, sent him to Madrid, Spain, and required him to sign the Treaty of Madrid. Under the terms of the treaty Francis abandoned all French claims to Italy, gave up Burgundy, and renounced his rights to Flanders (a region in the Low Countries) and Artois (a region in northern France). With Italy now in the hands of the Spanish, Venice's ambitions of taking over more territory came to an end.

Status as sea power lost Venice's sea empire was also declining. Venetian trade routes were still being threatened by Ottoman expansion in the eastern Mediterranean. Not only did Venice lose its ports in Albania and Greece in 1503, but it also gave up the Aegean islands north of Crete in 1540 and ceded control of Cyprus to the Ottomans in 1571. The Ottomans took over Crete itself in 1669. The Venetian sea empire collapsed completely when Venice lost the Peleponnesus, a peninsula in Greece, to Turkey in 1715. In addition, Venice's trading monopoly was being challenged by Portugal, which had emerged as a sea power in Asia. In 1498 Portuguese navigator Vasco da Gama (c. 1460–1524) found an Atlantic Ocean route to Asia around the Cape of Good Hope at the tip of South Africa. Another significant development was the discovery of America, in 1492, by Genoan navigator Christopher Columbus (1451–1506), who sailed on behalf of Spain. Columbus's voyages to America opened Atlantic routes to the New World (the European term for North America and South America). These routes were increasingly utilized by Spain, Portugal, France, England, and the Netherlands in the sixteenth century. The rise of the Dutch merchant city of Antwerp (in present-day Belgium) in the 1500s further disrupted Venetian trading routes in northern Europe. Thus European sea commerce had shifted away from the Mediterranean to the Atlantic, reducing Venice to the status of a minor trading state.

Although Venice was no longer the most powerful state in Italy, it remained politically stable and independent. The Venetians developed an effective diplomatic corps and maintained a strong fleet. In 1571 Venice briefly revived its standing as a sea power by helping Holy League commander John of Austria (1547–1578) defeat the Turkish fleet at the battle of Lepanto. In this decisive naval engagement the Christians fought the Turks at the mouth of the Gulf of Patras, off the coast of Lepanto, Greece. The Christian victory prevented the Ottomans from gaining total control of the Mediterranean. In 1576 Venice was struck by an outbreak of the plague. The population of the republic was reduced from 180,000 to less than 150,000. After 1583 the old nobility, which had once controlled Venetian politics, lost its power to the Senate. The republic of Venice gave up its independence in 1797 at the end of the first phase of the French Revolutionary Wars (1792–1802; a series of conflicts between France and Austria), when it was dissolved and divided between Austria and France.

Mantua

Mantua was another northern Italian city-state that made important contributions to the Renaissance. Although not so great as Milan and Venice, Mantua became a center for artistic and intellectual life under the Gonzagas, the family that ruled the state for more than four centuries. The city also played a role in the political history of the Italian Renaissance.

Gonzagas have long rule The site of Mantua was originally part of Etruria, an ancient country in central Italy, and later became a Roman town. In the twelfth and thirteenth centuries it was a free commune. At the beginning of the fourteenth century the population had reached thirty thousand. In 1328 Luigi Gonzaga (1267–1360) seized control of the government and transformed the territory into a hereditary lordship, establishing Gonzaga rule that lasted for nearly four hundred years. In 1433 Holy Roman Emperor Sigismund (1368–1437; ruled 1433–37) made the Mantuan state a fief of his empire, which meant that the Gonzaga family was forced to pay homage (tribute) to the empire while they ruled the area.

During the fifteenth and sixteenth centuries, Mantua struggled to remain independent from its larger neighbors, Milan and Venice, which were trying to take over Mantuan territory. The Gonzaga family achieved independence through well-timed alliances with one or the other of these two states. At this time Mantua also became involved in the Italian Wars, a struggle between Spain and France for control of Italy (see "Italian Wars dominate the Renaissance" section previously in this chapter). Both Spain and France claimed they had a right to the throne of Naples. During this conflict the Gonzagas formed alliances that benefited Mantua. In 1494, during the first phase of the Italian Wars, King Charles VIII of France invaded northern Italy in a march to Naples. Although Charles VIII entered Naples, he did not have the support of the people and was forced to leave Italy.

The following year Francesco Gonzaga (1466–1519), marquis of Mantua, sided with Spain and led allied forces against the retreating French at the battle of Fornovo in northern Italy.

Seeking to retain the independence of Mantua, however, Francesco later fought for the French against the Spanish during the second phase of the wars. King Francis I of France signed the Treaty of Cambrai in 1529, thus bringing the wars to a temporary halt. In 1530 Francesco's son, Federico Gonzaga (1500–1540), was appointed duke of Mantua by Holy Roman Emperor Charles V, who was also the king of Spain and a member of the House of Habsburg. Federico then established a close alliance with the Habsburgs, which remained in effect when the Italian Wars resumed again (1542–44 and 1556–57). Spain finally emerged victorious after the Treaty of Cateau-Cambrésis in 1559.

The Gonzagas continued to rule Mantua as a fief of the Holy Roman Empire until Vincenzo II, the last of the original Gonazaga line, died in 1627. Vincenzo's death led to the decline of the duchy of Mantua. A war of succession, known as the Mantuan War (1627–30), then erupted over the question of who should rule the duchy. This dispute became part of the Thirty Years' War (1618–48), a series of conflicts fought mainly in Germany over many issues. France supported Carlo I (1580–1637), a representative of a French branch of the Gonzaga family, the Gonzaga-Nevers. Carlo succeeded in becoming duke, but not before his rival's forces sacked the city.

Mantua never fully recovered from the destruction. In 1707 the last Gonzaga duke of Mantua, Ferdinando Carlo (1652–1708), was exiled by the Habsburgs for supporting King Louis XIV of France in the War of the Spanish Succession (1701–13). The duchy of Mantua, which had remained an imperial fief, then went to the Habsburgs.

Mantua and the Renaissance During the Renaissance, Mantua was the scene of important cultural developments. In 1423 the Gonzaga family invited the humanist Vittorino de Feltre (1378–1446) to establish a school of the humanities (which then included literature, philosophy, rhetoric, and ethics) for the education of their children and those of other notable families in the area. This school became the model for many of the later humanist schools. The Gonzagas were great art lovers, so they invited numerous painters to Mantua to help decorate their palaces. Antonio Pisanello (1395–1455) painted scenes from the English legend of King Arthur; Andrea Mantegna (1431–1506) created numerous frescoes (wall paintings) that are among the greatest works of fifteenth-century Italian art; and Leonbattista Alberti (1404–1472) designed the new Basilica of Sant' Andrea and the church of San Sebastiano. In the sixteenth century Francesco Gonzaga and his wife, Isabella d'Este (1474–1539), established a famous court at Mantua, which attracted prominent Renaissance artists and literary figures. Giulio Romano (1499–1546) held the post of chief architect of Mantua

Isabella d'Este

Isabella d'Este and her younger sister Beatrice were born into one of the most respected families in Europe. When they were children, the sisters split their time between Ferrara, Italy, where their father was duke, and Naples, Italy, where their grandmother was a member of the royal court. Both received an excellent classical education, but Isabella proved herself to be especially good with languages. By the time she was a teenager, she had mastered Greek and Latin grammar, could recite large sections of the works of the ancient poets Homer and Virgil from memory, and was knowledgeable about politics. She was also an accomplished lute player (a stringed instrument that is an ancestor to the modern guitar), a skillful dancer, and a flawless embroiderer.

Isabella was engaged to Francesco Gonazaga, who was marquis of Mantua from 1494 to 1519, for ten years before they were finally wed. As the marchioness (feminine form of the title marquis) of Mantua, Isabella became the very model of the accomplished Renaissance woman. She was expected to be intellectual, articulate, and politically aware. Gonzaga shared Isabella's passion for learning and culture, and their royal court quickly became a great center of artistic and literary life. A number of talented artists and writers from throughout Italy were attracted to their court, mainly because of Isabella's library, which was one of the finest in Italy, and because she was a dedicated patron of the arts.

under Duke Federico Gonzaga (1500–1540) and his brother Cardinal Ercole Gonzaga (1505–1563). Romano's works there include the Palazzo del Te on the outskirts of the city, the remodeled interior of the Cathedral of San Pietro, and the monastery church of San Benedetto in Polirone.

Mantua held a significant place in the Renaissance religious history as well. The younger sons of the Gonzaga family played an important role in church politics as bishops of Mantua and cardinals. Starting with Cardinal Francesco Gonzaga (1461–1483) a series of ten Gonazaga rulers held the

post of cardinal. All of them combined the interests of their family with the policies of the church. During the sixteenth century, Protestantism, a religious reform movement rebelling against the Roman Catholic Church, was gaining momentum throughout Europe. It captured the imagination of merchants, peasants, nobles, and even church officials because of corrupt practices within the church. Benedetto Mantova (died 1541), a Mantuan scholar, wrote Il Beneficio di Cristo ("the benefit of Christ's death"; published 1543), the most significant book on reform efforts in Italy. The Gonzagas' commitment to Roman Catholicism,

Isabella d'Este by Titian. ©*Burstein Collection/ Corbis. Reproduced by permission of the Corbis Corporation.*

In 1509 Francesco was captured in a war against Venice, and Isabella was forced to rule in his place. She became such an able leader that Francesco was jealous of her success. Francesco was not released from prison for several years, a fact he blamed on his wife. Their marriage suffered until his death in 1519. Isabella ruled for another six years in the place of her nineteen-year-old son, Federico, who felt he could not rule as well as his mother. Her diplomatic skills ensured Federico the title of duke from Holy Roman Emperor Charles V. Her influence also won her younger son, Ercole, a place in the papacy as a cardinal. When Isabella died on January 13, 1539, she was honored as the "first lady of the world."

however, prevented Protestantism from becoming a major force in Mantua.

Rome and the Papal States

The Italian Renaissance was supported by the popes in Rome, which was the base of the Roman Catholic Church and the Papal States. In ancient times Rome was the seat of the Roman Empire, and after the rise of Christianity in the sixth century it became the headquarters of the church. Throughout history the city had therefore been the center of the Western (non-Asian) world. At the beginning of the Renaissance, however, Rome had gone into decline and was not even one of Italy's greatest cities. For instance, during the third century more than a million people had lived in Rome, but in the early fifteenth century only one hundred thousand people resided there. Rome's economy was largely based on the city being the home of the papacy, which attracted thousands of pilgrims who made religious journeys to receive the blessing of the pope. The municipal, or city, government was frequently unstable, as wealthy families fought amongst themselves and with the popes for control. Rome's government also suffered from extensive corruption because the families often attempted to seize the papacy itself through bribes (payments in return for favors) and political blackmail (threat to expose an embarrassing or illegal act if payment is not made).

Babylonian captivity and the Great Schism The decline of the city of Rome began in 1307, when Pope Clement V moved the headquarters of the church to the Papal State of Avignon in his native country of France. The Italian scholar and poet Petrarch was alarmed at this development, and he wrote extensively about it, declaring Avignon to be the "Babylon of the West." He was referring to the story in the Old Testament (the first part of the Bible) about the Jews being captured by the Babylonians and held in Babylonia (an ancient country in Asia, located between the Tigris and Euphrates Rivers) for seventy years. According to Petrarch, Catholics were being held captive in Avignon just as the Jews had been kept against their will in Babylonia. This situation resulted in ongoing conflicts between France and Italy. The papacy remained in Avignon until 1376—a period known as the Babylonian captivity because it also lasted seventy years—when Pope Gregory XI (1329–1378; reigned 1370–78) returned it to Rome. Gregory was horrified to discover deep corruption in the Italian church, however, and he made plans to return the papacy to Avignon. He died in 1378 before the move could be made. Mobs in Rome then forced the sacred college of cardinals (a committee of high-ranking church officials

who elect the pope) to name Urban VI (c. 1318–1389; reigned 1378–89) as the next pope.

Urban VI was determined to end corrupt practices in the church, particularly among cardinals. Ranking just below the pope, cardinals were appointed by the pope himself and therefore had acquired considerable power and wealth. The French cardinals feared Urban's reform efforts, so they claimed that his election was invalid because pressure had been put on the sacred college by the mobs. In 1378 the French cardinals elected a new pope, Robert of Geneva (1342–1394), who had been a cardinal from the French-speaking city of Geneva, a city in southwestern Switzerland that was surrounded by French territory. He became Clement VII (reigned 1378–94), and the French cardinals returned to Avignon with him. Clement was called an antipope because Urban was still the pope in Rome. Clement intended to establish Avignon as the center of the church once again. Urban refused to recognize the legitimacy of the new pope, so he excommunicated the French cardinals and Clement. Urban then appointed new cardinals to replace those who had been banished. For the next thirty-seven years, the rival camps in Rome and Avignon each elected new popes and hurled accusations of heresy (violation of church laws) at one another. This dispute is known as the Great Schism (also the Schism of the West). The Great Schism came to an end in 1417 when church officials met at the town of Constance in Switzerland and

The Papal States

The Papal States (also known as the States of the Church or Pontifical States) were territory in Italy under the direct rule of the pope. The Papal States originated in the sixth century A.D., when popes became unofficial rulers of the city of Rome and the surrounding area. In 754 Pepin the Short, king of the Franks, officially awarded this territory to Pope Stephen II. During the next seven hundred years papal holdings were increased by gifts to the church as well as the church's own purchases and conquests. For instance, Avignon, France, was a Papal State that played an important part in the Babylonian captivity and the Great Schism in the thirteenth and fourteenth centuries. At the end of the Great Schism, Avignon was still under jurisdiction of the pope, but the people ruled themselves. At the height of the Renaissance, in the fifteenth century, the Papal States occupied most of central Italy and, in addition to Rome, comprised the cities of Bologna, Urbino, Rimini, and Assisi. At various times papal domains also included such duchies as Verona, Padua, and Ferrara in northern Italy. The Papal States were dissolved in 1870, when the king of Italy, Victor Emmanuel II, annexed nearly all of the territory, including Rome, into the united nation of Italy. The area ruled by the pope was confined to the Vatican. In protest against the Italian occupation of Rome, popes were voluntary prisoners in the Vatican until 1929. At that time the Lateran Treaty recognized the Holy See (office of the pope) in Vatican City as an independent state.

elected Pope Martin V (1368–1431; reigned 1417–31). They declared him to be the only rightful leader of the Roman Catholic faith.

Revival fuels Renaissance

Pope Martin moved the papacy back to Rome, and church officials decided to return the city to its former glory. For the rest of the century popes focused their attention on revitalizing church buildings and promoting the arts. Martin planned an ambitious building program, which was later carried out by Pope Nicholas V (1397–1455; reigned 1447–55). During Nicholas's reign a new Vatican palace (the residence of the pope) was built, remodeling was begun on Saint Peter's Church (also called Saint Peter's Basilica; the principal church in the Roman Catholic world), and preliminary plans for a Vatican Library were started. Pope Sixtus IV (1414–1484; reigned 1471–84) initiated the building of the Sistine Chapel in Saint Peter's Church. In 1506 Pope Julius II (1443–1513; reigned 1503–13) decided that Saint Peter's Church should be entirely rebuilt, a project that took eighty-four years to complete.

Saint Peter's Church Rebuilt

In 1506 Pope Julius II decided that Saint Peter's Church should be entirely rebuilt. Spread over eighty-four years, the project involved five renowned architects—Donato Bramante, Raphael, Antonio da Sangallo, Michelangelo, and Giacomo della Porta. Julius appointed Bramante to draft the design of the new church. Records show that Bramante originally planned the building in the shape of a symmetrical Greek cross topped by a great dome at the center. This design caused considerable controversy throughout the sixteenth century, however, since many people wanted the church to be built in the shape of a Latin cross. In 1547 Michelangelo completed the building up to the dome. Porta then altered the design (he may have used a model made by Michelangelo) and completed the dome in 1590. Finally, supporters of the Latin cross design won, and Carlo Maderno added a nave and facade (1607–14). But critics were not pleased with the results, since his additions obscured the dome from view.

The revitalization of Rome helped spread the Italian Renaissance. One of the most important innovations was a new style of architecture. In the sixteenth century architects such as Andrea Palladio went to Rome and sketched ancient ruins, then adapted them to design buildings that featured the domes, columns, arches, and vaults used by the Romans. Throughout Italy—and eventually Europe—town halls, palaces, and villas were built according to the designs of Palladio and other architects.

The city of Rome was once again the center of culture and politics in Europe. As a result of these advances, the city survived a devastating attack by the army of Charles V, the Holy Roman Emperor, in 1527 (see "German Fury" section previously in this chapter). In the second half of the sixteenth century, Rome became one of the fastest-growing cities in all of Europe because of the papacy's patronage, or support, of artists. Talented and influential artists flocked to the city, seeing it as the center of the Italian Renaissance.

Corruption in the papacy

Although the church was promoting a cultural rebirth, corruption was still a problem. It reached a peak when Rodrigo Borgia (pronounced BOHR-jeh;1431–1503), an Italian cardinal, became Pope Alexander VI (reigned 1492–1503) in 1492. Borgia was the nephew of Pope Calixtus III (1738–1458; reigned 1455–58). Having been surrounded by high church officials for most of his life, Borgia rose quickly through the ranks. In June 1460, when he was still a young cardinal, Borgia received a letter from Pope Pius II (1405–1464; reigned 1458–64). The pope reprimanded the young man for his sexual activities with several married women. Despite his behavior, and the fact that many in the church were aware of it, Borgia managed to gather enough support to be elected pope.

Once Borgia became Alexander VI, he continued to indulge in his previous behavior. He held extravagant parties, dined on the finest foods, and used church funds to sponsor bullfights (sporting events in which men called matadors challenge bulls in an arena). Violence flourished in Rome during his reign. Gangsters ruled the streets, and reports indicate that Alexander had personal knowledge of more than 250 murders. He made little effort to improve Rome or the lives of its citizens, except for his four illegitimate children, who were all given careers and whose mother lived like a queen on church money.

The most ambitious and destructive of Alexander's children was Cesare Borgia (1476–1507), a vicious youth who was made cardinal at the age of fourteen. Cesare murdered his older brother and the second husband of his sister, Lucrezia (1480–1519). Capitalizing on his father's influence and power, Cesare began to establish a vast state in central Italy. In 1498, during the Italian Wars, he formed an alliance with King Louis XII of France, who had invaded Italy to restore it to French control. Cesare married a French woman and received the title Duke of Valentinois. After establishing a French presence in the region, he continued to expand his state. His finances were severely limited, however, by the death of Alexander in 1503. The new pope, Julius II, was Alexander's bitter enemy. Julius had set his

Alexander VI was one of the most corrupt popes to have lead the Catholic Church.
Renaissance Alinari-Art Reference. Reproduced by permission of Art Resource.

sights on expanding the Vatican's empire into the area of central Italy where Cesare had established his estate. Cesare's empire quickly fell apart and, in 1504, he was imprisoned in Spain. He died three years later.

Julius became notorious for his love of war, his seemingly endless energy, and the amount of respect he earned from those around him. Known as "Papa Terrible" because of his passion for battle, Julius attempted to expand papal holdings by conquering lands in central Italy. In 1505 he marched his forces through cities formerly controlled by Cesare Borgia. In November 1506 Julius forced the city of Bologna to surrender. Through negotiation and influence, he assembled a massive army to drive the French out of central Italy. While accomplishing all of these things, Julius still found time to commission timeless pieces of art from Michelangelo, Bramante, and other painters. Julius died of a fever in 1513.

The "German Fury"

During its long history Rome had frequently been attacked by invaders. In 1527 the city was invaded again, this time by the forces of Holy Roman Emperor Charles V. The attack was the outcome of a complex situation involving the emperor's war with France over control of territory in Italy (see "Italian Wars dominate the Renaissance" section previously in this chapter). It also involved the religious reform movement started in 1516 by German priest Martin Luther (1483–1546), which was underway in Germany and eventually resulted in the Protestant Reformation. Luther had gained many followers, called Lutherans, and a large percentage of the population in the German states were Lutherans. They posed a threat to both the church and the Holy Roman Empire. The church was faced with the possibility that the Lutherans would break away and form a separate Christian faith. The empire would be further weakened by the spirit of the Lutheran movement, which supported the independence of the German states—a large portion of the empire in northern Europe. In 1521 the imperial diet (meeting of the supreme council of representatives of states in the Holy Roman Empire) was held at the German city of Worms to discuss these problems. The diet issued an official statement called the Edict of Worms, which outlawed Luther and his followers.

Charles signed the edict, but he was so preoccupied by the war against France that he failed to prevent the spread of Luther's doctrines. Charles had also been having problems with the popes, who felt that their power and independence were being threatened by Holy Roman Empire dominance in Italy. In 1525 Charles's forces defeated the French at Pavia, in Lombardy (a province in northern Italy), and captured Francis I, the king of France. The next year Francis signed the Treaty of Madrid, which forced him to give up French claims to land in Italy and transferred Burgundy (a region in present-day eastern France) to Charles V. The Holy Roman Emperor was certain that he now had total control of Italy.

When Francis was released from captivity, however, he renounced the Treaty of Madrid. He then organized the League of Cognac in opposition to the Holy Roman Empire. The Papal States, Venice, Milan, and Florence joined the league along with England, which was allied with France at the time. In retaliation, Charles sent an army, composed mostly of German Lutherans, into Italy. In 1527 Charles's army defeated the forces of the League

Lucrezia Borgia

Lucrezia Borgia is considered one the most notorious figures in European history. According to legend, she engaged in numerous crimes and vices, such as conspiring in family plots to kill political enemies and having sexual relationships with her father and brother. Although historians have found no basis for most of these stories, they are certain that Lucrezia's corrupt family used her as a tool to advance their political schemes.

Lucrezia was the illegitimate daughter of Rodrigo Borgia, who later became Pope Alexander VI. He took advantage of his position as head of the Roman Catholic Church to establish an empire in northern and central Italy. Lucrezia's brother, Cesare Borgia, capitalized on their father's influence to gain power for himself. When Alexander VI began his reign as pope in 1492, he formed an alliance with the Sforza family of Milan against the Aragon family of Naples. To secure the support of the Sforzas, he arranged for thirteen-year-old Lucrezia to marry Giovanni Sforza. Alexander VI then turned against the Sforzas and made an alliance with Naples. The Sforzas formed ties with French noblemen, who had acquired power in the region because of Cesare's alliance with Louis XI, the king of France. Giovanni feared that the Borgias would kill him, so he fled from Rome, becoming an enemy of the Borgias.

Alexander annulled (declared invalid) Lucrezia's marriage to Giovanni in 1497. Giovanni later charged that Lucrezia had sexual relations with Alexander. In an effort to strengthen ties with Naples, the Borgias arranged for Lucrezia to marry seventeen-year-old Alfonso, duke of Bisceglie and nephew of the king of Naples. In 1500 Alfonso was murdered by one of Cesare's servants as part of a plot to break off relations with Naples.

After Alfonso's death, Lucrezia moved away from Rome and was seen with a three-year-old boy named Giovanni (also called the *Infans Romanus*, or Roman Infant). A papal bull (official statement) recognized the child as the illegitimate son of Cesare; a second bull then declared that Alexander, not Cesare, was the father (some modern historians believe this was probably true). In 1501 Cesare arranged for Lucrezia to wed Alfonso I, duke of Este, in order to strengthen Borgia control of the Este region in northeastern Italy. After Alexander's death in 1503 Lucrezia no longer had any political usefulness. In 1505 Alfonso inherited the duchy of Ferrara in northern Italy, where Lucrezia established a court that attracted the foremost artists, writers, and scholars of the Italian Renaissance. She devoted her life to the court at Ferrara, which is regarded as her real contribution to history.

of Cognac, then marched on Rome in a siege that was called the "German Fury." The German soldiers ransacked the city and stormed the residence of Pope Clement VII (not to be confused with the Avignon antipope of the same name), who had supported the French. Although Charles claimed he had no involvement in the "German Fury," he managed to profit from the siege of Rome by taking land and money from the pope. He also retained control of Italy through the Treaty of Cambrai with France and the Peace of Barcelona with Clement (both signed in 1529).

Naples and Sicily

To the south of the Papal States were the mountainous kingdoms of Naples and Sicily. The kingdom of Naples was a vast area with cities on both the Adriatic and Mediterranean Seas. The kingdom of Sicily was located to the southwest of Naples, on the island of Sicily in the Mediterranean. The two kingdoms were ruled jointly by the king or queen of Naples and Sicily. Both areas had poor soil and relied on their port cities to support the economy. At the beginning of the Renaissance, Naples was one of the greatest cities in Europe, since a majority of the ships sailing in the Mediterranean used its port. During the sixteenth century Naples would become one of the largest cities in all of Europe.

War of the Sicilian Vespers Both Naples and Sicily had troubled and turbulent political histories. Many of the problems were caused by the fact that the region was vulnerable to invasion from the sea: the kingdom of Naples occupied most of the Italian peninsula, which juts into the Adriatic and the Mediterranean, and Sicily sits in the Mediterranean. Both areas had been attacked repeatedly during the Middle Ages, first by Muslims (followers of the Islamic religion who lived in Asia) from the east and then by Normans (Scandinavian conquerors of Normandy, a region in present-day France) from the west. Stability briefly returned when Holy Roman Emperor Frederick II (1194–1250; ruled 1212–50) attempted to rule his northern empire, which was located north of the Alps, from his base in Sicily. After his death, Italy's ties with the Holy Roman Empire began to weaken. Charles I (Charles of Anjou), the youngest brother of King Louis IX of France, took over the thrones of Sicily and Naples in 1266. The reign of Charles and his family was known as the Angevin dynasty.

Charles was a cruel and dictatorial king. Unpopular with the local peasants, he was considered an illegitimate ruler because of his desire to place all of Italy under French control. Charles clung to power until a bloody uprising against the French erupted on Easter Day 1282. The uprising began when a French soldier sexually assaulted a young married woman on her way to vesper (evening worship) services at a church in the town of Palermo. A violent conflict broke out, and soon the area was engulfed by war. Charles's claim to the throne of Sicily was supported by the papacy, which supplied him with military forces. The revolutionaries in Sicily had the support of the kings of Aragon, a region in Spain. Sicily was placed under the rule of Peter III of Aragon (c. 1239–1285), whose successors were known as the Argonese. The conflict was known as the War of the Sicilian Vespers. When it ended in 1306 Charles retained control of Naples, while Peter's successors continued to rule Sicily.

The Angevin and the Argonese were rivals throughout the fourteenth and fifteenth centuries. One of the Angevin rulers in Naples, Robert the Wise (1278–1343; ruled 1309–43), gave many hope that the family would be able to unite Italy. These hopes vanished when Robert's granddaughter, Joanna I (1326–1381; ruled 1343–81), ascended to the throne and triggered a complex string of events. At the age of five Joanna had been married to her cousin, seventeen-year old Andrew, prince of Hungary. As she grew into adulthood, Joanna became increasingly bored with her husband. By most accounts, Andrew was an unremarkable and unintelligent match for the spirited Joanna. She had numerous lovers, and one of them murdered Andrew in 1345. Now nineteen years old, Joanna was forced to go to Avignon, France, and prove to antipope Clement VII that she had no part in Andrew's murder. (These events took place during the so-called Babylonian captivity, when there were two popes—the traditional pope in Rome and an antipope in the Papal State of Avignon) Although Joanna was declared innocent, suspicion followed her back to Naples. (Some modern historians believe she actually did arrange for her husband to be killed.) Seeking revenge, Andrew's brother, King Louis I of Hungary (1326–1382; ruled 1342–82), mounted two unsuccessful invasions of Naples. Joanna made peace with Hungary in 1352.

Joanna married two more times after Andrew's death, but she had no children. She had adopted Charles of Durazzo (1345–1386), the grandson of Charles II (1248–1309; ruled 1285–1309) of Naples. Joanna designated the child as the heir to the throne of Naples and later sent him to live with Louis I in Hungary. In 1380 the Italian pope, Urban VI, urged Charles, who was now thirty-five, to overthrow Joanna. Urban was displeased with Joanna's support of Clement VII, the antipope at Avignon. Joanna disinherited Charles, renouncing him as her heir, and named a Frenchman, Louis Duke of Anjou (1339–1384), as her successor to the throne. In 1381 Charles conquered Naples, captured Joanna, and put her in prison. He was then given the kingdom of Naples by Urban and crowned Charles III (ruled 1381–86). Upon Charles's orders Joanna was strangled with a silken cord, and her body was hung in the market place to show what would happen to anyone who supported the French.

The overthrow of Joanna marked the beginning of the Durazzo line. When Charles died, his son,

Alfonso I, king of Naples, was a great promoter of Renaissance arts and education. *Reproduced by permission of Hulton Archive.*

Ladislas (also known as Lancelot), was named king of Naples. Although Ladislas (c. 1376–1414; ruled 1386–1414) was a minor (below the legal age to rule on his own), he successfully defended his throne against Louis of Anjou. As Ladislas grew older, he became a brilliant military leader. Capitalizing on the confusion caused by the Great Schism, he expanded his kingdom into central Italy. He seized the cities of Latium and Umbria, then in 1408 he took Rome before moving north to Florence. Fearing a takeover, Florence allied with the house of Angevin to stop Ladislas.

Finally, Naples and Florence agreed to peace terms with Ladislas in 1411. Three years later, after the death of Ladislas, Joanna II (1371–1435; ruled 1414–35) ascended the throne as the queen of Naples. Joanna was a corrupt woman with an appetite for power. In July 1421 she convinced her lover, Alfonso V (1396–1458), to support her in a campaign against the French in return for being named the heir to the throne. Alfonso, who was already king of Aragon and Sicily, battled with René Duke of Anjou (1409–1480), for nearly a decade. René, who had the support of Pope Eugenius IV (c. 1383–1447; reigned 1431–47), was finally defeated in 1442. Alfonso took the throne of Naples as Alfonso I (ruled 1442–58). For a brief time he was able to unite the three crowns of Aragon, Sicily, and Naples. This union provided a degree of stability that had been lacking in war-torn southern Italy and paved the way for new artistic achievements. Alfonso was a great promoter of the arts and scholarship. Known as Alfonso the Magnanimous, he founded a university at Catania and helped support a number of respected scholars such as Lorenzo Valla (1407–1457), who wrote philosophical studies and produced Latin translations of works by ancient writers Homer, Herodotus, and Thucydides.

After Alfonso's death, his illegitimate son Ferdinand I (1423–1494; ruled 1458–94) became king of Naples while Alfonso's brother, John I (1397–1479; ruled 1458–79), took over Aragon. Ferdinand was regarded by many as a cruel and unforgiving man, a reputation that came mainly from enemy propaganda rather than his own behavior. Unlike his father, Ferdinand was not interested in promoting the arts, and he focused his attention on diplomatic strategy. He made several intelligent political moves, including lending his support to Florence, which was led by Lorenzo de Medici (see "Florence" section previously in this chapter). Ferdinand also married the daughter of the king of Hungary in order to strengthen political ties with that country.

When Ferdinand died in 1494 the throne was challenged by King Charles VIII of France, who invaded Italy. He started the Italian Wars, a conflict between France and Spain over control of Italy. Ferdinand's unpopular son, Alfonso II of Spain (1449–1496; ruled 1494–95), sent an army to northern Italy under his own son, Ferdinand II (1467–1496; ruled 1495–96), known as Ferrandino, to head off the French forces. Charles VIII easily avoided the Neopolitan army (as the forces of Naples were called) and continued his march to Naples. Alfonso abdicated, or abandoned, his throne in January 1495. For a year, Ferrandino unsuccessfully attempted to rally support in Naples. He fled in February as Charles entered the city. Only three months later, in May 1495, Charles left Naples and never returned. The remaining French forces were defeated by the Neopolitan armies in June 1496. Ferrandino, however, died in October of the same year and was succeeded by his uncle, Frederick (1452–1504; ruled 1496–1501).

Despite Frederick's ruling abilities, his reign was ended by cooperation between King Louis XII of France, whose army invaded Italy around 1499, and Frederick's cousin, Ferdinand II of Spain (called the Catholic; 1452–1516). Ferdinand II (not to be confused with the Ferdinand II of Naples, called Ferrandino) was a member of the house of Aragon, and his alliance with France ended the unity Alfonso V had established in 1442. France and Spain divided the kingdom with the Treaty of Granada in 1500. In 1502, however, Spanish forces mounted an attack against the French forces, driving them completely out of Italy in 1503.

Spanish control of Naples lasted from 1504 until 1713. While there were a variety of leaders during this time, Naples had its most stable period under Spanish rule. Feudalism was completely destroyed as a result of Spanish rule. A new class of nobles who were loyal to the government emerged, and landowners no longer had the freedom to establish their own laws and customs. Although the monarchy ruled from Spain, the Council of Italy was established in 1558 and the king of Naples governed in conjunction with the Spanish king. The new class of nobles played an instrumental role in running the government. While political independence from Spain was impossible, the Spanish occupation did provide political stability in Naples.

The Rise of Monarchies: France, England, and Spain

3

One of the most significant developments in the three centuries leading up to the Renaissance period was the collapse of feudalism. This social and economic system had emerged during the ninth century in the Carolingian Empire (pronounced care-eh-LIN-jee-ehn), which was centered in the region that is now France. (See "Feudalism" in Chapter 1.) Eventually feudalism (a term derived from the medieval Latin word *feudum,* meaning "fee") spread throughout Europe and served as a unifying institution for all aspects of life. Under feudalism, which was based on an agricultural economy, distinct social classes were dependent on one another through a complex system of pledging loyalty in exchange for goods and services. At the top were kings, who owned the land. Beneath them were lords (noblemen) and clergymen (church officials), who were granted tracts of land called fiefs (pronounced feefs) by the king. Below the lords were vassals (knights), who held smaller amounts of land awarded to them by lords. At the bottom were serfs (peasants), who farmed the fiefs but were not given land of their own. Land occupied by churches, monasteries (houses for men called monks, who dedicated themselves to the religious life), and other religious establishments of the Roman Catholic Church were also considered fiefs.

Feudalism began to decline in the eleventh century with the rise of capitalism, an economy based on investing money and earning profits from business ventures. Capitalism is considered one of the major contributions of the Renaissance. Under feudalism there were few cities, and most communities consisted of small towns and rural areas clustered around castles, which served as centers of government and social life (see "Castle as center of community" in Chapter 1). Capitalism brought about the rise of cities, which were built as hubs in a network of trade routes throughout Europe. The cities replaced fiefs as population centers. The growth of the new economy posed threats to the feudal system. Serfs started escaping to urban areas in search of work. A middle class, consisting of merchants and bankers, was taking power away from noblemen.

Although feudalism had been replaced by a new economic system, social and political structures were still based on the fief. When the Renaissance began in the mid-fourteenth century in Italy, Europe was divided into hundreds of independent states, each with its own laws and customs. The result was absolute chaos, as leaders of states vied for more power and larger territories. In the south, the Italian peninsula was turned into a battleground. Numerous wealthy city-states competed for trade rights around the Adriatic and Mediterranean Seas, and the Italian Wars (a conflict between France and Spain for control in Italy) raged for sixty-four years (see "Italian Wars dominate Renaissance" in Chapter 2). As the Renaissance moved north of Italy in the fifteenth century, northern and central Europe was even more fragmented. The power of the Holy Roman Empire had dwindled, and princes (noblemen who ruled states)—particularly in the more than two hundred principalities of Germany—were seeking independence. At the same time religious reformers, first in Germany and then in the Netherlands and Scandinavia, were leading a movement against the practices of the Roman Catholic Church. Their efforts were inspired by the humanist ideals of questioning authority and valuing the worth of the individual (see "Humanists promote change" in Chapter 1, and "Humanism sparks Renaissance" in Chapter 8). This reform movement resulted in the revolution known as the Protestant Reformation, which eventually spread throughout Europe.

Monarchs (kings and queen with supreme rule) in France, England, and Spain responded to the chaotic situation in Europe by consolidating their power. A significant development in all three of these monarchies was the rise of nationalism, or pride in and loyalty to one's homeland, which was a distinctive feature of the Renaissance period. In France, the Capetians (pronounced cuh-PEE-shuns) gained control of nearly all duchies (fiefs) by staging internal wars and defeating England in the Hundred Years' War. They established a line of strong monarchs that lasted for eight hundred years and elevated France to the status of a major power. Although England was exhausted by the long conflict with France, the Tudor monarchs began a new dynasty after emerging victorious from the War of the Roses, a struggle between two families for the throne of England. During the sixteenth and seventeenth centuries, the Tudors reigned over the English Renaissance. Their era produced one of the greatest cultures in the world and led to the creation of the British Empire in later centuries. In Spain, the monarchs Ferdinand II of Aragon and Isabella of Castile laid the foundation for an immense empire by uniting several independent provinces. In the sixteenth century, during the reign of King Charles I (Holy Roman Emperor Charles V), the Spanish empire spread east from Spain to include the kingdoms of Germany, Hungary, Bohemia, Naples, and Sicily. It also extended south and west to include possessions in North Africa and the Americas.

France

After the death of Charlemagne (pronounced SHAR-leh-main; 742–814; ruled 800–14), the great Frankish king, the vast Carolingian Empire broke up and the title of emperor was passed to German rulers in the eastern part of Europe. Territory that is now France was invaded by tribes from Scandinavia (Norway,

Denmark, and Sweden). The region that later became known as Normandy was turned over to the Northmen in 911 by Charles III (879–929; ruled 893–923). At the end of the tenth century, Hugh Capet (c. 938–996; ruled 987–96) founded the line of French kings that ruled the country for the next eight hundred years. Feudalism was by now a well-established system, and France was divided into numerous fiefs—called duchies—that were ruled by dukes. The Capetians were a family who controlled the Île-de-France, a region centered on Paris that extended roughly a three days' march in all directions around the city. At first the Capetians' control over the other duchies of France was mostly in name only because many were semi-independent kingdoms. Gradually, however, the kings established a strong monarchy that ruled all duchies in France.

Capetians establish strong monarchy

One of the most powerful Capetians was William II (c. 1028–1087), the duke of Normandy, a duchy in northwestern France. He expanded his territory by crossing the English Channel (a body of water between France and England) and launching the Norman conquest of England (1066–70). Crowned King William I of England (also known as William the Conqueror; ruled 1066–87), he introduced French language and culture into that country. The Capetians gradually extended their control over the duchies of

France during the eleventh and early twelfth centuries. Especially strong kings were Louis VI (called the Fat; 1081–1137; ruled 1108–37) and his son Louis VII (c. 1120–1180; ruled 1137–80). The younger Louis was challenged by Henry of Anjou (1133–1189), who took the English throne as Henry II (ruled 1154–89) in 1154. At that time he was feudal lord of a greater part of France, including Normandy, Brittany, and Anjou in the northwest and Aquitaine in the southwest. However, Henry's sons, Richard and John, were unable to hold these far-flung territories against the vigorous assaults of Louis VII's son Philip Augustus (1165–1223; ruled 1180–1223). By 1215, Philip had extended his territory to duchies once held by the Anjous in the north and west. He also increased his power in Languedoc and Toulouse in the south. Philip's grandson, Louis IX (1214–1270; ruled 1226–70), had a long reign. He firmly established the strength of the monarchy by enforcing his royal powers.

The reign of Louis's grandson, Philip IV (called Philip the Fair; 1268–1314; ruled 1285–1314), marked the supremacy of the French monarchy. Philip the Fair quarreled with the popes (heads of the Roman Catholic Church) over control of the French clergy and other aspects of the monarch's sovereignty (independent rule). For instance, Philip argued that he, as king, should be able to appoint bishops (officials who head church districts) and make governmental decisions without the consent of the pope. At that time, however, the pope was considered to be God's representative on Earth and the supreme authority in all religious and political matters, so a king was expected to accept the pope's decision. When the popes would not give in to Philip's demands he resolved the situation by having his agents arrest Pope Boniface VIII (c.1235–1303; reigned 1294–1303). After Boniface's death in 1303, Philip succeeded in having the seat of the papacy (office of the pope) moved from Rome, Italy, to Avignon, France. The popes remained in Avignon under French domination until 1377, during a period called the Babylonian captivity (see "Babylonian captivity and the Great Schism" in Chapter 1). Philip the Fair was followed by three sons, each of whom reigned only briefly and left no direct male heirs. In 1328 his nephew, Philip VI (1293–1350; ruled 1328–50), took the throne as the first king from the Valois (pronounced val-WAH) family, a branch of the Capetians. Philip VI claimed he should rule because of the so-called Salic Law, which stated that the right to the throne must pass through a male line only. Philip reasoned that since there were no longer any Capetian male heirs and since he was related to the Capetians through the Valois line of the family, he had the right to be named king. Philip was challenged by Edward III (1312–1377; ruled 1327–77) of England, whose mother was the daughter of Philip the Fair. In 1337 Edward claimed the right to the throne through his mother's line—ignoring the Salic Law—and named himself king of France. As a sign of his authority he had lilies, the official symbol of France, painted on his shield.

France versus England: The Hundred Years' War

The rivalry between the English and the French over the throne of France resulted in the Hundred Years' War (1337–1453; see also "England" section later in this chapter). Actually, the struggle did not last a full one hundred years but instead consisted of a series of conflicts interspersed with periods of peace. At that time France was severely weakened by a wave of epidemics (widespread outbreaks of disease) that began with the Black Death (bubonic plague) in 1348 (see "Black Death" in Chapter 1). It is estimated that between 1348 and 1400 the population of France dropped from sixteen million to eleven million. Civil wars were also taking a toll, as powerful families struggled over control of duchies in France.

In 1346, Edward III won a notable victory at Crécy in a battle that showed the superiority of English ground troops and longbows (oversized stringed weapons used to shoot arrows) against the French knights in armor. In 1356 French forces were defeated at Poitiers. Under terms of the peace agreement, the Treaty of Brétigny (1360), the kingdom of France was divided and the southwest region was formally given to the king of England. The great soldier Bertrand du Guesclin (pronounced gay-klahn; c. 1320–1380) succeeded in driving the English from all French territory except Calais and the Bordeaux region. France was then ravaged by an internal war between the Orléanists (a family in the duchy of Orléans, in north central France) and the Burgundians (a family in the duchy of Burgundy, in northeastern France), who were both claiming the right to the French throne.

Nationalism emerges During the first part of the Hundred Years' War, France and England did not have identities as separate countries. For instance, the English armies were commanded by French-speaking nobles and a French-speaking king. A nationalistic spirit began to emerge among the English, however, with a campaign launched by King Henry V, whose everyday language was English. Taking advantage of the civil war between the Orléanists and the Burgundians, Henry invaded France in 1415. He won a decisive victory at Agincourt (now Azincourt), a village in northern France, and instantly became a hero in England. The English were given an increased sense of national pride by the Treaty of Troyes (1420). The treaty required France's King Charles VI (1368–1422; ruled 1380–1422), an Orléanist, to give his daughter, Catherine of Valois (1401–1437), in marriage to Henry. Charles also had to declare Henry and Henry's descendants heirs to the French crown. Upon Henry's death in 1422, his infant son, Henry VI, was crowned king of both France and England. (See "England" section later in this chapter.)

By this time the French were also consumed by a nationalistic spirit. Shortly after the death of Henry V, Charles VII (1403–1461; ruled 1422–61), who was Charles VI's son, slowly began to regain French territories from the English. In 1429 the country was dramatically energized by Joan of Arc (c. 1412–1431), who was known as the Maid of Orléans. Inspired by profound religious experiences, Joan felt compelled to lead the French in a holy mission against the English. Under her command, the French won several important battles. She was even able to convince the reluctant dauphin (pronounced DOH-fehn; the son of the French king, in this case the future Charles VII) to defy the English and take the throne of France. Joan stood near Charles VII as he was crowned king at Rheims, France, in 1429. Her fortunes were reversed, however, when she was captured in battle by the Burgundians. She was sold to the English, who then turned her over to the Inquisition, an official church court appointed to punish heretics (those who violate church laws), at the French city of Rouen. (See "The Inquisition" in Chapter 1.) Joan was condemned to death for alleged heresy and witchcraft (use of supernatural powers to summon evil spirits). She was burned at the stake in 1431. Over the next thirty years the French armies continued to advance, winning major battles against the English. By the time Charles died in 1461, the English had been driven from all French territory.

The next king, Louis XI (1423–1483; ruled 1461–83), set France on a course that eventually destroyed the

The Battle of Crécy during the Hundred Years' War was a notable victory for England because it showed the superiority of English ground troops and longbows against the French knights in armor. *Reproduced by permission of Hulton Archive.*

power of the great feudal lords. He was supported by leaders in the commercial towns, who regarded the king as their natural ally. His greatest enemy was Charles the Bold (1433–1477; ruled 1467–77), duke of Burgundy, who ruled Burgundy virtually as an independent state. For many years Charles commanded far more resources than the king of France himself. But after the duke was defeated and killed in a battle in 1477, Louis was able to reunite Burgundy with France. Louis's son, King Charles VIII (1470–1498; ruled 1483–98) then married Anne of Brittany (1477–1514) and merged Brittany, the last remaining quasi-independent province, into royal lands. The consolidation of the kingdom of France under one ruler was now complete.

Charles VIII launches Italian Wars

In 1494, during the reign of Charles VIII, France embarked on the first phase of the Italian Wars (1494–1559), a series of conflicts between France and Spain that took place in Italy (see also "Italian Wars dominate Renaissance" in Chapter 2). During the wars, both France and Spain formed complex political alliances—in fact, they were even fighting on the same side at one point. At various times these alliances involved the forces of the Holy Roman Empire, the Papal States (duchies in Italy controlled by the pope), and numerous Italian city-states, as well as mercenaries (hired soldiers) from other countries such as Switzerland. The dispute over whether France or Spain had the right to rule Naples and Sicily had been going on since the thirteenth century. In 1266 King Charles I of France (Charles of Anjou; 1227–1285; ruled 1266–85), the youngest brother of King Louis IX, took the thrones of Naples and Sicily (called the Kingdom of the Two Sicilies). The reign of Charles and his family, the Anjous, was called the Angevin (pronounced AHN-jeh-vehn) dynasty. Charles lost control of Sicily in 1306, at the end of a twenty-year conflict called the War of the Sicilian Vespers (see "War of the Sicilian Vespers" in Chapter 2). In

1282 Sicily had been placed under the rule of Peter of Aragon, a member of a royal family in the Aragon region of Spain. Peter and his successors were called the Argonese. In the sixteenth century the Argonese cause was adopted by the Habsburgs (a royal family with branches in Austria and Spain) when Charles I, a member of the Habsburg family, became Holy Roman Emperor Charles V (see "Spain" section later in this chapter).

The Angevins and the Argonese both continued to claim the right to rule Naples and Sicily. In 1489 Charles VIII was offered the crown of Naples by Pope Innocent VIII (1432–1492; reigned 1484–92). Charles felt he now had the right to move into Naples. The Italian Wars began in 1494, when Charles was asked by the Sforzas, the family that ruled the city-state of Milan, to join them and Swiss mercenaries in seizing Florence from the Medici family (see "Milan" in Chapter 2). Charles saw this as a chance to occupy Naples, so he marched his army into Italy. Pope Alexander VI (1431–1503; reigned 1492–1503) took the side of the Medicis and convinced King Ferdinand of Aragon to send in Spanish troops to fend off the Sforzas, the French, and the Swiss. The Spanish drove the French out of Italy in 1495. The French returned in 1499, however, this time to take Naples and Sicily from the Sforzas. Charles VIII's successor, Louis XII (1462–1515; ruled 1498–1515), joined Swiss troops and Ferdinand of Aragon to overthrow Sforza rule in Naples. The French and Spanish monarchs then had a falling-out because Louis XII also claimed a right to rule in Italy because his grandmother, Valentina Visconti, was a daughter of Gian Galeazzo Visconti, duke of Milan. This conflict led to overwhelming Spanish victories at Barletta, Cerignola, and Garigliano. By 1503 the French were once again driven out of Italy, and the Spanish took possession of the Kingdom of the Two Sicilies.

Francis I renews conflict in Italy

The Italian Wars were continued with renewed vigor under King Francis I (1494–1547; ruled 1515–47), who became known as a Renaissance prince during his long reign. (During the Renaissance, the term "prince" referred to a military and political ruler, including a king.) Francis had grown up in the court of King Louis XII and was called the dauphin. He married Louis's daughter, Claude de France, in 1514. In 1512, when France went to war with Spain, the king gave the eighteen-year-old Francis command of an army. The Spanish king, Ferdinand II of Aragon, had conquered and annexed the small kingdom of Navarre, situated between France and Spain on the Bay of Biscay (see "Spain" section later in this chapter). The French were now trying to recapture Navarre. Although Francis had able military advisers, he failed to score a victory. Then in 1513 Swiss troops inflicted a humiliating defeat on the French at Novara, a province in northwest Italy. On December 31, 1514, Louis died, and on the first day of 1515 Francis I took the throne of France.

Renaissance prince Francis I, king of France, continued the Italian Wars with renewed vigor. *Photograph courtesy of The Library of Congress.*

Francis's reign had an impressive beginning. Determined to avenge the defeat at Novara by taking Spanish-held Naples, the young king personally led an army into Italy. On September 13 and 14, 1515, at Marignano (now Melegnano) near Milan, Francis won the greatest triumph in what was to be his long career as a military leader. His troops annihilated Swiss mercenaries hired by Massimiliano Sforza (1493–1530), duke of Milan (see "Milan" in Chapter 2). In the aftermath of Marignano, Francis took the duchy of Milan, and Pope Leo X

Francis I: Renaissance King

King Francis I became known as a Renaissance prince during his long reign. His childhood was remarkable because of his enlightened, humanist education. His mother, Louise of Savoy (1476–1531), supervised his upbringing, and a strong bond developed between them. The young boy learned the Spanish and Italian languages, and he spent his time reading mythology, history, and literature and admiring art. Francis also received a proper noble education in the art of war. Surrounded by young playmates, he learned the strategy and methods of Renaissance warfare and showed signs of unusual talent at the craft. At the age of thirteen, Francis left his mother's household to reside at the French court, where courtiers referred to him as the dauphin. King Louis XII granted Francis the duchy of Valois, created from the vast estates of the house of Orléans.

When Louis died in 1515, Francis became king. Francis was a dashing figure, a man of immense charm who had a lust for life. He was daring and courageous in battle, to the point of folly. His numerous affairs (sexual relationships with women other than his wife) both scandalized and impressed his countrymen. His compassion and leniency toward his subjects were uncharacteristic of the age, and he did much to improve the cultural life of his country during the Renaissance. Yet there was a darker side to the gallant French king. He often broke treaties, and on occasion he even allied with Muslims and Protestants to oppose Catholic Spain. He neglected to reward several of his best lieutenants for their services, and as a result he lost their support. Finally, he became so obsessed by his rivalry with Holy Roman Emperor Charles V that he lost all sense of proportion, spending heavily on unsuccessful wars against Spain.

(1475–1521; reigned 1513–21) gave him neighboring Parma and Piacenza. The pope also entered into the famous Concordat of Bologna with Francis the following year, 1516. According to the terms of the agreement, the Catholic Church in France came under direct control of the French crown. The Concordat marked a high point in the struggle over the question of the monarch's sovereignty, which had divided France into two camps. Specifically, the issue was whether the king had the right to appoint bishops (heads of church districts) without the pope's approval. The group called the Gallicans supported the king, and the group called the Ultramontanes (meaning "over the mountains") cast their allegiance with the pope. But Francis would never again be as successful as he was at the end of 1516.

Rivalry between two young kings

Francis became his own worst enemy

when he began competing against Charles I, the young king of Spain. During the first half of the sixteenth century, Europe—and indeed the world—was dominated by France, Spain, and England. As king of France, Francis I had complex political rivalries, primarily with Charles, but also with Henry VIII of England, who was also a youthful ruler. Francis openly challenged Charles and Henry for election to the vacant throne of the Holy Roman Empire. The three young monarchs bitterly competed for the title of Emperor, but the rivalry was especially intense between Francis and Charles. Charles's advisers bribed the German princes who served as electors, however, and in 1519 Charles took office as Holy Roman Emperor Charles V. As both the king of Spain and head of the Holy Roman Empire, Charles was now the most powerful ruler in Europe. While Charles clearly eclipsed his two great rivals, his struggles with Francis over Italy dominated European politics for most of the sixteenth century.

In order to avenge the slight of not being named emperor, Francis initiated the first of five wars with Spain and the Holy Roman Empire (Charles was head of forces for both Spain and the empire). In August 1520 he met with Henry VIII in Calais, France, at the Field of the Cloth of Gold, hoping to win Henry's support in the war against Spain. Henry declined to join the French effort. Meanwhile, Charles V had formed an alliance with Pope Clement VII (1478–1534; reigned 1523–34). In late 1520, Francis secretly backed an assault on Luxembourg

As both the king of Spain and head of the Holy Roman Empire, Charles V was the most powerful ruler in Europe.

(now in Belgium), a city in the Holy Roman Empire. The French also occupied the province of Navarre during the Comuneros Revolt in Spain. The Comuneros had formed the "Holy League of Cities" and were protesting the policies of Charles's government (see "Spain" section later in this chapter). The revolt was distracting Charles's attention, so the French were able to move into Navarre and wage war with Spain.

During the next four years, however, the war with Spain went poorly for Francis. His men won a few battles, at Parma and Fuenterrabia, but they were soundly defeated at Ezquiros and Pamplona and driven out of Navarre. The Spanish then invaded France, taking Toulon and other parts of southeast France. In northern Italy, Spanish forces won victories against the French at Tournai, Lodi, Cremona, Genoa, and Alessandria. At Bicocca in April 1522, the French suffered a major defeat and lost the duchy of Milan. Complete disaster awaited Francis at Pavia, a city near Milan, in February 1525. He led an army of 37,000 men against a Spanish army of equal numbers. The Spanish lost 1,000 men. Between 10,000 and 14,000 Frenchmen died, and many others were taken prisoner, including Francis himself.

More losses for France

Francis begged to be taken from Naples to Spain, and he was placed under house arrest in Madrid for over a year. The French king was not confined like most prisoners: He hunted regularly, enjoyed the companionship of his nobleman comrades, and attended numerous dinners given in his honor. He gained his release in March 1526 by agreeing to relinquish all claims to Italy and by giving up the duchies of Burgundy, Flanders (now part of Belgium, France, and the Netherlands), and Artois (a region in northern France). When Francis swore as a gentleman to return to captivity if he failed to live up to his end of the bargain, Charles agreed to set him free. Once he had returned to France, however, Francis declared the

Treaty of Madrid to be null and void. His excuse was that he was forced to sign the document at a time when he could not think clearly.

Francis's violation of the treaty made another war with Spain inevitable. Francis quickly organized the League of Cognac (1526), which allied France, England, Milan, Venice, the Papal States, and the republic of Florence against Charles. But in this second war, which began in 1527, Charles was destined to win an even greater victory. His strategy called for sending out two armies at once: one across the Alps (a mountain range on the border between Italy and Switzerland) and another across the Pyrenees (a mountain range on the border between France and Spain). To counter the Spanish offensive, Francis planned for Swiss troops in the employ of Clement VII and Venice to attack Spanish holdings on the Italian peninsula. The French would meanwhile send a fleet to take Genoa and Naples. At first all went well for Francis. Genoa fell to his naval forces, led by admiral Andrea Doria (1466–1560). Doria was a soldier-for-hire who hailed from Genoa but, in 1527, held the post of commander of French naval forces. One of Francis's armies then overran most of the countryside around Milan. But in May 1527, Charles's soldiers made a massive assault on the city and caused extensive damage. The siege has often been called the "German Fury" because the majority of the marauding soldiers were German Lutherans. Charles's spokesmen claimed the troops had moved on Rome against the emperor's wishes. According to an official report, when the soldiers reached the city they were so upset by the corruption of the Roman clergy that they committed atrocities. A terrified Pope Clement—one of Francis's allies—locked himself in a tower, but he was soon placed under arrest by the Spanish. He surrendered to Charles in the Treaty of Barcelona. Henry VIII, whose heart had never really been in the war, also quickly came to terms with Charles.

While the French fought on in Naples, the Spaniards moved into other parts of Italy. The French effort collapsed in 1528. The Spanish won two battles at Genoa and were victorious at nearby Savona and at Aversa in the south. By 1529, Francis had signed the Treaty of Cambrai, which repeated the humiliating terms of the earlier Treaty of Madrid. It also called for Francis's two sons to be held in Madrid for a ransom (money paid for releasing a hostage) of two million gold crowns (a large sum of Spanish money).

Francis is patron of the arts

For six years, Francis remained in France, where he became an enthusiastic patron of the arts. In the process, he helped bring the Italian Renaissance to France. A pet project was the renovation of the royal palaces at Blois, Chambord, Fontainebleau, and the Louvre. Purchasing the works of Italian painters Michelangelo, Raphael, and Titian, Francis also invited some of the finest Italian artists of the day to come to France. Among them were

Leonardo da Vinci, Benvenuto Cellini, and Andrea del Sarto. Francis corresponded with the Dutch humanist Desiderius Erasmus and sponsored a royal lecture series that supported promising scholars. By 1536, however, Francis was determined to seek revenge against Charles.

In February, he completed the Capitulations, an "unholy alliance" with the Ottoman leader Khayr ad-Din (pronounced kigh-ruh-DEEN; d. 1546), who was called Barbarossa by Europeans. This move shocked and offended most Christians in Europe, even many of Francis's longtime supporters. Although they appreciated his will to resist the mighty Spanish kingdom, they felt that Francis was committing heresy by allying with what Christians considered "infidel" Turks to slaughter fellow Christians.

Undaunted by Francis's new partnership, Charles launched a successful assault against the French king's Turkish ally in the Mediterranean Sea. Spanish forces led personally by Charles took La Goletta (now Halq al-Wadi), a seaport town in northeast Tunisia. Charles liberated thousands of Christian prisoners and soon thereafter captured the port of Tunis. Barbarossa fled to Algiers (now Algeria), in North Africa, with the remnant of his fleet. Charles then turned toward Italy, landed in Sicily in August, and advanced with ease toward the Alps. He also invaded Provence, a region in southeast France, and areas of northern France. By 1538, when a peace agreement was signed in Nice, France, both sides were financially exhausted. In one year alone, Francis had spent 5.5 million livres (the French unit of currency at that time) on the war. He had neither won nor regained any territory.

Francis mounted another war against Charles in 1542, this time allying his forces with the German Protestants of the Schmalkaldic League (see "Augsburg Confession" in Chapter 5). At Mühlberg, Germany, however, Charles won his greatest victory over Francis and the Lutheran princes. Although Francis had sided with Protestants against his great rival Charles V, he turned against the Waldensians, a group of Protestants in his own country. (Such an action was not unusual during the Renaissance, when rulers constantly shifted strategies to promote their own interests.) The Waldensians were advocates of the views of Peter Waldo (also known as Pierre Valdés; d. before 1218), an early French religious reformer who protested against corruption in the Catholic Church. A brutal campaign against the Waldensians demolished twenty-two towns and killed four thousand people. Francis issued a list of banned books and established a court to punish heretics. The court burned hundreds of Huguenots (French Protestants) at the stake.

Francis died of gout and liver disease at Rambouillet, France, in 1547. At the time of his death, the French crown was six million livres in debt. Ten years later, France declared bankruptcy (a lack of funds to pay bills). The Italian Wars finally ended after a seventh war, which lasted from 1547 until 1559. It was waged by the successors of Francis and Charles. In these wars, Spanish armies were victorious for the sixth time. As a result, Spain was given control of Italy in the Treaty of Cateau-Cambrésis in 1559.

Tensions between Catholics and Protestants

Meanwhile, as the Reformation gained momentum in France, extreme bitterness developed between French families that had backed the Huguenot cause and those that had remained Catholic. The policy of the French monarchy was to suppress Protestantism at home while supporting it abroad as a counterbalance to Habsburg power. Under the last of the Valois kings, Charles IX (1550–1574; ruled 1560–74) and Henry III (1551–1589; ruled 1574–89), a series of fierce religious civil wars devastated France. Paris remained a stronghold of Catholicism, and on August 23 and 24, 1572, thousands of Protestants were slaughtered in the massacre of Saint Bartholomew's Day.

Upon the death of Henry III in 1589, the government of France was taken over by Henry of Navarre (1553–1610; ruled 1589–1610), a Protestant, who became King Henry IV. He was the first of the Bourbon line of rulers. Unable to capture Paris by force, Henry embraced Catholicism in 1593 and entered the city peacefully the following year. In 1598 he signed the Edict of Nantes, which guaranteed religious freedom to the Huguenots. Henry succeeded in restoring prosperity to France. Assassinated in 1610 by a Catholic fanatic, Henry was followed by his young nine-year-old son Louis XIII (1601–1643; ruled 1610–43). Louis's mother, Marie de Médicis (1519–1589), acted as regent (interim ruler) in the early years of his reign.

Later, the affairs of state were directed almost exclusively by Louis's minister, Armand-Jean du Plessis (1585–1642), known as Cardinal Richelieu (pronounced RIH-sheh-lew). Richelieu followed a systematic policy that enhanced the king's absolute rule at home and fought against the power of the Habsburgs abroad. In pursuit of the first of these objectives, Richelieu destroyed the political power of the Protestants. In pursuit of the second he led France, in 1635, into the Thirty Years' War (1618–1648), a series of conflicts fought mainly in Germany over many social, political, and religious issues (see "Thirty Years' War" in Chapter 6). France allied with the Protestants and against the Austrians and the Spanish. Richelieu died in 1642, and Louis XIII died a few months later. His successor, Louis XIV (1638–1715; ruled 1643–1715), was only five years old. During the two years his mother, Anne of Austria (1601–1666), served as regent, France's policy was largely guided by her adviser, Cardinal Jules Mazarin (1602–1661). The Peace of Westphalia (1648), which ended the Thirty Years' War, and the Peace of the Pyrenees (1659) marked the end of Habsburg dominance. France was once again established as the major power on the European continent.

French Exploration

During the reign of Francis I, French explorers became part of the age of European exploration, one of the great achievements not only of the Renaissance period but also in Western history. In 1534 French navigator Jacques Cartier (1491–1557) joined the search for a Northwest Passage to China. He explored the St. Lawrence River—gateway to the Great Lakes—but his voyages never took him farther west than the site of modern-day Montreal, Canada. Nevertheless, his thorough exploration and charting of the Gulf of Saint Lawrence led the way for further exploration by one of his countrymen, Samuel de Champlain (c. 1567–1635). In fact, most of the major exploratory work in North America was done on inland water routes by the French. Beginning with Champlain in 1600, the French pushed their way down the Saint Lawrence River to the Great Lakes. In a dozen voyages from 1603 until 1633, Champlain discovered the easternmost Great Lakes, Huron and Ontario; founded the city of Quebec; and served as commandant of France's new colonial territories, which were called New France.

England

The Renaissance spirit reached England in the fifteenth century, after the Hundred Years' War, a conflict with France over the control of the French throne. The Hundred Years' War was not actually a single war that lasted one hundred years. Instead, it was a series of conflicts mixed with periods of peace that began in 1337 and ended in 1453. The Hundred Years' War was the outcome of disputes between the ruling families of England and France, the Plantagenets (pronounced plan-TAJ-eh-nets) in England and the Capetians (pronounced keh-PEE-shehns) in France. Since 1066 the English had controlled rich agricultural areas in France, and the two countries had often fought over these territories. In the 1300s marriages between English and French nobles meant that both English and French kings had a claim to the French throne. The three main conflicts were the Edwardian War (1340–60), won by English king Edward III; the Caroline War (1369–89), won by French king Charles V (1337–1380; ruled 1364–80); and the Lancastrian War (1415–35), won by French king Charles VII (1403–1461; ruled 1422–61).

During the Edwardian War the English took control of large areas of southwestern France and the northern coastal city of Calais. Although England was smaller than France, it was able to gather a large army. Equipped with longbows and arrows that could pierce French armor, the English defeated the French cavalry. During the Caroline War, the French regained much of the territory lost during the Edwardian War. This success was due to able military leadership, development of a full-time professional army, and a taxation system that supported the army. During the Lancastrian War,

the English allied with Philip III (called Philip the Good; 1396–1467, ruled 1419–67), the duke of Burgundy, to conquer most of northern and western France. The tide changed, however, when Philip formed an alliance with the French. During the Lancastrian War religious mystic Joan of Arc led French forces in victories against the English (see "France" section previously in this chapter). The use of newly invented cannons also significantly aided the French war effort. The uncrowned French king, Charles VII, then took the throne in 1429. Although the English maintained control of Calais until 1558, they were never again a serious threat to French sovereignty, or independent rule.

War of the Roses

The English were weakened by their loss to the French during the Hundred Years' War. Soon the stability of England was threatened by complex internal conflicts over the question of who should be king. Two rival houses (royal families), York and Lancaster, each claimed to have the right to the throne. Each house used the image of a rose to represent itself—a red rose for Lancaster and a white rose for York. For this reason the conflict is known as the War of the Roses. Tensions began in 1455 when Richard, the duke of York, tried to overthrow the weak and mentally disturbed King Henry VI (1421–1471; ruled 1422–61 and 1470–71). The king was a member of the house of Lancaster, and many blamed him for the loss of the Hundred Years' War. Henry's wife, the strong and determined Margaret of Anjou (1430–1483), gathered those loyal to the house of Lancaster and asked them to support the king. When Richard of York was killed in 1460, his son, Edward (1442–1483), continued the campaign against the Lancasters. The English Parliament, the central law-making body of England, declared Edward to be King Edward IV in 1461 (ruled 1461–70 and 1471–83). Henry and Margaret fled to Scotland, where she continued her opposition to the house of York.

Edward was a talented military leader, but his weaknesses were laziness, cruelty, and a hesitancy to call meetings of the Parliament. This left many members of Parliament feeling that they were being ignored. Edward began to lose support, even in the house of York. Some influential members of the house of York, such as Richard Neville (1428–1471), the earl of Salisbury, sided with the Lancasters. In 1470, with the support of King Louis XI of France (1423–1483, ruled 1461–83), the house of Lancaster managed to return Henry VI and Margaret to the throne. After a six-month battle, however, Edward's forces killed Neville and proclaimed victory. Edward was returned to the throne. Margaret was exiled to France, and Henry lived the rest of his life imprisoned in the Tower of London (a prison for members of the royalty and nobility). Edward ruled England for twelve more years, until his unexpected death in 1483. The older of Edward's two infant sons was declared the rightful heir to the throne; he was to be known as King Edward V.

Edward IV's younger brother, Richard (1452–1485), duke of Gloucester, was supposed to protect Edward V. Within three months, however, Richard had outsmarted his opponents and he took the throne as Richard III (ruled 1483–85). The child king was placed in the Tower of London along with his brother; those who had opposed Richard were executed. Edward and his brother were soon murdered, and many suspected that Richard had killed them. Henry Tudor (1457–1509), earl of Richmond, became the champion of those who felt that Richard had wrongly taken the throne. Although he lived in exile, he was considered the king. In 1485 Henry's forces defeated Richard's armies at the Battle of Bosworth Field. Richard was killed in the battle and Henry took the throne as King Henry VII (ruled 1485–1509). He was a member of the house of Lancaster, but after he married Elizabeth of York, the War of the Roses officially ended. A new royal house, the Tudors, began with this marriage. Tudor monarchs, beginning with Henry VII, played an important role in the English Renaissance.

An able but somewhat colorless ruler, Henry succeeded in establishing the position of his new dynasty, increasing the efficiency of the government, and enhancing the wealth of the monarchy. He was not interested in intellectual affairs, though his mother, Margaret Beaufort (1443–1509), countess of Richmond and Derby, did provide patronage for

Henry VIII: Renaissance Prince

Renaissance ideas became dominant in England in the 1530s, during the reign of King Henry VIII. Henry is now considered the true English Renaissance prince. Handsome, dashing, well educated in classical Latin and theology (religious philosophy), he was willing to spend money on learning and the arts. Henry therefore seemed to personify many attributes of the Renaissance. The great humanist Thomas More served as his lord chancellor (chief secretary) in the 1530s. The German artist Hans Holbein was Henry's court painter, and the English scholar Thomas Elyot was one of his secretaries. The Renaissance palace at Hampton Court was the scene of many splendid entertainments. Saint Paul's School was founded early in Henry's reign by John Colet, the learned dean (head) of St. Paul's Cathedral. It was the first grammar school to provide rigorous instruction in the classical languages. The Latin grammar written for Saint Paul's by William Lily was the first text of classical Latin (the language used by ancient Romans). Elyot's dictionary (1538) was the first to provide English equivalents for all the words in the classical Latin vocabulary. The grand tour of Europe, which often included extended visits to Rome and Florence, became part of the education of young English aristocrats and gentlemen.

scholars. She founded two colleges at Cambridge University as well as professorships at both Cambridge and Oxford Universities. The humanist ideas associated with the English Renaissance had begun to filter into England before Henry took the throne but were firmly established only during his reign. For these reasons Henry VII was once considered England's first Renaissance ruler, and the English Renaissance was often dated to the beginning of his reign in 1485. Modern scholars have altered this view, however, concluding that Renaissance ideas became dominant in the 1530s during the reign of Henry VII's brother, Henry VIII (1491–1547; ruled 1509–47). Henry VIII is now considered the true Renaissance prince.

Henry reforms church

Shortly after becoming king, Henry enacted a pro-Spanish and anti-French policy. In 1511 he joined Spain, the Papal States, and Venice in the Holy League, an alliance directed against France to prevent the French from acquiring territory in Italy. Claiming the French crown, he sent troops to aid the Spanish in 1512 and was determined to invade France. The bulk of the preparatory work fell to Thomas Wolsey (c. 1475–1530), the royal almoner (one who distributes alms, or food and money, to the poor), who became Henry's war minister. Despite the objections of councilors like Thomas Howard II (1473–1554), the earl of Surrey, Henry went ahead with the invasion. The king personally commanded English troops at the famous Battle of the Spurs (1513), in which the French made a hasty retreat, leaving several towns in northern France under English control. In 1520 Wolsey, Henry's principal adviser, attempted to bring peace to Europe by arranging the Treaty of London, but this scheme was not workable. Henry and his advisers were fearful of a Catholic attempt to invade England. They spent vast amounts of money on fortifications and on renewed wars against France and Scotland (a traditional ally of the French).

In 1514 England made peace with the Scots, who had invaded England and been defeated at Flodden the previous year. The English also formed an alliance with France and, to seal the treaty, Henry's sister Mary became the wife of King Louis XII of France. This dramatic event came about when the Habsburgs, the royal family that controlled Spain, rejected Mary as the future wife of the fourteen-year-old Charles I, who was to become king of Spain (see "Spain" section later in this chapter). Increasingly, Wolsey handled state affairs; he became archbishop of York in 1514, chancellor and representative to the papacy (office of the pope) in 1515. Not even his genius, however, could win for Henry the crown of the Holy Roman Empire. The king was competing with Francis I of France and Charles I of Spain for the coveted position of emperor (see "France" section previously in this chapter). Henry was deeply disappointed when the title was bestowed on Charles, who became Holy Roman Emperor Charles V, in 1519.

Henry VIII, king of England, founded the Anglican Church when the pope refused to grant him a divorce from his first wife, Catherine of Aragon. ©Gianni Dagli Orti/Corbis. Reproduced by permission of the Corbis Corporation.

Establishes Anglican Church Henry VIII is best known today for establishing the Anglican Church (Church of England) after the pope refused to let him get a divorce from his first wife. Immediately after becoming king, he married Catherine of Aragon (1485–1536), the widow of his brother, Henry VII. For more than a decade Henry and Catherine were happy together. They had a daughter, Mary, but the king wanted a son because he did not believe Mary would be accepted as his successor to the throne. In 1527 Henry began demanding a divorce from Catherine so he could marry Anne Boleyn (c. 1507–1536), an attendant in the court of Queen Claude of France. Henry was having a secret affair with Boleyn, and he hoped she might bear him a son. England was still a Catholic country and the pope's consent was required before Henry could get a divorce. However, Pope Clement VII refused to grant the divorce because Catherine's nephew, Holy Roman Emperor Charles V, had invaded Italy earlier that year. During the invasion Charles's troops had sacked Rome and stormed Clement's residence. The emperor now controlled Rome and had power over the pope. Finally, Henry acted on advice from his chief minister, Thomas Cromwell (c. 1485–1540), and simply announced that the pope had no authority in England. Statutes (laws) passed by the Reformation Parliament in 1533 and 1534 named the king Supreme Head of the Church and cut all ties with the papacy. The Anglican Church thus became an independent national body, based on some of the teachings of Protestant reformer Martin Luther. Previously, Henry had opposed Luther and was rewarded by the pope with the title "Defender of the Faith." Now he accepted a number of Lutheran doctrines, such as rejection of the pope as God's sole representative on Earth.

Closing of monasteries

One of the most important events of Henry VIII's reign was the closing of monasteries. At the beginning of the Tudor era the religious houses owned as much as one-fourth of all land in England. These estates had been given or bequeathed (granted in wills) to monks by religiously devout men and women in exchange for prayers for their souls after they died. Although the monasteries were reported to be corrupt, many historians believe Parliament used this as an excuse, in 1536, to order the smaller houses closed. Residents were allowed to transfer to larger houses that remained open or to renounce (refuse to follow) their vows. Most chose to renounce their vows. The great abbeys (churches connected with monasteries) were suppressed one by one in the next few years. A second statute, passed in 1540, legalized these closures and mandated the seizing of all remaining property. Former monastic possessions were managed by a new financial bureau, the Court of Augmentations. The court paid small pensions (financial allowances for retired people) to the former monks and nuns, and larger ones to the former abbots and priors (heads of monasteries) who had cooperated in the closing of their houses. By the time of Henry VIII's death in 1547, most of the monastic land had been sold to noblemen and members of the gentry. These people would thus profit from the continuation of the Reformation.

The loss of the monasteries was felt in various ways. Earlier they had been great centers of learning and the arts, but now the great monastic libraries were divided and sent to other locations. Some collections remained in cathedrals that had earlier been associated with monasteries, like Canterbury and Dudiam, while others were acquired by Oxford and Cambridge universities or by private collectors. Much of the wealth seized from the religious houses was spent on warfare.

Henry granted divorce

In May 1533 Henry's divorce was granted by Thomas Cranmer (1489–1556), the new archbishop of Canterbury (head of the Anglican Church). Henry and Anne Boleyn had been secretly married in January, and their daughter Elizabeth was born the following September. In 1536 Henry discovered that Anne had been unfaithful to him and he had her beheaded. Catherine of Aragon died a natural death in the same year. Henry finally had a male heir in 1537, when his third wife, Jane Seymour (c. 1509–1537), gave birth to their son Edward. Jane died of complications following childbirth, but Henry waited until 1540 to marry again. Cromwell was eager to form an alliance against Charles V by joining England with one of the Protestant states in Germany. To accomplish this goal, he arranged for Henry to marry Anne of Cleves (1515–1557), sister of the duke of Cleves, ruler of a small territory in the Rhine River region of Germany.

Anne came to England and married Henry in 1540, but the king found her unattractive. Cromwell therefore declared the marriage invalid shortly after he conducted the wed-

After becoming archbishop of Canterbury, Thomas Cranmer granted Henry VIII's divorce from Catherine of Aragon.
Photograph courtesy of The Library of Congress.

ding ceremony. Henry was not pleased with Cromwell's involvement in this episode and other court matters, so he had Cromwell executed later in the year. On the very day of Cromwell's death Henry married Catherine Howard (c. 1520–1542). Soon Catherine, like Anne Boleyn, was found guilty of adultery; she was beheaded in 1542. Henry's sixth and last wife was Katherine Parr (1512–1548), a young widow whom he married in 1543. She cared for the aging king and tried to be a mother to his children. Both Katherine Parr and Anne of Cleves outlived Henry, who died in 1547.

Edward takes throne

Henry stated in his will that any of his three children—Edward, Mary, and Elizabeth—could succeed him to the throne, even though his daughters had earlier been declared illegitimate when he divorced their mothers. Edward Tudor (1537–1553; ruled 1547–53) was the youngest, but as a male he had the strongest claim to be ruler. (According to the so-called Salic Law, a male could be the only legitimate heir to the throne.) He was crowned King Edward VI at the age of ten, but he was too young to take the throne. Henry had named a large council of regents to rule England until Edward was old enough to be king. Nevertheless, Edward's uncle, Edward Seymour (c. 1550–1552), duke of Somerset, took control of the government. Called Protector, Somerset virtually ruled England for several years, but he found it difficult to deal with several rebellions that broke out in 1549. He lost power to John Dudley (1502–1553), earl of Warwick, who was the most important figure in the government for the remainder of Edward's reign.

Both Somerset and Warwick approved of further reform in the church. Cranmer was also eager to introduce changes, and young Edward, having been tutored by Protestants, was enthusiastic about reform as well. Renaissance ideas had dominated his education. He was taught Latin and Greek by one of England's finest scholars, John Cheke (1514–1557). He was instructed in religion by Richard Cox (c. 1500–1592), later the bishop of Ely. Protestantism now reached its highest point in English history. Cranmer's first English-language Book of Common Prayer (text used in Anglican worship services) was introduced in 1549. It was moderate in tone—that is, it did not reflect drastic changes from the Roman Catholic worship services—but a revision issued in 1552 was radically different. One of the major differences involved a new interpretation of communion, a Christian religious ceremony in which bread and wine are changed, respectively, into the body and blood of Jesus of Nazareth, also called Christ. The revised Book of Common Prayer regarded communion as simply a reenactment of the Last Supper, the final meal that Christ shared with his disciples, or followers. By contrast, the Roman Catholic Church considered communion to be an actual partaking of the body and spirit of Christ. The revised Book of Common Prayer also ordered the destruction of stone altars associated with the Catholic Mass (worship service in which communion is taken).

Edward died in 1553 at the age of sixteen, probably from pneumonia (a disease of the lungs) and possibly tuberculosis (a bacterial infection of the lungs). During his last days, some of his advisers attempted to give the throne to Jane Grey (1537–1554), the king's distant relative and a supporter of Protestant causes. They knew that

Edward's sister, Mary Tudor, would restore the Catholic faith because she had always been a Catholic. Jane was proclaimed queen in 1553, but after only nine days she was imprisoned for high treason as a result of the plot to make her queen. She was beheaded, along with her husband, Guildford Dudley, in 1554.

"Bloody Mary" is queen

Mary Tudor (1516–1558; ruled 1553–58) took the throne as Queen Mary I in 1553, after Jane Grey's nine-day reign. Like her mother, Catherine of Aragon, Mary was pro-Spanish and Catholic. Soon after being crowned, she married Philip of Spain (soon to be King Philip II), but Parliament prevented him from taking the English throne along with his wife. Mary had widespread popular support, and she immediately began undoing the Reformation in two stages. In 1553 she restored the Latin Mass and the following year she recognized the jurisdiction of the pope in England. Cranmer was dismissed from office and placed under house arrest, while Reginald Pole (1500–1558) was brought back to England to take the archbishop's place. Pole was an English aristocrat who had lived in Italy since Henry VIII's break with the papacy. Many people supported Mary's restoration of the Catholic faith, believing that Edward's reign had gone too far in abolishing cherished ceremonies and beliefs.

Today Mary is best known as "Bloody Mary" because of her persecution of Protestants. During her brief five-year reign, nearly three hundred people were burned at the stake. This method of punishment, which was introduced by the Inquisition (an official Catholic Church court charged with finding heretics) supposedly drove evil spirits out of the sinners (see "Inquisition" in Chapters 1 and 7). Many who refused to reject Protestant beliefs continued to worship in underground churches or fled to countries on the European continent. Others became involved in a series of plots against Mary's government. Protestant leaders looked to the queen's half-sister, Elizabeth, as a possible Protestant replacement. Mary then had Elizabeth arrested and sent to the Tower of London (a prison for members of royalty and the nobility), and later to Woodstock. Five years later Mary, who was now near death, named Elizabeth to be her successor. Thus, on March 17, 1558, the last Tudor monarch of England ascended the throne.

Elizabeth

The reign of Queen Elizabeth I (1533–1603; ruled 1558–1603) is known as England's golden age. In 1559 Elizabeth restored the Anglican Church, taking the title Supreme Governor of the Church. She did not call herself Supreme Head, possibly because it was believed a woman could not head a church. Nevertheless, she followed the religious policies of her father and brother. The Elizabethan Book of Common Prayer was based on Cranmer's second version, but it was modified to allow individual wor-

Elizabeth I, queen of England. Elizabeth's reign is known as the golden age of England. *Reproduced by permission of Archive Photos, Inc.*

dominated literature. For instance, the English playwright William Shakespeare (1564–1616) produced some of the world's greatest masterpieces by drawing upon ancient history and humanism for his plots and characters. Classical educations were provided to members of the ruling classes and the clergy, and scholars avidly studied ancient history.

Philip II declares war

Following Mary' death, Philip II had suggested that he marry Elizabeth. When she refused his proposal he realized that England could never be a Catholic country. For the rest of the century England and other Protestant states were involved in conflict with Spain and the papacy. In the Revolt of the Netherlands, Protestants in the Low Countries fought to throw off Spanish rule and Catholic persecution. Initially reluctant to become involved, Elizabeth finally accepted the argument that England, as the chief Protestant power in Europe, had an obligation to aid Protestants elsewhere.

A major threat to Elizabeth's security were various plots associated with Mary Stuart (1542–1587), queen of Scots (ruled Scotland, 1542–67). Mary was a Catholic who had been driven from Scotland by Protestants. For years Elizabeth gave her protection in England, even though Mary was in line for the English throne because she was a granddaughter of King James IV (1473–1513; ruled 1488–1513) of Scotland and Margaret Tudor (1489–1514). But the discovery of a

shipers to hold diverse views about such matters as communion. Elizabeth was highly educated. She knew the Greek and Latin languages, and she occasionally embarrassed foreign diplomats when she understood comments they made in their own languages. She was an accomplished performer on the virginal, the keyboard instrument named in honor of her status as the Virgin Queen—Elizabeth refused to get married because she had devoted her life to her country. During her long reign Renaissance ideas conspiracy to assassinate Elizabeth in 1586 led to Mary's execution at Fotheringhay castle in 1587.

English defeat Spanish Armada

The execution of the Catholic queen was a signal to Philip that he must seize the throne of England. He began organizing the famous "Invincible Armada," a fleet of 130 heavily armored ships that carried 30,000 men, for an invasion of England (see "Spain" section later in this chapter). In 1587, even before the Armada could set out, the English seaman Francis Drake (c. 1540–1596) launched a surprise attack on the Spanish ships, which were anchored in the port of Cádiz, Spain. The destruction was so great that the invasion was delayed for a year. In May 1588 the Spanish Armada set out from Lisbon, but storms forced the fleet into La Coruña in northwestern Spain. The ships did not set sail again until July. By this time pandemonium had broken out in England, and Elizabeth's advisers urged her to prepare for the impending attack. English seamen rushed home from all over the globe to defend their homeland for their beloved Gloriana (the nickname given to Elizabeth). Among them were Drake, John Hawkins (1532–1595), and Martin Frobisher (c. 1535–1594). At the town of Tilbury, Elizabeth reviewed her small land army, which was clearly inadequate to take on the Spanish forces. She inspired the soldiers by saying that though she had "the body of a weak and feeble woman," she had "the heart and stomach of a King."

When the Armada began moving up the English Channel in early August, the English main fleet took advantage of a favorable wind and made three assaults on the Spanish ships. They did not inflict any serious damage, so on August 6 the Armada anchored at Calais (a French town on the Strait of Dover on the Channel) to await reinforcements. The following night the Spanish fleet commander, Alonso Pérez de Guzmán, duke of Medina-Sidonia, made a serious mistake. He improperly anchored the fleet, thus leaving an opening for a squadron of English fire ships to set the Armada ablaze. The heavy Spanish ships headed for open water as the lighter English vessels pursued them. The Armada was doomed when a powerful storm, which the English called the "Great Protestant Wind," swept through the Channel. Medina-Sidonia retreated, taking his ships north around the British Isles. Many Spanish ships broke up on the west coast of Ireland, and only half of the Armada eventually returned to Spain.

Queen confronts problems

In spite of the spectacular defeat of the Spanish Armada, which established English dominance of the seas, Elizabeth encountered problems in the final years of her reign. During the 1590s, she struggled to keep her government from going bankrupt. Yet she also spent excessive amounts of money on the "Cult of Gloriana," staging grand pageants and spectacles to impress the English people. Her final years were dominated by controversy surrounding one of her favorite courtiers (members of the court), Robert Devereux (1566–1601), earl of Essex. Essex had numerous clashes with two of the queen's most able ministers, William Cecil (1520–1598) and his son, Robert Cecil (1563–1612). When William Cecil died in 1598, Elizabeth snubbed Essex and awarded her highest council post to Robert Cecil. Then in 1599 she placed Essex in command of a military force and sent him to Ireland to subdue Tyrone's Rebellion. This movement, led by Hugh O'Neill (c. 1540–1616), earl of Tyrone, was designed to gain Irish independence from England. But Essex botched the job miserably. Not only did he refuse to follow Elizabeth's orders, but he also signed an unauthorized truce with the rebels.

When Essex returned to England, Elizabeth reluctantly withdrew her patronage from him. In 1601 he attempted to stage a coup (overthrow of government) that would oust Cecil's party and put his own party in power around the queen. He sought aid from the army in Ireland and from King James VI of Scotland. The plot failed, however, and Essex was arrested. He was put on trial and sentenced to death. After Elizabeth reluctantly signed the death warrant, Essex was executed. The queen died two years later. Since she had no heirs, the Tudor dynasty came to an end. Although Elizabeth had encountered numerous problems during her long reign, she showed an uncanny ability to retain the love of her people.

James I known for Bible

Elizabeth was followed by James VI of Scotland, who became King James I of England (ruled 1603–25). He was the son of Mary, queen of Scots, and Henry Stewart (1545–1567), who was the grandson of Henry VII. James was married to Anne of Denmark. A learned man himself, James wrote two studies of political theory, *The True Law of Free Monarchy* (1598) and *Baslikon doron* ("Royal gift"; 1599). He enjoyed delivering lectures on history and politics. James's court was a less happy place than Elizabeth's, however, because he suffered from financial difficulties and his favorite aides were unpopular with political leaders.

James also had to contend with religious unrest. As he rode from Edinburgh to London in 1603, shortly after becoming king, he was met by a group of Puritans (members of the Anglican Church who advocated strict reforms). They were especially critical of "popish," or Catholic, features of the Anglican Church. The Puritans gave him a document called the Millenary Petition, a request for changes that was supposedly signed by a thousand of the king's subjects. Among the reforms they demanded were simplified services, less elaborate church music, simpler vestments (robes worn by clergymen), and more preaching. They also wanted to end the use of wedding rings, which were believed to be popish because Catholics wore them. Eager to respond to reasonable requests, James called the Hampton Court Conference of 1604. Here Puri-

Elizabeth's Legacy

The forty-five-year reign of Elizabeth I was darkened by the executions of her cousin Mary Stuart (Mary, Queen of Scots) and of her favorite courtier, Robert Devereux, earl of Essex. Yet Elizabeth is best remembered for her accomplishments, such as strengthening the Anglican Church and keeping government finances stable. Most of all, she embodied the spirit of her people—a determination to survive and indeed prosper in the face of enormous odds. Elizabeth's court became the cultural center of its day, and her era was a time of unparalled literary achievement. Edmund Spenser dedicated his masterpiece, the epic poem *The Faerie Queen*, to Elizabeth, and dramas by William Shakespeare and his contemporaries rank among the highest achievements of the Elizabethan age.

During Elizabeth's reign England also began emerging as a great sea power, which eventually gave rise to the expansion of the British Empire over the next three centuries. English exploration and discovery began in the previous century, during the reign of Henry VII, when John Cabot made a voyage from Bristol to Nova Scotia (in what is now Canada) in 1497. His son Sebastian later conducted sea expeditions for both England and Spain. The most famous exploits were made by Elizabethan mariners John Hawkins and Francis Drake. Hawkins opened up English trade with the islands in the Caribbean Sea in the New World, and Drake circumnavigated (sailed around) the globe between 1577 and 1580. Attempts were made to colonize Virginia, the territory in North America named in Elizabeth's honor (she was called the "Virgin Queen"). English settlers made three failed attempts to start a colony at Roanoke, an island off the coast of Virginia. The last group of colonists mysteriously disappeared. The first successful English colony in North America was Jamestown, Virginia, which was started in 1607 during the reign of Elizabeth's successor, James I. Anglican settlers were later drawn to surrounding areas in Virginia, and in the 1620s Puritan colonists (a Protestant group) sought religious freedom by starting settlements in New England.

tan leaders met with the king and some of the officers of the Anglican Church. Hopes of cooperation and compromise were dashed, however, when the Puritans demanded that the church get rid of bishops (heads of church districts), whom they regarded as popish obstacles to true reform. Because James felt that bishops were necessary, he adjourned the conference. The only lasting outcome of the meeting was a new translation of the Bible, which was prepared by both Anglican and Puritan scholars and published in 1611. Although it was called the King James Bible, James himself had little to

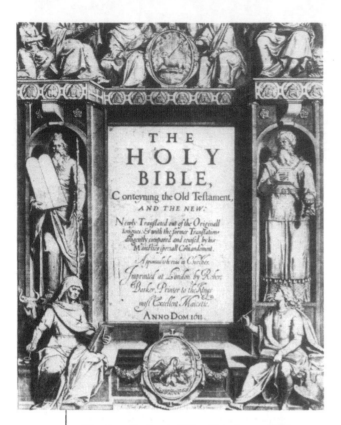

The frontispiece of the King James Bible. Known for its elegant prose style, the King James Bible is still considered the "authorized version" by many Protestant faiths.
Reproduced by permission of Hulton Archive.

do with the translation. Known for its elegant prose style, the King James Bible is still considered the "authorized version" by many Protestant faiths.

Involvement in Thirty Years' War

James's reign was troubled by his insistence upon ruling by divine right (the concept that a king is chosen directly by God). From the time he took the throne he had problems with Parliament, which he refused to recognize as the law-making body of Eng-

land. In fact, in 1614 he dissolved Parliament, then ruled for seven years without one. In 1621, however, Parliament reconvened in order to vote funds to aid Frederick V of Bohemia (1596–1632). Frederick was married to James's daughter Elizabeth. In 1619 Protestants in Bohemia had ousted their Roman Catholic king, Ferdinand (Holy Roman Emperor Ferdinand II), and replaced him with Frederick. Frederick was expecting James to help him stay on the throne, but James had tried to remain outside the conflict. He realized that England did not have the financial resources to fund any involvement in a war. In 1620 Frederick lost the throne of Bohemia (he was nicknamed the "Winter King" because he ruled for only one winter) and was stripped of all his territories in the Holy Roman Empire. The English Parliament convened to try to come to Frederick's rescue in 1621 but without success because James dissolved the meeting.

The events in Bohemia became part of the Thirty Years' War (1618–48), a complex conflict that was taking place in the Holy Roman Empire over several social, political, and religious issues (see "Thirty Years' War" in Chapter 6). James again tried to remain free of the war by arranging an alliance with a Catholic country. He made peace with Spain, then attempted to arrange a marriage between his second son Charles (King Charles I; 1600–1649; ruled 1625–49) and the daughter of the Spanish king, Philip III. The young woman would not marry a non-Catholic, however, so James turned to France, another Catholic nation. In

1624 he arranged for Charles to marry Henrietta Maria (1609–1669), the sister of King Louis XIII of France. This marriage did not allow England to be free of the war, though, since many English people believed it was necessary to aid Protestants on the European continent. James could not prevent Parliament from voting funds for a campaign against Spain. England was also dragged into several unsuccessful naval campaigns against Spain and France during the course of the Thirty Years' War.

English Renaissance continues

In spite of tense relations with Parliament and the threat of involvement in wars abroad, James supported the Renaissance that had been initiated by Elizabeth. During his reign classical learning continued to dominate education and literature. Court masques (plays in which actors wear masks), some of them written by the dramatist Ben Jonson (1572–1637), were based on classical myths. They often involved elaborate scenery and costumes as well as music. Prominent members of the royal family and the court frequently played roles in these productions. An important revolution in English architecture was begun by Inigo Jones (1573–1652). Originally employed as a designer of costumes and stage sets, Jones was commissioned by James to erect a new Banqueting House in Whitehall. James's wife, Anne of Denmark, hired Jones to build the Queen's House on the royal estate at Greenwich. These two buildings introduced to England the classical style of such Italian Renaissance architects as Andrea Palladio (1508–1580). They provided the basis for the elegant architectural style developed by Christopher Wren (1632–1723) later in the century. James also supported settlement in the New World. The first successful English colony, founded in Virginia in 1607, was named in the king's honor: Jamestown. Renaissance ideas were still dominant in England when James died in 1625. During the reign of Charles I, England was embroiled in a civil war between the Puritans and supporters of the monarchy. Charles was executed in 1649 and the Puritans took control of the government, bringing about the decline of Renaissance values in England.

Spain

Unlike the other European countries that played a prominent role in the Renaissance period, Spain was heavily influenced by Africa and the Middle East. Spain had often attracted the attention of people from North Africa as a promising new land. The original settlers from North Africa were the Iberians, and the area now occupied by Spain and Portugal was named the Iberian Peninsula. The Iberians were followed by the Carthaginians. The third group from North Africa were Muslim Arabs and Berbers (wandering tribes) called Moors. In A.D. 711 twelve thousand Moors, led by Tāriq ibn Ziyād (died c. 720), crossed the Strait of Gibraltar and invaded Spain. By that time Germanic tribes, called the Visigoths, had carved up Spain into numerous small regions, each controlled by a feudal lord. These lords were constantly fighting among themselves. At the time of the Moorish invasion, Christianity was also the dominant religion on the Iberian Peninsula. After winning several major battles, the Moors conquered the Visigoth capital of Toledo in 712 and soon pushed the Germanic lords and their armies into the northern frontiers of Spain.

The Moors established a new culture on the Iberian Peninsula. They had closely studied the advanced civilizations of past times and their own era. Moorish farming techniques brought the dry land to life. Moorish architects renewed cities with intricately decorated mosques, lush gardens, and paved streets. They built the Great Mosque (Muslim house of worship) of Córdoba in 786 and the Alhambra (a grand palace) in Granada in the 1300s. The Moors introduced the secrets of making medicine and of producing steel, skills they had learned from the Far East (countries in Asia). Their philosophy made the cities of Toledo, Córdoba, and Granada important centers of learning.

Jews link Muslims and Christians

The Jews were another important group that shaped the culture of Spain. They had arrived on the peninsula by A.D. 300, becoming both urban and rural dwellers. Records such as reports from the Christian Council of Elvira in 313 show that Christians immediately began pressuring Jews to

convert to Christianity. Thus, from the outset of their arrival in Spain, Jews were separated from Christians. The Jews therefore welcomed the invading Moors in 711. The Muslim conquest was economically attractive to Jews, since it opened the markets of North Africa as well as of the entire Muslim world as far away as India. Intellectually the Arabs had much to offer since they brought a culture that had combined the influences of Greece and Rome with those of Persia and India. Jews became highly influential in Spain from the tenth through the twelfth centuries, a period that is often called the "Golden Age" of Jewish history. During this time Jews not only produced great works of philosophy, poetry, liturgy (texts for worship services), theology (philosophy of religion), and literature, but they also served as the vital intellectual link between the Muslim Middle East and Christian Europe.

Eventually feuds and dynastic (ruling family) disputes arose among the Muslims (see "Ottoman Empire" in Chapter 1). In the eleventh century Christian states in the north of Spain, even though they were not unified, took advantage of Muslim unrest and set out to recapture territories conquered by the Moors. The Moors surrendered Toledo to the Christians in 1085. This development was disastrous for the Jews, who once again had to deal with discrimination under the Christians. Yet the Jews found Berber conquests even more threatening. In 1150 a new group of Berber conquerors, the Almohades, came to

Spain and forced the Jews to convert to Islam. As a result, many Jews fled from the region.

Inquisition reaches Spain

During the Christian reconquest of Spain, the Roman Catholic Church launched the Crusades (1096–1291), a series of holy wars against "pagans." (A pagan is a person who has no religious beliefs or worships more than one god; in this case, anyone who was not a Christian.) The Christians were trying to recapture the Holy Land (called Palestine at the time; the territory is now in parts of Israel, Jordan, and Egypt), which they considered sacred because it was the place where Jesus of Nazareth founded Christianity. In 1071 Muslim Turks had seized Jerusalem—the center of the Holy Land and a city considered sacred to Jews, Muslims, and Christians—when they conquered the Byzantine Empire (the eastern part of the former Roman Empire, based in Constantinople, which is now Istanbul, Turkey). After retaking Jerusalem from the Muslims during the First Crusade, the Christians began establishing Crusader kingdoms around the Mediterranean Sea.

In 1233 Pope Gregory IX (c. 1170–1241; reigned 1227–41) established the Inquisition (now known as the medieval Inquisition; see "Inquisition" in Chapter 1). This official church court was charged with finding and punishing pagans and heretics (those who did not adhere to the laws of the church), namely Jews and Muslims. During the Inquisition thousands of non-Christians were killed by mobs, while thousands more tried to save their own lives by converting to Christianity. Some Jews, called Marranos, pretended to convert while secretly practicing Judaism (the Jewish religion). "Converted" Muslims who still practiced Islam were called Moriscos. Religious fanaticism soon intensified. For a time Jews' property was seized, but they did not receive any further punishment. The situation changed after 1474, however, when Pope Sixtus IV (1414–1484; reigned 1471–84) gave Spanish monarchs Ferdinand II (1452–1516) and Isabella I (1451–1504) permission to conduct the Spanish Inquisition, which was separate from the medieval Inquisition.

Ferdinand and Isabella seek to unite Spain

With the marriage of Ferdinand of Aragon and Isabella of Castile, Spain's two largest Christian kingdoms, Aragon (in central Spain) and Castile (in eastern Spain), were united into a powerful force. Ferdinand and Isabella ascended to the throne as the Catholic Monarchs of Spain in 1474. Their reign, which lasted until Isabella's death in 1504, marked the end of the Middle Ages and the beginning of the Renaissance in Spain.

Ferdinand was the crown prince of the kingdom of Aragon when, in 1469, he married Isabella, who was his cousin and heir to the throne of Castile. The noblemen of Castile opposed the marriage because they knew a strong monarchy would limit their power. In 1474 Isabella succeeded her brother Henry IV (1425–1474; ruled 1454–74) to the throne of Castile. Ferdinand became king of Aragon when his father, King John II (1397–1479; ruled 1458–79), died in 1479. Thus the two largest Christian kingdoms in Spain were united. The marriage contract stated that Ferdinand and Isabella would rule their own kingdoms and that Aragon and Castile were not to be merged. Nevertheless, the monarchs were able to apply the same policies to both kingdoms. Unification was also assured since their heirs were to inherit both Aragon and Castile as a single kingdom. The Catholic sovereigns had specific goals: they wanted to bring the remainder of the Iberian Peninsula under their control, crush opposition groups, centralize the government, and unify the Spanish kingdoms. They had the support and advice of Isabella's priest, Francisco Jiménez de Cisneros (1436–1517), and Gonzalo Fernández de Córdoba (1453–1515), the foremost military leader of his day.

Ferdinand and Isabella first waged war against the Moorish kingdom of Granada, on the southern end of the peninsula. In 1492, after conquering this last outpost of Moorish rule in western Europe, they annexed Granada to Castile. In the early 1500s they continued the crusade against the Moors into North Africa with a series of military expeditions. Ferdinand's most brilliant military and political successes were achieved in Italy during the Italian Wars, a series of conflicts in which Spain and France were fighting over control of Naples and Sicily (see discussion of the Italian Wars in "France" section previously in this chapter). After the French invasion of Italy in 1494, Ferdinand was able to intervene in the affairs of Naples and Milan. He took complete control of Naples by 1504. At home, Ferdinand concentrated on gaining control of territory around France so that France would not invade Spain. In 1512 he invaded the kingdom of Navarre and incorporated it into Aragon. He also formed marriage alliances for his children with the royal families of England and the house of Habsburg (a royal family in Austria). He made similar alliances with Portugal.

Ferdinand and Isabella were able to centralize most of the government, although Aragon successfully resisted any changes that would increase royal authority. Most reforms took place in Castile, the larger and stronger of the two kingdoms. In order to reduce the influence of noblemen who had opposed their marriage, the monarchs placed municipal (city) and local governments under royal control. They rarely called meetings of the Cortes (Parliament, or central lawmaking body) and they appointed middle-class people to government offices. Ferdinand and Isabella also took over a municipal league known as the Santa Hermandad (Holy Brotherhood), which had provided mutual assistance and protection to its members for several centuries. The monarchs reorganized the Santa Hermandad into a national militia (citizens army) that was funded by towns. They used the militia to put down noblemen's efforts to revolt. Armed resistance from the most troublesome nobles was crushed by Fernández de Córdoba's armies.

Jews and Muslims expelled from Spain

The Catholic sovereigns' most controversial actions involved Jews and Muslims. Isabella believed that only Catholicism could unite the separate provinces of Spain. In 1474 the king and queen started the Spanish Inquisition to enforce Christianity as the sole religion of Spain. Their adviser was Tomás de Torquemada (pronounced tor-kay-MAH-thah; 1420–1498), a Dominican monk (member of a religious order founded by Saint Dominic). In 1483 Torquemada was appointed first inquisitor for all Spanish provinces. In 1487, when he was named grand inquisitor (supreme head of the court), he set out to rid Spain of "converts" who did not actually practice Christianity. Those who did not confess their sins or undergo genuine conversion were severely punished or executed. Practicing Jews were segregated and forced to wear an identifying badge.

On March 30, 1492, heeding the advice of Torquemada, the king and queen ordered all Jews to leave Spanish territory by July 30. Those who chose to stay in Spain had to submit to baptism (a ceremony marking admission into the Christian religion) or be put to death. Jews were forbidden to take most of their possessions with them if they chose to leave the country. Jewish leaders such as Abra-

The expulsion of the Jews from Spain in 1492 by command of King Ferdinand and Queen Isabella. ©Bettmann/Corbis. Reproduced by permission of the Corbis Corporation.

ham Senior, Isaac Abrabanel, and others tried in vain to have the order revoked. The Jews were expelled and went mainly to North Africa. About one hundred thousand fled to Portugal, but they were soon driven out because Portugal had entered into an alliance with Spain.

In 1502 Moriscos were also given the choice of converting to Christianity or leaving the dominion of Castile. This policy continued for more than twenty years. Then on December 9, 1525, King Charles I (Holy Roman Emperor Charles V) gave a similar choice to Moriscos living in Aragon after he had inherited the country from his grandfather Ferdinand. The following year he established an Inquisition court at Granada, a heavily Muslim province, as a final effort to force Moriscos to accept Christianity or leave Spain. The church then sent Franciscans and Jesuits (members of Catholic religious orders) into Granada and Valencia to apply pressure on the Moriscos. Many Moriscos paid considerable sums of money to Catholic Church officials so they could stay in the country. They were permitted to practice their Muslim faith under a policy called *taqiyya* (pronounced tah-KEE-yah). By the mid-1500s, between 350,000 and 400,000 Moriscos were living in the Spanish provinces. While they were less numerous in Catalonia, Castile, Estremadura, and Andalusia, Moriscos comprised about one-fifth of the population (50,000 people) in Aragon and one-third of the population (100,000 people) of Valencia. The majority of Moriscos were farm laborers, though many worked in trades such as the silk and leather industries. Some had even entered the ranks of nobility.

Tensions between Spain and the Ottomans had reached a peak in the mid-1500s. Christians were becoming impatient because only a few Moriscos had actually converted. Moriscos were also fiercely opposing the efforts of the Inquisition. On De-

cember 24, 1568, Moriscos in Granada staged a rebellion and fought royal armies for nearly two years. During the standoff, in 1569, King Philip II ordered all Moriscos—including those who were not involved in the conflict—out of Castile, Estremadura, and central Andalusia. More than 80,000 people were deported. Government and church officials then debated what to do about Moriscos in the rest of Spain. Some contended that conversion was the best policy. Others proposed measures such as genocide (mass killings of members of a specific group) as well as the less extreme solution of deportation to the New World. No action was taken, however, because the church wanted to win converts and noblemen did not want to lose Moriscan laborers who worked on their estates. By the early seventeenth century, however, Spanish people had become convinced that Moriscos were plotting with Muslim and Protestant enemies to overthrow the Catholic state. On April 9, 1609, King Philip III signed a decree of expulsion. From 1609 until 1614, between 300,000 and 350,000 Moriscos were forced to leave Spain. Most settled in North Africa, while others went to Turkey, France, and Italy. Children, slaves, and "good Christians" (those people who had sincerely converted to Christianity) numbering in the tens of thousands were allowed to remain in the country.

Monarchs back Columbus's voyage

In 1492 Ferdinand and Isabella became leaders in the European

Portugal

Portugal was a rival of Spain during the age of exploration and discovery. The country occupies the western part of the Iberian Peninsula, next to Spain. The name Portugal comes from the ancient port city of Portus Cale (now Porto), at the mouth of the Douro River, where the Portuguese monarchy began. The country's early history is indistinguishable from that of the other Iberian peoples. Lusitanians were successively overrun by Celts, Romans, Visigoths, and Moors (711). In 1094 Henry of Burgundy was given the county of Portugal by the king of Castile and León for his success against the Moors. Henry's son, Alfonso I (c. 1109–1185), became king and achieved independence for Portugal in 1143. Thus began the Burgundy dynasty. By the mid-thirteenth century, the present boundaries of Portugal were established and Lisbon became the capital.

King John I (c. 1357–1433; ruled 1385–1433) was the founder of the powerful Aviz dynasty. He was married to the English princess Philippa of Lancaster. After the Portuguese defeated the Spanish in a war over the throne in 1385, John established a political alliance with England under the Treaty of Windsor (1386) that has endured to the present day. This victory inaugurated the most brilliant era in Portuguese history. Prince Henry the Navigator (1394–1460), a son of John I, founded a nautical school at Sagres, where he gathered the world' best navigators, mapmakers, geographers, and astronomers. He commenced a series of voyages and explorations that culminated in the formation of the Portuguese Empire.

In the golden age of Portugal, during the fifteenth and sixteenth centuries, Portuguese explorers sailed most of the world's seas. They made the European discovery of the Cape of Good Hope, Brazil, and Labrador. They also founded Portugal's overseas provinces in western and eastern Africa, India, Southeast Asia, and Brazil and poured the vast riches of the empire into the homeland. In 1580 and 1581, Philip II of Spain claimed the throne of Portugal, conquered the country, and acquired its empire. National sovereignty was restored by the revolution of 1640. King John IV (1604–1656; ruled 1640–56), founder of the Bragança dynasty, then took the Portuguese throne. John IV ushered in Portugal's silver age, the seventeenth and eighteenth centuries, when the wealth of Brazil once more made Lisbon one of the most brilliant European capitals.

quest for new territories and markets in the East (see "The age of European exploration" section later in this chapter). They commissioned Christopher Columbus (1451–1506), a navigator from Genoa, Italy, to find a sea route to the Indies (Asia). Columbus's ships went off course and he did not reach Asia. Nevertheless, he did come upon a continent that was then unknown to Europeans. When Columbus returned from this "New World," Ferdinand and Isabella asked Pope Alexander VI to recognize Spain's authority over these new lands. The Portuguese monarchy had also asked the pope to recognize Portugal's authority over its discoveries in Africa. These requests raised a question about rights to sea routes. In a papal bull, or decree, Alexander drew a line from north to south one hundred leagues (approximately 240 miles, or 386 kilometers) west of the Azores Islands. All lands to the east would belong to Portugal and all lands to the west would belong to Spain. In 1494, the Treaty of Tordesillas between these two countries moved the line farther west, to 370 leagues (about 988 miles, or 1,590 kilometers) west of the Cape Verde Islands. The new line would give Portugal authority over Brazil when it was discovered five years later. The pope also gave Ferdinand and Isabella the authority to convert the people of these new lands to Christianity and to govern them.

Habsburg alliance with Spain

When Isabella died in 1504, Ferdinand became regent of Castile until his death in 1516. Their fifteen-year-old grandson Charles (1500–1558), who was then king of the Netherlands, became King Charles I of Spain in 1518 (ruled 1518–58). The crowning of Charles as king of Spain was the climax of a bitter dispute that resulted from the marriage contract between Ferdinand and Isabella. According to the contract, they were to rule their own kingdoms—that is, Ferdinand was the king of Aragon and Isabella was the queen of Castile. Although there was no mention of heirs, Spanish law stated that the monarchs' heir would inherit both kingdoms. The problems started when Isabella died in 1504. Ferdinand and Isabella's son John had been the heir to the throne of Castile, but he had also died. The next in line was their daughter Joanna (1479–1555), who was married to Philip I of Austria (1478–1506), son of Holy Roman Emperor Maximilian I. Ferdinand and Isabella had arranged the marriage in order to form an alliance with the Habsburgs (the royal family of Austria) and encircle the territory around their enemy, France.

Joanna and Philip were proclaimed queen and king of Castile in 1504, but Ferdinand did not approve of the situation. He disliked having Philip, a foreign prince, on a Spanish throne. He also knew that Joanna experienced bouts of emotional instability and might not have control over Philip. Another concern was that the noblemen of Castile supported Philip because they hoped he would rule in their favor. They wanted to regain power that had been taken from them by Ferdinand and Isabella over the past twenty years. Ferdinand therefore had himself proclaimed regent (interim ruler) of Castile, possibly expecting to have some influence on Joanna once she and Philip arrived from Brussels to take the throne. Shortly after the new monarchs reached Spain in 1506, Philip suddenly died. Having been deeply in love with her husband, Joanna was completely devastated and could not rule. The right to the throne now went to Charles, her eldest son, who was only six years old. Joanna retired to a castle in Tordesillas, where she mourned her deceased husband until her own death in 1555.

Ferdinand remained regent of Castile. The prospect of having Charles someday take the thrones of both Castile and Aragon disturbed Ferdinand. The main problem was that Charles was a foreigner. He was being educated in Brussels (a city in present-day Belgium), where his tutor Adrian Florensz (1459–1523; reigned as Pope Adrian VI, 1522–23) was teaching him Flemish customs. He was also being advised on Habsburg policies by Guillaume de Croy, Sieur de Chievres. In addition, Charles would inherit lands in Burgundy (a region of France) that belonged to Maximilian I, and he was in line to become Holy Roman Emperor. At one time, the Holy Roman Empire had encompassed nearly all of Europe. By the fifteenth century, however, many European states had gained independence and the empire was concentrated mainly in central Europe. Nevertheless, the emperor was still the most powerful political figure in the Christian world.

Charles is king, then emperor

Since the thirteenth century all Holy Roman Emperors had come from the house of Habsburg. Ferdinand feared that the Habsburgs would influence Charles to place their own interests above the needs of Spain. In an effort to prevent this outcome, Ferdinand brought Charles's younger brother, Ferdinand, from Flanders to Spain. He had the boy trained in Spanish customs and politics and even made out a will naming the young Ferdinand as his heir. The Castilian nobility were alarmed by this development because they knew a Spanish king would limit their power. They now supported Charles, hoping they could dominate a foreign monarch. Giving in to pressure from the noblemen and Charles's Flemish advisers, Ferdinand rewrote his will and named Charles as his heir.

When Ferdinand died in 1516, Charles was named king of Castile and Aragon, becoming the first official monarch of a united Spain. The aged Jiménez de Cisneros, who was now archbishop of Toledo, acted as regent of Castile until Charles arrived in Spain. By this time most Spaniards were having second thoughts about the new king: Charles had never been to their country, and he could not even speak Spanish. Like Ferdinand, they also feared that he would be more interested in expanding Habsburg territory and becoming Holy Roman Emperor than in ruling Spain. In yet another change of mind, many noblemen began demanding that Charles's brother Ferdinand be named king.

Early in 1518 the eighteen-year-old Charles took the throne of Spain. The Spaniards' worst fears were realized when Charles's political advisers arrived in Spain. Spanish officials were dismissed and replaced by men

Banker Jakob Fugger supplied the loan used by Charles's advisers to bribe imperial electors into voting Charles as the Holy Roman Emperor. *Reproduced by permission of Archive Photos, Inc.*

from Flanders. The following year, after extensive manipulation by his Habsburg advisers, Charles was elected as Charles V, Holy Roman Emperor (he was not officially crowned until 1530). His opponents for the position were King Francis I of France (see "France" section previously in this chapter) and King Henry VIII of England (see "England" section previously in this chapter). Charles's victory started a rivalry among the three young kings that was to last for the rest of their lives. To take on his duties as emperor Charles had to move to Aachen, Germany. The parliaments of Castile and Aragon were immediately called into session so Charles could request money to finance his trip to Aachen. His advisers also needed to pay back a loan of 850,000 florins (the Italian unit of currency) they had received from Jacob Fugger (1459–1525), a wealthy German banker. They had used the borrowed money to bribe imperial electors, the voting representatives who selected Charles as emperor. The Cortes of Castile announced that, before they would approve any funds, Charles had to give Spain priority over the Holy Roman Empire. Their efforts were defeated after the king's agents bullied and bribed the majority of Cortes members. Charles received funding for both the trip and the bribe. Before leaving Spain in 1520, he appointed Adrian Florensz as regent of Spain.

The Comuneros Revolt

Revolts broke out as soon as the king left the country. Juan de Padilla (c. 1490–1521), a representative from Toledo, organized leaders in other cities into a "Holy League of Cities." Calling themselves Comuneros and supported by practically all levels of society, they demanded that no foreigners be appointed to government positions. They also declared that Spain's foreign policy must promote Spanish interests and that the Cortes should meet every three years. Adrian did not respond to their demands, so the Comuneros formed an army under Antonio de Acuña, bishop of Zamora.

Adrian sent a royal army to put down the revolt. While preparing to confront Adrian's forces, the Comuneros discovered that they were divided among themselves. Leaders of both the nobility and the middle class feared that their property would be seized by government forces, so they had lost the motivation to champion their political cause. With the Comuneros fractured by internal bickering, the royal army easily crushed Acuña's army at the Battle of Villalar in April 1521.

Charles returned to Spain from Germany in 1522. One of his first acts was to execute 270 people who had been involved in the Comuneros revolt. The king also established completely new policies that would appeal to Spanish pride. Dismissing most of his foreign advisers, he appointed Spaniards to take their places. As both the Holy Roman Emperor and the king of Spain, Charles—at the age of twenty-two—was now the most powerful man in Christendom (the term then used for Europe). States occupied by the Holy Roman Empire also came under the rule of Spain and the Habsburgs. For the next eight years Charles increased his power and expanded Habsburg territory. In 1526 he inherited the thrones of Hungary and Bohemia when the Ottoman Turks killed King Louis, the ruler of those provinces. That same year he married Isabella of Portugal. Charles also continued the war against France in Italy. Pope Clement VII joined Francis I of France and Henry VIII of England in the League of Co-

Conquistadors Are Ruthless

While Charles was securing his empire in Western Europe, his military generals—called the conquistadors—were winning tremendous lands and wealth in the Americas. In what became known as New Spain (present-day Mexico), Hernán Cortés (1485–1547) led Spanish forces against the ancient Aztec empire. He marched his army through Mexico in 1519 to the Aztec capital of Tenochtitlán (modern-day Mexico City). Sitting on horses in their gleaming armor, the Spaniards looked like gods to the Aztec. Moctezuma II, the Aztec ruler, gave gifts of gold and silver as peace offerings. But Cortés wanted more treasures, and over the next two years he massacred the Aztec, finally destroying Tenochtitlán in 1521. Even more ruthless than Cortés was Francisco Pizarro. Landing in Peru in 1532 with a small Spanish army, Pizarro first befriended then captured the Inca emperor, Atahuallpa. After receiving a tremendous ransom for the emperor's release, Pizarro murdered Atahuallpa, then claimed the Inca empire for Spain, killing all the Inca who did not cooperate.

gnac, an alliance against Spain and the Holy Roman Empire. Infuriated that the pope had sided with France, Charles sent his Spanish and German troops into Rome in 1527. The soldiers were equally angry—not at the pope but at Charles—because they had not received their wages. They went on a rampage that is now called the "German Fury" and sacked Rome. The horrified Clement, who had been locked away in a tower for his own safety, quickly joined Henry in making peace with Charles. Francis was also forced to make peace by 1529. The war between Spain and France continued until 1559, when Italy was placed under Habsburg rule by the Treaty of Cateau-Cambrésis.

Emperor confronts reformer

In 1530 Clement VII officially crowned Charles V as Holy Roman Emperor. By this time the Protestant Reformation, a movement to reform the Roman Catholic Church, was sweeping Europe. The Reformation had begun thirteen years earlier, just before Charles became king of Spain. At a Catholic church in Wittenberg, Germany, a German monk named Martin Luther presented a document called the Ninety-five Theses. (Over the years the story has been told that Luther nailed the Theses to the door of the Wittenberg Castle church, but many historians refute that story.) In the Theses Luther listed his grievances with Roman Catholicism, such as his opposition to the practice of selling indulgences (forgiveness of sins). Soon he had many enthusiastic followers called Lutherans, who joined him in initiating the Protestant Reformation. At the time Charles was preoccupied with campaigning for the position of emperor and with putting down the Comuneros revolt, so he dismissed Luther as an insignificant heretic. For

the next four years, however, the Lutheran movement gained momentum, especially in Germany and the Netherlands.

In 1521, after Charles had become Holy Roman Emperor, he summoned Luther before the Imperial Diet at Worms, a meeting of representatives of states in the Holy Roman Empire held in Worms, Germany. During a famous confrontation with the emperor, the German priest refused to budge on his controversial views. Charles denounced Luther as a heretic who could never be returned to the church. Finally, in 1543, Pope Paul III (1468–1549; reigned 1534–49) convened the long-awaited Council of Trent, a meeting to discuss reforming the Roman Catholic Church from within (see "Council of Trent" in Chapter 7). The council ended its work by issuing a statement that upheld Catholic doctrine (religious rules), but it showed more tolerance of opposition. Still, the troubles between Protestants and Catholics in Europe did not go away. Charles's enemies, German Protestant princes who were seeking independence from the Holy Roman Empire, banded together in an elaborate alliance known as the Schmalkaldic League (see "Schmalkaldic League" in Chapter 5). Charles V won his greatest victory as seventy thousand imperial soldiers annihilated the forces of the German Protestant princes at Müberg. Although hostilities ended for a time, by 1551 the German princes had found another ally in the new king of France, Henry II (see "France" section previously in this chapter).

A Spanish galleon of the mid-sixteenth century. Ships such as this brought silver, gold, and gems to Spain from the New World. *Reproduced by permission of Hulton Archive.*

Charles ends long reign

After the battle at Müberg, Charles V concentrated his foreign policy on forming alliances rather than on waging war. In 1554 he formed an alliance between Spain and England by arranging for his son Philip II (1527–1598; ruled 1556–98) to marry the Catholic English queen, Mary I (see "England" section previously in this chapter). In 1555 Charles officially turned rule of the Netherlands over to Philip. The Netherlands had always been the Spanish territory closest to Charles's heart, and many noblemen wept during his speech.

The following year Charles retired to a monastery and Philip became king of Spain. Charles's younger brother, Ferdinand, was named Ferdinand II, Holy Roman Emperor in 1558. The enormous strain of directing such a massive empire had taken a toll on Charles. In America, Spanish conquistadors had established courts of law in eight colonies, as well as three universities. Tons of silver from the mines of Potosi as well as Mexican and Peruvian gold and gems were streaming into Spanish ports aboard giant galleons (the large, heavy ships used by Spain). Charles had firmly consolidated Spanish hold on far-flung territory that was eight times the size of Castile and held one-fifth of the world's population. Charles spent his final years as an adviser to Philip, who soon earned the nickname of the "Prudent King" because he made decisions slowly and with great deliberation. Just one year before Charles died, Philip decisively ended more than a half-century of Spanish-French conflict regarding Italy. Philip's forces demolished the French at Saint Quentin. Spain and France signed the Treaty of Cateau-Cambrésis in 1559.

Numerous problems confront Philip II

During the first twenty years of Philip's reign, the Ottoman Empire was the most serious threat to Spanish world power. Charles had left Philip in charge of an unresolved war with the Muslim Turks, which had begun in 1551 over control of the Mediterranean Sea. In 1560 the Spanish attempted unsuccessfully to take Tripoli, a port city in northwest Lebanon, from the Turks. In 1563 and 1565, Philip's troops managed to repel Turkish attacks on Oran, a port city in Algeria, and on the island of Malta, a Spanish stronghold in the Mediterranean near Sicily. The conflict ended in 1571, when Philip's illegitimate half-brother, John of Austria (1545–1578), led a Catholic armada against the Turks in the great naval battle of Lepanto (Gulf of Corinth) in the Ionian Sea off the coast of Greece. The Spaniards took 127 Ottoman ships and thousands of soldiers and seamen. The Ottoman

Empire was no longer a threat to Spain's rich possessions in Italy and along the Mediterranean.

While Spanish forces were defeating the Ottomans, Philip was contending with the Revolt of the Netherlands, which broke out in 1566 (see "Netherlands" in Chapter 4). Although the revolt did not end until 1648 with Dutch independence, the Spanish had many military victories in the Netherlands during Philip's reign. The uprising began when Dutch Protestants staged violent riots and smashed statues of Catholic saints. In 1567 Philip introduced the Spanish Inquisition in the Netherlands and sent Fernando Álvarez de Toledo, duke of Alba (c. 1507–1582), to crush the revolt. Alba initiated an extremely repressive policy. Arresting two rebel leaders, Lamoral, count of Egmont (1522–1568), and Philip de Montmorency, count of Hoorn (c. 1518–1568), Alba established the Council of Troubles. Alba had Egmont and Hoorn executed along with perhaps twelve thousand other rebels. Other notable leaders fled to safety in Germany. Among them was William I Prince of Orange (1533–1584), the spiritual leader of the rebellion. Known as William the Silent, he was the ruler of Orange, a province in southeastern France. William was a member of the Nassau family, who were based in the Netherlands, and he had acquired Orange through inheritance. Alba's repression continued unchecked, but by 1573 Philip had seen enough. He recalled Alba and replaced him with Luis de Requesens (pronounced ray-kay-SAINS;

1528–1576). In 1577 Requesens was replaced by John of Austria.

In 1568, at the height of his Dutch troubles, Philip experienced several other misfortunes. He lost his third and most beloved wife, Elizabeth of Valois, as she was delivering a baby daughter. The Moriscos revolted in Granada and had to be forcibly restrained. Philip's only son, Carlos, was exhibiting bouts of severe mental instability. For instance, he threw a servant out of the window when the young man crossed him. He frequently attacked his father's ministers, including the duke of Alba, with a knife. Carlos also made a shoemaker eat a pair of boots because they were too tight. The troubled young man was finally locked away in a tower, where he went on a series of hunger strikes and died later in the year.

Special mission to defend faith

The Dutch troubles worsened in 1578 when Philip approved the assassination of Juan de Escobedo (died 1578), John of Austria's dangerous and ambitious secretary. Two years later, Philip issued a royal proclamation condemning William of Orange as an outlaw and the main source of unrest in the Netherlands. The king's announcement also offered a reward of 25,000 ducats (coins used in various European countries) for the capture of William of Orange. William responded with a document that accused Philip of incest (having sexual relations with family members), adultery (having sexual relations outside marriage), and the murders of both Carlos and Elizabeth of Valois.

Philip was convinced, however, that God had chosen him for a special mission to defend the Catholic faith. Indeed, it seemed to many Europeans that "God had turned into a Spaniard" by 1584. That year an assassin killed William of Orange in his home in Delft. In 1585, Alessandro Farnese (1545–1592), the duke of Parma, surpassed the military skill of even the bloody Alba when he captured the great walled town of Antwerp (a city in present-day Belgium). The successful siege ended a five-year Spanish offensive that conquered more than thirty rebel Dutch towns and maintained Spanish and Catholic control of the southern provinces of the Netherlands until 1714.

Meanwhile, in 1580, Philip had claimed the throne of Portugal. Forced to fight for what he considered to be his hereditary rights (his mother was the princess of Portugal), he had sent Alba into Portugal with twenty-two thousand troops. The old and brutal duke was again successful, and the vast dominions of Portugal fell into Philip's hands. Then, in a crowning victory, Philip's navy, under Álvaro de Bázan (1526–1588), the marquis de Santa Cruz, smashed a combined English-French force off the coast of the Azores in 1582 and 1583. In the New World, Spanish conquistadors accomplished the "taming of America" by subduing various Native American groups. To many Europeans at the time, this was Philip's most impressive achievement.

Spanish Armada defeated

Just as Philip was on the verge of reclaiming the northern provinces of the Netherlands, his attention was diverted by war with England. The English Protestant queen, Elizabeth I, was worried about the Catholic advance in the Low Countries. In 1585 she openly supported the Dutch rebels. Philip immediately began organizing the famous "Invincible Armada," a fleet of 130 heavily armored ships that carried 30,000 men, for an invasion of England. Leading the venture would be an experienced admiral, the marquis of Santa Cruz. The plan called for the Armada to sail from Lisbon, Portugal, into the English Channel. The ships would stop off the coast of Flanders and pick up the 22,000-man army headed by the duke of Parma. The Armada would then sail on to England and stage a massive sea assault.

Almost from the beginning, things went wrong with the complicated Spanish plan. In 1587, even before the Armada could set out, the English seaman Francis Drake launched a surprise attack on the Spanish ships, which were anchored in the port of Cádiz, Spain. The destruction was so great that the Spanish invasion was delayed for a year. In the meantime, Santa Cruz died and Philip replaced him with the inexperienced Alonso Pérez de Guzmán (c. 1550–1619), duke of Medina-Sidonia. Medina-Sidonia was an army commander, so he protested that he was unqualified to lead a naval fleet. Philip brushed his reservations aside, insisting that only a man of Medina-Sidonia's stature would be obeyed by the captains of the Armada ships.

In May 1588 the Spanish Armada set out from Lisbon, but storms forced the fleet into La Coruña in northwestern Spain. The ships did not set sail again until July. By this time Elizabeth had prepared the English fleet and organized a dedicated but small land army. In August, sailing against strong winds, the Armada began moving up the English Channel toward Flanders. Medina-Sidonia had been ordered not to engage in battle with the English until he had made contact with Parma. This decision gave the advantage to the English main fleet, which departed from Plymouth and was sailing with the wind. Once within range of the Armada, the English ships were able to fire their weapons at the Spanish vessels from a relatively safe distance. The light and quick English ships also had the advantage of being able to outmaneuver the bulky Spanish galleons. The English made three assaults on the Spanish, but they did not inflict any serious damage. On August 6, Medina-Sidonia anchored his fleet at Calais to await contact with Parma. But Medina-Sidonia made a fatal mistake on the night of August 7. He had not secured all of the anchors, so some ships drifted in the water and left an opening for a squadron of English fire ships to move in and set the Armada ablaze. One by one the Spanish ships broke their cables and headed for open water. The smaller English ships darted in and out of the flames, pouncing on stragglers.

Then a powerful storm—the "Great Protestant Wind," as the English called it—swept through the Channel and forced the Spanish vessels away from England. Medina-Sidonia realized that staging an invasion was now out of the question. He did his best to save the fleet, and the Armada sailed north. Storm after storm seemed to come from nowhere to pound the galleons as they desperately tried to sail around the British Isles. Many of the Spanish ships broke up on the west coast of Ireland. Nearly three months after the battle, Geoffrey Felton, secretary for Ireland, went walking on the coast of Sligo Bay. Although the secretary had seen slaughter and bloodshed during Irish wars with the English, he reported that he had seen nothing like the carnage that awaited him that autumn day. In walking less than five miles, he counted more than eleven hundred Spanish bodies. Half of the Armada was lost and so was Philip's dream of making England into a Catholic province.

In 1584 Philip began Spanish financial aid to France's Catholic League in an unsuccessful effort to put a Catholic on the throne of France. Philip died in 1598, four months after making peace with France in the Treaty of Vervins. He believed he had left to his son, King Philip III (1578–1621; ruled 1598–1621), a nation relatively free from international difficulties. Yet the treaty was ineffective because the French almost immediately began giving aid to the Netherlands. Claiming also that the treaty applied only to the continent of Europe, the French continued to encroach on Spanish commerce in the Atlantic Ocean.

Philip III heads Renaissance

After Philip III took the throne in 1598, Spain began going into decline. Like his father, he was a devout Catholic, yet he lacked Philip II's intelligence and commitment to work. He was more interested in pursuing his own pleasures, so he turned the government over to his favorite adviser, Francisco Gómez de Sandoval y Rojas, duke of Lerma (pronounced fran-THES-koh GO-mahth day sahn-doh-VAHL ee RO-hahs; 1553–1625). Spain made peace with England in 1604 and reached a truce with the United Provinces of the Netherlands in 1609. Spain resumed wars in Italy (1615–16), however, and then entered the Thirty Years' War by sending troops into Germany (see "Thirty Years' War" in Chapter 8). Philip III reigned during a glorious Renaissance period that produced such great figures as the novelist Miguel de Cervantes (1547–1616), the dramatist Lope de Vega (1562–1635), and the painters El Greco (1541–1614) and Francisco de Zubarán (1598–1664).

Empire in decline

When King Philip III died in 1621, the decline of Spain was becoming more evident. Long years of fighting Habsburg wars in central Europe had depleted the Spanish treasury, despite gold and silver shipments from the New World. Although aware of these difficulties, the new king, Philip IV (1605–1665; ruled 1621–65), continued his father's policy of turning over the government to a court favorite. In this case the favorite was Gaspar de Guzmán (1587–1645), who was given the title of count-duke of Olivares. Olivares had plans for far-reaching reform that he hoped would solve Spain's economic and political problems. First, he wanted to distribute taxes throughout the country and, second, he wanted to abolish privileges given to certain provinces.

Olivares's plans caused revolts in Catalonia, a region of Aragon. Once the thriving center of sea trade on the Iberian Peninsula, Catalonia and its capital city Barcelona had been declining since the middle of the fifteenth century. In the 1300s the Catalans had been given the privilege of taxing themselves and voting subsidies (additional funds) for the crown only if they wanted to do so. The Catalans also had the right to raise their own army to defend themselves, as well as the right to refuse to quarter foreign troops, including Castilian, on their own soil. Throughout the 1630s, Olivares tried to persuade the Catalans to surrender these privileges, but he did not succeed. In 1639 a French army invaded Catalonia, and in 1641 the Catalonians declared their independence from Spain and gave their allegiance to King Louis XIII of France. While the Catalan revolt was going on, the Portuguese took advantage of the confusion and declared their independence from Spain. A similar movement emerged in Andalusia. Thus, Olivares's usefulness

had come to an end. In 1643 the king dismissed him and appointed his nephew Luís de Haro as the new chief minister. By the late 1640s, the Catalans had tired of French rule, and Haro offered to restore Catalan privileges. In 1652 Philip sent an army under his illegitimate son John of Austria (1629–1679) to Barcelona. The city surrendered and Catalonia was restored to Spain. Yet the Catalan revolt and the Andalusian independence movement, along with the loss of Portugal, showed that Spain was losing its status as a major world power.

The age of European exploration

Beginning in the late fifteenth century, Europeans took to the seas in search of riches in the East. Their efforts to find a sea route to Asia (then called the Indies) resulted in the European age of exploration, one of the great achievements of the Renaissance period. The forerunner to the European explorers was the Venetian traveler Marco Polo (1254–1324). In the 1300s he had left a record of his journeys to the faraway lands of China (then called Cathay), India, and the Spice Islands. In these lands Europeans could find exotic merchandise and foods that had never been known in Europe. After Marco Polo's explorations, the Mongols, who ruled all of Asia and parts of the European continent, had allowed free overland access to European merchants. Although it was a long and difficult journey across the entire Asian continent, scores of European traders managed to return from Cathay and the islands with valuable goods.

The Mongolian empire fell apart at the end of the fourteenth century, and the rulers of the Persian and Muslim kingdoms closest to Europe no longer gave outsiders access to their territory. Denied land routes to some of their most treasured goods, the Europeans had to find a route to Asia in the uncharted oceans. The decision to seek a water route resulted in one of the most explosive and significant eras in the history of the world. By the mid-eighteenth century, virtually all of the world, including the continents of the Americas, became known to Europeans. Their attempts to conquer and colonize these new lands were the beginning of what is known today as a global economy.

Europeans begin expansion

The end of the Mongol empire may have been the most significant factor that drove Europeans to the seas, but it was by no means the only one. In the early 1400s the Renaissance was spreading across Europe. Renaissance thought emphasized pursuit of the arts and sciences, the achievement of personal glory, and commercial expansion. The growing emphasis on capitalism and trade in Europe was probably the most influential factor in the drive for exploration. Increasingly, a nation's power and prestige had become dependent upon money and material wealth, and the best way to become a world power was to build a

trade empire. Also the Christian nations of Europe had long been devoted to converting the rest of the world to Christianity. Some European explorers were inspired by the myth of Prester John, a Christian king rumored to be living somewhere in eastern Asia. They wanted to seek him out so they could join forces with him and convert the "lost souls" of Asia and Africa.

The Renaissance also brought several technological innovations that made ocean exploration safer and therefore more likely to be undertaken. For example, the magnetic compass and other advances made it possible for navigators, who had previously been forced to rely on the Sun and the stars, to travel in bad weather and poor climates. Reliable maps of the known world, which previously had been closely guarded as state secrets, were becoming available to seafarers. Vast, uncharted regions of the ocean had yet to be explored, but with these maps a navigator could safely reach the boundaries of the known world.

Portuguese exploration and colonization

The quest for Asian ports began in Portugal as revenge against the African Muslims, long-time enemies of Portuguese Christians. The Muslims lived across the Strait of Gibraltar from Portugal, at the port city of Ceuta. In 1415 Henry the Navigator, son of the Portuguese king, led an armada against Ceuta and won a battle that left thousands of Muslim bodies piled in the streets of the city.

Only eight Portuguese were killed. After this bloody victory, while looting the city, Henry first glimpsed the riches of African trade that had come from the Indies: cinnamon, pepper, cloves, ginger, and other spices. Unlike Asia, Africa's kingdoms had never allowed Europeans to penetrate the interior. After the battle at Ceuta, Henry became obsessed with gaining access to exotic markets in Africa.

Henry the Navigtor believed the mission would be dangerous if undertaken by sea. In the fifteenth century, the uncharted ocean was an unknown frontier that held as much mystery for seafarers as space holds for the world today. Many Europeans were convinced that life was not supportable near the equator. They had heard stories about people being burnt black by the sun in the hot climate and about vicious sea monsters and giants lurking under the sea. Nevertheless, Henry managed to recruit many able sea captains to go on his venture. In expedition after expedition, Portuguese ships inched their way down the African coast. Along the route, the Portuguese started trading posts and supply stations, often by fighting off natives who tried to repel the intruders. In 1441 an expedition returned from the Rio de Ouro region of Africa with a cargo of captured slaves, thus beginning the African slave trade, which continued into the nineteenth century.

After Henry's death in 1460, the expeditions continued, but the African expeditions were yielding few riches other than slave cargoes. King John II of Portugal therefore decided to have his captains circumnavigate (sail around) the African continent and reach India by way of the ocean. This feat would not happen until 1488 when the Portuguese seaman Bartolomeu Dias (c. 1450–1500) rounded what he called the Cape of Storms (known today as the Cape of Good Hope). Dias's voyage, however, did not match the 1497 journey of Vasco da Gama (c. 1460–1524), who went across the southernmost tip of Africa and sailed all the way across the Indian Ocean to Calicut, on the Malabar Coast of India.

The merchants of India were immediately suspicious of this highly organized expedition from Europe. When Gama returned to Calicut in 1502, with the purpose of turning it into a Portuguese colony, the city's head administrator, or Samuri, sent a ship full of envoys (representatives) to discuss the captain's intentions. Gama responded by seizing a number of traders and fishermen from the harbor, killing them, and sending a boat filled with their body parts back to the Samuri. He included a note suggesting that the Samuri use the body parts to make himself a curry (an Indian dish with spices).

Gama's handling of the Samuri's diplomatic efforts was only a hint of the brutality later committed by the Portuguese invasion force in Asia and the Indies. The Portuguese viceroy placed in charge of Portuguese colonization, Alfonso de Albuquerque battered his way across the Indian Ocean. He set up a line of fortified outposts from the Persian Gulf all the way to the Malaccan Strait, the most popular route to China and the Spice Islands. Many of the natives near these garrisons were forced to convert to Christianity. Less than fifty years after Gama's discovery of the eastern route to Asia, trade between Europe and the ancient lands of the Orient was controlled by Portugal, a small kingdom that was more than a year's journey away from Asia.

"Discovering" the Indies

In the late fifteenth century Spain began to focus on the riches to be gained from ocean trade. Yet Africa and the eastern route to the Indies were off limits because Pope Alexander VI had granted total control of these areas to Portugal (see "Spain" section previously in this chapter). The only way another country could reach the Indies would be by a western route. The Genoan seafarer Christopher Columbus believed that the western route would actually be shorter. He theorized that one did not need to sail east for a year to reach the Indies. Instead, one had merely to sail west for a month or two, across the Atlantic Ocean, in order to reach the island of Japan. In 1492 Queen Isabella, the monarch of Spain, commissioned Columbus to prove he could find the western route. He returned about a year later with the news that he had discovered the Indies. Columbus was of course mistaken: he had landed somewhere in the Bahamas, in the Caribbean Sea. Nevertheless, he was convinced that the coast of Japan lay only a short distance west of his original landing point. He made three more

voyages to the "Indies" (in 1493, 1498, and 1502) to confirm his theory and to colonize the islands he had already explored. Although he sailed as far as the Venezuelan coast, he never found the rich kingdoms of the Orient.

Spain claims Americas

In 1501 Amerigo Vespucci (1454–1512) sailed far down the coast of South America. He proved that Columbus had landed nowhere near the Indies but instead had discovered an entirely new continent. North and South America were later named for Vespucci. His discovery made possible two other historic events: the conquest and colonization of the American continents and the circumnavigation of (completely go around) the globe.

The conquest of the American natives by Spanish conquistadors happened within a few decades. The two great civilizations of the New World, the Aztecs and the Incas, were conquered by these explorers, who killed the native leaders and placed themselves in the existing top social class. Other native tribes were quickly brought under control by the conquistadors, and for the next three centuries Spain built up an empire in the New World. Vasco Nuñez de Balboa (1475–1519) traveled across the Isthmus of Panama, and Juan Ponce de León (1460–1521) searched for the mythical Fountain of Youth in Florida. Hernando de Soto (c. 1496–1542) navigated the Mississippi River, and Francisco de Coronado (1510–1554) traveled through territory that is now northern Mexico and the southwestern United States. Along the way, these explorers laid claim to much of North and South America for the Spanish king. At the same time, the Portuguese were establishing a colonial presence in Brazil, the easternmost part of the South American continent.

Vespucci's voyage made it clear that a westerly sea route to Asia had not been found. The stage was set for what was then, and is perhaps still, the greatest ocean voyage ever accomplished: the circumnavigation of the globe. In September 1519 the Portuguese navigator Ferdinand Magellan (c. 1480–1521), sponsored by King Charles I (Holy Roman Emperor Charles V) of Spain, set out from Seville, Spain, with five ships bound for the coast of South America. He reached the continent in November. A year later, in October and November 1520, Magellan navigated the treacherous straits (now known as the Straits of Magellan) at the continent's cape and sailed across the Pacific, the world's largest ocean. The following month Magellan was killed in a skirmish with the island natives. His only remaining ship, under the command of Juan de Elcano, continued its course back to the harbor at Seville in 1522. Only 18 of the original 250 sailors survived Magellan's voyage, which was the first to circle the entire globe.

The Latecomers: England, France, and the Netherlands

Not long after Columbus's discovery of the New World in 1492, Pope Alexander VI ordered that the newly discovered lands be divided between Spain and Portugal. The Spanish had rights to all lands west of the longitudinal Line of Demarcation, while Portugal could claim everything to the east. The Treaty of Tordesillas in 1494 made this division official and granted Portugal possession of what is now Brazil. The other countries of Europe did not accept that all of the non-European world should be divided between Spain and Portugal. Driven by increasing prosperity, the emerging powers of northwestern Europe—England, France, and the Netherlands—decided to invest in exploration.

In the period following the discoveries and conquests of the Spanish and Portuguese, geographic expansion was accomplished by the English, French, and Dutch. During the next two hundred years, nearly every remaining land mass in the world, with the exception of Antarctica, was explored and mapped by explorers from these countries. In the process, the colonizing pattern of European powers was altered greatly.

The problem with being a latecomer to world exploration and conquest was that most of the good lands were already occupied and defended by superior Spanish and Portuguese navies. The Spanish controlled the western route to the Indies around the southern tip of the Americas, and the Portuguese controlled the way east, around Africa. Consequently, the earliest efforts at exploration by the English, Dutch, and French concentrated on lands unclaimed by either country, in North America. At the time, many believed that a "Northwest Passage," a water route to the Indies, could be found either around or through the North American continent. One of the first to seek the Northwest Passage was John Cabot, an Italian navigator financed by King Henry VII of England. Cabot's exploration of Newfoundland, in 1497, yielded sparse information about the new continent's northernmost regions. Also in search of the Northwest Passage was French navigator Jacques Cartier (1491–1557). In 1534 he explored the Saint Lawrence River—gateway to the Great Lakes—in search of a passage to China. Cartier's voyages never took him farther west than the site of modern-day Montreal, Canada, but his thorough exploration and charting of the Gulf of Saint Lawrence led the way for further exploration by one of his countrymen, Samuel de Champlain (c. 1567–1635).

French explore inland water routes
Nearly sixty years later, and farther north, Henry Hudson (died 1611), a British captain sailing for the Dutch, led his expedition in search of the Northwest Passage. Hudson's expedition wound through the strait and into the huge bay, now in upper Canada, that now bear his name. Originally, the Hudson Bay, the Hudson River, and the river valley were settled by the Dutch, who controlled entrance to the river at the fortress town of New Amsterdam, on what is now Manhattan Island. After Hudson's expedition, most of the major exploratory work in North America was done on inland water

routes by the French. Beginning with Champlain in 1600, the French pushed their way down the Saint Lawrence River to the Great Lakes. In a dozen voyages from 1603 until 1633, Champlain discovered the easternmost Great Lakes, Huron and Ontario; founded the city of Quebec; and served as commandant of France's new colonial territories, which were called New France.

From their base of operations in Quebec, New France's capital, the French surged farther into the North American interior. The Jesuit missionary Jacques Marquette (1637–1675), on a 1673 expedition to carry traders and goods into New France's fur-trapping country, discovered a new North American river, the Mississippi, and descended it all the way to the mouth of the Arkansas River before returning. Marquette's accidental voyage convinced the French that the Mississippi flowed into the Gulf of Mexico, a suspicion that was confirmed in 1682, when René-Robert Cavelier de La Salle (1643–1687) traveled down the Mississippi to its mouth, where he founded the city of New Orleans. In 1684, La Salle lay claim, on behalf of France, to the entire Mississippi River basin, from the Illinois country to the Gulf of Mexico. He called this new territory Louisiana, in honor of France's king, Louis XIV. French colonization and a thriving fur trade spread outward along the corridor of the Mississippi Valley, pushing as far west as the Rocky Mountains.

For the time being, the English were content to settle along the eastern coast of North America. After a couple of failed attempts, English settlements were established in Virginia and Massachusetts, later spreading into Maryland and Pennsylvania. The English colonies, especially in the South, would later establish a plantation economy, producing chiefly tobacco and cotton, that relied heavily on the use of African slaves.

The other European powers now had land and a certain amount of income from their colonies, but they still did not have what they wanted: the spices, sugar, and precious metals owned by Spain and Portugal. Growing bolder in their quest for riches, these countries attacked Portuguese and Spanish treasure ships wherever they could find them—in the Caribbean, along the Spanish-American coast, and in the English Channel. Nevertheless, Spain's empire was never seriously threatened on land. In fact, only the Dutch had any success in attacking European empires in America. In 1630 the Netherlands seized some coastal towns in northern Brazil. For about twenty years the Netherlands maintained virtual control of Brazil and its sugar production, before being thrown out by an increasingly independent Brazilian population.

Five European empires

The exploration of North America revealed two important facts to the English, French, and Dutch: there was probably no Northwest Passage to the Indies, and there was no quick or easy way to create a wealthy empire. At the beginning of the seventeenth century, these countries were shifting their attention to the riches of the Indies. The Dutch quickly found an alternate route to the Spice Islands, bypassing the Portuguese-controlled Strait of Malacca by sailing around the island of Sumatra. Once a Dutch presence had been established in the Spice Islands, ships commissioned by the Dutch East India Company assaulted Portuguese ports from the Indian Ocean to China. By 1615, the Dutch possessed the Spice Islands and were forced to face the threat of the British East India Company. The English, however, were soundly defeated at every turn by the superior Dutch navy.

Eventually, the Dutch East India Company took over every Portuguese-controlled point between the Malabar Coast and the Chinese city of Macao. Although the fiercest fighting over African colonies would not occur until the eighteenth century, English and French expeditions managed to take control of various slaving stations along the coast of Africa. By the year 1700, there were not two, but five important European empires with influence throughout the world: Spain, Portugal, England, France, and the Netherlands.

Central and Northern Europe

4

During the fifteenth through seventeenth centuries, strong monarchs in France, England, and Spain consolidated their territories into nations. A similar situation slowly developed in the rest of Europe—about two-thirds of the continent—which was divided into hundreds of independent states. The borders of these states shifted constantly because of power struggles among emperors, kings, princes, and religious leaders. In general, this part of Europe consisted of the following main geographic regions: In central Europe were Germany, Austria, and Switzerland. Northern Europe was composed of the Low Countries (the Netherlands, Belgium, and Luxembourg) and Scandinavia (Denmark, Sweden, and Norway).

In the 1400s commerce and trade flourished around the coast of the Baltic Sea (called the Baltic region) and in the Rhineland region (areas along the Rhine River and the Danube River in Germany). Throughout northern, central, and eastern Europe, culture was influenced by Italian humanists, members of the intellectual and literary movement that had sparked the Renaissance in Italy (see "Humanists promote change" in Chapter 1, and "Humanism sparks Renaissance" in Chapter 8).

The Italians had journeyed north to work as diplomats (official representatives of governments), secretaries, and university lecturers. Inspired by the innovations of the Italian Renaissance, thinkers and artists traveled from other parts of Europe to Italy to study with prominent figures. These travelers then returned to their northern homes and began making their own cultural contributions, which became known as the northern Renaissance. For instance, humanists in Germany and the Netherlands expanded on the work started by the poet Petrarch and his followers in Italy. The ancient art of oil painting was refined by artists in the Netherlands, who in turn influenced painters in other countries.

Despite these innovations, however, the states in northern, central, and eastern Europe were engulfed in political and social chaos that virtually halted the Renaissance by the mid-1500s. This situation was caused by the disintegration of the Holy Roman Empire, which resulted in numerous independence movements, and by the rise of the Protestant Reformation, which permanently transformed Europe. These events also had an impact on France, England, and Spain, but the rest of the continent was more directly affected. The reason was that Austria and Germany, located in the center of the continent, were at the heart of the Holy Roman Empire.

The Holy Roman Empire

The Holy Roman Empire was a vast state that extended from France in the west, to Denmark in the north, and to Poland and Hungary in the east. In northern Italy, all territories except Venice were part of the empire. Although the emperor ruled most of Europe, he was actually a mere figurehead. He had no real power in France, southern Italy, Denmark, Poland, or Hungary. He ruled in name only in England, Sweden, and Spain. His control of northern Italy and Germany was sometimes nonexistent, sometimes firm. Countries such as Hungary were headed by the emperor or an imperial prince (a nobleman who ruled in the name of the emperor), but they remained outside the empire. Others, including Flanders (territory now in parts of Belgium, France, and the Netherlands), Pomerania (now in Russia and Poland), and Schleswig and Holstein (a region in western Germany), were part of the empire but were ruled by foreign princes who were granted control of these territories by the emperor.

Problems had existed in the Holy Roman Empire since it was founded in 962 by the Saxon (Germanic) king Otto I. He wanted to unify territories that are now the nations of Germany and Italy. From the beginning, the Holy Roman Empire was closely connected to the Roman Catholic Church (see "Holy Roman Empire" and "Roman Catholic Church" in Chapter 1). The emperor was crowned by the pope, the supreme head of the church, who had the final word in the appointment of all emperors. The emperor was considered to be God's representative on Earth in state affairs, just as the pope was God's representative on Earth in spiritual matters. After Otto's death, German kings served as Holy Roman Emperors. Eventually, when a king was elected by German princes, he automatically wanted to be crowned emperor by the pope. Even though kings and Holy Roman emperors were supposed to be elected, these positions gradually became hereditary, or passed on from father to son. From time to time German princes were able to exercise their authority in deciding who would become king, but final approval always rested with the pope. After 1045 a king who was not yet crowned emperor was known as king of the Romans, a title that gave him the right to the throne of the Holy Roman Empire. All such kings did not become emperors, however, because the popes often chose someone else, especially when an election was in dispute.

Feudalism in decline

The main reason the Holy Roman Empire went into decline, however, was the collapse of feudalism (see "Feudalism" in Chapter 1). Feudalism was the social and economic system that dominated Europe in the Middle Ages. Under feudalism, tracts of land called fiefs (pronounced feefs) were granted by kings to lords and church officials in exchange for loyalty. In the eleventh century, capitalism, an economic system based on business and profit, began replacing feudalism, which was based on agriculture. Nevertheless, the fiefs remained in place as the basic social and political structure, so that Europe consisted of hundreds of independent states, or fiefs, that each had its own ruler. These states also had their own customs and laws. Continuing warfare in Italy and the weakness of monarchs in other kingdoms increased the power of German princes. In 1338 the German princes proclaimed that their appointed electors (those who voted for emperor) had the right to choose the emperor without the intervention of the pope. In 1356 Holy Roman Emperor Charles IV issued an official declaration called the Golden Bull, which supported the princes' decision by recognizing electors and regulating election procedures.

Holy Roman emperors were also confronted with conflicts between noblemen and merchants. Trade and commerce were flourishing along the coasts of the North Sea and the Baltic Sea, and German merchants were becoming wealthy. They were gaining more political power, which alarmed the princes. Partly as a defense against the princes, merchants in the twelfth century began forming a network of trading associations known as the Hanseatic League. They established cities, called Hansa cities, that served as trading centers. Since the Holy Roman emperors were already having problems with unruly princes, they tended to side with the merchants. In an effort to increase their power base, the emperors declared the Hansa to be free cities that came under the direct control of the emperor and were given voting rights in the diet (a meeting of church officials and representatives of states).

Another problem was that Holy Roman emperors put more effort into maintaining a dynasty (rule by members of the same family) than in governing the empire. This situation arose because the emperor's throne was usually given to the king who had the most land and wealth. Over time, as kingships became hereditary and kings accumulated vast estates, the throne was held by emperors from a few families. Most prominent were the Luxembourgs and the Habsburgs. After 1438 all Holy Roman emperors were members of the powerful Habsburg (also spelled Hapsburg) family, which was based in Austria. They were frequently accused of being more interested in expanding family territories than in unifying the empire. The problem reached a crisis during the Renaissance period, when Habsburg emperor Maximilian I ruled as the king of the German nation. The German princes became concerned when Maximilian seemed to be placing the Habsburgs' interests above the welfare of the empire. He was also involved in the Italian Wars, a conflict between Spain and France over rich and divided territories in Italy (see "Italian Wars dominate Renaissance" in Chapter 2). Victory in this war could have resulted in expansion of Habsburg territory into Burgundy, a region in present-day eastern France. In 1495 the princes established a supreme court of justice to impose Roman law throughout the empire. Five years later they forced Maximilian I to place administration of the empire in the hands of an imperial council, which would control all external and internal affairs.

These measures simply slowed the disintegration of the Holy Roman Empire. Most of the states were seeking independence, a trend that was encouraged by the Reformation, a movement to reform the Catholic Church that began in Germany in the early sixteenth century. The Reformation resulted in Protestantism being established as a religion separate from Catholicism. The German princes accepted Protestantism, while the emperors remained Roman Catholic. This situation led to the Thirty Years' War (1618–48), a complex religious, political, and social conflict. In this war, which involved all of Europe, the Holy Roman emperors joined Spain against the German Protestant princes, who were allied mainly with Sweden and France (see "Thirty Years' War" in Chapter 6). The struggle ended in 1648 with the Peace of Westphalia, a treaty that recognized the sovereignty (right to self-rule) of the states in the Holy Roman Empire. The only limitation was that the princes could not form alliances against the empire or the emperor. The states still belonged to the Holy Roman Empire, but the emperors exercised their power mainly as monarchs in their home regions. From this point onward the Holy Roman Empire existed in name only. (The empire ended officially in 1806, when Francis II of Austria renounced the title of emperor.)

The Protestant Reformation

The Holy Roman Empire and its religious strongholds in Europe

Early reformers

The most influential religious reformers were Meister (Johannes) Eckhart, John Wycliffe, Martin Luther, Huldrych Zwingli, and John Calvin. Their efforts started the movement that became known as the Protestant Reformation (the term "Protestant" came from "protest"). In addition, the invention of "moveable type" and the mass production of the Gutenberg Bible in the mid-fifteenth century spread word concerning a key aspect of Protestant beliefs: that every person could understand the Bible without the help of a priest. Wycliffe was a major figure in the early Protestant movement. He was the first person to translate the Bible from Latin into English so that lay readers—those who were not church officials—could read it. Wycliffe, whose followers were called Lollards, also denied the Catholic belief in communion, the ceremony in which bread and wine represent the body and blood of Jesus Chris, as a "miracle." Eckhart, a German Dominican mystic, argued that conversion came through a personal relationship with God. Because of the power of the Roman Catholic Church, both Wycliffe and Eckhart were quickly condemned as heretics—those who go against Church teachings—as were many of their followers.

The early protests against the Roman Catholic Church did not really attract a popular following until the lifetime of Martin Luther, a German monk who was a teacher at the University of Wittenberg. At the time, Germany was one of a few European countries with no strong central government, making it especially vulnerable to the corruptions of the church. Outrage among the citizens concerning this corruption made this region especially ripe for religious change.

began to unravel after the period known as the Babylonian Captivity and the Great Schism in the Roman Catholic Church (1348–1417; see "Crisis in the papacy" in Chapter 1). During this time there were as many as three popes—one in Rome, a second in France, and a third in Pisa, Italy. By 1500 the papacy, or office of the pope, had been returned to Rome, but it had become extremely corrupt. Popes were involved in raising taxes and tithes (contributions consisting of one-tenth of church members' income) to support the standing army of the Papal States, the territories ruled by the pope. Popes were also selling church offices, or positions. Most controversial of all was the selling of papal indulgences (payments made by church members in exchange for forgiveness of sins by the pope). Simultaneously, the death toll caused by the plague (1348–1700s; see "Black Death" in Chapter 1) was destroying both the social and spiritual lives of Europe's peasant and working classes. To make matters even worse, two of Europe's great political and religious powers, France and England, were engaged in the bloody Hundred Years' War (1337–1453), which brought further turmoil. Indeed, it seemed to many Christians that the church had failed its promise, and that the time was ripe for a "reformation" of both the church and the Holy Roman Empire.

Luther starts Reformation

An important early figure in the movement that came to be known as the Protestant Reformation was John Wycliffe (c. 1330–1384). He was the first person to translate the Bible from Latin into English so that the general population—all those who were not church officials—could read it. Wycliffe's ideas differed from the Catholic Church in terms of the meaning of communion, the sacred ceremony in which bread and wine represent the body and blood of Jesus Christ. Wycliffe did not believe communion was a "miracle" as the Catholics did. Although Wycliffe played an important role reforming some of the ideas of the Catholic Church, the Reformation actually began with Martin Luther (1483–1546), a Catholic monk who was on the faculty at the University of Wittenberg in Saxony. In 1513 Luther had an intense spiritual experience that eventually led him to leave the Catholic Church. He came to realize that faith in Jesus Christ was all that was required for one to be saved. He called this "justification by faith alone." Rejecting the involvement of

the church in personal spiritual matters, he introduced the concept of a "priesthood of all believers." Luther also began preaching against the Catholic Church's belief that the pope was God's sole representative on Earth. Luther argued that Christians should rely only on the Bible for spiritual guidance, and he encouraged the reduction of the seven Catholic sacraments (communion, baptism, confirmation, penance, anointing of the sick, marriage, and holy offices) to only two (baptism and communion). Luther differed with Wycliffe on the Catholic concept of transubstantiation. According to Catholic teachings, when the priest raises the bread and wine during the communion service, these elements become the flesh and blood of Christ. Wycliffe actually believed that the bread and wine are simply symbolic representations and do not literally become Christ's body and blood. Luther, on the other hand, believed that the body and blood of Christ are present in the bread and wine, but they are transformed only by the word of God as found in the Scripture and not by a priest. Luther called this process "consubstantiation."

The Reformation began when Luther took a stand against the sale of papal indulgences. Indulgences had long been granted to parishioners, or church members, as a form of forgiveness for confessed sins. After performing an act of faith or good works, a parishioner was given a pardon and a "free pass" out of purgatory, the Christian concept of the region between heaven and hell, after death. Since the beginning of the Renaissance in Italy, several popes had begun selling indulgences as a way to finance church projects (see "Rome and the Papal States" in Chapter 2). The practice had become widespread in Germany. In October 1517 Luther presented a document titled Ninety-five Theses at Schlosskirch Church in Wittenberg, inviting Catholic officials to discuss his beliefs about the sale of indulgences. Luther had intended to influence church reform rather than leave the church entirely. In 1521, however, he was called before the diet, a meeting of German princes and Holy Roman Emperor Charles V, in Worms, Germany. Charles denounced Luther as an "outlaw," but Luther was not punished and he continued to call for reforms.

Inspires other reformers Movements against the Roman Catholic Church soon sprang up elsewhere in Europe. Huldrych Zwingli (1484–1531), a Swiss priest with a passion for music and women, protested against the church's requirement that priests not get married. In direct defiance of church leaders, Zwingli was married in 1524. He also enraged church officials by challenging their rule that only they could interpret the Bible. He went further and called for separation of church and state. Zwingli was killed in 1531 by Catholics in Switzerland who feared and resented his growing support. Switzerland was the adopted home of another famous Protestant, John Calvin (1509–1564), whose radical views would also earn him a permanent place in the reform move-

ment. Born in France as Jean Cauvin in 1509, Calvin became a renowned biblical scholar and translator. He based his faith on his own readings of the Bible in the original Greek and Hebrew languages. He was the first Protestant leader who had not been a clergyman (priest) in the Catholic Church. Calvin and his followers, called Calvinists, made Geneva, Switzerland, a stronghold of Protestant activity. Calvinism's guiding principle was "predestination," or the belief that a small minority of people were "elected" before birth to become the chosen who would enter heaven. Calvin's followers carried his teachings to eager reformers throughout Europe, especially in France, where Calvinists were called Huguenots, and England, where they inspired the Puritan movement.

Protestantism became a rallying point for peasant and noble classes alike; members of both classes wanted to escape the oppression of the church and the governments that supported it. By the end of the sixteenth century, the Scandinavian countries had become predominantly Lutheran. In 1555 Emperor Charles V held a diet—a meeting of representatives, called electors, of states in the Holy Roman Empire—at Augsburg. The diet issued a statement called the Peace of Augsburg, which stated that each of the more than three hundred German principalities would adopt the religion of its local ruler. This left more than half of Germany to the Lutherans. In France nearly a quarter of the population had converted to

Calvinism as Huguenots. During the Saint Bartholomew's Day Massacre on August 24, 1572, in Paris, ten thousand Huguenots were massacred by Catholics. In the Edict of Nantes (1598), King Henry IV of France granted religious freedom to Calvinist sects, or small religious groups.

Soon many splinter movements began to form throughout Europe. Because the basic tenets of Protestant reform generally gave power to individual believers, lay preachers and others were suddenly "converted." By 1600 hundreds of new Protestant sects had formed and re-formed, basing their new churches on their own interpretations of the Bible. Recognizing the close connection between religion, politics, and economics, lay preachers began to press for social, trade, tax, and land reforms. The Reformation thus spread to all aspects of life, and the Christian world found itself in the middle of the most profound upheaval since the Catholic Church was founded around A.D. 600.

The Habsburg Empire

The history of Europe during the Renaissance and Reformation was dominated by the Habsburg family. The Habsburgs were based in Austria, which comprised the eastern portion of central Europe, and they also held lands in Burgundy, areas along the eastern border of France. Because all Holy Roman emperors at this time were Habsburgs, the family also controlled the Holy Roman Empire in central Europe. The Habsburg dynasty (line of rulers from the same family) began in 1438 and continued until 1740. One reason the Holy Roman Empire went into decline, however, was that Habsburgs were more concerned about expanding or holding onto their territories than in ruling the empire. In the fifteenth century they extended their possessions into Bohemia, Moravia, and Hungary in eastern Europe. During the reign of Charles V, the Habsburgs united Austria with Spain, the strongest monarchy in Europe at the time. Charles also took over the Netherlands in the name of Spain, and conquistadors (Spanish soldiers) expanded the Spanish empire into the Americas. Charles and the Habsburgs now controlled the largest empire in the history of the world. Nevertheless, Charles and his successors were confronted by numerous problems, including challenges to their rule from European monarchs, princes, and noblemen. They also had to contend with the continuing threat of invasion by the Ottoman Empire, a vast kingdom ruled by Muslims (followers of the Islam religion, founded by the prophet Muhammad) in Asia and North Africa (see "Hungary" section later in this chapter).

Perhaps the greatest challenge came from Protestant reformers, who were demanding radical changes in the Roman Catholic Church. The Habsburgs, who were staunch Catholics, struggled to hold onto their power by becoming leaders in the Catholic Reformation (also called the Counter Reformation), a systematic effort by the

Catholic Church to combat the Protestant Reformation. The Protestant movement also triggered a complex string of events that resulted in the Thirty Years' War. The war began in Bohemia with a struggle between Catholics and Protestants over control of the Bohemian throne (see "Bohemia" section later in this chapter). It soon escalated into a conflict that involved political, social, and economic issues. Reaching into every level of society throughout Europe, the Thirty Years' War severely diminished the power of the Habsburgs.

The Habsburg dynasty

The Habsburg dynasty lasted for 219 years, from 1438 through 1657. This era was ruled by ten members of the family: Frederick III, Maximilian I, Charles V, Ferdinand I, Maximilan II, Rudolf II, Matthias, Ferdinand II, and Ferdinand III.

Albert II The first Holy Roman Emperor in the Habsburg dynasty was Albert II (1397–1439). He was crowned in 1438 after the death of his father-in-law, Emperor Sigismund (1368–1437; ruled 1433–37). Albert was also the king of Hungary, Germany, and Bohemia (present-day Czechoslovakia). Although he served as emperor for only a year, he worked to promote stability in the empire. In 1438 he called a diet at Nuremberg, Germany, and ended the practice of kings and lords settling feuds with private wars. He also appointed arbiters (judges) to help resolve disputes. Albert died in

Habsburg emperors during the Renaissance

Below are listed the Habsburg emperors and the years they ruled, from 1438 through 1657.

Albert II	1438–39
Frederick III	1440–93
Maximilian I	1493–1519
Charles V	1519–58
Ferdinand I	1558–64
Maximilian II	1564–76
Rudolf II	1576–1612
Matthias	1612–19
Ferdinand II	1619–37
Ferdinand III	1637–57

1439 during a campaign against the Ottoman Empire.

Frederick III Albert's successor was the German king Frederick III (1415–1493). Although Frederick had numerous problems during his reign, he made the house of Habsburg a powerful force in European politics. The son of Duke Ernest of Austria, Frederick inherited the Habsburg possessions of Inner Austria (Styria, Carinthia, Carniola, and Gorizia) upon his father's death in 1424. Frederick was elected German king and uncrowned emperor in 1440, but he was confronted with conflicts among his relatives and challenges from rebellious nobility. These problems caused Frederick to withdraw almost completely from German affairs. He had more satisfactory relations with the church, and in 1452 he became the last emperor to be crowned in Rome by a pope.

Frederick was unable to keep the Ottomans out of eastern Europe (then the Byzantine Empire) because his empire was financially and militarily weak. The Ottomans took Constantinople (now Istanbul, Turkey), the capital of the Byzantine Empire, in 1453, and moved into Styria and Carinthia. Beginning with Frederick's reign, the Habsburgs presented themselves as the champions of Christianity in the war against Islam. They continued to play this role for more than three centuries.

Frederick's greatest achievement came in 1477 when he arranged a marriage between Maximilian and Mary of Burgundy (1457–1482), daughter of Charles the Bold, duke of Burgundy. This union gave the house of Habsburg a large part of Burgundy and made the Austrians a European power. In 1486, when his son Maximilian became king of Germany, Frederick assumed a less active role in affairs of state. Like many rulers in the Renaissance period, he occupied his time with astrology (prediction of future events according to the positions of the stars), magic (conjuring of supernatural spirits), and alchemy (attempted manufacture of gold from base metals). He also collected books and precious stones and associated with prominent humanists.

Maximilian I Maximilian (1459–1519) restored the power of the Habsburgs.

His intense interest in the arts and in elaborate public ceremonies earned him a place in legend as well as history. Maximilian appears to have been more of a storybook king than a hardworking ruler. He spent a great deal of time and money on books and portraits that promoted an image of himself as a heroic knight (a medieval warrior who vowed to uphold a complex code of honor and duty) He also wrote several romantic versions of his own life.

Maximilian's marriage to Mary of Burgundy plunged him into a conflict with King Louis XI of France over control of territories in Burgundy (see "France" in Chapter 3). While holding his own against Louis, Maximilian also had to put down revolts in Flanders (see "The Netherlands" section later in this chapter). His son and heir, Philip I (1478–1506), became the recognized prince of the Low Countries (the Netherlands, Belgium, Luxembourg, and Flanders) upon his birth. When Mary died in 1482, Maximilian held onto his Burgundian lands. In 1490 he recaptured Austria from Hungary. Six years later he arranged for Philip to marry Joanna (1479–1555), the daughter of Ferdinand and Isabella of Spain. This union linked the house of Habsburg with the most powerful monarchy of Europe (see "Spain" in Chapter 3).

Maximilian was more successful in establishing a Habsburg dynasty than in asserting his power as emperor. His rule had been limited by the imperial council that was formed by

Habsburg Austria

Austria appeared on the map of Europe as a sovereign, or independent, state only after World War I (1914–18). At the beginning of the sixteenth century, Austria belonged to the Habsburgs, who called themselves the house of Austria. The state covered the eastern part of central Europe—the regions that are now Lower Austria, Upper Austria, Styria, Carinthia, and Carniola (largely part of present-day Slovenia). Austria also included the Tyrol (also Tirol) and Vorarlberg, two regions on the eastern border of Switzerland, as well as scattered Habsburg holdings in southwestern Germany.

The Habsburgs had come into possession of these lands in the thirteenth and fourteenth centuries. Primogeniture (the giving of an entire estate to the eldest son upon the death of his father) was not in effect until the reign of Emperor Ferdinand II. Before that time the Habsburgs routinely divided their lands among all their sons. The first of the Habsburgs to come to the territory was Rudolf I (1218–1291; ruled 1273–91), a German king and Holy Roman Emperor. The next Habsburg to become

Holy Roman Emperor was Albert II, who was crowned in 1438. From that time until 1740, all emperors were Habsburgs. As emperors, the Habsburgs also ruled Germany. For that reason scholars have found it difficult to fix a dividing line between Austria and Germany.

Beginning with the reign of Charles V in the sixteenth century, the Habsburgs ruled the largest empire in the history of the world. Nevertheless, they struggled to maintain their hold over Austria because German princes were constantly seeking independence. The Protestant Reformation also had a profound impact on Austria. Except for the Tyrol (a province between Austria bordering Switzerland), which remained Catholic, the entire region was divided between Catholics and Protestants. The Habsburgs had ongoing financial problems as well; they found that their expenses were much higher than their income, so they were always searching for cash and loans to run the empire. After the Thirty Years' War, which concluded with the German states being awarded sovereignty, the power of the Habsburgs was confined to Austria.

the princes to control all external and internal affairs of the empire. He also suffered numerous military setbacks that further eroded his authority in Europe. During the Italian Wars, a conflict between France and Spain over control in Italy (see "Italian Wars

dominate Renaissance" in Chapter 2), Maximilian led his troops against the French in three separate battles in Italy—in 1496, 1499, and 1500. Each time he was soundly defeated. Between 1500 and 1504 Maximilian was busy putting down rebellions in Germany (see "Germany" section later in this chapter). Then the sudden death of his son Philip in 1506 brought problems over the rule of the Netherlands, adding to Maximilian's difficulties in Germany and Italy. In 1508 Maximilian fought the French once again in Italy, but this time he was stopped by resistance from the city-state of Venice. The emperor retaliated by entering into the League of Cambrai with France and the Papal States against Venice (see "Venice" in Chapter 2). In 1510, however, Pope Julius II decided to consolidate his own power in Italy and rejected the League of Cambrai. Maximilian continued to face the rising power of France until his death in 1519.

Charles V The next Holy Roman Emperor was Charles V (1500–1558; ruled 1519–58), grandson of Maximilian and son of Philip I, ruler of the Low Countries. Charles's mother, Joanna of Castile and Aragon, suffered from a mental illness, so after Philip died in 1506 Charles was raised in Flanders by his aunt, Margaret of Austria (1480–1530). When he turned fifteen, he became ruler of the Netherlands. Just a year later, when his grandfather Ferdinand II of Aragon died, he inherited Spain and its empire. Charles traveled to Spain in 1517 to assume the rule there, but he was still very young. He knew neither the language nor the customs of his Spanish subjects, and he surrounded himself with Flemish (the name given to people from Flanders) advisors. This action angered many people in Spain. When Maxim-

ilian died in 1519, Charles became the heir not only to Habsburg territories but also to Burgundy. At the age of nineteen he was also named the new Holy Roman Emperor (he was officially crowned in 1530). He won the position after his advisers bribed electors with 850,000 florins (the Italian unit of currency at the time).

Early in his reign as emperors Charles was confronted with the growing Protestant movement. The revolt had started in 1517, the year Charles became king of Spain, when Martin Luther presented the list of ninety-five complaints against the Roman Catholic Church at Wittenberg, Germany (see "Luther starts Reformation" section previously in this chapter). Although Charles was a devout Catholic, he paid little attention to Luther at first. Finally, in 1521, Charles and the German princes summoned Luther before the Diet at the town of Worms. Charles and the princes demanded that Luther change his views. When Luther refused, Charles and the Diet declared him an outlaw of the Church. This declaration did little to stop Luther, though, who escaped punishment and continued to call for reforms.

Charles could not keep a check on Luther because he had to focus his attention on the Italian Wars. In 1521 he invaded areas in northern Italy controlled by France, but the French king, Francis I, angrily fought back. In 1525 Charles defeated Francis at the battle of Pavia, captured him, and then held him prisoner for a year (see "France" in Chapter 3). After his release Francis again opposed Spanish control in Italy, this time joined by Henry VIII of England and Pope Clement VII. But Charles's imperial forces, gathered from his vast empire, were too strong. They brutally attacked Rome in 1527. Thus, Francis, Henry, and the pope were forced to recognize Charles's position in Italy. In 1530 Clement VII crowned Charles Holy Roman emperor at Bologna, Italy.

Faces challenges to his rule For the remainder of his reign, Charles had to fight to secure his empire. Turks from the Ottoman Empire challenged his authority in the Mediterranean and in central Europe. The Turks killed Louis II, the king of Hungary and Bohemia, at the Battle of Mohacs in 1526 (see "Hungary" section later in this chapter). As a member of the Habsburg family, Charles inherited those kingdoms, and his brother Ferdinand I was named the new king. The Turks continued to threaten Europe, however, so Charles met them in battle in 1529 and again in 1532. He captured the Turkish stronghold at Tunis (a city in present-day Tunisia in northern Africa) in 1535. The Turks did not give up though, continuing to attack the Italian coast. After suffering a defeat in 1541 at a Turkish base in Algiers in northern Africa, Charles had to sign a truce with the Ottoman Empire.

After the truce, Charles tried to restore Catholic unity to his empire. In response, German Protestant princes formed an alliance known as the Schmalkaldic League. Under the protection of the League, the Reformation spread through most of Germany. Charles's imperial army defeated the forces of the German princes at the Battle of Mühlberg in 1547. Nevertheless, the ideals of the Reformation were strong enough to carry on. As a result, Charles's empire would never be fully Catholic. Having grown tired of running his vast empire, he stepped down from the throne in 1555, but he did not formally retire as emperor until 1558. The majority of his lands went to his son Philip II (see "Spain" in Chapter 3). The lands controlled by the Habsburg family and the title of emperor went to his younger brother, Ferdinand I. Charles retired to the monastery of Yuste in western Spain where, on September 21, 1558, he died clutching a crucifix (a carved image of the crucified Christ on the cross).

Ferdinand I Ferdinand I (1503–1564; ruled 1558–64) was brought up in Spain and lived for a long time in the shadow of his brother Charles. When their grandfather, Emperor Maximilian I, died in 1519, Charles inherited a large empire, while Ferdinand received only the Habsburg possessions in Austria. Ferdinand's brother-in-law Louis II was king of Bohemia and Hungary. When Louis was killed at the Battle of Mohacs in 1526, Ferdinand became king of Bohemia and Hungary. His position was complicated because he was a representative of the Holy Roman Empire while at the same time being a German prince and the independent king of Hungary.

In 1531 Charles had Ferdinand elected king of the Romans, that is, Ferdinand was designated as the next emperor. Although Ferdinand was a Catholic, he acted as a mediator between his brother and the Protestant princes. He led forces in Charles's triumph over the Schmalkaldic League at the Battle of Mühlberg in 1547. Five years later, when Charles was betrayed by a former ally, Maurice of Saxony (see "Saxony" section later in this chapter), Ferdinand arranged the Treaty of Passau (1552). This treaty was the first step toward the Treaty of Augsburg of 1555, which granted religious freedom to the Lutheran princes. Charles refused to accept the terms of the Treaty of Augsburg and soon stepped down from the throne. Ferdinand then became emperor and continued his efforts to unite Catholics and Protestants. He died in Vienna in 1564.

Maximilian II Ferdinand was followed as emperor by his son, Maximilian II (1527–1576; ruled 1564–76), who was married to Charles V's daughter Maria. Maximilian took the throne in 1564 under a cloud of controversy. Although Ferdinand had served as emperor for the past six years, the way had not been cleared for Maximilian to follow him. This situation had been created by both Charles and Maximilian himself. Charles had made arrangements to keep the line to the throne open for his own son, Philip II of Spain. Maximilian was therefore excluded from the line of succession, and a deep division was created between the two main branches of the Habsburg family. A complicating factor was that Maximilian had embraced Protestantism, and he was on good terms with the German princes who had defeated Charles in 1552.

After Ferdinand succeeded Charles in 1558, he tried to bring Maximilian back into the Catholic Church. Maximilian refused, however, and by 1560 his relations with his father were near the breaking point. Maximilian then tried to rally the Protestant princes against Ferdinand. After finding no support, he gave in and agreed to return to the church. Many people doubted his commitment to Catholicism and warned that he would favor Protestantism if he ever became emperor. Nevertheless, in 1562 Ferdinand made sure Maximilian would be named emperor by having him elected king of the Romans. Two years later Maximilian took the throne. He was now in a position to help Protestants overtake the empire, but he made no real efforts to reform the church. Maximilian's dealings with the German Protestants were made more difficult by ferocious hostilities among various Lutheran sects and between the Lutherans and Calvinists (followers of French reformer John Calvin). Maximilian wanted to maintain good relations with the Spanish branch of the Habsburg family, so he sent his oldest son, Rudolf II, to Spain for a Catholic education. In 1574 Maximilian designated Rudolf as the next emperor, thus assuring that Habsburg lands and the Holy Roman Empire would remain under Catholic control.

Rudolf II When Maximilian died in 1576, Rudolf II (1552–1612; ruled 1576–1612) became the new emperor. He was also the king of Bohemia and Hungary. Although Rudolf reigned for thirty-six years, he was a weak ruler. He suffered from bouts of severe depression, which limited his ability to tend to state affairs. Soon after becoming emperor he moved to Prague, the capital of Bohemia, where he lived in seclusion and devoted his time to the arts and sciences.

During the first twenty years of Rudolf's reign the empire was torn apart by disputes between Roman Catholics and Protestants. When the Protestant movement began in the early 1500s, the Habsburgs took the role as leaders of the Counter Reformation, or Catholic Reformation (the name given to attempts to change the Catholic Church from within). By 1600 they had to a large extent eliminated Protestantism from Austria. Bohemia was their next target, but Bohemia had become increasingly Protestant and most of the influential nobility were anti-Catholic. Reversing Maximilian II's tolerant policies, Rudolf tried to limit the political privileges of the Protestant Estates (representatives of the four social classes: nobility, clergy, middle class, peasants) that were granted in the Peace of Augsburg.

In 1607 Rudolf quarreled with his brother, Matthias, over control of Habsburg lands. The Habsburg archdukes (noblemen who ruled provinces) designated Matthias as the next emperor. The following year they made

Matthias Corvinus had already proven to be an incompetent ruler by the time he became emperor of the Habsburg dynasty in 1612.
Reproduced by permission of Hulton Archive.

Rudolf give up Hungary, Austria, and Moravia to Matthias. Although Rudolf promised to give Matthias the crown of Bohemia, he turned to the Bohemians for support against Matthias. In order to gain their loyalty, Rudolf issued the Bohemian Estates a Letter of Majesty (emperor's official order) in 1609. Under this decree, religious freedom was granted to all Bohemians, and they had the right to construct churches and schools on Habsburg land. Nevertheless, the emperor quickly removed Protestant officials from key offices in Bohemia and replaced them with Catholics. But his transparent concessions to religious freedom did little to strengthen Rudolf's position. Finally, in 1611, imperial troops attacked Bohemia with Rudolf's support. The Bohemian Estates called for assistance from Matthias, whose army virtually held Rudolf prisoner in Prague until he yielded Bohemia to Matthias. Although Rudolf prevented Matthias from being elected king of the Romans, Matthias did become emperor after Rudolf's death in 1612.

Matthias Matthias (1557–1619) had already proven to be an incompetent ruler by the time he became emperor in 1612. In 1577 the Catholic nobles in the Spanish Netherlands invited him to serve as governor general of their province. At that time Protestant reformers there, led by William of Orange, were seeking independence from Spain (see "The Netherlands" section later in this chapter). Matthias was unable to make peace between Spain and the Protestants, so he returned to Germany in 1581. Five years later Rudolf named Matthias governor of Austria. Matthias continued Rudolf's policy of suppressing Protestantism, and he successfully put down several rebellions between 1595 and 1597. Yet he never won any substantial victories over the Protestants. In 1598 Matthias appointed Melchior Khlesl (1552–1630), a Catholic cardinal (a church official who ranks below the pope) from Austria, as his chief adviser.

After Matthias became emperor he withdrew from public life and Khlesl soon took over major policy matters. The imperial diet (representative assembly) had been paralyzed since 1608 as a result of disputes between Protestant and Catholic princes. When Matthias and Khlesl failed to resolve the conflict, Habsburg archdukes took the side of the Catholic princes in Germany. The archdukes then decided that Matthias's cousin, Archduke Ferdinand of Styria, should succeed Matthias as emperor. Matthias had no children, so there were no sons who could follow him to the throne. Ferdinand was a threat to Bohemian religious liberty, however, because he was the most ardent Catholic among the Habsburgs. Since the divided Bohemian Estates had no candidate of their own, they reluctantly agreed to accept Ferdinand, who would share the title with Matthias. Ferdinand was named king of Bohemia in 1617 and crowned king of Hungary in 1618. Matthias and Khlesl urged Ferdinand to make concessions to the Protestants, but Ferdinand refused to compromise. Matthias died the following year.

Ferdinand II Ferdinand II (1578–1637; ruled 1619–37) had been educated by the Jesuits (a Catholic religious order) at Ingolstadt in Catholic Bavaria, a region that is now part of Germany. The Jesuits were enormously influential in forming Ferdinand's conception of his duties as the Christian prince of Styria (a region in southeast Austria). When he was old enough to rule he dedicated himself to restoring the Roman Catholic faith in his lands. In 1602 he expelled Protestant teachers and preachers from Styria, closed or destroyed their churches, and gave his non-noble Protestant subjects the choice of conversion or exile. When his cousins, the emperors Rudolf II and Matthias, died childless, Ferdinand inherited the Habsburg dominions in Austria, Bohemia, and Hungary. In 1617 he was elected king of Bohemia and in 1618 became king of Hungary. His Protestant subjects, fearing an attack on their right to worship, refused to swear loyalty to him. In May 1618 the Bohemian nobility staged the revolt known as the "Defenestration of Prague" (see "Hungary" section later in this chapter). With the support of Maximilian of Bavaria and the forces of the Catholic League (an alliance of Catholic noblemen), Ferdinand suppressed the Protestant rebels in Austria and Bohemia in 1620.

Ferdinand's efforts to restore Catholicism initiated the Thirty Years' War, a European conflict in which the religious issue ultimately became submerged in a conflict for domination of the continent. In 1629 and again in 1635 Ferdinand was in a position to dictate a favorable peace in Germany. But both times he refused to make compromises with the Protestant princes and their powerful foreign protectors, France and Sweden. He died in Vienna in 1637 and was succeeded as emperor by his son, Ferdinand III.

Ferdinand III As Holy Roman Emperor, Ferdinand III (1608–1657; ruled 1637–57) headed the so-called peace party at the Habsburg imperial court during the Thirty Years' War. He signed the Peace of Westphalia, the treaty that ended the war in 1648.

The eldest son of Ferdinand II and Maria Anna of Bavaria, Ferdinand III was named archduke of Austria in 1621 at the age of thirteen. He was crowned king of Hungary in 1625 and became king of Bohemia in 1627. When Generalissimo Albrecht von Wallenstein (1583–1634) prevented him from taking command of Ferdinand II's armies, Ferdinand joined a conspiracy against Wallenstein. Wallenstein was dismissed from his position and killed in 1634. Ferdinand was partly responsible for the generalissimo's death. Ferdinand then took over as commander of the Habsburg armies, though the actual general was Matthias Gallas (1584–1647), a leader in the plot against Wallenstein. In 1634 imperial forces captured Regensburg, a town in southeast Germany, and defeated Swedish forces (who were supporting the Protestant effort in Germany) at the first Battle of Nördlingen in the same year. Ferdinand headed the peace party at the Austrian court, encouraging negotiations that led to the Peace of Prague in May 1635 (see "Thirty Years' War in Chapter 6). This treaty was an attempt to reunite Catholics and Protestants by addressing disputes over rights to Habsburg lands. Protestants were also given amnesty, or freedom from punishment for past offenses against the empire. Although the German princes agreed to the Peace of Prague, warfare soon broke out again. Cardinal Richelieu (Armand-Jean du Plessis), the French leader, felt that the Holy Roman Empire and the house of Habsburg were still too powerful. French and Swedish forces therefore continued the fight against the imperial armies.

Ferdinand was elected king of the Romans in 1636 and became emperor when his father died the next year. In 1648 he agreed to the Peace of Westphalia, the treaty that resulted from seven years of negotiations and ended the Thirty Years' War. Considered the first modern peace conference, the Peace of Westphalia reduced the power of the Holy Roman Empire and the house of Habsburg. The German states were granted independence and the empire continued in name only. France then emerged as the major European power. Ferdinand died in 1657 and his second son, Leopold I (1640–1705), the king of Hungary, succeeded him as emperor (ruled 1658–1705).

Germany

By the fifteenth century Germany consisted of more than three hundred separate states that were crowded into four main regions: Brandenburg in the north, along the Baltic Sea; Hesse in the west, on the southern border of the Netherlands; Saxony in the central area, between Hesse and Silesia; and Bavaria in the south between Austria and the Tyrol.

Brandenburg

The history of modern Brandenburg began during the Renaissance when, in 1417, Holy Roman Emperor Sigismund gave the title of elector (a German prince entitled to take part in the election of the Holy Roman Emperor) to his loyal lieutenant Frederick I of Hohenzollern (1371–1440). Frederick's descendants would rule Brandenburg, and later Prussia and Germany, until 1918. Frederick I was succeeded by his eldest son, Frederick II (1413–1471; ruled 1440–70), known as "Iron Tooth" because he was a strict ruler. Beginning in 1442 Frederick II brought the cities of Berlin and Cölln under his control. He also caused all Brandenburg cities to leave the Hanseatic League, and he signed a concordat (agreement) with Pope Nicholas V (1397–1455; reigned 1447–55). The concordat gave Frederick extensive rights in the appointment of bishops in the three dioceses (church districts) of Brandenburg (Lebus, Brandenburg, and Havelberg). The next ruler was Frederick II's brother, Albert Achilles (1414–1486; ruled 1470–86), who issued the *Dispositio Achillea* (1473), which established primogeniture (the giving of an entire estate to the eldest son upon the death of his father). Albert Achilles was frequently absent from Brandenburg, so he entrusted the government to his eldest son, John Cicero (1455–1499; ruled 1486–99), who welcomed Italian scholars and tried to improve the education of his subjects. He had to contend with repeated attacks from his neighbors, however, and rebellious Brandenburg noblemen were constantly challenging his rule.

Reformation and Renaissance John Cicero was followed by Joachim I

The Hanseatic League

The Hanseatic League was a trading network formed by German towns after 1100. A major reason for the league's development was the lack of a powerful national government that could support extensive commerce and provide safe passage for merchants when they traveled to foreign lands. As a result, companies of merchants made agreements that guaranteed mutual protection, exclusive trading rights, and trade monopolies (domination without competition) whenever possible. Implementing these agreements, the merchants began building towns that were closer together. At first the league was controlled by a dozen or so German towns (known as Hansa) in the Baltic and Rhineland regions. Originally "hansa" referred to an association of warriors, but the term soon denoted a tax imposed on foreign merchants. Gradually, the word came to mean a group of merchants in a particular city who were engaged in trade with foreign lands. Finally the German "Hansa" signified a vast community of urban merchants who did business in the Baltic Sea and the North Sea. Three stages marked the expansion of the Hanseatic League: it was initiated during the period 1100 to 1200; it reached its height in the years 1200 to 1350; and its influence gradually decreased during the two centuries from 1350 to 1550. After 1550 the commercial unity of the Hansa fell apart, though certain cities such as Lübeck, Bremen, and Hamburg continued to prosper far into the modern period (centuries that followed the beginning of the Renaissance in the mid-1300s).

(1484–1535; ruled 1499–1535), who founded the University of Frankfurt on the Oder, called the Viadrina. In 1517 the first rector, or leader of the school, Konrad Koch (c. 1460–1531), brought John Tetzel (c. 1465–1519) to Viadrina. Tetzel was the Dominican priest who sold indulgences and provoked Martin Luther's Ninety-five Theses, the list of charges against the Roman Catholic Church that started the Protestant Reformation. The university also attracted champions of the new Renaissance learning, among them Ulrich von Hutten (1488–1532), a poet and later supporter of the Reformation. Viadrina began to decline, however, when the faculty opposed Luther's reforms. The plague also struck Frankfurt repeatedly and students increasingly flocked to Wittenberg University, which became a center of humanist learning (see "Saxony" section later in this chapter). Joachim I's brother, Albert II (1490–11545), was a true Renaissance prince. The archbishop (head church official) of Magdeburg and Halberstadt, Albert admired the Dutch humanist Desiderius Erasmus (c. 1466–1536) and patronized the leading artists of the time, including the German painters

Lucas Cranach the Elder (1472–1553) and Albrecht Dürer (1471–1528).

Joachim and Albert both blamed Luther for the outbreak of the Peasants' War (1524–26), a social and political revolt staged by the poorer classes in Germany. After it was quashed in 1526 Joachim and Albert joined the dukes of Brunswick and Saxony in the Anti-Lutheran League of Dessau. Joachim continued to oppose Protestantism for the rest of his life. Upon his death in 1535 his son, Joachim II (1505–1571; ruled 1535–71), became the ruler of Brandenburg. In 1539 Joachim II issued an order that supported Protestant beliefs. Nevertheless, he kept many of the ceremonial features of the Roman Catholic Church, such as exorcism (a ceremony in which a priest gets rid of evil spirits) and the use of chrism (consecrated oil) in baptism (a ceremony in which a person is admitted into the church). Joachim was such an effective diplomat that Brandenburg received approval from both the Protestant reformer Martin Luther and the Catholic champion Emperor Charles V.

A significant shift in Brandenburg's religious orientation began during the reign of Joachim Frederick (1546–1608; ruled 1598–1608). Joachim Frederick's advisers were Calvinists (followers of the French Protestant reformer John Calvin), and he advocated a foreign policy that opposed the Holy Roman Empire. This process was completed by his successor, John Sigismund (1572–1619; ruled 1608–19), who converted to the Reformed faith (a branch of Protestantism founded by Calvin) in 1613. In the early part of the Thirty Years' War, Brandenburg was the leading Reformed state and supported independence of Germany from the Holy Roman Empire. By embracing the Reformed church, however, John Sigismund alienated the Lutherans. The Lutherans did not accept the simpler forms of worship advocated by the Reformed movement, so Brandenburg was divided by further religious conflict. John Sigismund's son George William (1595–1640; ruled 1619–40) was unable to unify the state, and by the time of his death in 1640 he had surrendered political control to Adam zu Schwarzenberg, a Catholic who sided with the empire. Brandenburg suffered heavy losses in the Thirty Years' War, but after the war it became the leading Protestant state in Germany.

Hesse

Hesse became a powerful province during the reign of Ludwig (1413–1458), a member of the house of Brabant. Ludwig unified the two core areas of Lower Hesse on the Werra River and Upper Hesse on the Lahn and laid claim to the counties of Katzenelnbogen on the Rhine River. Ludwig also renewed the important *Erbverbrüderung* (union of great noble houses) with the Wettin family in Saxony (see "Saxony" section later in this chapter). This union was Hesse's most important alliance during the Renaissance. Ludwig's heirs centralized the government, and by 1500 a powerful Hessian state emerged that roughly resembled the present federal state of Hesse. Connected to the world market by the Rhine and its merchants, Hesse produced wool and linen textiles for export, as well as grains, raw wool, iron, and salt.

Hesse reached its peak under Philipp the Magnanimous (1504–1567), who made it the major protector of emerging Protestant churches. Hessians were also active in opposing Charles V's attempts to strengthen Habsburg power. In 1526 Philipp sought a Protestant political alliance to defend the new Protestant churches. In 1529 he held a conference called the Colloquy of Marburg to bring religious unity between two disputing Protestant groups, Zwinglians (followers of Swiss reformer Huldrych Zwingli) and Lutherans (followers of German reformer Martin Luther). When Philipp's policies were finally adopted in 1531, he played the leading role in the new Schmalkaldic League, an alliance of German Protestant princes (see "Schmalkaldic League" in Chapter 5). In 1541 Philipp's influence was severely weakened, however, by his notorious bigamy (marriage to more than one wife). Along with other factors, this led to the defeat of the league and his imprisonment (1547–52).

After Philipp's death in 1567, Hesse was divided among his four legitimate sons. However, growing religious discord and competition among the brothers caused divisions between the two regions. The major figures in the conflict were Wilhelm IV, who ruled Lower Hesse until 1592, and Ludwig IV, who ruled Upper Hesse until 1604. Since none of Philipp's sons had any male heirs, in 1604 Upper Hesse and Lower Hesse were consolidated into Hessen-Kassel and Hessen-Darmstadt.

Saxony

Saxony was created in 1423 when Holy Roman Emperor Sigismund granted the duchy (territory ruled by a nobleman called a duke) of Saxony-Wittenberg to Frederick of Meissen and Thuringia. Frederick was head of the Wettin family. In 1485 these territories were divided between Frederick's grandsons, Ernest and Albert, resulting in the foundation of the two main lines of the house of Saxon—Ernestine Saxony and Albertine Saxony. The two lines were never reunited. Ernest, the elder brother, was named elector and received Saxony-Wittenberg, central and southern Thuringia, the Franconian lands (Coburg), and parts of the Vogtland. Albert received Meissen and northern Thuringia. Ernestine Saxony was centered in Wittenberg and Albertine Saxony was governed from Dresden. This arrangement created complex and confusing boundaries that became the root of future conflicts.

Wittenberg is center of humanism Under the leadership of Elector Frederick III, known as Frederick the Wise (1463–1525; ruled 1486–1525), Saxony-Wittenberg prospered and quickly became the most influential principality in the Holy Roman Empire. In 1502 Frederick founded a new university at

Wittenberg for the training of civil servants (government workers) and church officials. The university offered a curriculum based on scholasticism (a scholarly method that combined Christian teachings with Greek philosophy; see "Saint Thomas Aquinas" box in Chapter 1). Renaissance scholars were also on the faculty. Among them was the humanist Nicholas Marschalk, who set up a printing shop in Wittenberg and generated enthusiasm for the Greek language and the study of classical texts. The arrival of the Augustinian monk Martin Luther gave humanistic studies an even greater boost. Luther possessed qualities of intellect and leadership that soon made him the unchallenged leader of the Wittenberg academic community. Although he was not a humanist, he used humanist methods to explain the Bible, and in the process became a relentless critic of scholasticism. In October 1517 Luther presented his famous Ninety-Five Theses, a list of charges against the Roman Catholic Church. By the following summer he was beginning to attract attention as a religious reformer.

In 1518 the appointment of Philipp Melanchthon (1497–1560) to the newly created professorship in Greek lent further impetus to these changes. Melanchthon advocated replacing scholasticism with the humanist method, which relied on the individual intellect rather than the teachings of expert scholars. As Luther found himself increasingly involved in religious controversies, Melanchthon not only became his chief theological supporter but also the leader of educational reform. By 1521 these reforms changed Wittenberg from a scholastic and Roman Catholic school into a humanistic and Protestant one. It emerged as one of the most popular universities in Germany.

Frederick and his successors, John the Constant (ruled 1525–32) and John Frederick the Magnanimous (ruled 1532–54), protected Luther's movement against the church and the emperor. Ernestine Saxony thus became the center of the Reformation. By contrast, Duke George of Albertine Saxony (ruled 1500–39) remained a staunch defender of the Catholic Church. Deeply shaken by the Peasants' War, he joined with the rulers of Brunswick and Brandenburg in the Anti-Lutheran League of Dessau in 1525. Ernestine Saxony and Albertine Saxony were also separated by economic and political differences. While Ernestine Saxony was essentially agricultural, Albertine Saxony was more densely populated and profited greatly from textile production, mining, and trade. Duke Henry V (ruled 1539–41) finally introduced the Lutheran Reformation in Albertine Saxony. His son and heir, Maurice (ruled 1541–53), continued to push for church reform, but he did not join the Schmalkaldic League. Instead, he sided with Holy Roman Emperor Charles V. He was rewarded by receiving the title of elector along with most of the Ernestine lands, including Wittenberg and its university.

Maurice leads princes' rebellion Maurice supported the Augsburg Interim of 1548 (an order to restore Catholicism in Protestant areas), which provoked a series of controversies. Soon Maurice became alarmed about the emperor's efforts to take over territories in Germany and restore the Catholic religion. Maurice then entered into a secret alliance with King Henry II of France, an enemy of Charles V. In 1552 Maurice's forces suddenly attacked Charles's imperial army, leading a rebellion of German princes. A defeated Charles was forced to sign the Treaty of Passau (1552), which required him to give up his plans for keeping Germany in the empire and restoring the Catholic Church. The center of power in Saxony now shifted from Wittenberg to Dresden. Benefiting from administrative reforms that brought a thriving economy, Albertine Saxony became the empire's leading Protestant state. Universities flourished in Albertine Saxony, though Wittenberg, in Ernestine Saxony, continued to be popular among supporters of the Reformation.

The next elector, August I (ruled 1553–86), was Maurice's brother and one of the best rulers Saxony ever had. The city of Leipzig especially benefited from his reign and became a center for the arts. August worked hard to achieve greater harmony within the Lutheran movement. His efforts were successful and resulted in the Formula of Concord (1577), which brought about the banishment of all suspected Calvinists from Saxony. In the Thirty Years' War, Elector John George (1585–1656; ruled 1611–56) took the side of Catholic Emperor Fer-

dinand II, but then he switched sides and attempted to lead a neutral party that fought with Sweden against Ferdinand's imperial forces. In 1635 John George signed a separate peace treaty with the Habsburgs, but during the last ten years of the war his lands were devastated. When the lengthy conflict ended with the Peace of Westphalia in 1648, neighboring Brandenburg had replaced Saxony as the leading state in northern Germany.

Bavaria

Bavaria was created as a duchy in 1180 when Holy Roman Emperor Frederick I (ruled 1152–90) granted the territory to his ally Otto of Wittelsbach. Wittelsbach's descendants reigned in Bavaria until 1918. By the early 1400s the duchy was divided into four smaller duchies: Bavaria-Ingoistadt, Bavaria-Landshut, Bavaria-Munich, and Bavaria-Straubing. Disputes and wars among Wittelsbach brothers and cousins plagued Bavaria during the fifteenth century. In 1445 the duchy of Bavaria-Ingoistadt was taken over by Duke Heinrich of Bavaria-Landshut. When Heinrich's grandson, George the Rich, died without male heirs in 1503, Heinrich sought to leave his duchy to his son-in-law, Rupert of the Palatinate (a region on the Rhine River). This plan was opposed by Albrecht IV of Bavaria-Munich (1447–1508; ruled 1467–1508), who claimed the duchy for himself, saying he was the next direct male heir to Wittelsbach. Following Albrecht's victory in the Landshut succession war (a conflict in 1504 to determine who would rule Bavaria), the Upper Palatinate was given to Rupert, but the rest of Bavaria came under the control of Albrecht. Bavaria was once more a united duchy. In order to prevent future divisions of the territory, Albrecht established primogeniture.

Throughout this period Bavaria's economy remained firmly rooted in agriculture, with more than 80 percent of its population composed of peasants who lived in small villages and worked on farms. Land ownership was divided among the Wittelsbach dukes, the Roman Catholic Church, and numerous Bavarian noblemen. The two largest cities were Munich and Straubing. Munich had a population of approximately twelve thousand, and the population of Straubing was around four thousand. Munich supported a modest textile industry and was a minor trade center linking Italy and the Tyrol to southeastern Germany, Austria, and parts of Switzerland. In the second half of the sixteenth century, high taxation and the expulsion of Protestant artisans and merchants from many towns hampered economic growth.

Catholicism re-established The power of Bavarian dukes increased during the sixteenth century, which in turn led to a decline in the Bavarian Estates (composed of high churchmen, nobles, and burghers, or middle-class citizens), whose role in government had expanded in the 1400s. The dukes assumed greater judicial powers, extended their authority over the church, and established a centralized administration made up of a privy council, council of war, spiritual council (to oversee the church), and *Hofkammer* (treasury department). Protestantism was slow to gain support in Bavaria, but in the 1550s pro-Lutheran nobles and burghers in the estates petitioned Albrecht V for reforms in the church. Among the reforms was the right of church members to take communion (the worship ceremony in which bread and wine represent the body and blood of Jesus Christ, the founder of Christianity). At that time in the Catholic Church, the wine was being drunk only by the priest. They also asked that priests have the right to marry.

Although staunchly Catholic himself, Albrecht at first agreed to such demands in return for the estates' financial support. But by the 1560s, after he discovered (but never proved) a pro-Lutheran conspiracy among the nobility, Albrecht hardened his attitude toward Protestantism. He encouraged the activities of the Capuchins and Jesuits (Catholic religious orders that were seeking to convert Protestants), established strict censorship, and promoted the decrees of the Council of Trent (a conference called by the Catholic Church to respond to the threat of the Protestant Reformation). He also established a spiritual council, made up of laypeople (as opposed to priests and other church leaders), to oversee church affairs. By the 1580s, Lutheranism had virtually disappeared in Bavaria, which became a center of Catholicism in Germany.

During the late sixteenth century Wittelsbachs were named bishops (heads of church districts) in Freising, Regensburg, Passau, and Eichstadt. In 1583 the Wittelsbach family was given the archbishopric (office that supervises bishops) of Cologne. In 1609 Duke Maximilian I (1573–1651; ruled 1597–1651) was instrumental in the formation of the alliance of Catholic princes known as the Catholic League, becoming its first political and military director. When the Thirty Years' War began in 1618, Maximilian allied himself with his cousin, Holy Roman Emperor Ferdinand II. Maximilian's army of thirty thousand men played an important role in many victories achieved by the empire in the early stage of the war. In 1623 Maximilian was elevated to the status of imperial elector and received the Upper Palatinate. From 1632 until the close of the war in 1648, Bavaria suffered invasion and devastation by Swedish and French armies. At the Treaty of Westphalia (the conference that ended the war), however, Bavarian Wittelsbachs retained the Upper Palatinate and the position as elector.

Bohemia

Bohemia had been part of the Holy Roman Empire since the tenth century, when it was placed under the control of Germany. The country was ruled by kings of the house of Luxembourg from 1310 until 1437. In the early 1400s, Bohemia was the scene of religious revolts that are considered the first stage of the Protestant Reformation. The revolts were led by Hussites, followers of religious reformer Jan Hus (c. 1372–1415). Hus was a Czechoslovakian priest who had attended the Council of Constance, a conference held in 1414 to solve problems in the Roman Catholic Church.

The meeting was called by Sigismund of Luxembourg, who wanted to end the Great Schism (see "Great Schism" in Chapter 1). Sigismund was the king of Hungary (ruled 1387–1437), the king of the Romans (1410–37), and later the Holy Roman emperor (1433–37). The Great Schism was a period of deep divisions within the church, when there were as many as three popes at the same time—one in Rome; one in Avignon, France; and one in Pisa, Italy. Sigismund wanted the papacy to be controlled by a council, not by a pope who made his own decisions. This idea had been suggested years earlier, but it had not been accepted by church officials. Sigismund hoped to get enough backing to accomplish his goals. In 1414 he assembled several important churchmen at the town of Constance in Switzerland. The council met until 1417, when it was decided that all of the existing popes should be removed and a new one elected. Pope Martin V (1368–1431; reigned 1417–31) was then named the only rightful leader of the Roman Catholic faith. The other popes did not want to step down, but none of them had enough support to stay in power. The Great Schism came to an end with the Council of Constance.

Hus becomes Czech hero Although the Council of Constance had ended the Great Schism, it resulted in another serious challenge to the church, which was initiated by Hus. In 1410 Hus had been excommunicated (expelled) from the church. One of his crimes was criticizing the practice of selling indulgences, which were partial pardons of sins in exchange for money. Hus believed that people who purchased indulgences should suffer the full penalty of their actions and should not be allowed to buy God's forgiveness. He claimed that a truly penitent, or sorrowful, soul would be cleansed in purgatory. Indulgences were therefore not only useless but also wrong. Hus's view angered many church leaders and state officials, who often split the money raised by the selling of indulgences. This practice had been especially important during the Great Schism, when various popes were competing for support from monarchs. The monarchs frequently depended on the money to fund their wars or to help finance their kingdoms.

Hus continued to be outspoken in his demands for church reform, and he made many powerful enemies. After being excommunicated in 1410, he retired to the Czech countryside to write. Hus had the support and protection of King Wenceslas (1361–1419; ruled 1378–1419; Holy Roman Emperor 1378–1400) of Bohemia. While in the countryside, Hus composed his most famous work, *De ecclesia,* in which he claimed that Scriptures (text of the Bible), not the pope, had supreme authority over the church. He also wrote that the pope was not a perfect being who was always correct, and that the state had the right and

duty to supervise the church. When Hus was invited to the Council of Constance, he was told that no harm would come to him. Nevertheless, many officials were still angry about his daring to challenge the church. Shortly after arriving in October 1414, Hus was arrested and imprisoned. He was kept in prison until June 1415, at which time he was finally given an opportunity to go before the council. When he tried to explain his views, he was shouted down. A month to the day after his original meeting with the council, Hus was once again given a chance to withdraw his criticism of the church. He refused. He was then stripped of his clerical robes and forced to wear a paper crown painted with three demons and the words "We commit thy soul to the Devil." Hus was led to the town square, where he was burned alive. The members of the council claimed that fire was the only way to cleanse his soul. Hus is regarded as one of the forefathers of the Protestant Reformation.

After Hus's execution, nobles in Bohemia sent an angry letter to the council and Sigismund, protesting the actions against Hus. Sigismund replied that he would eliminate all Hussites. Sigismund and Pope Martin began a crusade against the Hussites, who then retaliated by blaming Sigismund for the death of a Czech hero. Rebellion and chaos soon spread throughout Bohemia and Moravia (now a territory in the Czech Republic), leading to the Hussite Revolt (also called the Hussite Wars). The Hussite Revolt lasted from 1420 until 1434. The Hussites issued their demands to Sigismund and Martin in the Four Articles of Prague (1420). They called for freedom of preaching, limits to property holding by the church, and civil punishment of mortal sin (a sin causing spiritual death), among other religious reforms. The Hussites were led by Bohemian nobleman Jan Žižka (c. 1346–1424), who headed their military efforts even after he was blinded in battle. In 1431 the Council of Basel was called for the purpose of drafting an agreement between the church and the Hussites. The war continued, however, as the Hussites argued among themselves; eventually they split into two factions (opposing sides). Despite this division, Sigismund was unable to achieve victory.

The two Hussite camps continued fighting, with the side known as the Ultraquist Hussites finally winning out in 1434 and ending the hostilities. During peace talks the Ultraquist Hussites demanded that Bohemia and Moravia be granted independence from Germany. They also wanted their own religious practices to be recognized by the Roman Catholic Church. The Council of Basel, not wanting to lose its influence, agreed to these demands. In 1436 the Ultraquist Hussites signed the Compact of Jihlava (also Iglau), in which they agreed to accept Sigismund as king of Bohemia. As a result, Bohemia became independent from Germany. Moravia came under the rule of Bohemia. Most of the political and religious issues involved in the struggle remained unsolved, but the Hussite movement stimulated nationalist sentiments among the Bohemians, checking a previous trend toward Germanization.

The Defenestration of Prague In 1471 Bohemia came under the control of the Jagiellonian (pronounced yag-yeh-LOH-nee-un) dynasty of Hungary, which ruled until 1526 (see "Hungary" section later in this chapter). During the Jagiellonian period the religious situation was tense but quiet. A dramatic change occurred in 1526, when Holy Roman Emperor Ferdinand I, a member of the Habsburg family, was elected king of Hungary and Bohemia. The Protestant Reformation was now spreading from Germany to other parts of Europe, and the Catholic Habsburgs were intolerant of the growing Protestant movement in Bohemia. Tensions between Catholics and Protestants reached a climax in 1609. The conflict arose over two Protestant churches that had been built on Habsburg lands in Bohemia—one in Hrob (Klostergrab) and the other in Broumov (Braunau). The Protestants felt Holy Roman Emperor Rudolf II had given them the right to build the churches in a Letter of Majesty (official order) in 1609. The Habsburg authorities rejected this argument, and in 1617 the churches were ordered closed. The one at Hrob was even torn down. The matter caused such an uproar that a radical wing—a group with extreme political views—of the Bohemian Estates, or representative assembly, staged a revolt against the Habsburgs in 1618. The revolt was led by Count Matthias Thurn, Baron Colona Fels, and Wenceslaus Ruppa.

Although a royal order prohibited Protestants from assembling, Protestant leaders met on May 21, 1618, and continued in session for two days. On May 22, they demanded a redress of grievances over the churches that had been shut down, but the Habsburg government rejected their demands. Thurn, Ruppa, and Fels then planned the murder of the deputy governors of Bohemia, Count Jaroslav Martinitz and Count Wilhelm Slavata. Martinitz and Slavata were leaders of the Catholic, pro-Habsburg faction in the Bohemian Estates. An armed band of more than one hundred Protestants marched to Hradcany Castle in Prague and confronted Martinitz and Slavata. Both officials denied any personal involvement in rejection of the Protestant demands. Heated words were exchanged. Suddenly, Thurn and others stepped forward, seized the two deputy governors, and hurled them through a castle window into the refuse-filled moat forty feet below. Miraculously the victims survived the fall and managed to escape.

This incident is known as the "Defenestration of Prague" ("defenestration" comes from the Latin phrase *de fenestra,* which means "from the window"). It triggered a widespread revolt against the Habsburg regime. Thurn and Ruppa became leaders of a revolutionary government in Bohemia and mobilized fighting forces. In August 1619 Bohemia formed a confederation with Moravia, Silesia, and Lusatia. This confederation arranged a pact of mutual assistance with the Protestant states of Upper and Lower Austria. The Protestant alliance then overthrew Ferdinand, the Catholic king, and replaced him with a Protestant, Frederick V (1596–1632), prince of the Rhenish Palatinate (a region in southwest Germany on the Rhine River).

Frederick's rule lasted only seven months and was known as "the reign of the Winter King." His time on the throne was brief because Holy Roman Emperor Matthias died in March 1619, and Ferdinand was elected to succeed him in August. Ferdinand was determined to put down the Protestant revolt in Bohemia and put the country under Habsburg control again. He defeated the Bohemian army at the Battle of the White Mountain on November 8, 1620, ending Bohemia's bid for independence. Frederick was removed from the throne and replaced with a Catholic, Maximilian I (1573–1651) of Bavaria. German was enforced as the national language of Bohemia. Although fighting ceased for the time being, it later resumed and initiated the Thirty Years' War.

Switzerland

Switzerland became part of the Holy Roman Empire in 1032. In the thirteenth century, it was placed under the Habsburgs, whose harsh domination resulted in the rebellion of several cities. In 1291 an "eternal alliance" was formed between three cantons (provinces) of Switzerland: Schwyz, Uri, and Unterwalden. This agreement was the first step toward forming the alliance called the Swiss Confederation. The Habsburgs invaded the three provinces but were defeated by the Swiss at Morgarten Pass in 1315. By 1353, five other cantons—Luzern, Zürich, Glarus, Zug, and Bern—had joined the confederation. Now unified into a larger force, the cantons won four victories over the Habsburgs (in 1386, 1388, 1476, and 1499) and defeated Charles of Burgundy, whose ambitions threatened their independence until his death in 1477. The confederation continued to grow, and by 1513 it included thirteen cantons as well as several affiliated cities and regions. Switzerland now reached south of the crest of the Alps (a mountain range between France and Italy) to the Ticino River (between Switzerland and Italy). The Swiss also controlled many of the vital passes in the Alps that linked southern and northern Europe.

Confederation weakened by Protestantism

The power of the confederation was undermined by conflicts stemming from the Protestant Reformation. The Reformation started in Switzerland in 1518, when reformer Huldrych Zwingli began to denounce the sale of indulgences by the Roman Catholic Church. Under Zwingli's leadership, the city of Zurich asserted its independence from the church. By 1524 Zwingli was turning Zurich into a Protestant city. Those who disagreed with him were forced either to comply or to leave. As early as 1524, disagreements surfaced among some of Zwingli's friends and followers. Among them were the Anabaptists, who formed a separatist movement, known as the Swiss brethren, which was seen as a threat to the Zwinglians. The Anabaptists believed that "even the atheist had a right to his unbelief as long as he obeyed Civil Law." They also strictly separated the state from the church. One of the main sources of disagreement between Zwinglians and Anabaptists was the Anabaptist concept of Believer's Baptism. (Contrary to both the Protestant and Catholic practice of baptizing children, the Anabaptists asserted that only adults who voluntarily accepted Christianity could be baptized.) A dispute in 1525 led to the suppression of the Anabaptist movement in Zurich and later to the banishment of its members. They were prosecuted, and in 1527 one of their leaders, Felix Mantz, was among those executed.

What had begun as a religious dispute rapidly developed into a force dividing the Swiss Confederation. Zurich, in turn, sought possible allies and defenders of its cause. In 1526 a Catholic-dominated conference was held in Baden. Zwingli himself did not attend because he was concerned for his personal safety. The conference condemned Zwingli's reforms, dealing a blow to his followers in Zurich. Zwingli's absence, in the eyes of his opponents, was considered an act of cowardice.

On January 6, 1528, a public religious debate was held in Bern. It was the largest state of the confederation, which had remained indifferent to the reforms in Zurich. All clergymen from Berne and the Catholic bishops were invited and so were the four bishops of Lausanne, Sion, Basel, and Constance. Many Catholics refused to attend. The debate lasted until the end of January, but the participants could not reach an agreement. It soon became obvious that Zwingli's reforms would be carried out in Berne. Zwingli had reached the summit of his power and influence, and states were looking to him for guidance. By this time, however, Zwingli and Martin Luther were not on friendly terms. Luther was not actively involved in reform efforts and was devoting his time to translating the Bible into German. Zwingli was now leading the challenge to the Catholic Church, but Luther had little regard for Zwingli's abilities as a biblical scholar. Luther was a regular priest who was said to have had a haughty manner when speaking to Zwingli. He thought Zwingli a coarse fanatic trying to show off his knowledge of Greek and Latin because his German was so bad. When they finally met at the Colloquy of Marburg in 1529, on the first day they were said to have parted without shaking hands. Finally, the participants at the conference drew up fifteen articles describing the Protestant faith.

The Kappel Wars

The Marburg meeting took place between the two Kappel Wars. In 1528 Zurich had extended its influence to the territories of Saint Gall and Thurgau and to the Lake of Constance.

In 1529 Zurich declared war on the Catholic military alliance called the Catholic Confederates, and the two armies met near the village of Kappel. The Protestant troops far outnumbered the Catholics. Only a few moments before the actual fighting, the leaders of the opposite sides were called in for peace negotiations. A truce was drawn up and signed by both parties. Yet neither side seemed completely satisfied: the Catholics felt defeated by people they felt were heretics, or those who go against church teachings, and Zurich remained committed to expanding Protestantism.

Soon Protestant opponents of Zwingli joined the Catholic states of Switzerland in resisting reform. Zwingli proposed a quick military campaign to put down opposition once and for all. Yet the Bernese allies interfered, suggesting an economic blockade instead. (A blockade is a ban on trading activity.) The blockade proved very hard on the Catholic Confederates, whose well-being largely depended on prosperous trade in Zurich. The Protestant side suffered as well: by 1531 Zwingli's popularity had begun to diminish as merchants, millers, bakers, and other artisans complained of the damaging effect the blockade had on their trade. The army of the Catholic Confederates gathered near the city of Zug. Hastily, Zurich's troops hurried in from all sides, but on such short notice it was impossible to form orderly units. No time remained to ask the Protestant allies for support. Facing the well-prepared Catholic troops near Kappel in

Religious reformer Huldrych Zwingli's death during the Battle of Kappel. *©Bettmann/Corbis. Reproduced by permission of the Corbis Corporation.*

October 1531, the Protestant army of about 1,500 fought bravely but without a chance of success. After only a few days, the Protestant alliance was defeated. Zurich lost about 500 men in battle, among them its spiritual leader, Huldrych Zwingli.

Calvin makes Geneva a Protestant center

In the meantime, Protestantism continued to spread to other Swiss cities. In 1536 Geneva revolted against the duchy of Savoy, an independent state between Italy and France that controlled the area around Lake Geneva in Switzerland. Geneva refused to acknowledge the authority of its Roman Catholic bishop. That same year the French theologian John Calvin, one of the main leaders of the Reformation, visited Geneva. The local Protestant preacher, Guillaume Farel, persuaded Calvin to stay and drive Catholics out of the city.

Calvin and Farel established their own church, but their methods were extremely strict. They enforced rigid moral codes and implemented Calvin's concept of the "elect," which dictated that only a few people were chosen by God to enter heaven. These

Calvin Stops for a Visit

One evening in June 1536, John Calvin stopped in Geneva, Switzerland, to spend the night. He fully intended to continue on his journey the following day. But the local Protestant preacher, Guillaume Farel, had another idea. He convinced Calvin that it was his duty to God to remain where he was most needed. The task was to expel the remnants of Catholicism from the city, which had recently won its independence from the Catholic Church. Together Farel and Calvin directed the Reformation in Geneva. Within a couple of years, both were expelled for being too strict and for encouraging French immigration. Calvin went to Strasbourg, France, where he taught at an academy, preached, and developed his ideas on the nature of the ideal Christian church. In 1540, while living in Strasbourg, Calvin married Idelette Bure, a widow of one of his converts. She had a son and a daughter from her previous marriage. Unfortunately for the couple, their only child together died shortly after birth in 1542. After Idelette died seven years later, Calvin never remarried. Little is known of their lives together, though Calvin's relations with women were not entirely warm. In fact women were typically the most outspoken opponents of his moral reforms.

the city. Calvin went to teach at a university in Strasbourg, France, where he continued his reform efforts. In 1541, he returned reluctantly to Geneva in response to a call from the floundering Protestant church. After receiving assurances that he would be given the freedom he felt was necessary to build God's kingdom on Earth, he soon organized a highly disciplined social network. Despite considerable opposition within the city, Calvin's influence grew steadily as he defeated theological and political opponents alike. In 1553, Michael Servetus (c. 1511–1553), a Spanish religious philosopher, came to Geneva in spite of Calvin's earlier warnings that he was not welcome. Often called the first Unitarian (a Protestant denomination), Servetus denied the divinity of Christ and the doctrine of the Trinity (the Christian concept of the Father, the Son, and the Holy Spirit). His views alienated him from both Catholics and Protestants. When Calvin recognized his foe sitting within the crowd listening to one of his sermons, he promptly had Servetus arrested and put on trial. As the "Defender of the Faith," Calvin demanded that Servetus be executed. His order was supported by the city government, and on October 27, 1553, Servetus was burned alive for heresy.

Soon Calvin overcame most remaining opposition, and in 1555 his Consistory, a kind of moral court, was accepted and given effective powers by the city. Henceforth, moral discipline was strictly enforced. Taverns were closed and replaced with *abbayes* in which patrons were closely scrutinized

elect few were to guide the majority of other believers to salvation, or forgiveness of sins. After a couple of years Calvin and Farel were expelled from

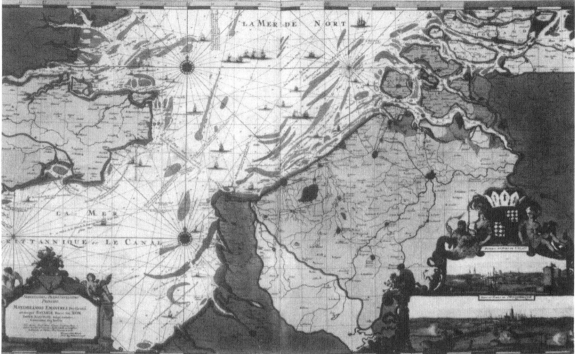

A map of the Netherlands, which came under the control of the house of Habsburg in 1477.
©Historical Picture Archive/Corbis. Reproduced by permission of the Corbis Corporation.

for signs of excessive consumption of alcoholic beverages. Indeed, throughout Geneva, citizens monitored each other's behavior, ready to report any sort of wrongdoing. In 1559 Calvin established the Genevan Academy (now the University of Geneva) for the training of clergymen. Calvin did not limit his reform efforts to Geneva. He was soon spreading the Reform movement abroad, especially within his native France. Under his direction, Geneva became a haven for persecuted Protestants and the unofficial center for growing Protestant movements in countries as far away as Scotland.

During the Thirty Years' War the Swiss cantons remained neutral (they did not fight on either side). Switzerland was recognized as an independent state by the Peace of Westphalia, the treaty that ended the Thirty Years' War in 1648.

The Netherlands

Soon after the disintegration of the Carolingian Empire in 814, several duchies and counties were founded in the Low Countries (the Netherlands, Belgium, and Luxembourg).

With the coming of the Middle Ages, Holland (present-day North and South Holland provinces in the Netherlands) became the most important region. The ancient bishopric of Utrecht (regional capital of the Roman Catholic Church) was another important principality. As the Middle Ages drew to a close, individual cities such as Amsterdam, Haarlem, and Groningen rose to eminence, together with the Duchy of Gelderland. In the fifteenth century, the dukes of Burgundy (a region in France) acquired most of the Low Countries. The Burgundian dynasty came to an end when there were no more male heirs. The Netherlands then came under the control of the house of Habsburg in 1477, when Mary of Burgundy married Archduke Maximilian I of Austria.

Their grandson, Charles, became King Charles I of Spain in 1516 and Holy Roman Emperor Charles V in 1519. In 1547 he united the Netherlands and Austria. Two years later he joined the Netherlands with Spain. By the end of his reign in 1555, Charles was master of the Low Countries. His son and successor, Philip II of Spain, concentrated his efforts on increasing the power of Spain (see "Spain" in Chapter 3). To bring the Low Countries under his direct control, he tried to stamp out the rising force of Protestantism and suppressed the political, economic, and religious liberties long cherished by the population. As a result, both Roman Catholics and Protestants rebelled against him under the leadership of William the Silent, prince of Orange (1533–1584; ruled 1579–84), who had inherited territories in the Low Countries.

William earns nickname "the Silent"

William was born at Dillenburg in the German principality of Nassau and originally raised as a Lutheran. He inherited the territories of Orange and Nassau at the age of eleven. Because of the importance of the inheritance, Charles V insisted that the young prince of Orange be raised as a Catholic. Moving to Breda and then Brussels, William was raised at the court of Mary of Hungary, the regent of the Low Countries. He also served as a page, or attendant, in the court of Charles V. William was taught French and Dutch and readily adopted the customs of the Dutch people. The teachings of the Christian humanist, Desiderius Erasmus (1466–1636) of Rotterdam, held particular significance for the young prince and later played a large part in the religious toleration for which William was renowned.

At the age of eighteen William married Countess Anne of Egmont, gaining several additional territories in the Netherlands. He enjoyed considerable favor at the court during the reigns of both Charles V and Philip II in Brussels. In 1559 the Treaty of Cateau-Cambrésis ended the Italian Wars and made Spain a major power in Europe. Philip then named William to his prestigious Council of State and the Order of the Golden Fleece. In 1561 Philip appointed William as *stadholder* (governor and captain-general) in the important provinces of Holland, Zeeland, Utrecht, and Franche-Comté. Soon serious dissension arose in the Netherlands. Two issues were of paramount importance: religion and the king's rigid policies. Philip's rule contrasted sharply with the relative independence allowed the Dutch nobles under Charles V. By 1565 the Dutch opposition was led by a faction, or small group, of low-ranking nobles called the Gueux (pronounced GOH), or Beggars, which was organized with William's assistance. Unlike the higher-ranking nobles, they were more inclined toward violence as a possible solution for their grievances. While most of the higher-ranking nobles quickly divorced themselves from the Gueux, William retained his ties to them.

Despite William's pleas for moderation, open revolt against Spain erupted in August 1566. Frenzied mobs attacked Catholic churches throughout the provinces, smashing religious idols and vandalizing church property. Philip responded by summoning the famous Spanish general, Fernando Álvarez de Toledo (1507–1582), the duke of Alba, to crush the revolt. William himself quelled a Calvinist riot in Antwerp (now in Belgium), Europe's richest city. He then closed the city's gates and denied access to both the rebels and the king's forces. In 1567 William withdrew to his family's estates at Dillenburg, where he gained his famous nickname "the Silent" by remaining neutral in the conflict.

William leads independence movement Alba created the Council of

Erasmus: Christian Humanist

The teachings of Dutch humanist Desiderius Erasmus had a profound impact on William I of Orange, who led the independence movement in the Netherlands. In 1516 Erasmus published *Novum instrumentum,* an edition of the New Testament (the second part of the Bible) that featured texts in Greek and revised Latin side by side. The first published Greek text, Erasmus's New Testament was a landmark for scholars and reformers. It paved the way for the literary and educational classics of other Christian humanists, scholars who believed that individual Christians could rely on their intellect to understand the Bible.

Another dimension to Erasmus's writing also appeared in 1516. He was serving briefly as an adviser to the future Holy Roman Emperor, sixteen-year-old Charles V. Following current humanist practice, Erasmus prepared *Institutio principis Christiani,* a guide for educating princes to rule justly. In 1517 he composed *Querela pacis,* condemning war as an instrument of tyranny. He warned rulers to fulfill their obligation to preserve Christian harmony.

Troubles to arrest, try, and execute religious "heretics." It came to be known as the Council of Blood after Alba executed as many as twelve thousand people. William himself was summoned to appear before the Council of Troubles, but he refused to appear. Alba

William III, prince of Orange, gained his famous nickname "the Silent" by remaining neutral in the conflict between Dutch nobles and Philip II, king of Spain. *Reproduced by permission of Hulton Archive.*

the only way he could receive support from French, German, and English Protestants. In 1572 he succeeded in convincing Queen Elizabeth I of England to send troops and money to help the Dutch Protestant rebels (see "England" in Chapter 3).

In 1572 Calvinist Holland and Zeeland joined the rebellion and called for the prince of Orange to lead them. In accepting leadership, William insisted upon equal protection for both the Catholic and the Calvinist faiths. William's brother, Louis of Nassau (1538–1574), supported the rebels by moving into the southeastern provinces at Mons. Alba rushed to confront him. William meanwhile marched virtually uncontested into the Brabant (a region in the southern Netherlands and northern Belgium) and captured several strategic towns. By late 1572, however, Alba had overcome both Louis and William at Mons. The prince of Orange then moved to the northern provinces to reorganize his forces. In the meantime, Philip had become alarmed at Alba's brutality, so he recalled the general to Spain in 1573.

William formally became a Calvinist, but he would not go along with the Calvinist provinces in declaring Catholicism illegal. In 1576 he took control of the States-General and arranged for acceptance of the Pacification of Ghent. This agreement united the seventeen provinces of the Netherlands and supported religious moderation. Philip then installed his half-brother, Don John of Austria (1547–1578), as the new ruler in the

then confiscated William's possessions and deported one of William's sons to Spain. This harsh treatment pushed the prince of Orange into becoming a rebel. William organized an army and marched on the Low Countries in 1568. Alba met and crushed William's forces at the Ems River. The prince of Orange then fled to sanctuary in a Huguenot (Calvinist) region of France. Although he despised the strictness of the Calvinist faith, he gradually came to realize that accepting Calvinism was

Low Countries. Don John was not overly concerned with suppressing the revolt because he was preoccupied with planning an invasion of England to restore Catholicism in that country (see "Spain" in Chapter 3). Upon Don John's death in 1578, Alessandro Farnese (1545–1592), the duke of Parma, became governor-general of the Netherlands and began subduing the southern provinces. In 1579 the Treaty of Arras united the southern provinces under Spanish rule and Catholicism. William then agreed to the Union of Utrecht, which united the northern provinces under the Calvinist faith. William still wanted to unite all of the Dutch provinces, so he turned for assistance to Alençon, the duke of Anjou, heir to the French throne. Alençon's Catholic troops then joined the Dutch Protestants.

Dutch gain freedom

In 1580 Farnese captured more than thirty rebel towns along with the city of Antwerp, bringing Holland and Zeeland to the brink of defeat. Philip issued a royal proclamation condemning the prince of Orange as an outlaw and the instigator of trouble in the Netherlands. William responded by accusing Philip of incest (having sexual relations with a family member), adultery (having sexual relations outside of marriage), and the murder of his son and third wife. On July 10, 1584, a Catholic extremist shot and killed William of Orange in his home on the Delft River. William's son Maurice (1567–1625; ruled 1584–1625) became governor of the republic. He carried on a successful campaign against Spain. Final recognition of Dutch independence by the Spanish government was not obtained until the Peace of Westphalia, at the end of the Thirty Years' War, in 1648. The southern provinces had remained loyal to Spain and to the Roman Catholic Church, and they were thereafter known as the Spanish Netherlands.

In the seventeenth century, the United Provinces became the leading commercial and maritime power in the world. Its prosperity was nourished by Dutch settlements and colonies in the East Indies, India, South Africa, the West Indies, South America, and elsewhere. The government was oligarchic (ruled by a small group of leaders) but based on republican and federative principles, principles that acknowledge the government's responsibility to citizens, and the citizens' right to have a voice in their government. The Dutch were noted for their religious freedom. They welcomed religious refugees, Spanish and Portuguese Jews, French Huguenots, and English Pilgrims. Arts, sciences, literature, and philosophy flourished alongside trade and banking.

Scandinavia

The Scandinavian countries— Sweden, Denmark, and Norway—were politically united by the Union of Kalmar in 1397. Under this arrangement Scandinavian noblemen, who had similar languages and cultures, agreed to choose their kings by elections. They also agreed to fight off the efforts of German princes to gain influence over them. The Union frequently broke down throughout the 1400s, but it continued to function into the 1500s.

Denmark

In the late twelfth and early thirteenth centuries, Denmark conquered most of the southern coastal region around the Baltic Sea. The Danes (the name given to the people of Denmark) established a prosperous kingdom that was twice the size of present-day Denmark. During this time merchants and craftsmen and a number of guilds gained political power. A growing discord developed between the Danish king and the nobility. In 1282 noblemen forced King Erik V (c. 1249–1286; ruled 1259–86) to sign a charter (a document that serves as the basis of government) that made the Danish ruler subordinate, or answerable, to law and created an assembly of noblemen called the Danehof. A temporary decline in Danish dominance came after the death of King Christopher II (1276–1332; ruled 1320–26, 1330–32) in 1332. During the reign of Christopher's son Valdemar IV Atterdag (c. 1320–1375; ruled 1340–75), Denmark once again became the leading force on the Baltic Sea. However, the Hanseatic League, a commercial federation of European cities, controlled trade.

Union of Kalmar collapses In 1380 Denmark and Norway were joined in a union under one king, Olaf II (1370–1387), a grandson of Valdemar IV. After Olaf's death in 1387, his mother, Margaret (1353–1412), became the ruler. In 1389 she obtained the crown of Sweden, and in 1397 she formed the Union of Kalmar, which united Denmark, Sweden, and Norway. Denmark was the dominant power, but Swedish noblemen repeatedly sought independence. The Kalmar Union lasted until 1523, when Sweden won its freedom in a revolt against Christian II (see "Sweden" section later in this chapter). The revolt was led by Gustav Vasa, who was elected king of Sweden as Gustav I in that year. Also in 1523, Christian II was driven from the Danish throne and replaced by Frederick I.

A period of unrest followed as Lübeck, the strongest Hanseatic city, interfered in Danish politics. With help from Gustav I, Lübeck's interference was ended and Christian II's successor, Christian III (1503–1559; ruled 1534–59), consolidated his power as king of Denmark. Christian III supported the Reformation, and during his reign the Lutheran Church was established as the state religion. At this time the Danish kings began to treat Norway as a province rather than as a separate kingdom. Denmark's commercial and political rivalry with Sweden for domination of the Baltic Sea resulted in conflicts that are sometimes called the Nordic Seven Years' War (1563–70) and the War of Kalmar (1611–13).

In the 1620s King Christian IV (1557–1648; ruled 1588–1648) drew Sweden into the Thirty Years's War when he supported the Protestant cause in Germany. Continued rivalry between Denmark and Sweden for primacy led to the Swedish Wars (1643–45 and 1657–60). Denmark was badly defeated and lost several of its Baltic islands and all of its territory on the Scandinavian Peninsula except Norway. Economic setbacks resulting from these defeats had a widespread impact in Denmark. The growing commercial class, which was hard hit by the loss of foreign markets and trade, joined with the monarchy to curtail the power and privileges of the nobility. In 1660 King Frederick III (1609–1670; ruled 1648–70), son of Christian IV, overthrew the Council of the Realm (the governing assembly made up of noblemen). The monarchy, which until then had been largely dependent for its political power on the noblemen, was made hereditary. In 1661 the monarchy became absolute, that is, the king had the sole authority to make and administer laws. The tax-exemption privileges of the nobility were ended, and nobles were replaced by commoners in the government.

Sweden

The Union of Kalmar was brought to an end by a conflict between the Danish king Christian II and the popular Swedish leader Sten Sture (called the Younger; c. 1492–1520). In 1520, after a series of battles, Christian invaded Sweden and seized the throne. Sten Sture had already been acting as an independent monarch of Sweden, but he ruled on behalf of the Danish king. Christian was eager to consoli-

Gustav Vasa was elected king of Sweden after the Danish king Christian initiated the "bloodbath of Stockholm." *Reproduced by permission of Archive Photos, Inc.*

date his power by uniting Denmark and Sweden, so in 1517 he bypassed Sten Sture and attacked Sweden directly. Sten Sture defeated Christian II on the battlefield of Brännkyrka in 1518. Among his troops was the courageous soldier Gustav Vasa (1496–1560). In the treaty that followed this conflict, Sten Sture handed over Gustav to the Danish king as a pledge of his good intentions. Christian took Gustav back to a mild form of captivity in Denmark. When Gustav heard news of renewed fighting between Denmark and

Sweden, he escaped and made his way to the port of Lübeck, a wealthy trading city in the Hanseatic League. He wanted to go back and fight with his countrymen, so he obtained financial assistance for his cause from wealthy merchants in Lübeck. In 1520 Sten Sture was killed in battle. Christian then seized the Swedish city of Stockholm, and on November 8, 1520, he presided over the "bloodbath of Stockholm." During a rampage Danish soldiers chopped off the heads of nearly one hundred prominent Swedes who had supported Sture. The massacre continued in the Swedish provinces in the weeks that followed.

Gustav Vasa gains power The surviving Swedes called upon Gustav Vasa to be their new leader. Gustav regained control of the country in 1523 and was elected king. He gave major trading advantages to Lübeck in exchange for its support in the war. Although Gustav was obligated to Lübeck, he also made trading agreements with Holland and Prussia in 1526 in an effort to expand Sweden's own trading networks. He saw the advantage of adopting Protestantism as the national religion. Gustav had many debts from the war with Denmark, but he had hardly any money to repay them (at that time, monarchs financed wars themselves). In contrast, the Catholic Church had significant wealth, receiving almost five times as much as the king's income in tithes (one-tenth of church members' income) alone. It also owned estates and castles and had other forms of wealth in abundance.

Gustav was determined to lay his hands on this wealth, so he began to support Lutheranism as a way to break the power of the Catholic Church. In 1527 he called a meeting of the Swedish Estates (assembly of nobles, middle-class citizens called burghers, clergymen, and peasants) in the city of Västerâs. The Estates agreed to let Gustav take over the church. Gustav's men entered churches and took gold and silver plates, candlesticks, and other objects that could be converted into money. The king also seized estates, castles, and lands that had been church property for centuries. This policy led to an uprising of Catholic nobles and peasants in the southwestern provinces of Sweden in 1529, but Gustav soon outwitted the rebels and executed their ringleaders.

Gustav's next challenge was paying off huge debts to the city of Lübeck, but he resisted because he wanted to break Lübeck's trading monopoly. In 1534, after extensive negotiations, Lübeck declared war on Denmark and Sweden. Gustav responded by again allying with Frederick I of Denmark. The Swedish navy won victories in 1535, inaugurating the growth of Swedish naval and maritime power. In 1539, Gustav declared the Lutheran Church to be the national religion. Five years later the Swedish Estates granted Gustav's request to make his elective monarchy into a hereditary one. They also approved his plan to create a citizen-army that would replace hired soldiers. Thus a Vasa dynasty was established and Sweden became the first country in Europe to have a permanent army composed of its own farmer-soldiers. From that time until his death in 1560, Gustav's throne rested secure. His son, who took the name Erik XIV (1533–1577; ruled 1560–68), was able to carry on the expansion of Swedish power.

In 1587 Sigismund Vasa (1566–1632), heir to the Swedish throne, accepted the invitation of the Polish nobility to be their king (ruled 1587–1632). A convert to Roman Catholicism, Sigismund simultaneously held the crowns of Sweden and Poland after 1592. He faced powerful opposition in staunchly Lutheran Sweden. The religious issue developed into a civil war between Catholics and Protestants. In 1600 Sigismund's uncle, Karl IX, took the throne of Sweden away from Sigismund. In 1611 Karl's son, Gustav II Adolf (ruled 1611–32), became king at the age of seventeen. As a condition for ruling under the legal age of eighteen, he accepted limitations on his royal powers known as the Charter of 1611. He promised to give the nobility a monopoly over state offices and to govern with the advice of the council and the constitutional bodies—the Diet (law-making body) and the Estates.

Gustav II Adolf: A great king Gustav is known as one of the great Swedish kings. His reign brought higher standards of government—better administration and tax collection—as well as the rule of law and educational advancement. In 1600 Sweden did not have a central government. By 1626 it boasted the most efficient and well-or-dered government in Europe. Gustav was also one of the world's leading military geniuses. He is credited with creating the first modern army. During his reign he defeated Poland and conquered Livonia. By winning a war with Russia he also acquired Ingermanland (a region in northwest European Russia) and Karelia (a region in northeast Europe between Finland and Russia). In 1620 Sweden entered the Thirty Years'War to join France against the Holy Roman Empire and the Catholic Habsburgs. At this time Sweden was the foremost Protestant power on the European continent. Although Gustav was killed at the Battle of Lützen in 1632, his policies were carried on during the reign of his daughter Christina (1626–1689; ruled 1632–54). She was assisted by his prime minister, Axel Oxenstierna (1583–1654).

Under the terms of the Peace of Westphalia (1648), which ended the Thirty Years' War, Sweden acquired a large part of Pomerania, the island of Rügen, Wismar, the sees of Bremen and Verden, and other German territory. (A see is the seat of a bishop's office.) This acquisition entitled the Swedish sovereign to three votes in the diet of the Holy Roman Empire. Sweden then became the greatest power in the Baltic area. In 1654 Queen Christina abdicated, or formally gave up the throne, naming her cousin Charles X Gustav (1622–1660) as her successor. She lived the rest of her life in Rome. Charles declared war on Poland, initiating the conflict known as the First Northern War (1655–60). Sweden was victorious

The first modern army

King Gustav II Adolf is credited with creating the first modern army. By 1630 his Swedish army had evolved into the premier fighting force throughout the world. Gustav rejected the traditional method of massing soldiers into square groups and sending them to confront the enemy. Instead he introduced linear formations, whereby the infantry (foot soldiers) marched in several ranks (long parallel lines) onto the battlefield. He trained his men to move rapidly according to a specific tactical plan. Another innovation was the use of musketeers (soldiers carrying large pistols called muskets), who were followed by pikemen (soldiers carrying long spears with sharp points). To increase firepower and intimidate the enemy, Gustav integrated easily movable artillery pieces (weapons such as cannons) into the formations of soldiers, employing various weapons in coordinated functions during battle. He also made effective use of the cavalry (soldiers mounted on horses), a tactic he had learned from Polish generals when he fought against Poland.

Gustav would start a battle by sending in lines of musketeers, who advanced in a "rolling barrage" toward the enemy. The artillery pieces would provide additional weapons support to the muske-

teers. Next, the pikemen rushed forward to open gaps in the enemy line. Finally, the cavalry would move in to complete the combined arms attack. Swift mobility on the battlefield demanded incessant training and a high degree of organization. Modern military organizations—companies, battalions, brigades—and the basic chain of command originated with Gustav.

Gustav developed the first professional army. Officers were carefully nurtured by Gustav and were expected to show initiative. The nucleus of the army—Swedish and Finnish regiments—came from a system of national conscription (the requirement of all men above a certain age to serve in the military), which was unique to Sweden. Strict discipline was based on Gustav's "Articles of War," which forbade swearing, blasphemy (uttering oaths against God), drunkenness, and fornication (having sexual relations). A mixture of Lutheranism and the leadership of Gustav inspired the officers and men to fight for their country. With prayers twice a day and a chaplain, or religious adviser, in every company, the Swedish army brought a new spirit to war in Europe. In tactics, organization, and spirit, Gustav's army ushered in the era of modern warfare.

and, in 1660, under the terms of a treaty called the Peace of Oliva, Poland formally gave the province of Livonia to Sweden. Charles invaded

Denmark twice in 1658, regaining provinces in southern Sweden that Denmark had acquired in the sixteenth century.

Hungary

The region that now comprises Hungary has a complex history. Once a part of the ancient Roman province of Pannonia, it was occupied by the Germans, the Huns, the Avars (an Asian people), the Moravians (a Slavic tribe), the Franks (people from the region that is now France), and the Magyars (pronounced MOHD-yahrz; a tribe that originated in eastern Europe). In 955 the Magyars were defeated by the Saxon king Otto I, who became Holy Roman Emperor in 962. The Magyars maintained friendly relations with the Holy Roman Empire, however, and Christianity and Western culture began to spread into Hungary. In 975 the Hungarian duke Géza was converted to Christianity. His son Stephen I (977–1038) was formally recognized as king of Hungary by Pope Sylvester II in 1001 or 1002. A new era began during Stephen's reign. Christianity became the official religion, the government was centralized, and the country was divided into counties. For many centuries most of the burden of labor and taxation was imposed on non-Magyar people, who were treated as inferior. When Stephen died in 1038 there was no direct heir to the throne. Struggles for the throne and revolts by non-Christians caused instability in the country over the next three centuries.

In 1308 Charles Robert of Anjou (1288–1342; ruled 1308–42) became king of Hungary as Charles I and established the Angevin dynasty. Ruling until 1342, Charles restored order, limited the power of noblemen, and consolidated Hungarian territory. He also incorporated Bosnia and part of Serbia into Hungary. By marrying Elizabeth, the sister of Kazimierz III, king of Poland, he extended Hungarian control into Poland. Upon Robert's death in 1342, his son Louis I (1326–1382; ruled 1370–82) was crowned king of Hungary and Poland. During Louis's reign Hungary acquired new territory through a series of wars, becoming one of the largest kingdoms in Europe. Louis further limited the power of noblemen and promoted the development of commerce, science, and industry. In his last years as king the Ottoman Turks moved onto the Balkan Peninsula. They took control of several provinces in the southern part of Hungary, the buffer zone between Europe and the Ottoman Empire. Louis's successor, Sigismund, launched a crusade, or holy war, against the Ottomans, but he was defeated in 1396. Hungary endured numerous other setbacks, including defeats by the Venetians and struggles with the Hussites, religious reformers in neighboring Bohemia (see "Bohemia" section previously in this chapter). In 1433 Sigismund became Holy Roman Emperor (ruled 1410–37) and carried out a persecution campaign against the Hussites.

Hunyadi is national hero

Sigismund was followed as king of Hungary and Holy Roman Emperor by his son-in-law, Albert II, a member of the Habsburg family. Albert was killed in a battle with the Turks in 1439. Hungary was saved from Ottoman domination by the military leader János Hunyadi (c. 1407–1456), who is now considered a national hero in Hungary. Hunyadi defeated the Ottomans when they attacked the Hungarian city of Belgrade in 1456. Despite strong opposition from supporters of Holy Roman Emperor Frederick III, Hunyadi's son Matthias I Corvinus (1443–1490; ruled 1458–90) was elected king in 1458. Matthias was one of the greatest rulers of his time. He initiated government reforms, formed a standing army, and supported commercial and cultural development. An able military leader, he took Austria from the Habsburgs in the 1480s and moved his residence to Vienna. He acquired other territory, including Moravia, Silesia, and Lusatia. These acquisitions made Hungary the strongest kingdom of central Europe. After the death of Matthias in 1490, noblemen regained the status they had held under feudalism, a change that led to strife among social classes in Hungary, including a peasant rebellion. General political chaos intensified during the first two decades of the sixteenth century, making Hungary unable to defend itself against foreign invaders. In August 1521 an Ottoman army under Sultan Süleyman I (pronounced seu-lay-MAHN; c. 1494–1566; ruled 1520–66) captured Belgrade and Sabac (both now in Serbia), the chief strongholds of the kingdom in the south. In 1526 Süleyman crushed the Hungarian army at Mohacs, a plain in southern Hungary.

Süleyman crushes Hungary

The Battle of Mohacs had its roots in the late 1400s, when the Habsburg dynasty set out to create a world empire. After forming marriage alliances with Burgundy and Spain, the Habsburgs in 1515 concluded a similar union with the Jagiellonian dynasty (see "Poland" section later in this chapter). Two marriages were actually involved, but the most important was the union between Ferdinand I of Habsburg and Anne Jagiello, sister of the future Jagiellonian king Louis II (1506–1526; ruled 1516–26). This union was designed to pave the way for Habsburg control of Bohemia and Hungary in the event of the extinction of the male Jagiellonian line.

By the time the marriage took place in 1521, war had broken out between the major European powers, France and the Habsburgs. King Francis I of France (see "France" in Chapter 3) and Holy Roman Emperor Charles V had been rivals since Charles had defeated Francis in the contest for emperor. They had met in battle on several fronts in western Europe. Meanwhile in the East, Süleyman was about to capture the city of Belgrade, the gateway to Hungary and to the Austrian states to the north. In addition, the Lutheran revolt was sweeping the Holy Roman Empire. These problems forced Charles V to divide his vast holdings with his brother Ferdinand, who received Habsburg possessions in Austria. By 1526 Charles had triumphed over Francis. Francis then formed an alliance with Süleyman, which was known among Christian Europeans as "the sacrilegious union of the Lily and the Crescent." In other words, they considered this an affront to the Christian God because the Christian nation of France (whose symbol was the lily) had joined forces with Muslims (whose symbol was the crescent), whom Christians regarded as pagans (those who have no religion). For the first time, though not the last, Europe witnessed the union of France and the Ottomans against their common enemy, the Habsburgs.

Süleyman tried to come to the assistance of France in the French effort to drive the Habsburgs out of Italy (see "Charles VIII launches Italian Wars" in Chapter 3). When Hungary refused to grant him free passage through its territory, he directed his wrath against that country instead. Süleyman set out from Constantinople (now Istanbul, Turkey) in April 1526 at the head of some two hundred thousand men. Among them were the sultan's elite troops, the Janissaries (*Yeniçeri,* meaning "new army" in Turkish), a highly skilled unit composed of non-Turks. His vast army moved slowly northward until, in mid-August, they stood some thirty miles from the plain of Mohacs in southern Hungary. Awaiting the Ottomans was the disorganized Christian army of some twenty-six thousand Hungarians and assorted allies, under the unsteady leadership of King Louis II. In a battle that lasted for only an hour and a half, the Ottomans wiped out the Hungarian army. Hungary was devastated by this loss. After his army captured the city of Buda on September 10, 1526, Süleyman withdrew from Hungary.

Hungary divided

The misery visited upon the Hungarian people by the invading

 The Battle of Mohacs

The Battle of Mohacs was a conflict between the twenty-six-thousand-man Christian army of Hungary and two hundred thousand Muslim troops of the Ottoman Empire. The Hungarians were led by King Louis II, and Ottoman forces were commanded by Sultan Süleyman. The battle took place on August 29, 1526, and lasted an hour and a half. Within that short period of time, the Ottoman Turks decimated the Hungarian army. At the outset of the fray, the Hungarian cavalry broke the Turkish center, only to be held up by the Sultan's elite Janissaries. Meanwhile, other strong Turkish units surrounded the Christian army and annihilated it. More than twenty thousand Hungarians perished. No prisoners were taken, and few men escaped. Louis drowned in a stream while fleeing the field. In following up his victory, Süleyman mercilessly ravaged the countryside, wiping out a Hungarian force of some twenty-five thousand peasants. He temporarily occupied Buda, the capital of the country. On the homeward march to Constantinople a few weeks later, his troops took two hundred thousand men, women, and children to be sold into slavery.

Turks was matched only by the political chaos that ensued in Hungary after their departure. Süleyman had not intended to make the country part of his empire, but instead planned to retain it as a dependent state. But Ferdinand now asserted his claims as a Habsburg to the vacated thrones of Bohemia and Hungary. For more than 150 years after the defeat at Mohacs, Hungary was the scene of almost continuous conflict. The Habsburg Holy Roman emperors seized control of the western portion of their former kingdom, while the Ottomans took over the central region. Groups of noblemen, especially Magyars in Transylvania, strived to keep the Habsburgs and the Ottomans from conquering all of Hungary. The Magyars had abandoned the Catholic Church during the Protestant Reformation, offending the Catholic Habsburgs. After the middle of the sixteenth century and the beginning of the Counter Reformation (attempts to reform the Catholic Church from within), confrontations between the Protestant Magyars and the Catholic Habsburgs became increasingly violent. At the end of the conflict called the Long War (1593–1606), Holy Roman Emperor Rudolf II was forced to grant the Magyars of Transylvania political and religious autonomy, or independence. Transylvania became the center of Protestantism in eastern Europe. During the Thirty Years' War, Transylvania sided with France and Sweden against the Habsburgs. At first they were led by Gabriel Bethlen (1580–1629), prince of Transylvania (1613–29) and king of Hungary (1620–21). In 1630 Bethlen was succeeded as prince by George I Rákóczi (1593–1648; ruled 1630–48), who fought against Habsburg domination of western Hungary. In alliance with the Swedes and the French, Rákóczi invaded Austrian territory in 1644. Emperor Ferdinand III was forced to meet many

of Rákóczi's demands, which included freedom of religion for all Hungarians under Habsburg rule.

George II Rákóczi (1621–1660; ruled 1648–60) became the next prince of Transylvania. During his reign the Ottomans expanded their control into Transylvania. In the meantime, the Habsburgs had sent Catholic missionaries into their part of Hungary, and many people returned to the Roman Catholic Church. Repressive measures were then taken against Protestants. These actions led to an uprising headed by Count Imre Thököly (1657–1705), who won a series of victories over the forces of Emperor Leopold I. In 1682 Thököly obtained military support from the Ottomans, but Leopold's armies succeeded in driving the Ottomans from most of Hungary and defeating Thököly's troops. Leopold punished the rebel leaders and forced the Hungarian legislature to give the crown of Hungary forever to the house of Habsburg. Under the Treaty of Karlowitz in 1699, Transylvania was granted to the Habsburgs and the Ottomans kept only the Hungarian Banat (a region in southern Hungary), which they had lost nineteen years earlier.

Poland

The country now known as Poland was created by rulers of the Piast dynasty around the middle of the tenth century. In 999 the Piast ruler Boleslaw I (c. 966–1025; ruled 992–1025) established Poland as a Christian country. Under Casimir III

(1310–1370; ruled 1333–70), the last of the Piast rulers, Poland reached its height as a nation. Casimir made peace with the Teutonic Knights, added Galicia (a former territory in east central Europe) to the Polish realm, and welcomed Jewish refugees who were expelled from Spain (see "Spain" in Chapter 3). He established a system of laws, centralized the government, and founded a university at Kraków (also Cracow) in 1364. In 1386 Poland was united with Lithuania when Jagiello, grand duke of Lithuania, became the king of Poland. Jagiello ruled Poland as Ladislas II (1351–1434; ruled 1386–1434) and started the Jagiellonian dynasty. Jagiellonian territory extended from the Baltic Sea to the Black Sea, encompassing territories in central Europe, notably West Prussia and Pomerania. The combined forces of the union annihilated the Teutonic Knights (a German military religious order founded in 1190) in 1410, at the Battle of Grunewald. In order to preserve the union during the reign of Sigismund II Augustus (1520–1572; ruled 1548–72), the last of the Jagiellonians, provisions were made for a monarch to be elected by a single parliament (called the *Sejm*) for Poland and Lithuania. The country was officially called the Commonwealth (*Rzeczpospolita*).

Sigismund Augustus was the only son of Sigismund I Stary (1467–1548; ruled 1506–48) and Bona Sforza. Sigismund I Stary is often considered the father of the Polish Renaissance. Bona Sforza was from the Sforza family, great patrons of the arts in Milan, Italy

Sigismund I Supports Renaissance

Sigismund I Stary brought important Renaissance artists to Kraków, the capital of Poland and Lithuania. He had stayed at his brother Wadislav's court in Bohemia from 1490 until 1493, where he could have come into contact with Italian art and culture. Sigismund initiated many major architectural and sculpture projects that used Italian styles. Even before taking the Polish throne in 1506, he may have called Francesco Fiorentino (died 1516), a stonemason from Florence, to Kraków. Fiorentino designed the tomb of Sigismund's older brother, King Jan Olbracht, which was the first major work in Poland to exhibit the new Italian style. Sigismund I also commissioned German, Polish, and Dutch craftsmen to create paintings and decorative artworks.

(see "Milan" in Chapter 2). The young Sigismund Augustus therefore grew up in a Renaissance atmosphere. Tutored by the finest Polish and Italian humanist scholars, he quickly learned to appreciate art, literature, and architecture. Wasting little time, his ambitious mother nurtured him to become king. By the age of two, he was elected the future grand duke of Lithuania. By the age of nine, in 1529, he was officially recognized as the future king of Poland. Following his election, Sigismund Augustus moved to Wilno and began his reign as the Grand Duke of Lithuania. Thus, for nearly two decades there were two

King Sigismunds—the father, Sigismund I, in Kraków and the son, Sigismund II Augustus, in Wilno. This dual kingship remained in place to insure that Sigismund Augustus would face no opposition from the Polish magnates (high-ranking noblemen) of the Sejm and to assure his ascension to both the Polish and Lithuanian thrones. With the death of Sigismund I in 1548, Sigismund Augustus took control of both states.

Last of the Jagiellonians

Sigismund Augustus is best known today as the last of the Jagiellonians. He did not have any children, so the dynasty came to an end when he died. According to historical accounts, Sigismund's mother poisoned his first two wives because they did not produce an heir. In 1553 Sigismund was married for a third time, to his first wife's sister, Princess Katherine of Habsburg. The marriage was a catastrophe from the start. Soon after the ceremony a frightened Sigismund learned first-hand that Katherine was subject to epileptic episodes (known as seizures; a disorder caused by disturbances in the central nervous system); thereafter he avoided any intimacy with her. Queen Bona did not remain in Poland long enough to decide whether Katherine should be poisoned. In 1556 Bona retired from Polish political life and returned to her native Italy. Since Sigismund could not take another wife, no Jagiellonian heir could be born to take the Polish throne.

When Sigismund became king, the noblemen expected him to quickly enact much-needed political and social reforms. To their disappointment, the reforms were not realized until late in Sigismund's reign. Despite Sigismund's numerous failures and countless conflicts with the nobles of both Poland and Lithuania, he ultimately secured his place in history with the Union of Lublin. Signed near the end of his reign on July 1, 1569, in the Polish town of Lublin, the act bound all Polish and Lithuanian lands together under a single constitution (system of laws). This agreement formed the republic known as the Polish-Lithuanian Commonwealth. The Union of Lublin not only joined the two states but also provided for a system of government. Following 1569, the king of Poland also held the office of grand duke of Lithuania and governed both states as one nation. The king would rule from the new Polish capital of Warsaw and be elected by a joint Polish-Lithuanian Sejm.

Dissent brings decline

The sixteenth century marked the golden age of Polish literature and scholarship. Protestantism also gained many converts among the nobility in the mid-1500s, but it ceased to be significant after 1600. Poland began to decline when a series of political reforms resulted in noblemen gaining influence and power at the expense of the king. Meeting in the Sejm, they adopted a practice whereby a single dissenting voice was sufficient to prevent the passage of laws. The nobility imposed such far-reaching limitations upon the monarchy that national unity could not be maintained. The nation was further weakened by internal disorders, such as the Cossack and peasant uprising (1648–49). Led by Ukrainian independence leader Bohdan Khmelnytsky (c. 1595–1657), this revolt protested against Polish domination of the Ukraine. It was particularly devastating to Polish Jews, many of whom had served as agents of the nobility in administering Ukrainian lands. In 1683 Polish and German troops led by Polish king John III Sobieski (1629–1696; ruled 1674–96) rescued Vienna, Austria, from a Turkish siege. This victory halted the Muslim threat to Christian nations in central Europe. But Poland fared poorly in wars with Sweden, Russia, and other states. A Russian, Prussian, and Austrian agreement in 1772 led to the division of Polish territory. By 1795 Poland was no longer an independent state. Galicia was ruled by Austria-Hungary, northwestern Poland by Prussia, and the Ukraine and eastern and central Poland by Russia.

5 | Martin Luther: Founder of Lutheranism

Martin Luther (1483–1546) is one of the most important figures in the history of Christianity (a religion founded by Jesus of Nazareth, also called Jesus Christ). Luther is credited with starting the Protestant Reformation, a movement to reform the Roman Catholic Church (a Christian faith based in Rome, Italy) that resulted in a worldwide revolution. Before turning to how Luther sparked the Reformation, however, it is necessary to consider the state of the Catholic Church in the early 1500s, when Luther called for reforms. By this time the church had dominated Europe for more than eight hundred years. The pope, the supreme head of the church, was one of the most powerful figures in the world. He was considered Earth's vicar, or representative, of Jesus Christ, as well as the lawgiver and judge for followers of the Catholic faith. The pope and other church officials were involved in virtually every aspect of religious, social, political, and economic life in Europe. Nevertheless, the church itself was highly unstable and corrupt. In fact, it had nearly been torn apart by two bitter conflicts, the Babylonian captivity (1306–76) and the Great Schism (1348–1417), which had taken place in the two centuries prior to Luther's life.

The Babylonian Captivity

The events leading up to the Babylonian captivity began in 1294, when church leaders were embroiled in a crisis over the selection of a pope. For eighteen months, since the death of Pope Nicholas IV (1227–1292; reigned 1288–92), the sacred college of cardinals (a committee composed of cardinals, the highest-ranking church officials, who elect the pope) had been divided into two opposing sides and could not reach an agreement on the election of the next pope. Neither side would recognize the legitimacy of the other. A schism, or division, of the church seemed inevitable. Then Pietro da Morrone (c. 1209–1296), an elderly Benedictine (member of a religious order founded by Saint Benedict), wrote the college a letter promising severe divine judgment if a pope was not elected soon. Terrified of God's wrath, the dean of the college called for Morrone to be elected pope. The cardinals agreed and quickly approved the decision. Morrone became Pope Celestine V (reigned 1294).

As a Benedictine, Celestine had been a hermit, a member of a religious order who retires from society and lives in solitude. He soon found that his new responsibilities did not allow the quiet, reflective life he had been leading before his election. He refused to move to the loud, congested city of Rome, where the papacy had traditionally been centered. Instead, he had a special wooden cell built at the papal castle located in Naples, Italy, so he could escape the constant attention of cardinals, bishops, and other officials of the church. Celestine became so depressed that he asked for advice from Benedetto Caetani (1240–1303), a respected member of the church and one of the cardinals who had elected him. Caetani, who had aspirations of his own, suggested that Celestine resign. On December 13, 1294, after only fifteen weeks as pope, Celestine stepped down.

On December 23 the college of cardinals met once again in Naples and elected Caetani the new pope. Taking the name of Boniface VIII, he returned the center of the papacy to Rome. Boniface focused on expanding his secular, or nonreligious, authority. In 1296 he found himself in conflict with King Philip IV of France (1268–1314; ruled 1285–1314) and King Edward I of England (1239–1307; ruled 1272–1307). Both kings had begun taxing clergymen in order to finance the Hundred Years' War, a conflict between England and France over the French throne (see "Hundred Years' War" in Chapter 6). This taxation had been started without the permission of Boniface. Outraged, the pope issued a decree (statement), known as the *Clericus laicos*, which forbade the taxation of clergy members without the permission of the papacy. The penalty for defying the order would be excommunication (forced to leave) from the church. Threats of excommunication had been used several times by popes to persuade monarchs to change their countries' political policies to those of the church. By the late thirteenth century, however, such threats carried less weight. Because the monarchs were supported by their nobles, Philip and Edward both refused to give in to Boniface's demands. The pope attempted to strike a compromise, but he was forced to back down when Philip stopped all French money collected for the papacy from leaving his kingdom and being sent to Rome.

In 1300 thousands of religious pilgrims flocked to Rome for a great church event called the jubilee celebration. The jubilee celebration was normally held every twenty-five years by order of the pope, and it was a time of formal celebrations and prayer. Boniface issued another decree, this one known as *Unam Sanctam*. The order stated that all human beings, regardless of religion or country, were subjects of the pope. In other words, all of Europe was now under the control of one man, the Roman Catholic pope in Rome. Philip was outraged by this claim. Gathering his nobles around him, he publicly accused Boniface of crimes such as committing murder, practicing black magic (use of supernatural evil forces), and keeping a demon (evil spirit) as his personal pet. For years prior, such stories had been spread by men loyal to Philip, thus making it easy for Philip's accusations to take hold. Boniface was soon seen as an evil pope attempting to overthrow a legitimate king. In 1303 Philip sent armed French soldiers to confront Boniface at his private home in Agnan, Italy. The soldiers ransacked the house, stealing everything of value. They attempted to force Boniface to return to France in order to stand trial. After three days, the pope was rescued from the soldiers. The ordeal proved to be too much for the aging Boniface. A few weeks later he died, suffering terribly from the humiliation and shock of the events.

Papacy moved to France

A new pope was soon elected. This time Bertrand de Got (pronounced deh GOH; c. 1260–1314), a Frenchman, was elevated to the highest post in the church and took the name Clement V (reigned 1304–14). King Philip and Clement, probably because they were fellow countrymen, had a good relationship. In 1306 Clement moved the headquarters of the papacy once again, this time to the city of Avignon in France, a Papal State (territory under the direct control of the pope) in his native country. The papacy remained in Avignon for seventy years. Since the city had not been equipped to house the papacy in the manner that popes had enjoyed in Rome, massive building projects commenced. Yet the papacy ran into considerable problems by moving the center of religious authority. Opposition to the move was sometimes violent in central Italy, and the popes serving during this period had to raise money for the troops needed to reclaim control there. Other Papal States lost money because of the move, and the various popes who served during this time were forced to find ways to return the lost revenue.

The massive financial pressure required the Avignon popes to rely on a practice known as simony, or the selling of church offices. Any nobleman who had enough money could become a bishop. For instance, Pope Clement VI (c. 1290–1352; reigned 1342–52) was once heard saying that he would make a donkey bishop if the donkey had enough money. The financial worries of the church began to take a heavy toll on the spiritual authority of the pope. One pope, John XXII (c. 1235–1334; reigned 1316–34), did try to raise money in ways that did not damage the respectability of the church. Although he had some success, the church's reputation had already been severely weakened. Furthermore, Rome was still regarded by many as the rightful home of the papacy. With the papacy (office of the pope) centered in Avignon, it was widely believed that church interests were controlled by the French monarchy.

The Italian humanist scholar Petrarch, one of the founders of the Renaissance, wrote extensively about conditions in the church. He declared Avignon to be the "Babylon of the West." He was referring to the story about Jews being held in captivity in Babylonia (an ancient country in Asia, located between the Tigris and Euphrates Rivers), which appears in the Old Testament of the Bible. According to Petrarch, Catholics were being held captive in Avignon just as the Jews were held against their will by the Babylonians. During the "Babylonian captivity" in Avignon, there were several attempts to move the papacy back to Rome, but arguments among church officials always prevented it from happening. Finally, in 1376, Pope Gregory XI (1329–1378;

Fearing Pope Urban VI's reform efforts, French cardinals declared his election invalid. The result of this action led to the Great Schism. *Reproduced by permission of Corbis-Bettmann.*

reigned 1370–78) returned the papacy to Rome because of mounting pressure from important Catholics. Avignon had been the center of Roman Catholic worship for seventy years, the same length of time as the original Babylonian captivity. Upon returning to Rome, Gregory was horrified to discover extensive corruption in the Italian church. He made plans to return to Avignon, but he died before he could carry them out. Mob rioting forced the sacred college of cardinals to elect an

Italian pope, Urban VI (c. 1318–1389; reigned 1378–89), in 1378.

The Great Schism

Pope Urban was determined to end the corrupt practices and extreme wealth of the cardinals. Fearing Urban's reform efforts, the French cardinals declared that his election was invalid because of the pressure put on the college by the mobs. In 1378 they elected as the new pope Robert of Geneva (1342–1394), who became Clement VII (reigned 1378–94). He had been a cardinal from the French-speaking city of Geneva, a city in southwestern Switzerland that was surrounded by French territory. The cardinals returned to Avignon with Clement, who was called an antipope because Urban was still the pope in Rome. While Clement intended to establish Avignon as the center of papal authority once again, Urban refused to recognize the legitimacy of the new pope and excommunicated Clement and the French cardinals. Urban then appointed new cardinals to replace those who had been banished. For thirty-seven years, the rival camps in Rome and Avignon each elected new popes and hurled accusations of heresy at one another. This dispute is known as the Great Schism (also called the Schism of the West).

The Roman Catholic Church was now deeply divided as each camp claimed to be the rightful heir to Saint Peter (the first pope) and the legitimate authority for Catholicism. All of western Europe was divided as well. With Catholicism as the only form of Christianity, a choice had to be made by monarchs of Catholic countries: Would they support the popes of Avignon or Rome? France recognized the popes of Avignon, as did Scotland, Sicily (an island off the coast of Italy), and Portugal. England, which was fighting the Hundred Years' War against France, supported the popes of Rome. The papacy in Rome was also recognized in parts of the Holy Roman Empire, northern and central Italy, and Ireland. Loyalty to the two camps was dependent on the individual interests and needs of a country, often changing when these interests were met by one side and not by the other.

Catholics confused about loyalties
During this turmoil Catholics across western Europe began to discuss questions concerning the fate of an individual's soul. Many wondered if they would be saved from damnation (being sent to hell after death) if they were represented by a false priest and a false pope. As time dragged on and it seemed that a compromise would never be reached, some Catholics suggested that a general council of church leaders should meet to provide a solution. Yet the popes at Avignon and Rome would not agree to be judged by followers from the other side. In 1409 the situation became even more complicated when a group of five hundred high-ranking bishops, called prelates, met in a council at Pisa, Italy. The prelates decided that both popes should be removed and a new one should be elected. The popes of Avignon and Rome would not ac-

cept this solution, and for a while there were three popes claiming to be the legitimate ruler of the Roman Catholic Church.

Sigismund of Luxembourg, the king of Hungary (1368–1437; ruled 1387–1437) and king of the Romans (1410–37; Holy Roman Emperor 1433–37), wanted the papacy to be controlled by a council, not by a pope who made his own decisions. This idea had been suggested years earlier but had not been accepted by church officials. This time Sigismund hoped to get enough backing to accomplish his goals. In 1414 he called a number of important churchmen to the Swiss town of Constance for a meeting. The council met until 1417, when it was decided that all of the existing popes should be removed and a new one elected. Pope Martin V (1368–1431; reigned 1417–31) was then named the only rightful leader of the Roman Catholic faith. The other three popes did not want to step down, but none of them had enough support to stay in power. Although the Council of Constance ended the Great Schism, the question remained whether future popes would be required to meet with councils before making decisions about church policy.

Church corruption causes protests

By 1500 the papacy had become so corrupted by power that most of its energies were exhausted by selling church offices, raising taxes and tithes (one-tenth of church members'

income) to support its standing army. Simultaneously, the Black Death (1348–1700s; a widespread epidemic of a disease called the plague) had devastated Europe. The plague had destroyed the social and spiritual lives of Europe's peasant and working classes, whose faith in the church's earthly power was needed for Catholicism itself to survive. To make matters even worse, two of Europe's great political and religious powers, France and England, were engaged in the Hundred Years' War, which brought further turmoil. Indeed, it seemed to many in Christendom (the name then given to Europe) that the Roman church had failed and that the time was ripe for a "reformation" of both the church and the political powers that helped implement its policies.

The most influential supporters of reform were Meister (Johannes) Eckhart (c. 1260–c. 1327), John Wycliffe (c. 1330–1384), Martin Luther, Huldrych Zwingli (1484–1531), and John Calvin (1509–1564). The protest movement that eventually became known as the Protestant Reformation is best understood through their works. In addition, the invention of "moveable type" and the mass production of the Gutenberg Bible in the mid-fifteenth century spread word concerning a key aspect of Protestant ideology: that every person might individually, without the help of a priest, discover Christian salvation through his or her own understanding of the Bible. Wycliffe, for instance, was a principal figure in the Protestant movement. He was the first person to translate the Bible from Latin into English so that lay readers—those outside the church—could read it. Wycliffe, whose followers were called Lollards, also rejected the Catholic belief in communion (a ceremony in which wine and bread represent the body and blood of Jesus Christ) as a "miracle." Eckhart, a German Dominican mystic (one who has intense spiritual experiences), put forth the idea of conversion through one's personal rapport with God. Because of the power of the Catholic Church at this point, both Wycliffe and Eckhart were quickly condemned as heretics (those who violate the laws of God and the church), as were many of those Protestants who followed them. Indeed, the growing schism, or break, between Catholics and non-Catholics would create a bitter and unresolved crisis in both religion and politics. Much more so than today, church and state were almost indistinguishable from each other in their function and power. For instance, the Holy Roman Empire, which had been founded in 962 as a uniting force in Europe, was closely allied with the church.

Luther starts Reformation

The early protests against the Roman Catholic Church did not really attract a popular following until Luther's lifetime. To understand the Protestant Reformation, one must first learn about Luther, the man who began the Reformation with a single defiant act: he dared to publicly criticize the church. At various points in his life Luther was an author, a professor, a friar (member of a religious order), a priest, a father, and a husband—in fact, he was so busy and so productive that many people claimed he must have seven heads. For some, Luther was a hero and the father of the most important religious revolution in Western (non-Asian) history, but to others he was a heretic who endangered the future of Christianity. Who, then, was this man who not only challenged the corrupt religious practices of the church, but also changed the course of human history?

Luther's early life

Martin Luther was born at Eisleben in Saxony (a duchy in northwest Germany) on November 10, 1483, the son of Hans and Margaret Luther. His parents were of peasant stock, but his father had worked hard to raise the family's social status. Hans Luther began his career as a miner, then became the owner of several small mines that brought the family a fair degree of financial comfort. This process took nearly a decade, however, and life for the nine Luther children (five boys and four girls) was sometimes difficult. Young Martin was severely beaten by both his mother and his father for relatively minor offenses. This type of discipline was common at the time, and the Luther children grew up in a family that firmly believed in "tough love." Around 1490 Martin was sent to the Latin school at Mansfeld, Germany. Seven years later he was sent to a better school in Magdeburg, Germany. In

1498, after he had shown academic excellence, he enrolled in a school located in Eisenach, Germany. Here he met Johann Braun, a dedicated cleric who became his role model.

Luther's early education was typical of late-fifteenth-century practices. To a young man in his circumstances, only the law and the church offered likely avenues to success. His parents believed that the financial success of their children would guarantee the elder Luthers comfort in their old age. Hans Luther had a dislike for the priesthood, a feeling that probably influenced his decision that Martin should be a lawyer. Hans believed that if Martin became a lawyer, he would be able to increase the Luther family's prosperity. Martin was enrolled at the University of Erfurt in 1501. He received a bachelor of arts degree in 1502 and a master of arts degree in 1505. In the same year he enrolled in the faculty of law, giving every sign of being a dutiful and possibly wealthy son. Although Martin seemed poised for a prosperous future in the legal field, he privately yearned to become a priest.

Religious conversion changes his life

The years between 1503 and 1505 were filled with religious crises that would take Luther away from the study of law forever. He was extremely pious, a quality that was instilled in him by his parents and early teachers. Aware that the material world was extremely close to the supernatural world, he believed the forces of good and evil had a direct effect on the everyday lives of human beings. A series of events would confirm this for young Martin and change his life. A serious accident in 1503 and the death of a friend a little later began to affect Martin's religious development. Then, on July 2, 1505, while Luther was returning to Erfurt after visiting home, he was caught in a severe thunderstorm. He fell to the ground in terror, and he suddenly vowed that he would become a monk if he survived. This episode, as important in Christian history as the equally famous (and parallel) scene of Saint Paul's conversion, changed the course of Luther's life. Two weeks later, against the opposition of his father and to the dismay of his friends, Luther entered the Reformed Congregation of the Eremetical Order of Saint Augustine at Erfurt.

Luther took his vows in 1506 and was ordained a priest in 1507. Upon ordination, a nervous Luther conducted his first mass, a worship service at which communion is taken. In attendance at the service was Hans Luther, who was still angered by his son's choice of vocation. Martin felt he was unworthy to be a messenger of Christ, but he explained to his father that he had to enter the monastery because of his experience in the thunderstorm. Martin was determined to prove himself to his father, and he dedicated himself to the rigorous life of a monk. His supervisor, Johann von Staupitz (1469–1524), recognized that Martin was academically brilliant, Staupitz urged him to become a teacher. Having reconciled with his father, Martin was selected for advanced theological (philosophy of religion) study at the University of Erfurt, which had connections with his monastery.

Luther at Wittenberg

In 1508 Luther was sent to the University of Wittenberg (founded in 1502) to lecture in arts. Like a modern graduate student, he was also preparing for his doctorate degree in theology while he taught. He lectured on the standard medieval texts, such as the *Book of Sentences* by the Italian religious scholar Peter Lombard (c. 1095–1160), a collection of teachings of early church fathers and the opinions of theologians. Luther also read for the first time the works of Saint Augustine (A.D. 354–430), one of the great champions of early Christianity. In 1510 Staupitz sent Luther to Rome as an official representative of the Eremetical Order of Saint Augustine. On October 19, 1512, Luther received his doctorate in theology. After completion of his degree came the second significant turn in Luther's career: he was appointed to succeed Staupitz as professor of theology at Wittenberg. Luther was to teach throughout the rest of his life. Whatever fame and notoriety his later writings and statements were to bring him, Luther's true work was teaching, a duty he fulfilled diligently until his death. By 1550, due to the efforts of Luther and his colleague Philip Melanchthon (1497–1560), Wittenberg was to become the most popular university in Germany. In 1512, however, it lacked

the prestige of Erfurt and Leipzig and was insignificant in the eyes of the greatest of the old universities, the University of Paris. Wittenberg was not the place for an academic who aspired to a prominent career, but Luther was dedicated to being a teacher, not to being financially successful. His rapid rise came from his native ability, his boundless energy, and his dedication to the religious life. Luther had a good relationship with the Duke of Saxony, also known as Frederick the Wise (1463–1525), who gave his full financial support while he attended the university. This relationship led to Luther becoming one of the most prestigious professors at Wittenberg, even before publishing his works on grace (a divine virtue given by God) and beginning the infamous indulgence controversy.

Continues to face religious questions

Luther had been exposed to two competing philosophical systems during his education: scholasticism and nominalism. Scholasticism was derived from the philosophies of the Italian religious scholar Saint Thomas Aquinas (1225–1274), who had in turn borrowed ideas from the ancient Greek philosopher Aristotle (384–322 B.C.). The main concept of scholasticism was that rigorous formal logic (thinking based on reason) should be used in all philosophical and theological inquiries. Any question could be answered by studying and thinking about it in a logical, organized way. Nominalism, on the other hand, was derived from the philosophies of the English scholastic William of Ockham (c. 1285–c. 1349) and his successors, and it was drastically different from scholasticism. Those who followed nominalism maintained that God was infinitely remote, or removed, from humans, and that the human intellect could not understand the majesty of God. Luther believed both of these philosophies held merit.

Luther dedicated himself to his studies, but he remained continuously afraid of God's wrath and power. While at the monastery he began to experience new religious crises that were based upon his acute awareness of the need for spiritual perfection and his equally strong conviction of his own human frailty. These conflicts caused him almost to despair before the overwhelming majesty and wrath of God. Nevertheless, Luther was a productive writer and he published his lectures on Peter Lombard in 1509. He went on to publish his lectures on the Bible: the Psalms (1513–15), Saint Paul's Epistle (Letter) to the Romans (1515–16), and the epistles to the Galatians and Hebrews (1516–18). During these years, his biblical studies became more and more important to him. Besides teaching and study, however, Luther had other duties. Beginning in 1514 he preached in the parish church and served as regent (member of the governing board) of the monastery school. In 1515 he became the supervisor of eleven other monasteries. Overwhelmed by his duties, Luther worried about the state of his soul.

Good deeds versus faith

Luther's crisis of conscience centered upon his fears of imperfection. He wondered how his personal efforts could begin to satisfy a wrathful God. These fears were intensified in 1519 when he began to closely study the works of Saint Paul. Luther began to despair while attempting to interpret the passage in Saint Paul's Epistle to the Romans, which says that the justice of God is revealed in the Gospels (four books in the New Testament that tell the story of Christ and his teachings). How can mankind satisfy this angry God, he asked himself. Soon he felt he had found the answer in Saint Paul's text. Luther claimed that God had to punish humanity because people were inherently sinful, yet because God was righteous he gave the gift of faith to those who would take it. Only faith in God's mercy, according to Luther, could save man. Good works became less important to him than faith. Luther used the term "works" to refer to both church liturgy and the more general sense of "doing good." According to Luther, the rituals of the Catholic Church should be secondary to the belief in God and his mercy. The idea that faith was more important than deeds was not new. An estimated forty-three other theologians, including Staupitz and Saint Augustine, had come to conclusions similar to Luther's. What was new, however, was Luther's relationship with God: unlike traditional Christians, he no longer found himself afraid of God, whom he believed to be a loving deity.

Indulgences

Indulgences began as gifts of money given to the clergy in appreciation or gratitude for forgiveness. Soon, however, indulgences began to represent an outward showing of grief for sins. People would pay for indulgences to prove to the church and others that they were truly repentant for their sins. The medieval church distinguished between guilt and punishment for a sin: a person could atone for guilt through Jesus Christ, but penance, or penalties, for sins could be ordered by a priest. Indulgences, therefore, could be used to reduce the penalties for sin. In the thirteenth century, the Catholic Church formulated what was called the "treasury of merits," which was a spiritual bank of sorts that "contained" the good works performed by Jesus Christ, the saints, and all pious Christians. In other words, because Jesus and the saints

had lived better lives than necessary to get into heaven, their good deeds had been left on Earth in the treasury of merits. Good deeds from this treasury could be redistributed in the form of indulgences. One would give money to his or her clergyman, who would in turn make a "withdrawal" from the spiritual bank. This system was supposed to reduce the punishments one suffered in purgatory (the place where believers feel the dead go to atone for their sins before either going to heaven or being cast into hell), but many did not understand it. Some thought they could buy their way out of hell and into heaven. By the fifteenth century many had begun purchasing indulgences for family members who were already dead. It was widely believed that people could sin as much as possible and still buy their way into heaven.

These new beliefs, which Luther formulated between 1515 and 1519, caused him to ask new theological questions, as well as to challenge certain elements of church life. The most famous of these is the controversy over indulgences (pardons for sins). In 1513 a great effort to dispense indulgences was proclaimed throughout Germany. In spite of reservations about this practice, indulgences were believed to be a way to escape punishment in the afterlife. This belief was held not only in Germany, but also across Catholic Europe. As Luther be-

came more and more convinced that indulgences were a threat to true faith, his comments about the issue brought him into direct conflict with the pope.

Can one man change a powerful institution?

In 1517 Pope Leo X (1475–1521; reigned 1513–21) announced his intentions to commission the building of a basilica, or church, over the supposed grave of Saint Peter in Rome. The church is now known as

Saint Peter's Basilica. Leo sanctioned the sale of indulgences to raise money for the construction. That same year, an experienced indulgence salesman, a Dominican friar named Johan Tetzel (1465–1519), arrived in a town not far from Wittenberg to begin raising money for the construction. Luther wrote a letter of protest to his archbishop, Albrecht von Bradenburg. Initially, Luther's protest fell on deaf ears, for the archbishop was sharing the profits of indulgence sales with the pope. Luther attached his Ninety-Five Theses, or propositions for debate, to the letter. He questioned the value of indulgence sales and reprimanded the church for its financial exploitation of Germany. As quoted in James Kittleson's *Luther the Reformer,* Luther asked why Pope Leo did not "build this one basilica of St. Peter with his own money rather than with the money of poor believers." Contrary to popular legend, Luther did not nail his theses to the door of the church.

Academic debates about theological questions were commonplace at Wittenberg, and had someone not translated Luther's theses from Latin into German they might have gone unnoticed. The translation made them accessible to theologians, scholars, and anyone else who could read German. Soon the theses gained worldwide attention. Most modern scholars agree that Luther never intended to begin a worldwide reform movement within the Catholic Church. He merely wanted to spark academic debate about a serious issue. In April 1518 Luther attended a convention of Augustine monks in Heidelberg, Germany. He had condensed his Ninety-Five Theses down to "Twenty-Eight Theses on Indulgences" and was excited about engaging in academic debate on the importance of salvation through faith. Luther wanted to put forth the idea that the Scriptures (the text of the Bible) are the sole authority for Christianity. He was warmly received by his fellow Augustine monks, who openly gave their support with cheers. Many of those in attendance would later become the first generation of Luther's followers. Among them were Martin Bucer (pronounced BUHT-zer; 1491–1551), who would head the reformation movement in Strasbourg, France, and Johannes Brenz (1499–1570), then a student at Heidelberg, who would later lead reform efforts in Württemberg (a province in central Germany). Luther quickly became a German folk hero, spearheading the campaign to end religious corruption.

Meanwhile, back at the Vatican, Pope Leo X—notorious for hobbies (such as hunting and traveling) that kept him away from his papal duties—realized that Luther's condemnation of indulgences represented a threat to the church's source of income. Leo, who was the son of the influential Italian banker Lorenzo de' Medici (see "Florence" in Chapter 2), intended to stop Luther from making more noise about the issue. He ordered a meeting for August 7, 1518. Luther asked his prince and supporter, Frederick the Wise, for guidance. Having already sought council from his own advisor, Frederick did not believe Luther to be a heretic and allowed him to stay at Wittenberg. As one of the seven electors of the Holy Roman Emperor (electors were German princes entitled to vote for an Emperor) and a leading Christian, Frederick put pressure on the Vatican for the hearing to be on German soil. Pope Leo X agreed and sent his envoy, Cardinal Cajetan (1469–1534) to Augsburg in October 1518.

Although nervous about the meeting, Luther was also excited to meet such a revered theologian. Luther was well versed in the writings of Thomas Aquinas, on which Cajetan was a leading expert. Luther hoped the two would be able to discuss Aquinas, which would serve as a launching point to dialogue about the new opinions of Luther. Upon meeting at the palace of the Fuggers (a wealthy banking family), the two men took an instant disliking to one another. While Luther looked for debate, Cajetan wanted Luther to submit to the authority of the church. Luther refused, and the two parted on bad terms. Hearing that he was to be arrested, Luther fled from Augsburg to the safety of Nuremberg. After a while, Luther returned to Wittenberg, where Frederick the Wise allowed him to continue teaching. Frederick hoped that the controversy would go away, and Luther agreed to stop writing or speaking publicly about his opinions on indulgences. Neither of them could foresee the controversy that was about to be unleashed.

Luther's troubles begin

In 1519 Luther agreed to a debate with the theologian Johann Eck (1484–1543) to be held at the University of Leipzig. Eck was a professor at the University of Ingolstadt and an extremely skilled debater. Eck realized he could earn celebrity and win favor with Rome by dismantling Luther's theological positions. A staunch supporter of the church, he was determined to defend the sacred institution. The debate, held in early July, was originally scheduled to take place between Eck and Luther's colleague Andreas von Karlstadt (1480–1541). When Eck quickly demolished all of Karlstadt's arguments, it was Luther's turn to join the debate. Eck outwitted Luther by challenging his positions, claiming they were similar to those of Jan Hus. Hus was a priest from Bohemia (now Czechoslovakia) who had been excommunicated from, or kicked out of, the church and executed in 1414 by the Council of Constance, a committee of Catholic officials meeting in the town of Constance, Switzerland (see "Bohemia" in Chapter 4). One of his crimes was criticizing the practice of selling indulgences. Hus angered many church leaders and state officials, who often split the money raised from indulgences. After Hus was executed he became a national hero and his followers went on to stage the Hussite Revolt (1420–34). He is now considered one of the forefathers of the Protestant Reformation.

Luther was pushed into a corner, and he was forced to declare that the Council of Constance had been

Renaissance Politics

Luther's prince and supporter, Frederick the Wise, was one of seven electors responsible for choosing a new emperor after the death of Maximilian I (1459–1519; ruled 1493–1519) on January 12, 1519. Three candidates were put forth: King Charles I of Spain (1500–1558), King Francis I of France (1494–1547), and King Henry VIII of England (1491–1547). Charles was a member of the house of Habsburg, a family of rulers based in Austria and in Spain. All Holy Roman Emperors were Habsburgs, so the family controlled not only their own vast territories but also the Holy Roman Empire. Charles had inherited the throne of Spain from his grandparents, Isabella of Castile and Ferdinand of Aragon, and had also inherited his rule over the Low Countries (present-day Netherlands, Belgium, and Luxembourg). Many politicians, the pope among them, felt that the naming of Charles to the throne would give too much power to the house of Habsburg. The same was true of Francis I of France, who belonged to the house of Valois. If made ruler of the Holy Roman Empire, the Frenchman would have a kingdom as large as that of Charlemagne, a ninth-century Frankish king who ruled much of Europe. Henry VIII, a Tudor, was not taken seriously because he had little support among the German princes.

Pope Leo was extremely worried about the election of a Habsburg or a Valois because each house controlled an Italian city-state that was close to Rome. Charles was king of Naples, and Francis ruled Milan, so either man would be ideally positioned to overtake the papacy. The pope asked Frederick the Wise to name himself as a candidate. Leo was certain that Frederick, a Saxon who was fiercely devoted to the church, was no threat to the papacy. Trying to be even more persuasive, Leo promised that if Frederick should be elected, he could chose any person he wanted to be made an archbishop. Leo was assuming that Frederick would choose Martin Luther for the post. Had Frederick chosen Luther, two problems could have been solved for Leo: he would have an emperor who did not want papal territory, and the condemnations of the church would stop; he assumed that if Luther were given a high-ranking position within the church, he would hesitate to publicly criticize the institution. Frederick was uninterested in the job, however, and he politely declined. Advisors of King Charles I of Spain bribed the electors and Charles was named Holy Roman Emperor Charles V. Charles promised to respect the traditions of Germany, and he appointed only Germans to imperial offices.

wrong in its condemnation of Hus. The University of Leipzig had been founded by student and faculty refugees who had fled from Prague during the height of the Hussite Revolt, and Luther's position proved unpopular with the audience. Luther refused to accept any reading of the

Luther, God, and Death

For years Luther was tormented by doubts about his ability to meet the demands of a righteous God. In 1545, a few months before his death, he wrote about this problem in a preface to an edition of his Latin works. He noted that after the disastrous debate in Leipzig in 1519, he studied the Psalms (a book in the Bible) and felt the joyful assurance that God did not demand righteousness from human beings. Instead, humans were made righteous by God's gift of Jesus Christ, a gift that was to be accepted by faith. Earlier Luther had taught that Christians who feared death were guilty of insufficient belief. He asked how one could be a Christian and doubt that God could raise the dead. After 1519, however, Luther taught that horror before death was a natural part of the human condition because death was a penalty for sin. According to Luther, a Christian could be terrified of death and yet trust God's graciousness despite this doubt and uncertainty.

Scripture that was decided by a council. (Luther's later movement, which grew out of this position, essentially ended the practice of convening church councils, known as conciliarism.) Luther lost the debate by an overwhelming margin. Luther's statements had been extremely dangerous, and he opened himself up to charges of heresy. Eck immediately began to capitalize on his victory, writing the *Exsurge Domine* (Arise Lord), the document that the pope later used as a basis for excommunicating Luther from the Church.

Continues assaults on the church

In 1520 Luther realized that he was intensely at odds with the church, but he felt it was his duty to defend his views and protect his growing group of supporters. He wrote powerful assaults on the papacy. In his *An den christlichen Adel deutscher Nation* (Appeal to the Christian Nobility of the German Nation), he asked the princes to take the duty of church reform over from the pope. He said that there was a "universal priesthood of all believers," who had a direct relationship with God. Those who were baptized in the faith were of equal standing with priests and had every right to address concerns about the state of their religion. He further argued that the clergy should be allowed to marry, a belief that shook Christendom to its foundations. In *De captivitat Babylonica ecclesiae* (Babylonian captivity of the church), he rejected the Catholic sacraments, or holy rites, of confirmation, marriage, ordination, and extreme unction (the act of anointing a person with oil before death). He claimed they had no scriptural basis and were merely conspiracies to keep Christians trapped within control of the church. He redefined penance to be a mutual assurance of divine forgiveness between Christians, and he argued for keeping only the traditional rites of baptism (the ceremony in which a person is blessed as a Christian) and communion.

At this time, there was considerable controversy among reformers about communion. Many debated whether there was a real presence of the body and blood of Christ in the bread and wine that was partaken during the ritual. Luther believed that the body and blood of Christ were combined with the substance of the bread and wine (known as consubstantiation), instead of the wine and bread being transformed into the actual body and blood (known as transubstantiation). In *Von der Freiheit eines Christenmenschen* (The freedom of the Christian), Luther held that the true Christian did good works not because of heavenly reward, but out of spontaneous gratitude to God for salvation.

In 1520 Pope Leo issued *Exsurge domine,* the bull (decree) written by Eck. The bull threatened Luther with excommunication if he did not recant his writings. On January 3, 1521, the pope issued another bull, titled *Decet Romanum Pontifecem* (It is fitting that the pope), and Luther was officially excommunicated from the church. Leo fully expected that the new Holy Roman Emperor, Charles V, would support the decree. Charles knew that the pope had objected to his election, and he wanted to gain favor with the church. On the other hand, Charles did not want to offend Frederick the Wise, Luther's supporter, or any other German prince. The emperor needed their help in his war against France (see "Italian Wars dominate Renaissance" Chapter 2). He was also

A group of men look on as Martin Luther burns the papal bull excommunicating him from the Catholic Church.

worried about the Ottoman Empire invading his Austrian lands (see "Ottoman Empire" in Chapter 1). Wanting to gain as much German favor as possible, Charles agreed to Frederick's request that Luther be given a hearing at the Imperial Diet of Worms.

Diet of Worms

Luther arrived in Worms and began studying with Jewish scholars to improve his Hebrew. He was working on a translation of the Old Testament, and he found that translating a Hebrew text directly to German would be more accurate than using a Greek translation as his master source. Luther was a firm believer in using original sources, a major theme of Renaissance humanism. When Luther presented himself before the council at Worms at 4 P.M. on April 17, 1521, he expected a theological debate. What he encountered was not what he had expected.

Luther was led to a room in which his collected writings were piled on a table. He was ordered to renounce them. He asked for time to consider, then left the room. He returned the next day to appear before Charles V. Luther gave this response to the council's command to renounce his views: "Unless I am proved wrong by the testimony of Scripture or by evident reason I am bound in conscience and held fast to the Word of God. Therefore I cannot and will not retract anything, for it is neither safe nor salutary to act against one's conscience. God help me. Amen." Luther felt strongly that his beliefs were completely supported by the Scriptures, and he refused to renounce them. One of Luther's students described his teacher at this period: "He was a man of middle stature, with a voice which combined sharpness and softness: it was soft in tone, sharp in the enunciation of syllables, words, and sentences. He spoke neither too quickly nor too slowly, but at an even pace, without hesitation, and very clearly.... If even the fiercest enemies of the Gospel had been among his hearers, they would have confessed from the force of what they heard, that they had witnessed, not a man, but a spirit."

Charles was unmoved by Luther's statements, seeing them as a threat to the stability of the church.

Nevertheless, Charles waited to condemn Luther publicly until after he had secured enough financial support to continue his military campaigns against the French and the Ottomans. Charles had been advised that Luther was extremely popular with the German masses, as well as with scholars throughout Europe, so he knew he had to bide his time. Finally, after receiving assurances from his allies, Charles issued an edict on May 26, 1521, that declared Luther to be an outlaw. The emperor forbade any of his subjects from helping Luther or his supporters. Luther, however, firmly believed that he was neither a troublemaker nor a heretic since he had never opposed indulgences or the papacy by using force. Instead, he stated that it was God's Word—meaning the scriptures—which Luther had taught, preached, and wrote about that actually weakened the papacy.

Occupied by threats from the Turks, the French, and rebels against his rule in Spain, Charles was unable to stop agents of Frederick the Wise from secretly taking Luther to Wartburg Castle. Luther hid there for almost a year, disguised as Knight George. Luther stayed in the castle and wrote many of the works that would define his career. In his treatise *De votis monasticis* (On monastic vows), he claimed that vows taken by Catholic monks and nuns were not binding, and he questioned the value of monks living in solitude and contemplation. In solitude, Luther thought, the Christian was open to attacks from Satan, the Christian concept of evil. While hiding in Wartburg castle, Luther also began translating the New Testament into German. The first edition appeared in September 1522 with prefaces explaining each book according to Luther's own views. His Old Testament translation was completed a decade later. Luther's German Bible became one of the influences on the modern German language.

Return to Wittenberg

Unrest in Wittenberg made Luther return there in March 1522. The discontent was caused by men, like Luther's former debate partner Andreas von Karlstadt, who had pushed to the limit Luther's idea that all religious authority came from the Bible. Since the Bible states that God condemned image worship and called upon prophets to destroy these objects, many people saw themselves as prophets called by God to destroy Catholic crucifixes (carved images of the crucified Christ on the cross) and statues of saints. The resulting violence and destruction threatened social order. Supported by Frederick, Luther decided to put a stop to it. Luther convinced Karlstadt that the Reformation would best be served by gradual and reasoned opposition to the church. Karlstadt, who had publicly declared that things were moving too slowly, heeded Luther's advice. Luther calmed down the mood at Wittenberg and returned to Wartburg Castle. In March 1522, Karlstadt began to once again spread a more radical doctrine than Luther, and Luther was forced to return to Wittenberg. He took over leadership of the Reformation in Wittenberg, and Karlstadt retreated to Orlamünde, Germany, where he led a more radical reform movement without the interference of Luther or Frederick. Luther, realizing that his message had been well received but badly interpreted, decided to start his own church.

The Knights' Revolt

Although Luther spoke out strongly against the corruptions and practices of the Catholic Church, he did not believe in violence as a solution to the problem. Luther wanted order to be maintained, both within society and within the church, and he did not advocate violent methods to achieve peace and harmony. Luther was alarmed that some wanted to use the sword to spread reform. Men like Franz von Sickingen (1481–1523) disagreed with Luther. Sickingen started the rebellion called the Knights' Revolt. (Under the system of feudalism during the Middle Ages, knights were warriors who swore allegiance to lords and kings and followed a strict code of honor called chivalry; see "Feudalism" in Chapter 1. Knighthood continued in many parts of Europe during the Renaissance and Reformation period.)

Sickingen and Ulrich von Hutten (1488–1523), a humanist knight who later helped write the *Letters of the Obscure Men,* were both lower nobles of the Holy Roman Empire. Like many nobles, they believed that the papacy should be under the control of

Different Interpretations, Different Problems

When Luther returned to Wittenberg from Wartburg Castle in December 1521, his message had already begun to take hold in religious practice. Greek scholar and Renaissance humanist Philip Melanchthon performed the Lord's Supper by distributing the ceremonial wine and bread to the laity (unordained church members). Melanchthon administered the ceremony in the spirit of Luther's concept of consubstantiation. Luther believed that, according to Scripture, the body and blood of Jesus of Nazareth (called the Christ) are present in the bread and wine taken during the service. This view was similar to the Roman Catholic teaching, known as transubstantiation, which holds that the bread and wine are transformed when held aloft by the priest during the service. The difference between Luther's theory and the Catholic teaching was that Luther refused to accept the role of the priest in changing the bread and wine into the body and blood of Christ.

He felt that only the world of God, as found in the Scripture, mad this change possible. The liturgy of Melanchthon's ceremony was similar to that of the traditional Catholic ceremony, but Melanchthon performed the first distinctly Protestant service. Other supporters of Luther, however, took more radical and experimental views. Marcus Stübner, one of Luther's former students, and two illiterate weavers from the town of Zwickau formulated their own interpretations of Luther's message. Seeing themselves as prophets, the three began preaching on the streets of Zwickau. While Luther did not deny that God could speak through common men, the fact that the three were proven to be alcoholics and liars did not help Luther's message. Luther spoke out against the Zwickau "prophets," and reemphasized his message about scriptural authority. This event, coupled with his disagreements with Karlstadt, led to Luther forming his own church.

the Holy Roman Emperor. They had watched helplessly as their land holdings declined in the economic turbulence of early sixteenth-century Europe. As the cost of living continued to increase due to inflation, many nobles began to attack merchants' caravans. Some of these robber knights, including Sickingen, started hiring themselves out as mercenaries (soldiers paid to fight in wars). In 1515 Emperor Maximilian I declared Sickin-

gen to be an outlaw. Maximilian was afraid to punish his friends in the lower nobility and was unwilling to lose his military experts, so he did not take proper action to support his declaration. In 1521 Sickingen sold his services to Charles of Spain (the future Emperor Charles V) in the war against King Francis I of France, a move that proved to be disastrous. Sickingen's military campaign was a dismal failure, and the Spanish government did not pay the 76,000 gulden Sickingen had been promised. He was forced to send many of his troops home without payment. Later that year, Sickingen was introduced to the ideas of Luther by Hutten. Moved by Luther's religious beliefs, Sickingen attempted to present his sword (a token of a knight' oath of loyalty) to Luther at the Diet of Worms. Although he politely declined the gesture, Luther did dedicate a later writing to Sickingen.

Luther's refusal of the sword did not curb Sickingen's own religious zeal. He was determined to spread the gospel (the word of God delivered by Jesus Christ) by waging war. In 1522 Sickingen attacked the western German city of Trier, including the home of the local archbishop. The military governor (known as a margrave), Philip of Hesse (known as Philip the Magnanimous; 1504–1567), was a strong supporter of Luther and did not agree with Sickingen's methods. Seeing violence as a threat to property and spirituality, Philip joined with the archbishop of Trier in seeking assistance from the Swabian League. The league was an alliance of cities, princes, knights, and church officials in Swabia, a region in southwestern Germany. It had been formed in the fourteenth century to protect trade and maintain peace in the region. Sickingen and his forces were driven out of the city and toward their own homes. One by one, the castles, or homes, of Sickingen and other knights fell under attacks from Swabian League forces. Sickingen was killed in 1523 when his castle was destroyed.

Hutten fled to Zurich, Switzerland, where he died of syphilis (a contagious disease spread by sexual contact or inherited from an infected parent). In the summer of 1523 the Swabian League continued to attack the castles of the robber knights, destroying a total of thirty castles. The actions of the Swabian League would serve as a rehearsal for the much more destructive Peasants' War of the mid-1520s.

A new pope and the Diet of Nuremberg

Meanwhile, Pope Leo X had died in 1521 and Adrian of Utrecht (1459–1523) became Pope Adrian VI (reigned 1522–23). A reform-minded native of the Low Countries, Adrian VI was the only non-Italian pope elected in the sixteenth century. (The next non-Italian pope was John Paul of Poland, who was elected in 1978.) Although Adrian had supported Luther's excommunication, Adrian agreed with some of Luther's charges against the Catholic Church. Adrian appointed a Reform Commission and indicated he would act on their recommendations. After only twenty months as pope, Adrian died of the plague, and with him died the hopes of peaceful reform within the Catholic Church. Many Catholics celebrated the death of Adrian, fearing the changes he had been poised to introduce. Clement VII (1478–1534; reigned 1523–34), a Medici, was named as Adrian's successor, but he never had the courage to implement reform in the church.

During the reign of Adrian VI and the early years of Clement's reign, a series of three Imperial Diets were held in Nuremberg, Germany, between 1522 and 1524. One of the central aims of the Diets was to discuss Luther and how to enforce the Edict of Worms declaring Luther an outlaw. The issue soon became secondary to the impending threat of the Ottomans. The city of Belgrade (present-day capital of Serbia) was an important fortress city in the Balkans (countries in eastern Europe) and had been sacked in 1521. When the island of Rhodes in the eastern Mediterranean was overtaken by the Ottomans, attention shifted from Luther to the potential fall of the Holy Roman Empire. Archduke Ferdinand (1503–1564) of Austria, the younger brother of Charles V and the future Holy Roman Emperor (Ferdinand I; reigned 1558–64), had been granted Habsburg lands in Germany. Ferdinand found it difficult to persuade the German princes and nobles to take definitive measures against Luther and his followers. In 1524, when Ferdinand insisted upon action, officials at the diet produced a document citing grievances against the church. A general council was called, and it issued an order stating that Catholic traditions would be observed until a church council met and made a final decision. Without a firm action or decree against them, Luther and his followers were able to continue winning supporters.

Lutheranism spreads into Nuremberg

Nuremberg was the site of three Imperial Diets as well as the seat of the Imperial Supreme Court (highest court of the Holy Roman Empire) and the Imperial Council of Regency (representative assembly of the Holy Roman Empire). The city was therefore essentially the center of the Holy Roman Empire. Nuremberg was also important to the humanist movement. A number of prominent humanistic thinkers lived there. Luther had visited the city twice in 1518, so many there had received early exposure to his ideas. The popularity of his message began to increase, and between 1520 and 1522 the city hired a number of church officials who had been Luther's students at Wittenberg. As Lutheranism continued to become more popular, city officials saw a chance to break from the authority of the Catholic Church. Having been given full rights to decisions regarding the city's churches by Pope Leo X in 1514, Nuremberg all but sealed its authority in religious matters by officially adopting Lutheranism in 1525. The city government already controlled the social aspects of life in Nuremberg and felt that control of the church was a logical next step. Nuremberg's decision to adopt Lutheranism served to fan the flames of reform, which quickly spread across all of Europe.

The German Peasants' War

The German Peasants' War was the greatest uprising of early German history. The conflict involved most of south Germany and parts of central Germany. Its high point was from January to June 1525, but preliminary activity and aftershocks extended from May 1524 to July 1526. Until April 1525 the rebellion was not based on military action; it was more a form of social protest than a call to violent conflict. Large gatherings and marches of commoners supported an armed boycott of clerical and lay lords. While there were scattered attacks on monasteries and castles, the aim was to acquire goods and money, not to kill or capture. To fully understand the German Peasants's War, the social, religious, and economic realities of the period have to be examined.

Most of the unrest was centered in the urbanized regions of the Holy Roman Empire, where a majority of the empire's food was grown. For years, noble landlords and clerics had been overworking and exploiting peasants who worked on farms, violating their rights and village customs. Artisans and common workers complained they were kept from markets of their choice by nobles and forced to sell food to their overlords at extremely low prices. In areas of upper Germany, populations were rapidly increasing while crops had been failing for more than two decades. With barely enough food to feed the population, misery and frustration spread. While crops were failing in some areas, most of western Europe had been experiencing an economic upswing since 1450. This fact did little to improve the life of the common landowner, but it increased the wealth of the nobility. A sharp division among the social classes quickly emerged. Landholding peasants controlled village government, dominated landless peasants, and subjugated common workers. In turn, however, the incomes of landholding peasants were reduced by landlords who collected rent, government officials who took taxes, and churchmen who expected tithes. (Peasants were allowed to hold land, but they could not own it.) Money was kept by the clerics, aristocrats, and nobles. Peasant landowners were given certain rights and privileges, but they were tightly controlled by those at the top. At the bottom was the common worker, who barely had enough to feed his family and had no personal wealth. As these injustices continued to mount, groups of peasant landowners across southern and central Germany began to unite in protest.

Peasants stage uprisings

The peasants had a number of complaints against the nobility. Local, self-ruled governments were rapidly being replaced by district officials. Towns and urban areas were being absorbed into larger territories and placed under the Holy Roman Empire. Wishing to create uniform rule and custom, officials of the empire replaced local laws with Roman law. In some areas, the practice of serfdom was once again instituted. Serfdom was a part of feudalism, a social and economic system in the Middle Ages, which required peasants to work all their lives for a landowner with no possibility of being freed (see "Feudalism" in Chapter 1). This change angered many peasants, who were also upset that noblemen were attempting to exclude them from hunting game in the local forests and meadows and from fishing in the local waterways. Selling game and fish was a traditional source of extra income for peasants, and the nobles' attempts to stop peasants from hunting and fishing directly affected the economic situation of many commoners. Peasants were also subjected to additional labor by the aristocrats who owned the land, keeping many peasants from making additional money to feed their families. Others objected to the excessive rents charged to live on the aristocrats' lands, and to the arbitrary penalties for offenses not mentioned in the law. New taxes on wine, beer, milling, and the slaughtering of farm animals greatly angered the peasants, who were also expected to pay the church a tithe, even when crops had failed. Overtaxed and overworked, underpaid and underfed, the peasants began to revolt.

In the early 1520s peasants staged armed uprisings against monasteries and castles. In the Black Forest, Upper Swabia, and Alsace, attacks were made on monastic landlords, demonstrating the widespread anger toward tithes. Other uprisings, also centered on monastic orders, occurred in 1523 and 1524. On May 30, 1524 peasants in the Black Forest region rebelled against the overlord, claiming they would no longer provide feudal services or pay feudal dues. In June laborers stopped working in the southern region of the Black Forest. Here the peasants were angered by the recent limits placed on local government, and when the local ruler would

not negotiate, peasant groups began to march through the Black Forest and called for rebellion. The movement soon began to gain support and increase in size.

The military phase of the Peasants' War, from April 1525 onward, was largely one-sided. Violence was usually squelched by the Swabian League and German princes. During this phase the rebel bands were successful in stealing the wealth of various monasteries, as well as destroying a number of castles belonging to aristocratic nobles. Some towns were forcibly occupied, but executions of nobles were extremely rare. The battles were usually slaughters in which commoners were killed. In May 1525, six thousand people were killed in Frankenhausen, Thuringia; eighteen thousand were killed in Alsace. Limited peasant uprisings continued into the seventeenth century, but the main rebellion essentially ended in 1525.

The Twelve Articles and the Federal Ordinance

Many factors contributed to the violence of the German Peasants' War. As already noted, anger toward the church and aristocratic nobles was central to the rebels' discontent. Several written works voiced these concerns and were adopted by the movement. The most significant were the Twelve Articles and the Federal Ordinance.

The Twelve Articles were written in March 1525, one month before the armed uprisings took place. This work expressed an opposition to tithes, and the authors used scriptural references to support their argument. The opening part of the Twelve Articles made the same point Luther had made years earlier, that any disorder resulting from the preaching of the gospel (that is, Lutheran gospel) should be blamed on those who resist it, not on those who preach it. According to this view, any violence or unrest that resulted from the Peasants' War was not the fault of the peasants. Instead, those who refused to hear their complaints were responsible. The peasants believed they were charged by God to rebel and fight for their rights. In addition to the Twelve Articles, there were other Reformation pamphlets that called for an end to the tithe and demanded that parishes have the right to choose and dismiss pastors. They insisted that pastors preach the Scripture as written in the Bible and not as it is interpreted by church officials.

The Federal Ordinance was a more complicated document because there were so many different versions. Some of these versions expressed different ideas about how the existing social and political structures should be changed. In versions found in Upper Swabia and the Black Forest, the authors wanted self-governing groups, or confederations, of local communities ("towns, villages, and rural regions") to be formed. Such a political and social organization was patterned on the Swiss Confederation of neighboring Switzerland (see "Switzerland" in Chapter 4). Switzerland had grown in size and power by absorbing smaller neighboring confederations on its borders. Some Germans even hoped to break away from Germany completely and become part of the Swiss Confederation. In larger territories, such as Württemberg or Tyrol, the authors wanted to have a peasants' estate join nobles and townsmen in the already established representative assemblies. In this system, peasants who owned land would be able to participate in the local government, essentially making them equal to the nobles and aristocrats who sat on the assemblies. (It was unusual, but by no means unheard of, for peasants to participate in representative assemblies during this time.) The rebels were not united under a common political goal; their ideas varied from region to region, and therefore there was not a united movement to change the political structure of Europe as a whole. Concerns were more regional, and desires for reform were usually tied to that region.

Religious concerns were also addressed in the Federal Ordinance. An appeal was made to fourteen leading Reformation theologians, such as Luther, Melanchthon, and Zwingli, to decide if the rebels had scriptural support for their rebellion. Thomas Müntzer (1490–1525) was the only prominent Reformation theologian to side with the rebels. Luther denounced them passionately, claiming they had not correctly interpreted his beliefs or the gospel itself. When the rebels refused to stop fighting, Luther wrote *Against the Robbing and Murdering Horde of Peasants* in May 1525. Luther called for authorities to end

Thomas Müntzer

Thomas Müntzer (1490–1525) was born at Stolberg in the Harz mountains of Germany. Little is known about his family background. He studied at the universities of Leipzig (1506) and Frankfort on the Oder (1512). Between 1517 and 1519 he was at Wittenberg, where he came into contact with Martin Luther. Müntzer was influenced by both Renaissance humanism and medieval mysticism (a religion based on intense spiritual experiences), and elements of both could be found in his writings. In 1520 and 1521 he preached at Zwickau. While in Zwickau, Müntzer became increasingly frustrated that the reform movement was moving too slowly. In April 1521 his radical beliefs caused him to be removed from his position as preacher at Zwickau. Later in 1521 he traveled to Bohemia; he preached at Prague and in November wrote his *Prager Manifest* (Prague protest), the first of his surviving documents. On Easter 1523 Müntzer became pastor of the church of Saint John in the small market town of Allstedt in Saxony. At Allstedt, Müntzer married the former nun Ottilie von Gersen. Here he also introduced the first liturgy (text used in worship services) written in German (the Catholic liturgy was written in Latin, the official language of the church, and could not be understood by common people). His Allstedt reform program was successful, and he soon enjoyed a wide following in the town and surrounding countryside, which led to conflict with local Catholic lords.

By the end of 1523, following an investigation into his reforms, Müntzer completely broke with Luther. In March

the rebellion by any means necessary. Some peasants felt that Luther had betrayed them and returned to the Catholic Church. While Luther felt the peasants had legitimate concerns and complaints, he felt the solution was to be found in the Gospels, not through violence. He thought that if a leader was to become a better Christian, he would become a better ruler. Despite his public statements against the rebellion, most German princes (both Lutheran and Roman Catholic) connected the Lutheranism movement with the German Peasants' War.

Early opponents of Luther had claimed that his appeal to the princes and the nobility to rebel against clerical authority would cause anarchy (total lack of order) across Europe. These opponents had also said that Luther's ideas would challenge the very rule of the princes and nobles he asked to support him. With the uprisings of 1525, many German princes believed these predictions were coming true. As a result, princes of all religious affiliations began to take greater control over the religious practices within their realms. As criticism of the

1524 a group of Müntzer's followers burned the small pilgrimage chapel at nearby Mallerbach. Müntzer defended the action and stopped the prosecution of the rebels by local officials. On July 13, 1524, he preached his famous *Fürstenpredigt* (Sermon to the princes; or, an exposition of the second chapter of Daniel) at the Allstedt castle before Saxon rulers and officials. These authorities called Müntzer and members of the Allstedt council for a hearing and ordered him to stop spreading his ideas. As a result, Müntzer fled Allstedt for Mühlhausen, a free imperial city in Thuringia, Germany, where he joined another radical reformer, Heinrich Pfeiffer. In late September 1524 city authorities expelled both reformers following their involvement in a rebellion. Later that fall, Müntzer's final writings against Luther were secretly printed in Nuremberg. Müntzer traveled to southwest Germany at this time, where he made contact with fellow radicals and preached to peasants who had risen in rebellion in the Klettgau and Hegaus regions of Germany. In early 1525 Müntzer returned to Mühlhausen. In March a new revolution in the city led to the formation of a new government. When the Peasants's War swept Saxony and Thuringia in April, Mühlhausen became an important urban center supporting the rebellion. Müntzer and Pfeiffer campaigned with rebel bands and worked hard to promote the cause of the commoner. Following the defeat of the peasants at the battle of Frankerhausen, Müntzer was captured. After interrogation and torture, he was beheaded outside the walls of Mühlhausen on May 27, 1525.

movement increased, Lutheranism was required to become more organized to defend itself against the attacks of opponents.

Luther gets married

During the Peasants' War, Luther met Katherine von Bora (1499–1552), a former nun. At the age of ten she had been placed in a convent by her father after he remarried. Young girls who were not wanted by their parents were frequently placed in convents to become "brides of Christ." Katherine did not find spiritual fulfillment in the church, however, and when she read Luther's writing against taking clerical vows she decided to flee the convent. Along with twelve other nuns, she hid in an empty barrel used to transport smoked herring (a kind of fish) and escaped on the eve of Easter 1523. Three of the nuns who had escaped were accepted back by their families, but Katherine and the eight remaining nuns could not return home. They found refuge at Wittenberg, where Luther was teaching.

Despite the Catholic Church's rule of the forbidding priests from getting married, Martin Luther married Katherine von Bora, a former nun. ©David Lees/Corbis. Reproduced by permission the Corbis Corporation.

Their situation was typical of a mounting problem: former nuns who were not wealthy and did not live with their families could not find husbands to support them. After two years, Luther decided to marry Katherine himself. Luther regarded the decision as having two benefits: he could please his father by taking a wife and upset the pope by getting married while he was still a priest.

Luther quickly settled into married life. The couple had six chil-dren, and Luther proved to be a tender husband and father. He was one of the first reformers to publicly support marriage for priests, and he greatly ad-mired his wife. Katherine had a talent for stretching her husband's meager income. She also started a boarding house and ran a successful farm. She brewed an excellent beer, which Luther greatly enjoyed, and she was not afraid to voice her opinion to her husband. Although always respectful, Katherine was known to openly dis-agree with Luther. As his respect for his wife and daughters grew, Luther became more vocal in his recognition of women's talents. He was one of the first advocates of schooling for girls, helping qualified women find jobs as elementary teachers. Although he sup-ported the right to education, Luther still believed that women should take care of the home and children and should not be allowed to be ministers or accept public responsibilities.

The Diets of Speyer: 1526 and 1529

The unstable political situa-tion in the Holy Roman Empire con-tributed to the success of the Reforma-tion movement. Holy Roman Emperor Charles V was continually threatened by the Ottoman Turks, so his military forces were busy fighting the war against the Turks in eastern Europe and were not available to keep order during the revolts in Germany. Some historians argue that if Charles had not been so preoccupied with the Ottomans, he would have stopped the reform movement. Political and military events of 1526 were therefore important to the continued spread of the Reformation throughout Europe.

In late June 1526 officials of the Holy Roman Empire met in the German Rhineland town of Speyer. Once again Charles V's brother, Archduke Ferdinand, presided in the emperor's absence. While they were meeting, reports of continued Ottoman aggression reached the council. Imperial officials were forced to make a decision regarding the empire's official stance towards the Reformation movement. So many churches and towns had turned "evangelical" (a term used to refer to the Reformation movement in Germany; those who practiced the new religion were called "evangelicals") that Ferdinand was forced to allow people to practice their chosen religion. In other words, the council decided that people should follow their own conscience as long as they did not break the laws of God and the emperor. Although this was neither a condemnation nor an approval of the evangelicals, the council declared it would be the official policy until the general church council was able to meet and establish more specific rules and regulations. Ferdinand and Charles both knew that taking a harsh stand against the evangelical movement could result in loss of support for their campaign against the Ottomans. The Turks were threatening Hungary, which was ruled by Ferdinand's brother-in-law, Louis II, and the council needed to act quickly. At

the Diet of Speyer it was decided that twenty-four thousand troops would be sent to assist Louis against the Ottomans. These efforts came too late, however, and the Hungarians were demolished by the Turkish forces (see "Hungary" in Chapter 4). Louis was killed on August 29, along with nearly twenty thousand troops and five hundred nobles. The Turks were unable to continue their campaign, however, because most of their forces were made up of noblemen who had to return home and attend to their own estates.

While the Turks were distracting Charles in eastern Europe, the evangelical movement was winning thousands of converts in Germany. Luther continued writing pamphlets that publicized the Lutheran cause. He also composed hymns that were based on the Psalms. These hymns made evangelical worship services more inspiring and attracted additional followers. (Luther's best-known hymn is probably "A Mighty Fortress Is Our God," which is based on Psalm 46. It is still sung in many Protestant churches today.) In the summer of 1527, as the evangelical movement presented mounting threats against the Catholic Church, an important event strengthened the ties between the emperor and the pope. Soldiers in Charles V's army sacked Rome when they had not been paid for their services. The mercenaries essentially held the city and Pope Clement VII captive until peace was restored. Charles was embarrassed by the actions of his men and the overall lack of discipline within his army. Nevertheless, he used the situation to promise protection to the pope, who had been opposed to Charles's efforts to bring Italy into the empire. In return, the pope had to give Charles control of Rome and the Papal States (territories ruled by the pope in central and northern Italy). After the new alliance was formed between the papacy and the Holy Roman Empire, the second Speyer meeting was held in March 1529. Both Charles and Clement were determined to strike a blow against the evangelical movement and its leaders.

By 1529 the evangelical movement had been weakened by internal fighting. Philip of Hesse and Duke John of Saxony (1468–1532) were both avid supporters of the Reformation, and they had been using their political positions to bring pressure on the Holy Roman Empire. They announced that they would withdraw support for the empire's campaign against the Ottomans if the Catholic Church did not respect the religious rights of the evangelicals. By 1529, however, the threat of Ottoman aggression had reached an alarming level. Philip and John of Saxony lost support, and with the evangelical movement splitting into different groups, imperial officials decided to act. On April 30, 1529, they repealed the Diet of Speyer compromise of 1526 and called for a return to the Catholic faith in all German provinces. Evangelical worship was no longer supported or allowed within the Holy Roman Empire.

A number of evangelicals protested the new policy, but both Ferdinand and Charles V rejected any compromise. It is because of these objections, or protests, that those allied with the evangelical movement became known as "Protestants." When a group of evangelicals who had gone to Spain to speak with Charles were placed under house arrest, it became clear that compromise was out of the question. Philip of Hesse and other supporters began to plan a Protestant military alliance. Philip realized that the only way political unity among the Protestants could be achieved would be if there were theological unity as well. Philip invited the leading Protestant theologians of the Roman Empire and Switzerland to his town of Marburg (present-day Maribor, Yugoslavia) for a meeting to be held on October 1, 1529. Luther, Melanchthon, and Zwingli all accepted. The meeting was the first time Luther had met Zwingli, who had started a successful reform movement in Switzerland and in parts of the Holy Roman Empire. After great debate, the two men were able to agree on many key issues. They still held differing views about the meaning of communion, however, and were unable to reach a compromise. Luther was adamant about there being a real presence of Jesus in the wine and bread used in the ceremony. Zwingli felt the ceremony was symbolic and nothing more. They agreed to disagree, but neither man ever trusted the other again. By the time the Holy Roman Empire announced another Imperial Diet in 1530, the Protestant movement had not become unified either politically or theologically.

Religious reformer Philip Melanchthon at the Diet of Augsburg. Melanchthon was appointed to write a statement detailing Protestant beliefs. *Reproduced by permission of Corbis-Bettmann.*

The Augsburg Confession: 1530

In the fall of 1529, the Ottomans had launched a full-scale attack against Vienna, Austria. The city was well-fortified and withstood the attack. After failing to take Vienna, the Ottomans focused their attention on conquering the remainder of Hungary. Ferdinand, who had presided over the previous three Imperial Diets for his brother Charles V, had been named the new king of Hungary. Charles announced that he would personally preside over the next meeting of the Imperial Diet, to be held in Augsburg, Germany. Outwardly, it seemed as though Charles was going to be more tolerant of the Protestants. He claimed he would be respectful of the Protestant theologians. While many Protestants still did not trust him, others hoped Charles would listen to their complaints, realize they were acting out of true faith, and leave them to practice their religion in peace. Charles had no intention of doing so. Permitting the Protestants to reject the authority of the pope would be the same as allowing them to reject the authority of the emperor. Like his grandfather Maximilian, Charles saw himself as a representative of Christ, and he would not allow his holy authority to be challenged.

Those who believed Charles had good intentions decided to take the invitation seriously. The Protestants were ordered to write a "confession," or statement, of their beliefs. The man charged with writing the confession was Philip Melanchthon, Luther's old friend. He was a respected theologian and the first priest to perform a Protestant communion. In 1521 Melanchthon had published the *loci communes,* (commonplaces) a well-respected text for the teaching of basic Protestant theology. He proved to be a good writer, and Luther respected his abilities. Luther was still an outlaw and was hiding in the safety of a Saxon castle, so he was unable to attend the Diet at Augsburg. He trusted Melanchthon to do a good job of representing Protestant beliefs.

Melanchthon's confession was not nearly so radical as many had expected. Charles V himself was surprised at the mild tone of the document. The situation became difficult, however, when followers of Zwingli and other theologians presented their own confessions, which were more unorthodox. Upset that the Protestants had been unable to come up with a single statement, Charles refused to address each of the confessions. Instead, he appointed a team of theologians to examine the Lutheran confession written by Melanchthon. The committee was headed by Johann Eck, Luther's opponent in the Leipzig

debates. After two weeks, Eck returned with a 351-page commentary on Melanchthon's confession. Eck's statement was so mean-spirited and unfair that Charles ordered Eck to rewrite it. Charles would not let the Lutherans see the manuscript until Eck had toned it down. The emperor had a reason for adopting this strategy: although the Ottoman threat was less severe by that time, he still needed Protestant support for his campaign against the Turks. On August 3, 1530, Eck presented Charles with a 31-page report, called the *Confutation,* which supported the decision of the 1529 Diet of Speyer. Charles insisted that the Protestants accept the *Confutation.* He ordered them to renounce their beliefs and return to the Roman Catholic Church. Failure to do so would result in the wrath of the empire. The Protestant theologians and diplomats claimed they needed time to read the *Confutation* and form an official response, but Charles refused to grant their request.

Officials of the Holy Roman Empire tried to divide the Protestants by sending some individuals expensive gifts to woo them back to the Catholic Church. These tactics did not work. Protestants such as John of Saxony left the Diet of Augsburg early out of frustration, while others stayed and participated. Although the council voted to supply Charles with forty thousand infantry (foot soldiers) and eight thousand cavalry (soldiers mounted on horses) in the war against the Ottomans, Protestants refused to abandon their religion. The emperor had set a deadline of April 15, 1531, for them to comply with the orders in the *Confutation*. Many feared the emperor might use military force against them. The threat of violence only strengthened the belief among most Protestants that they were right and the emperor was wrong.

The Schmalkaldic League

The Diet of Augsburg had been an effort to settle religious tensions within the Holy Roman Empire, but the meeting only intensified an already difficult situation. Frustrated and angry Protestants decided the time had come to form a military alliance. Philip of Hesse and others believed they could resist the emperor. They felt they were within their rights to do so, since they were rulers of their own areas. Those close to Luther were attempting to convince him that, whether he wanted it or not, conflict may be inevitable. As a pacifist, Luther did not advocate the use of violence under any circumstances. His beliefs were not shared by most Protestants. In late 1530 they gathered in the town of Schmalkalden, Germany, and formed the Schmalkaldic League for protection against Catholic forces. Philip of Hesse and seven other princes agreed that if one city-state were attacked, the remaining would come to its aid. Nuremberg, a large and important city, refused to join the Schmalkaldic League, as did neighboring Brandenberg-Ansbach. Despite these abstentions, many Protestants hoped the cities would eventually join the cause.

Philip Melanchthon. *Woodcut by Albrecht Dürer. Reproduced by permission of Archive Photos, Inc.*

At the Diet of Nuremberg in the summer of 1532, the league was so strong that Charles was forced to agree to a truce that continued the toleration of Lutheranism indefinitely. Philip of Hesse then took the offensive, and in 1534 he defeated the imperial troops, restoring Lutheranism to the territory of Württemberg. In northern Germany more princes and towns became Lutheran, including part of Saxony, which had been staunchly Catholic. Philip brought dishonor on himself in 1540, however, when he married a second time

Philip Melanchthon

Philip Melanchthon (1497–1560) was born in the trading center of Bretten, Germany, to Georg and Barbara Reuter Melanchthon. Showing a talent for language, Melanchthon mastered Latin and Greek at the age of twelve. By the time he was fourteen, he received his bachelor's degree of arts from the University of Heidelberg. He earned his master of arts at the University of Tübingen in 1514. In 1518 he became the first professor of Greek at Wittenberg University, which was still a relatively new school. At the beginning of the school year he gave his inaugural address, in which he proposed reform of the university curriculum. Melanchthon had been strongly influenced by humanism, and he wanted the new curriculum to be formed along humanist lines. He also proposed an emphasis on Latin, Greek, Hebrew, and on such disciplines as rhetoric (the art of speaking or writing effectively), dialectics (conversation based on discussion and reasoning), and history. Throughout his career at Wittenberg, he was successful in changing the general course of study for theology students. He came to be recognized as one of the greatest experts in Latin.

In 1519 he achieved the first theological degree, the *baccalaureus biblicus,* (bachelor of the Bible) at Wittenberg. By this time Melanchthon was a supporter of Martin Luther, having assisted the reformer in the Leipzig debates against John Eck. By 1527 many felt that evangelical theology would destroy the humanist movement. In response, Melanchthon wrote an important work titled *Encomium eloquentiae* (Praise of eloquence), in which he claimed that the gospel and humanism were both gifts from God. He emphasized that all students, including those studying theology, needed to be educated in languages and classical literature. Two years earlier he had been instrumental in founding a new Latin school in Nuremberg. In 1528 Luther and Melanchthon teamed up to write an explanation of the curriculum of local Protestant schools. He also made contributions in the area of rhetoric and revolutionized the use of oratory (public speaking). Throughout his life, Melanchthon published numerous works, mostly in Latin, and was widely regarded as a leading Reformation theologian, humanist, and scholar. Although his humanism was sometimes at odds with evangelical theology, scholars now maintain that Melanchthon was as important to Luther as Luther was to Melanchthon. Melanchthon lived in Wittenberg until his death in 1560.

without divorcing his first wife. Other Protestant princes condemned him for embarrassing the cause. Philip was now at the mercy of the emperor for having violated a fundamental civil and moral law. Charles forced him to restrain the Schmalkaldic League, which became sharply divided between militant and moderate factions, or opposing sides. Nevertheless, the Protestant forces remained strong and at another Diet of Speyer in 1544, Charles promised that all religious questions would be solved in the future by a German church council in which the Lutherans would be given a full voice. In 1545 another theological meeting was held at Regensburg, but when Catholics and Protestants failed to reach agreement, relations between the two groups worsened.

The Diet of Regensburg of 1546 was boycotted by members of the Schmalkaldic League, and Charles finally withdrew his earlier concessions. He won over Philip of Hesse's Protestant son-in-law, Maurice of Saxony (1521–1553), and declared war on the league. At first the Protestants were successful, but in April 1547, Charles captured John Frederick of Saxony (1503–1554). A short time later he also took Philip of Hesse captive, under promise of good treatment. He forced several recently converted Protestants to return to the Catholic Church, and he compelled other Protestant states to accept his authority. At the Diet of Augsburg in 1548, Charles issued the Augsburg Interim, which granted concessions to the Protestants, including the right of priests to marry, subject to papal approval. Most of the Protestant leaders were forced to accept the document, but they considered it unsatisfactory. The Augsburg Interim was largely ignored in the next few years, as resentment against Charles slowly built up. In 1551 Maurice, angry at the continued imprisonment of his father-in-law, organized a new Protestant League with French support. The league was successful. Charles was forced to release Philip and John Frederick and to issue another recess of the diet. Disgusted with the German situation, Charles left for the Netherlands and gave Ferdinand authority to conclude a settlement.

Luther's last years

Luther had aged rapidly during his hectic life. The stress of continual work and constant conflict with both Catholics and Protestants had taken a toll on him. After both of his parents died in 1530, he fell into a deep depression and his health declined. When the Schmalkaldic League formed in January 1531, Charles agreed to stop prosecution of Protestants who had not obeyed the *Confutation*. Once again the emperor needed the support of Protestants in his defense of Vienna against the Ottomans. The Protestant provided aid that helped the imperial forces defeat the Ottomans, and in June 1532 the Ottomans agreed to a peace treaty with the Holy Roman Empire. Even this turn of events did not lessen Luther's depression. His mood temporarily improved when he finally completed his translation of the German Bible in 1534. Until this point, German had been a clumsy language with many different spoken and written dialects. Luther's Bible became so popular that his style of Ger-

Martin Luther and Philip of Hesse

Philip of Hesse was instrumental in the formation of the Schmalkaldic League, as well as in the spread of Protestantism. He was a close friend of Martin Luther's and frequently sought religious advice from him. Philip was married to Christina, the daughter of Duke George of Saxony. Christina was a Catholic, and by 1540, the two had been married for sixteen years. The marriage was not a happy one, however, and Philip frequently complained to Luther that his wife was a cold, bitter alcoholic. Philip was a man with great sexual appetites, and he had been having affairs with ladies in his royal court for years. He often felt guilty about his behavior and confided this to Luther. In late 1539 he had contracted a dangerous sexually transmitted disease, syphilis, which had killed his father years before. He had also fallen in love with a seventeen-year-old member of his court, Margaret von der Saal, and wished to marry her. Philip went to Luther

for advice. In 1526 Philip had wanted to marry another of his court ladies, and Luther had refused to allow it. But when Philip met with Luther and several other Protestant ministers in 1539, the aging Luther agreed to the request. He and his colleagues felt that a bigamous (married to more than one woman at the same time) marriage was better than a divorce. They supported their claim by referring to men in the Old Testament who were married to several women at the same time. Bigamy was against imperial law, however, and Philip was told to keep his second marriage a secret. By 1540, news of the marriage became public, as did Luther's knowledge and support of it. Charles forced Philip to give up any positions within Protestant groups, promising Philip he would not be tried in court for bigamy. As a result the Schmalkaldic League lost one of its most important members, and Luther became linked with a scandal.

---

man became the basis of a unified German language.

Luther soon lapsed into despair again. He was greatly troubled that he had done little to stop the sinful behavior of man. He felt that he had given clear guidelines for peace and brotherhood through his teachings, but few accepted the truth that he had given them. During the last two decades of his life Luther spent as

much time arguing with other Reformation leaders as with his Catholic opponents. He longed for Christian unity, yet he could not accept differing views. In 1542, when his daughter Magdalena died from the plague, he publicly declared that he wished all his children would die. He was convinced the final judgment of God was coming and that the world would be destroyed. Luther began to write attacks against the Ottomans, the papacy, the Anabaptists (a Protestant group that opposed baptism of infants), and other religious groups. He was critical of the Council of Trent, one of the most important steps toward peace between Protestants and Catholics since the beginning of the Reformation.

Luther also began attacking Jews. In 1542 he wrote *Against the Jews and Their Lies,* calling upon authorities to burn Jewish synagogues (houses of worship) and to expel Jews if they did not convert to Christianity. These attacks were a drastic departure from Luther's earlier views. As a young man, he had studied with Jewish theologians when translating the Old Testament into German. In an age when most Catholics blamed Jews for the crucifixion of Jesus, Luther had written a pamphlet titled "That Jesus Christ Was Born a Jew," which defended the Jews against these charges. At the end of his life, however, he became one of their harshest opponents. Luther did nothing to stop John Frederick of Saxony, the son of John of Saxony, from expelling the Jews from his lands in 1536. In his last sermon, on February 15, 1546, Luther publicly declared that "the Jews are our enemies, who do not cease to defame Christ and would gladly kill us if they could." Despite these harsh words, he urged Christians to treat Jews with love and pray for their conversions. Three days after delivering the sermon, Luther died of a heart attack at the age of sixty-three.

The Protestant Reformation

6

As Martin Luther's reform movement gained momentum in Germany throughout the sixteenth century, other charges against the Roman Catholic Church sprang up elsewhere in Europe. Huldrych Zwingli, a Swiss priest, challenged the church's rule that priests could not marry. He also called for a separation of church and state. The famous French-born reformer John Calvin, who adopted Switzerland as the base of his "New Jerusalem," made the city of Geneva a stronghold of Protestant activity and Calvinism. His basic concept, later known as "predestination," was the belief that a small minority of people were "elected" before birth to become the chosen who would enter heaven (the concept of the place where the righteous go after death). His followers carried his teachings to eager reformers throughout Europe, especially in France, where Calvinists were called Huguenots, and in England, where they inspired Puritanism.

Radical Protestantism became a rallying point for peasants as well as nobles who desired to escape the oppression of the Catholic Church and the monarchs who supported it. In 1555 the Peace of Augsburg stated that each of the more than three hundred principalities in Germany would adopt the religion of its local ruler, leaving over half of Germany to the Lutherans. By the end of the sixteenth century, the Scandinavian countries had become predominantly Lutheran. In France nearly a quarter of the population were Huguenots. In 1598 King Henry IV granted religious freedom to Calvinist sects in the Edict of Nantes.

Soon hundreds of new Protestant sects were forming and re-forming. Among the strongest were the Anabaptists, who believed that baptism (the ceremony in which a person is blessed with water and admitted to the Christian faith) should be reserved only for adults who were fully aware of its significance. Others, like the Spiritualists, sought personal communion with the Holy Spirit (the spirit of God). The Evangelical Rationalists and Puritans of both Poland and England applied "right reason" (the use of reasoned thinking to interpret Scripture, as opposed to the blind acceptance of the teachings of theologians) to such concepts as the deity (godliness) of Jesus Christ, the Trinity (the Christian idea of God as the Father, Son, and Holy Spirit), and the existence of heaven and hell (place where sinners go after death). The Levellers and True Levellers, Ranters, Seekers, Muggletonians, Antinomians, and scores of other radical groups rose up, especially in England, Belgium, and France. They came to be known by both Catholics and conservative Protestants as "the lunatic fringe."

Lay preachers (ministers who are not officially ordained, that is, authorized by an established religion to head a church congregation) saw the close connections among religion, politics, and economics. They began to press for social and political reforms that they justified with passages from the Bible. The Reformation thus spread to all aspects of life, and the Christian world found itself in the middle of the most profound upheaval since Roman Catholicism was founded around A.D. 600. The Protestant Reformation had a far-ranging impact on most of the major European countries—Switzerland, Denmark, Sweden, the Netherlands, France, and England.

Switzerland

While Luther was taking his stand against the Catholic Church in Germany, Swiss pastor Huldrych (also Ulrich) Zwingli (1484–1531) was leading a similar movement in Zurich, Switzerland. In 1518 he denounced the church's practice of selling indulgences—partial forgiveness of sins—then he went on to attack other abuses. Zwingli expressed his views in sermons, private conversations, and public debates, called disputations, before the city council. Like Luther, he considered the Bible the sole source of moral and spiritual authority, and he set out to eliminate everything in the Roman Catholic system that could not be supported by the Scripture (books of the Bible). Zwingli eventually made Zurich the center of church reform. He died in battle against Catholic forces in 1531. Five years later the French reformer John Calvin estab-

While Martin Luther was challenging the Catholic Church in Germany, Swiss priest Huldrych Zwingli was leading a similar movement in Zurich. *Reproduced by permission of Archive Photos, Inc.*

When he was not tending to his congregation he devoted his time to classical studies. He also began reading the original text of the Bible, which was published by the Dutch humanist Desiderius Erasmus. Zwingli had been accustomed to reading the Bible commentaries of church "experts" instead of the text of the Bible itself, and he soon began to question traditional interpretations of the Scripture. This quest eventually led him to call for reforms in the church.

Zwingli's future was also shaped by his experience as a chaplain, or religious adviser, for the local army unit. In Zwingli's day, Switzerland was organized into the Swiss Confederation, an alliance of communities formed in the late thirteenth century for mutual protection in trading and in times of war (see "Switzerland" in Chapter 4). In 1499 the confederation declared its independence from the Holy Roman Empire. As the economy of Switzerland changed from a dependence on the dairy industry (the breeding of cattle to produce milk products) to agriculture (the growing of crops for food), many young Swiss men were unable to find jobs. They often signed up as mercenaries, or hired soldiers, in the armies of the pope or foreign kings and dukes. Mercenaries could make quite a bit of money, especially from raiding captured cities. During the time Zwingli was in Glarus, France was fighting against Spain (which was allied with the Holy Roman Empire) in the Italian Wars, a conflict over control of Italy (see "Italian Wars dominate Renais-

lished a Protestant movement in Geneva. Calvin soon became the most important figure in the Reformation, and his views gave a new direction to Protestant beliefs.

Zwingli: early reformer

Huldrych Zwingli began his career as a Roman Catholic priest in 1506, after graduating from the University of Basel with a master of arts degree. He was appointed as a parish priest in his home region of Glarus.

sance" in Chapter 2). Popes and foreign monarchs were also involved in these wars because they wanted to assert their own power. They did not commit themselves to one side or the other, however, and they formed alliances that seemed the most advantageous at the moment.

In 1513 men from Glarus joined a unit in the army of Pope Leo X, which was fighting in Italy against France on the side of Spain and the Holy Roman Empire. Zwingli went to Italy with the unit. After returning home, he recorded his impressions of the campaign in a fable (a story with animal characters that teaches a moral lesson) called *The Ox*. His message was that, for the security of the Swiss Confederation, it was essential not to sell out to foreign warlords. Rather, Switzerland should remain neutral in the power-plays of European wars. In 1515 the Swiss troops were defeated by the French in the Battle of Marignano. The following year they signed a treaty with the French king Francis I, in which they agreed to sign up as mercenaries in the French army—the former enemy—in exchange for economic benefits. When Zwingli's opposition to the treaty became public, he had to leave Glarus.

Questions church Zwingli then spent three years as a priest at a Benedictine abbey (a monastery run by members of the Catholic order founded by Saint Benedict) in Einsiedeln. In addition to taking care of the spiritual needs of the small community, he preached to hundreds of pilgrims, travelers who go on religious journeys. These pilgrims had come to do penance, or confess their sins, and receive absolution, or forgiveness of sins, for money. During his stay at the abbey, Zwingli continued to improve his knowledge of the Scripture by studying and imitating the works of Erasmus. By 1518 his preaching skills had been noticed at the Great Minster, the main church in the city of Zurich, where he was soon appointed a preacher. To help his audience better understand the word of God, in 1519 Zwingli began a series of lectures on the Gospel According to Matthew, a book in the New Testament, the second part of the Bible. In his lectures he used simple terms and incorporated references to events in everyday life. This approach was radical because Catholic priests were considered authorities on the Bible and they were not allowed to help their parishioners interpret the Scripture. Despite some opposition from traditional priests, Zwingli's unusual method was soon adopted by his fellow priests at Great Minster.

On March 5, 1522, in the home of the printer Christoph Froschauer (died 1564), some of Zwingli's friends and supporters broke the rule of fasting during Lent by eating sausages. Lent is a forty-day period prior to Easter, the celebration of Christ's rising from the dead. Christians devote this time to prayer, penance, and reflection. As a sign of fasting and additional penance, Catholics were not permitted to eat meat during Lent. Zwingli turned this event into a public issue in his sermon, which he followed with a pamphlet. Not only did he support the actions of Froschauer and the others, but he also claimed that it was the right of every individual to choose freely what to eat.

Leads debates This question of fasting triggered discussion of other issues, including clerical celibacy, the Catholic Church policy that does not permit priests to get married. Many clergymen of northern Switzerland were married, and Zwingli was among them. Secretly, he had married Anna Reinhart and had fathered several children. Together with ten other priests he sent a petition to the bishop of Constance (the official who headed the church district based in Constance) asking for church recognition of their marriages. To strengthen their argument, they pointed out that the "bishops," or founders, of the early Church had been married. Zwingli also took a stand against praying to saints—people declared as holy by the Catholic Church—for help and favors. Zwingli thought people could learn such qualities as humility, faith, and hope from the lives of the saints, but he believed in praying directly to God. Zwingli further questioned the belief that saints worked miracles. He had seen crowds of pilgrims flocking to shrines and praying for miracles, and he felt that the church was taking advantage of their superstition to get rich. Zwingli contended that pictures and statues of saints only encouraged idolatry—the worship of images, or false gods—so they should be taken down. Many of his most enthusiastic followers took his words literally, and from 1523 until 1525 they stripped decorations, statues, and pictures from all churches in Zurich. They frequently used violent tactics, causing disturbances in cantons (small territorial divisions in a country) that refused to adopt Zwingli's new methods.

In the sixteenth century, public debates called disputations were the generally accepted means for settling conflict. In January 1523 Zwingli invited the leading clergy of various cantons of the Swiss Confederation, including the bishop of Constance, to the Zurich town hall to discuss the recent issues. Most of his opponents refused to accept the invitation, and the bishop sent his personal adviser as an observer. Zwingli presented sixty-seven theses, which offered solutions to major problems in the church. Since the audience consisted mainly of his supporters, he easily convinced them to accept his plan. Zwingli's sixty-seven theses therefore became an outline for religious reform in Zurich. Among practices no longer acceptable were pilgrimages, processions (religious parades), incense, noisy hymns, and the purchase of prayers and indulgences. Zwingli also advised his audience not spend their money on such things as gambling and lavish clothing, but instead to use it to feed the poor and support widows and orphans. Additional reforms were decided upon at a second debate held later in the year. Among them were the closing of monasteries and the seizing of church property (land and wealth), which was to be given to the poor. The reformers also

The Sixty-Seven Articles of Huldrych Zwingli

In 1523 Huldrych Zwingli held a conference in Zurich to discuss reforms in the Roman Catholic Church. At the conference he presented sixty-seven theses, or proposed reforms, which became the basis of the Reformation in Switzerland. He began the list with this statement:

> I, Ulrich Zwingli, confess that I have preached in the worthy city of Zurich these sixty-seven articles or opinions on the basis of Scripture, which is called theopneustos (that is, inspired by God). I offer to defend and vindicate these articles with Scripture. But if I have not understood Scripture correctly, I am ready to be corrected, but only from the same Scripture.

Zwingli touched on nearly every practice of the Catholic Church. In theses 28 through 33, he addressed the issues of marriage of priests (he himself was a married priest), excommunication, and the giving of unclaimed property to the church.

The Marriage of Clergy

28. Everything that God permits or has not forbidden is proper. From this we learn that marriage is proper for all people.

The Impure Priest Should Take a Wife

29. All those who are in the church sin if they do not make themselves secure through marriage once they understand that God has granted marriage to them for the sake of purity.

Of Excommunication

31. No private person may excommunicate anyone else, but the church—that is, the communion of those among whom the one subject to excommunication lives—along with its guardians may act as a bishop.

32. The only one who should be excommunicated is a person who commits a public scandal.

Of Unclaimed Goods

33. Unclaimed goods should not be given to temples, cloisters, monks, priests, or nuns, but to the needy, if it is impossible to return them to their rightful owner.

Zwingli's sixty-seven theses became the basis for reform of the church in Zurich and, eventually, all of Switzerland.

Source: Mark A. Noll. Confessions and Catechisms of the Reformation. *Vancouver, B.C.: Regent College Publishing, 1997, pp. 42–43.*

wanted to change the interpretation of communion, the ceremony in which bread and wine represent the body and blood of Christ. According to Catholic tradition, the bread and wine became the actual body and blood of Christ (a process called transubstantiation). Zwingli and his supporters contended, however, that communion had only symbolic significance, nothing more.

Anabaptists

The Anabaptist movement arose in the early 1520s, mainly in Germany, the Netherlands, and Switzerland. Meaning "one who baptizes again," the name Anabaptist refers to the practice of baptizing adults, even if they had been baptized as infants. The Anabaptists called this believer's baptism because it was the voluntary choice of a mature person who was ready to accept Christianity. Calvinists and Lutherans often used "Anabaptist" as negative term for any sect (small religious group) that did not follow standard reform practices. Like the Calvinists and the Lutherans, the Anabaptists stressed the importance of personal communication with God, and they rejected the rituals of the Catholic Church. They were different from other Protestant groups, however, because they advocated nonviolence, opposed state churches, did not participate in state government, and refused to take oaths. Prominent Anabaptist leaders were Konrad Grebel in Switzerland and Hans Denck and Balthasar Hubmaier in Germany.

Closely related to the Anabaptists were the Hutterites (Moravian Brethren), a group founded by Jakob Hutter, an Austrian pacifist (one who is opposed to violence). The Hutterites established communities based on mutual Christian love and the sharing of goods. Another prominent Anabaptist group was the Mennonites. They were led by the Dutch reformer Menno Simons, the best-known Anabaptist theologian of the sixteenth century. Simons stressed the importance of living according to the teachings of Christ. Like the Hutterites, the Mennonites formed close-knit communities that lived apart from the rest of the world.

Anabaptism was embraced mainly by the poor and by uneducated peasants and artisans. Anabaptists were persecuted throughout Europe by the aristocracy and by mainstream Protestant reformers, who disapproved of their community-based religions and their opposition to state churches.

Makes Zurich evangelical city During the years to come, Zwingli turned Zurich into an evangelical city. ("Evangelical" was a term used to refer to the Reformation movement in Germany; those who practiced the new religion were called "evangelicals." They became known as "Protestants" in 1529, after many evangelicals protested the decisions of the second Diet of Speyer; see "Diets of Speyer" in Chapter 5.) Those in Zurich who disagreed with Zwingli were forced either to comply or to leave. As early as 1524, some of Zwingli's supporters claimed his reforms did not go far enough. Among them were the Anabaptists, who formed a separatist movement known as the Swiss Brethren. They were seen as a threat by the Zwinglians. The Anabaptists believed that even people who did not believe in God had this right as long as the obeyed the city's laws. They also strictly separated the state from the church. One of the main sources of disagreement was the Anabaptist concept of believer's baptism. Contrary to the Catholic and Lutheran practice of baptizing infants, Anabaptists asserted that only adults who voluntarily accepted Christianity should be baptized. This dispute led in 1525 to the suppression of the Anabaptist movement in Zurich and later to the banishment of its members. They were prosecuted, and in 1527 one of their leaders, Felix Mantz, was among those executed. This harsh policy, practiced by the reform council and supported by Zwingli, contributed to some loss of his popularity.

Religious disputes rapidly divided the Swiss Confederation. In 1524 the five central states formed a special alliance. Zurich, in turn, sought possible allies and defenders of its cause. In 1526 a Catholic-dominated conference was held in Baden. Zwingli, though invited, did not attend because he feared for his personal safety. The council condemned Zwinglian reforms as the works of the "Antichrist of the Great Minster." The conference's outcome was a blow to the reformers in Zurich. Zwingli's absence, in the eyes of his opponents, was considered an act of cowardice.

On January 6, 1528, a public religious debate was allowed to take place in Bern, the largest state of the confederation. All clergy from Bern were invited, as were the four bishops of Lausanne, Sion, Basel, and Constance. Zwingli and Johannes Oekolampadius of Basel, who had spoken on Zwingli's behalf, were to attend the debate. Many Catholic officials refused to attend, but several Catholics did come to the meeting. A main topic of discussion was the Catholic concept of the pope as God's representative on Earth. The Catholics argued that Jesus, before his death, had told his disciple (follower) Peter to organize a Christian church. Peter (later Saint Peter) then handed down this responsibility to popes, who were to appoint bishops, priests, and lay (unordained) members of the church. The reformers could not accept this reasoning because, as far as they were concerned, the church was the body of Christ and therefore Christ was its only head.

The debate lasted until the end of January, leaving no doubt that the reformation of the church, as Zwingli had demanded in Zurich, was soon to be carried out in the canton of Bern. One region, the Bernr Oberland, tried to resist the introduction of reforms, asking the neighboring states of Valais, Uri, and Unterwalden for spiritual and, eventually, military support. To reprimand the rebellious subjects, Bern sent in troops. The peasants of the Bernr Oberland soon gave up their resistance and accepted reforms that had taken place in Zurich. Zwingli had reached the summit of his power and influence. Those states willing to conform to Zurich standards were looking to him for guidance and advice. Realizing that his dream of a Protestant Swiss Confederation could be realized only with the help of foreign allies, he encouraged the council to form stronger ties with the cities of Muelhausen and Strasbourg. Although they were part of the German Empire, they had for some time been on friendly terms with the Swiss Confederation.

Popularity declines Neither Zwingli nor Luther had any doubts about his own interpretation of the Scripture. Luther was a regular priest who was said to have had a haughty way about him when speaking to Zwingli. He considered Zwingli a coarse fanatic—one who holds extreme beliefs—who was trying to show off his Greek and Latin only because his German language skills were so poor. When the two men finally met at a conference in Marburg in 1529, they reportedly parted without shaking hands. Nevertheless, the meeting was a success and the participants drew up fifteen articles that defined the Protestant faith. The Marburg meeting took place between the two Kappel Wars, religious conflicts between Catholics and Protestants. The first Kappel war began in 1528, immediately after Zwingli's successful appearance in Bern, Zurich had extended its influence to the territories of Saint Gall and Thurgau and to the Lake of Constance. Furthermore, Protestant villages in these areas were supported by Zurich. The Catholic cantons of Lucerne and Schwyz prohibited Zwinglian preaching within their borders. One reform preacher, Jacob Kaiser, who did not obey the Catholic cantons was sentenced to death by burning at the stake. On July 8, 1529, Zurich declared war on the Catholic cantons and the Protestant and Catholic armies met near the village Kappel. The Protestant troops far outnumbered the Catholics. Only a few moments before the actual fighting, the leaders of the opposite sides were called in for peace negotiations. Zwingli was disgusted. He warned the council against giving in to the pleading of the Catholics. A truce was finally signed by both parties, but neither side seemed completely satisfied.

When Zwingli returned home after the Marburg meeting, events seemed to develop in his favor. But soon thereafter open resistance from the Catholic cantons was combined with opponents in his own ranks. Zwingli proposed a quick military campaign to put down opposition once and for all. But allies in Bern interfered, suggesting an economic blockade instead. (A blockade is a ban on shipment of goods into a region.) This measure imposed a hardship on the Catholics, whose well-being largely depended on Zurich markets. It was not just the Catholics that suffered the effects of the blockade, however. Within Zurich, Zwingli's popularity began to shrink as merchants, millers, bakers, and other artisans complained of the damaging effect the blockade had on their trade. Zwingli asked the council to relieve him from his post. Although he was begged to stay, his position had been weakened.

Dies in second Kappel War Soon news reached Zurich that the Catholic forces had gathered near Zug, a region not far from Zurich. Hastily, Zurich's troops hurried in from all sides, but it was impossible to form orderly units on such short notice. No time remained to ask Protestant allies for support. Facing the well-prepared Catholic troops near Kappel in October 1531, the Protestant army of about fifteen hundred fought bravely, but with no chance of victory. After only a few days, the Protestant alliance was defeated. Zurich lost about five hundred men in battle, among them its spiritual leader, Huldrych Zwingli. After Zwingli's death, his colleague Heinrich Bullinger (1504–1575) became the pastor at Great Minster and the leader of the reform movement in Switzerland. In 1536 Bullinger played an important role in compiling the First Helvetic Confession, a statement of reform goals based largely on Zwingli's views. The Helvetic Confession reflected the differences between Zwingli and Luther on such issues as the communion ceremony. In 1549 Bullinger joined the French reformer John Calvin in drafting the Consensus of Tigurnius, which moved Swiss reform efforts toward Calvinism. Bullinger's later views were presented in the Second Helvetic Confession (1566), which was accepted in Switzerland, France, Scotland, and Hungary.

John Calvin: the most influential reformer

The next major figure in the Swiss Reformation was John Calvin (1509–1564), a French reformer who fled religious persecution (harassment for religious beliefs) in France and set-

John Calvin was perhaps the most influential of all religious leaders of the Protestant Reformation in sixteenth-century Europe. *Photograph courtesy of The Library of Congress.*

tled in Geneva. Calvin was perhaps the most influential of all religious leaders of the Protestant Reformation in sixteenth-century Europe. He was twenty-six years younger than Luther and had developed some important theological differences. Calvin believed in a sterner, more "puritanical" interpretation of Christianity. Under his tireless direction, Geneva became the focus of a far-reaching evangelical movement.

Calvin was born Jean Cauvin in Noyon, France, on July 10, 1509. His father, Gérard Cauvin, was an ambitious lawyer. His mother, Jeanne Lefranc Chauvin, was the daughter of a fairly well-to-do innkeeper. At an early age, Calvin was sent by his father to the University of Paris with the intention that he would one day enter the priesthood. But in 1528, his father ordered him to switch his emphasis from theology to law because law was a more practical profession. Calvin obeyed, leaving Paris for the University of Orléans and, later, for Brouges. Although he had already developed a passion for theology, Calvin embraced the study of law. In 1531 he published his first book, which showed his intellectual potential and promised a bright career. But the death of his father earlier that year was to change his life drastically. Returning to Paris, Calvin was now free to pursue his humanist and theological interests. During his studies he felt a personal challenge to become an instrument of God's will, and by 1533 he had converted from Catholicism to Protestantism.

Flees to Switzerland To escape persecution for being a Protestant, Calvin left France in 1534 and traveled under the assumed name of Martianus Lucianius. In Basel, Switzerland, he met people who shared his views. In 1536 he published the first edition of the *Institutes of the Christian Religion,* which outlined his beliefs and gained him attention as an important religious leader. For Calvin, the only spiritual authority was Scripture, both the New Testament and the Old Testament (the Christian name for the Hebrew Bible). According to Calvin, the

all-knowing and ever-present God had determined, from the beginning of time, who was to be saved and who was to be damned. All people, he felt, were sinful by nature and could never achieve salvation, or forgiveness of sins by God, through their own efforts. God had therefore selected a few people, called the "the elect," for salvation. The elect were to lead others, who had not been chosen by God, toward salvation. This concept was later called "predestination," but Calvin himself did not use the term. Calvin taught that the purpose of life was to strive to know or understand God as well as possible and then to follow God's will. This path could only be followed through faith (acceptance of truth without questioning), by which people pursue union with Christ, the embodiment of God on Earth. With this faith, then, all people were required to strive to live a moral life, out of hope that they were among the elect chosen by God. Calvin enforced strict moral discipline in pursuit of this goal.

One evening in June 1536, Calvin stopped in Geneva to spend the night. He fully intended to continue on his journey the following day, but the local evangelical preacher, Guillaume Farel (1489–1565), had another idea. He convinced Calvin that it was his duty to God to remain where he was most needed. The task was to expel Catholicism from the city, which had recently won its independence from the church. Calvin agreed to stay in Geneva, and with Farel he worked to establish Protestantism. Within a couple of years, however, both men were expelled for being too strict and for encouraging French Huguenots to move to Geneva. Calvin then went to Strasbourg, where he taught at an academy, preached, and developed his ideas on the nature of the ideal Christian church. Calvin's friends in Strasbourg urged him to find a wife. In 1540 he married Idelette Bure, the widow of one of his converts, who had a son and a daughter. The couple's only child together died shortly after birth in 1542. Idelette died seven years later, but Calvin never remarried.

Eliminates opposition In 1541 Calvin returned reluctantly to Geneva in response to a call from the now floundering church. After receiving assurances that he would be given the freedom he felt was necessary to build God's earthly kingdom, he soon organized the local church government with his *Ecclesiastical Ordinances*. With these, he began to develop a well-regulated social network within a morally disciplined society. Despite considerable opposition within the city, Calvin's influence grew steadily as he defeated theological and political opponents alike. In 1553 Michael Servetus (1511–1553), a Spanish theologian, or religious scholar, was traveling in disguise to avoid persecution for his scandalous religious ideas. Often called the first Unitarian (a present-day Protestant denomination), Servetus denied the divinity (godliness) of Christ and the doctrine of the Trinity (the Christian concept of God as the Fa-

ther, the Son, and the Holy Spirit). His views alienated him from both Catholics and Protestants. When Calvin recognized his foe sitting within the crowd listening to one of his sermons, he promptly had Servetus arrested and put on trial. As the "Defender of the Faith," Calvin demanded that Servetus be executed. His order was supported by the city government, and on October 27, 1553, Servetus was burned alive for heresy (not obeying the laws of God and the church).

Soon Calvin overcame most remaining opposition to his plans, and in 1555 the Consistory, which acted as a sort of moral court, was accepted and given powers by the city. Henceforth, moral discipline was strictly enforced. Taverns were closed and replaced with *abbayes,* in which patrons were closely scrutinized for signs of excessive drinking. Indeed, throughout Geneva, citizens monitored one another's behavior, ready to report any sort of wrongdoing. In this spirit, a strict moral order—based on Calvin's particular vision of truth—was built. Constantly preaching and writing, he involved himself in all aspects of Genevan affairs including education, trade, diplomacy, and even sanitation. In 1559 Calvin and the French scholar Theodore Beza (1516–1605) founded the Genevan Academy (now the University of Geneva) for the training of clergy. Calvin was not interested in Geneva alone but also in spreading the Reform movement abroad, especially within his native France. Under his direction, Geneva became a haven for persecuted Protestants and the unofficial center of growing Protestant movements in places as far removed as Scotland. Before Calvin died in 1564 he asked Beza to be head of the church of Geneva and to help promote Calvinism throughout the world.

Scandinavia

As Lutheranism spread northward from Germany, the Reformation was accomplished peacefully in the Scandinavian countries: Denmark, Sweden, and Norway. The kings of Denmark and Sweden sponsored the reform movement and broke completely with the papacy. In 1536 a national assembly held in Copenhagen, Denmark, abolished the authority of Roman Catholic bishops throughout Denmark and then in Norway and Iceland, which were ruled by Denmark. King Christian III of Denmark and Norway invited Luther's friend, the German religious reformer Johann Bugenhagen, to organize in Denmark a national Lutheran church on the basis of the Augsburg Confession, a statement of Lutheran beliefs written by the German reformer Philip Melanchthon in 1530 (see "The Augsburg Confession" in Chapter 5). In Sweden the brothers Olaus and Laurentius Petri led a similar movement, and in 1529 King Gustav I Vasa declared Lutheranism as the state religion. Sweden's Reformation, like that in England (see "England" section later in this chapter), left cathedrals, bishops, and priests in place, while gradually closing monasteries. There was relatively little debate about Protestant beliefs outside a small circle of theologians, especially by comparison with the Reformation in Germany, Switzerland, and England.

Denmark

The Reformation in Denmark was initiated during the reign of Christian II (1481–1559; ruled 1513–23), king of Denmark and Sweden. In 1520 Christian asked Frederick the Wise of Saxony, the patron of Martin Luther, to send one of Luther's followers to Denmark. Although Christian had not converted to Lutheranism, he wanted to reform the Roman Catholic Church. He issued several laws that limited the power of the church. For instance, he decreed that all spiritual cases were to be decided not by bishops but by the king and his council, who would act as a court of final appeal. He also prohibited the clergy from owning land. Christian's reform efforts and his support of Lutheranism were opposed by the bishops and by Danish noblemen. In 1523, after Christian used violent tactics to put down an independence revolt in Sweden, he was removed from the throne. Sweden won its freedom from Denmark and Christian was taken prisoner. He was succeeded by his uncle, King Frederick I (ruled 1523–33), who was also a Catholic. At first Frederick promised to stop the Lutheran movement, but he soon began protecting Lutheran preachers and reformers. He contended that even though a king had power over people's lives and property, he could not own their souls.

Frederick's policy permitted the spread of Lutheranism and the dismantling of the Catholic Church. Beginning in 1526, appointments of bishops were approved by the king instead of the pope in Rome. The king also allowed reformers to gain power in major cities, close monasteries, and destroy Catholic churches. He was influenced by his eldest son, Christian (1503–1559), duke of Schleswig and Holstein (then provinces in Denmark; now Schleswig-Holstein, a state in Germany), who was a Lutheran and encouraged the movement in his own territories. When Frederick died in 1533, Christian was prevented from taking the throne by a Catholic-dominated council that was in charge of electing a new king. Then the cities of Copenhagen and Malmö formed an alliance with the north German city of Lübeck to restore the imprisoned former Christian II to the throne. A civil war known as the Counts' War (1533–36) broke out when Lübeck's forces invaded Holstein, and soon Denmark was on the verge of collapse. Then Frederick I's son Christian achieved a victory over the invading forces with the help of Gustav I Vasa of Sweden, and in 1536 Christian became King Christian III (ruled 1534–59) of Denmark and Norway. He needed to pay off debts from the war, so he turned to the Catholic bishops, who were the wealthiest men in the country. They refused to give him any money, so he had them arrested and imprisoned, then seized their property. Although the bishops were released from prison, the king did not let them take their former positions.

Christian made an even bolder move in 1537, when he brought Johann Bugenhagen, a chief assistant of Martin Luther, to Denmark to head reform efforts. Christian asked Bugenhagen to crown him king, a function that was traditionally performed by the Catholic archbishop of Lund. Bugenhagen later ordained seven Lutheran clergymen, who were called superintendents, to replace the dismissed bishops. This act represented a definite break with the Catholic Church. Another step toward reform was the reopening in 1537 of the University of Copenhagen, which had been closed during the civil war. The university now had a Protestant faculty that trained ministers for Protestant churches. Bugenhagen was appointed professor of theology. In 1539 a commission of clergymen, chosen by the king and approved by Luther, issued a new Church Ordinance, which declared Lutheranism to be the state religion of Denmark. Christian III's Bible, the first complete translation of the Bible into Danish, appeared in 1550, nine years before the king's death.

Sweden

The Lutheran Church was established in Sweden by King Gustav I Vasa (Gustavus Eriksson; 1496–1560; ruled 1523–60). He came to power following a civil war that started in 1517, when King Christian II of Denmark (see "Denmark" section previously in this chapter) attacked Sweden. Christian was opposed by the popular Swedish leader Sten Sture (called the Younger; c. 1492–1520), who defeated

Johannes Bugenhagen

Religious reformer Johannes Bugenhagen (1485–1558) was instrumental in establishing the Lutheran church in Denmark. A native of Eastern Pomerania, he studied humanism in Greifswald, Germany, and was ordained as a Roman Catholic priest. He then became a teacher of religion. At first he did not agree with Martin Luther's criticism of the Catholic Church, but by 1523 he had become a supporter of the Reformation. He moved to Wittenberg, Germany, Luther's home and the center of the reform movement. Appointed as the town priest, Bugenhagen was also Luther's personal spiritual adviser and a theology lecturer at the Wittenberg University. He then became one of the foremost leaders of the Reformation in northern Germany and Scandinavia. In 1537 the Danish king, Christian III, invited Bugenhagen to head the church in Denmark. Two years later Bugenhagen was named superintendent general—head church official—of Saxony. He died in Wittenberg in 1558.

the king on the battlefield at Brännkyrka in 1518. Among Sten Sture's troops was the courageous soldier Gustav Eriksson. In the treaty that followed this conflict, Sten Sture handed over Gustav to Christian as a pledge of his good intentions. Christian took Gustav to Denmark as a captive. When Gustav heard news of renewed fighting between Denmark and Sweden, he es-

caped and made his way to back to Sweden. After Sten Sture was killed in battle in 1520, Christian seized Stockholm and declared himself king of Sweden. On November 8, 1520, he presided over the "bloodbath of Stockholm." During a rampage Danish soldiers chopped off the heads of nearly one hundred prominent Swedes, including two Catholic bishops, who had supported Sten Sture. The massacre outraged the Roman Catholic Church.

Gustav Vasa gains power The surviving Swedes called upon Gustav Eriksson to be their new leader. He regained control of the country in 1523 and took the throne as King Gustav I Vasa. Gustav immediately saw the advantage of adopting Protestantism as the national religion. He had many debts from the war with Denmark and very little money of his own to repay them (at that time, monarchs financed wars themselves). The Roman Catholic Church, however, had abundant wealth. The church received almost five times as much as the king's income in tithes alone, and it owned many valuable estates and castles as well. Gustav was determined to lay his hands on this wealth, and he confided his intentions to Bishop Hans Brask of Linköping. Brask protested that Gustav would be violating the law of God by taking such a step because Catholic officials were considered representatives of God on Earth. Nevertheless, Gustav was determined to break the power of the church.

Gustav's chancellor (secretary), Lars Andreae, had converted to

Lutheranism under the influence of Olaus Petri (1493–1552), a priest who had been a student in Wittenberg during Martin Luther's confrontation with the church. Within a year of becoming king, Gustav was defending the small circle of Lutherans in Stockholm. He also gave his approval to Petri's marriage, which went against the church ban on priests being married. Most Swedes opposed the Reformation, so Brask tried to coordinate opposition and stamp out Lutheranism. He also warned noblemen that the king would take away their privileges next if they resisted his efforts to break up the church. Gustav then promised the nobles that they could share church property with him. In 1527 he called a meeting of the Swedish Estates (assembly of nobles, middle-class citizens called burghers, clergymen, and peasants) in the city of Västerås. After the clever king burst into tears and threatened to abdicate (resign as king) if his plan was not approved, the Estates let him have his way.

Gustav's men entered churches and took gold and silver plates, candlesticks, and other wealth that could be converted into money. The king also seized estates, castles, and lands that had been church property for centuries. This policy led to an uprising of Catholics in the southwestern provinces of Sweden in 1529, but Gustav soon outwitted the rebels and executed the ringleaders. He then placed the church under the control of the state. Two years later the king appointed Laurentius Petri (1499–1573), brother of Olaus, as the first Lutheran Archbishop of Uppsala. Under Laurentius's guidance, the Bible was translated into the Swedish language in 1541 and became the most ambitious publishing venture in Swedish history at the time. In 1571 Laurentius issued a *kyrkoordning,* or church order, that defined the beliefs of the Swedish Lutheran Church. It was also the basis for keeping the church independent from the monarchy. The separation of church and state has continued to be a distinctive feature of Swedish government.

France

The leader of the religious reform movement in France was Jacques Lefèvre d'Étaples (c. 1450–1536), a Catholic priest and biblical scholar who was influenced by humanism. Lefèvre d'Étaples shared many of Martin Luther's views, such as the idea that the individual Christian is capable of interpreting the Scripture without the assistance of a bishop or priest. Like Luther, he also rejected the Catholic belief in transubstantiation, or the transformation of bread and wine into the actual body and blood of Christ during the communion service. Inspired by Luther's German Bible, Lefèvre d'Étaples translated the New Testament into French in 1523. Unlike Luther, however, Lefèvre d'Étaples advocated making reforms within the Catholic Church rather than starting a separate church. As Luther's teachings began to spread into France, however, Lefèvre d'Étaples and his followers were persecuted because church and government officials linked them with

Olaus and Laurentius Petri

Olaus Petri and his brother Laurentius Petri played important roles in the Reformation in Sweden. From 1516 until 1518, Olaus studied for the Roman Catholic priesthood at Wittenberg University, where faculty members Martin Luther and Philip Melanchthon were calling for reform of the church. Olaus adopted their views and, after he was ordained as a priest, he became an enthusiastic supporter of Lutheranism. By 1523, when Gustav I Vasa was crowned king of Sweden, Olaus was widely known for his preaching. He attracted the attention of the king, who was intent on breaking the power of the Catholic Church. Gustav's chancellor, Lars Andreae, had converted to Lutheranism under the influence of Olaus. Soon after being crowned king, Gustav began protecting the rights of the Lutherans in Stockholm. He also allowed for Petri's marriage, which broke the church law that prohibited priests from getting married. In 1531 Olaus served as the king's chancellor. Eventually he took a stand against Gustav's strict policies toward the church. He was condemned to death in 1540, but the sentence was not carried out and he was required only to pay a heavy fine. Olaus later regained the favor of the king and was appointed pastor of Storkyrkan (the Cathedral of Saint Nicholas) in Stockholm. Olaus produced most of the literature for the Reformation movement in Sweden, including a Swedish New Testament, a hymnbook, a church manual, the Swedish liturgy (text of the worship service), and many other writings.

Laurentius Petri was the first Protestant archbishop of Uppsala (1531–73) and had a great influence on the Reformation in Sweden. He oversaw the Swedish translation of the Bible, which was as important for Sweden as Luther's German translation was for Germany. Laurentius's *kyrkoordning* (church order) of 1571 defined the beliefs of the Swedish Lutheran Church. It was also the basis for keeping the church independent from the monarchy.

Lutheranism. Many French reformers fled to Switzerland, where they became involved in the movement led by John Calvin in Geneva (see "Switzerland" section previously in this chapter). Pastors trained by Calvin then began returning to France and promoting Protestantism. In 1559 delegates from 66 French Protestant churches met in Paris and issued a statement of faith based on the practices Calvin had established in Geneva. By 1567 more than 120 pastors trained by Calvin had returned to France. Known as Huguenots, the French Protestants grew into a powerful political force.

The Reformation period in France was marked by extreme violence. Efforts to suppress the Hugue-nots led to civil wars between Catholics and Protestants, called the French Wars of Religion (1562–98). The wars took place during the thirty years when Catherine de Médicis (1519–1589), the queen and widow of King Henry II, served as regent, one who rules for a king who is too young to take the throne. Henry was a member of the Valois dynasty. Catherine was the daughter of Lorenzo de' Médici, a pow-erful prince in Florence, Italy (see "Flo-rence" in Chapter 2). After Henry died in 1559, Catherine could not rule France because the Salic Law prohibited women from becoming monarchs. Nevertheless, she wielded great power during the reigns of her three weak sons—Francis II (1544–1560; ruled 1559–60), Charles IX (1550–1574; ruled 1560–74), and Henry III (1551–1589; ruled 1574–89). As a staunch Catholic, Catherine manipulated the religious prejudices of the nobility and the pub-lic in order to assure that the Valois family remained on the throne. She was partly responsible for many of the horrors of the French Wars of Religion in the 1560s and 1570s.

French queen Catherine de Médicis manipulated the religious practices of the nobility and the public in order to assure that her family remained on the throne. ©Bettmann/Corbis. Reproduced by permission of the Corbis Corporation.

France torn by religious wars

When Henry II died, his eldest son, Francis II, became king. During Francis's brief reign Protestants were ruthlessly persecuted. In 1558 Francis married Mary, Queen of Scots, a Catholic. The French government was in the hands of Mary's uncles, François of Lorraine, duke of Guise (1519–1563), and Charles of Guise, cardinal of Lor-raine (c. 1525–1574). At that time there

was considerable social unrest. After the Italian Wars, which ended in 1559, France was full of soldiers who had served in the wars. Many of the soldiers were unhappy because they had not been paid. Tax burdens on the peasants were also heavy. Calvinist preachers, therefore, with their message of pure faith that was not corrupted by politics, found a receptive audience. Huguenot noblemen took action, organizing a conspiracy to overthrow or at least dominate the court of Francis II. They obtained the support of England's new Protestant queen, Elizabeth I (see "England" section later in this chapter). Then, at the city of Amboise, their military uprising failed, and Francis's army arrested the leaders. In the presence of Catherine, her children, and Mary, Queen of Scots, fifty-seven of the Huguenot leaders were hanged or beheaded. This act only intensified religious and political conflicts as a powerful Huguenot family, the Navarres, and the Catholic Guises led factions (opposing groups) that competed for control of the government.

Upon the death of Francis II in 1560, Catherine became regent for her second son, Charles, who was crowned King Charles IX at the age of ten. For Catherine, religious differences were merely bargaining chips in a game to gain political advantage. She permitted Gaspard Il de Coligny (1519–1572), a famous admiral and an influential Huguenot, to act as Charles's chief adviser. In response, François de Lorraine and Charles de Guise formed an alliance to defend Catholicism against Coligny. In 1561, at the Colloquy of Poissy, Catherine tried to make peace between the Catholics and the Huguenots. Instead of reaching an understanding, the two parties hardened their differences. Open hostilities then broke out, initiating the first of three religious wars that raged for a decade.

Charles IX was an unstable character, and as he matured he came to dislike his mother and Henry, her favorite son. Catherine found it rela-tively easy to dominate Charles, despite his growing resentment. In the face of constant warfare she also tried to strengthen the kingdom for her sons' reigns. In 1565 she met with King Philip II of Spain, who was married to her daughter Elizabeth. Catherine wanted to discuss the continuing religious crisis in France, but Philip disliked her apparent willingness to pit Catholics and Protestants against one another. In his view, she should have been doing more to advance the Catholic Reformation (also called the Counter Reformation), a series of reform efforts undertaken by the Catholic Church to stop the Protestant Reformation. But Philip also knew that France's weakness was a strategic benefit for Spain. It made French intervention to aid the troublesome Dutch rebellion against Spain far less likely (see "The Netherlands" section later in this chapter). When Elizabeth died during childbirth in 1568, Catherine hoped Philip might marry her younger daughter Marguerite, but he was determined to take his French connection no further. Another blow to Catherine's politicking came the same year when Mary, Queen of Scots, was captured by her English enemies and imprisoned. This arrest left Scotland open to Protestant domination and ended Catholic efforts to encircle Protestant England.

Peace does not last

Throughout the 1560s, the two religious factions were at war while Catherine and Charles tried to avoid being associated with either side. The situation was complicated by an English invasion of France in alliance with the Huguenots. The war was further complicated by a feud among the major families, brought on when Coligny ordered the assassination of François of Lorraine in 1563. As the fighting continued, especially in the third religious war (1568–70), Huguenot armies attacked convents and monasteries, torturing and massacring their inhabitants. In retaliation, Catholic forces killed Huguenots in several districts. In 1570, following a decade of war, the two sides signed a treaty called the Peace of Saint Germain. The treaty specified that Catherine's daughter, Marguerite of Valois, should marry Henry of Navarre, a Huguenot leader. It also gave the Huguenots several strongholds throughout France and returned Coligny to his position as an adviser to the king. Catherine hoped that, as a moderate Huguenot, Coligny might curb the aggressions of his fellow Huguenots while she played the same role among Catholics. But Coligny quickly gained influence at court, becoming a friend of Charles IX. He aroused suspicions among Catholics, who were convinced that he was planning to take over the court. When Coligny discovered that Charles and his mother were at odds, he chose the king's side rather than Catherine's, provoking her furious resentment.

The city of Paris had remained friendly to the Catholic Guise party throughout the wars, and most Parisians resented the concessions to Huguenots made at the Peace of Saint Germain. The population was therefore restless and angry when a large Huguenot assembly entered their city in the summer of 1572 to celebrate the wedding of Marguerite and Henry. The bride herself was a stormy personality and a relentless intriguer. When Catherine had discovered earlier that Marguerite was having an affair with Charles of Guise, she and Charles IX had beaten her senseless. The motive for this marriage alliance was that Henry of Navarre, though a Huguenot, would have a strong claim to the French throne if neither Charles IX nor his brother Henry had a living heir. Marguerite was still in love with Guise, however, and resisted the planned marriage. She had also refused to give up her Catholic faith. During the negotiations, Henry of Navarre's mother, Jeanne of Navarre, died suddenly. Many Huguenots were ready to believe that Catherine had poisoned Jeanne, though that seems unlikely.

Saint Bartholomew's Day Massacre

In 1572 Catherine accepted an offer from a Catholic faction in the court to assassinate Coligny. She hoped that Coligny's death would shift power to the Catholics. The assassin shot Coligny but failed to kill him, and a distressed Charles rushed to his adviser's side. Catherine and her son Henry then convinced Charles that Coligny planned to overthrow the whole Catholic court and should now be finished off along with other Huguenot leaders. By careful prearrangement, church bells began to

An illustration of the Saint Bartholomew's Day Massacre in which more than three thousand men, women, and children were killed because of their religious practices. *Reproduced by permission of Hulton/Archive.*

ring at two in the morning of August 24, Saint Bartholomew's Day. The bells signaled Catholic troops to move in and kill the injured Coligny and other Huguenots. The attacks soon led to mass violence as all sense of order broke down. More than three thousand men, women, and children (including many people uninvolved in political and religious controversy) in Paris were shot or hacked to death. Similar massacres followed in the provinces, leaving more than seventy thousand dead and starting another civil war.

By a curious turn of events, Catherine's youngest son, Francis, duke of Alençon and Anjou (1554–1584), became the leader of the Huguenots in this phase of the French Wars of Religion. Placing himself at the head of the Protestant forces, he dreamed of becoming the king. He declared that Henry, who had just been elected to the throne of Poland, was no longer eligible to be king of France. (Catherine had previously arranged to have Henry appointed lieutenant-governor of Poland so he would be in line for the throne of that country.) Henry was less easily dominated and manipulated than Charles. He had spent the 1560s as a successful general in the wars against the Huguenots. His victories won him the envy of Charles IX, who was frail and could not go on military campaigns. Henry was homosexual (one who has sexual relations with a person of the same gender) and had had a long succession of lovers. Catherine tried to "correct" his behavior by ordering a banquet at which the food was served by naked women, but she could not succeed. Catherine tried to marry Henry to Elizabeth I of England, but the "Virgin Queen" declined the offer. (Elizabeth also refused to marry Francis, whom she called her "frog.") The only woman to excite Henry's interest, and to whom he sent ardent love letters signed in his own blood, was already married to a French prince.

At last Henry set out for Poland. His departure prompted another Huguenot uprising, in which Francis, Henry of Navarre, and Catherine's daughter Marguerite Valois were all implicated as conspirators. Catherine coordinated forces to put down the rebellion. Then, in 1574, Charles died at the age of twenty-four. Henry returned from Poland and was crowned Henry III in 1575. In the same year he married Louise of Lorraine, but they had no children to carry on the Valois line. From this time on, Catherine entrusted family fortunes to the Catholic Guise family. In 1576 she approved the formation of the Catholic League, which marched to triumph against the Huguenots. Henry's homosexual fa-

vorites dominated the court. When the Guises killed two of Henry's friends, the king developed an intense hatred of the Guises. Another round of feuding began despite Catherine's continued urging that Henry must settle his differences with the Guises for the sake of national and Catholic security. In 1589 Henry's bodyguards murdered Charles of Guise. By this time Catherine was in failing health, and shortly before her death she learned about the murder of Guise. She was devastated because her favorite son had destroyed her lifelong efforts to form an alliance between the Valois and Guise families. Later that year, Henry III was assassinated by a Dominican friar, Jacques Clement (1564–1589), who regarded the king as a traitor to the faith for joining Henry of Navarre against the Catholic League. In this way, the Valois dynasty came to an end.

Before dying Henry III had recognized Henry of Navarre as the legitimate heir to the French throne. Henry of Navarre then became King Henry IV (ruled 1596–1610), though he was not formally crowned. He still faced opposition from the Catholic League because he was a Calvinist. He promised to protect the Catholic Church and announced his willingness to receive Catholic instruction, which many Catholics took as a promise to convert. Wishing not to appear too opportunistic or insincere, he continually postponed receiving Catholic instruction. Eventually the Estates-General, which was dominated by the Catholic League, met to discuss the election of a new candidate as the Catholic king of France. This move forced Henry to make a decision. On July 25, 1593, his formal conversion to Catholicism was celebrated amid great pomp at Saint Denis, near Paris. Henry reportedly made the famous remark that "Paris is worth a Mass"—in other words, becoming the ruler of France was worth the small sacrifice of having to attend mass, the Catholic worship service. His conversion, however, did not end the civil wars. Many Catholics still doubted the sincerity of Henry's conversion. Half of the country was held by the Catholic League, which was being supported by Spain, and the city of Paris would not recognize him as king. After formally being crowned on February 27, 1594, at Chartres, Henry IV marched on Paris, which was occupied by Spanish troops. Encountering little resistance, he entered the city on March 22.

The Edict of Nantes

Yet the Spanish continued to support resistance to Henry IV. Thus, in January 1595, he declared war on Spain. Henry displayed great courage and leadership by beating back Spanish forces from Amiens, which is dangerously close to Paris. Finally, he led his troops into Brittany and easily defeated the remaining Spanish-backed resistance. Equally significant, on this trip he also issued the famous Edict of Nantes, which granted certain religious and civil liberties to Huguenots. They were given seventy-five fortified towns and other secure places where they could worship freely. They were also granted the right to worship on the lands of Huguenot noblemen. In addition, Huguenots were eligible for public office, and they had equal access with Catholics to schools and other facilities. Nevertheless, Catholicism remained the official religion of France, and Huguenots had only limited independence from the crown. Tolerance of Huguenots continued in France until 1685, when the Edict of Nantes was revoked by Henry's grandson, King Louis XIV. Protestantism was supposedly no longer practiced in France, but many Protestants continued to hold secret worship services. The prestige of the Roman Catholic Church was eventually damaged by Louis's harsh measures against the Protestants.

The Netherlands

In the Netherlands, Martin Luther's reform movement was welcomed by the prosperous middle class in the northern provinces (Holland, Zeeland, Utrecht, and Franche-Comté). The southern provinces (now Belgium) were predominantly Roman Catholic. At that time the Netherlands was controlled by the Habsburgs, a powerful family based in Austria and Spain. Holy Roman Emperor Charles V was a Habsburg as well as the king of Spain. He was also a Catholic, and he wanted to halt the spread of Protestant doctrines in the Netherlands. He held public burnings of Luther's books, and in 1522 he established the Spanish Inquisition to seek out heretics and force them to remain Catholics (see "Spanish Inquisition" in Chapter 7). These measures were unsuccessful, however, and by the middle of the sixteenth century Protestantism had a firm hold on the northern provinces. By this time the Dutch (the name given to inhabitants of the Netherlands) were seeking independence from Spain, and they embraced Calvinism as a way to give unity to their struggle.

William of Orange becomes leader

The leader of the independence movement in the Netherlands was William of Orange (also known as William the Silent; 1533–1584). He was born at Dillenburg in the German principality of Nassau, the son of Count William of Nassau and the Countess of Stolberg. William was raised as a Lutheran and inherited the territories of Orange and Nassau at the age of eleven. The Habsburgs wanted to maintain control of Nassau and Orange, so Charles V insisted that William be brought up as a Catholic. Moving to Breda and then Brussels, William was educated at the court of Mary of Hungary, the regent of the Low Countries (the Netherlands, Belgium, and Luxembourg). He was taught French and Dutch and readily adopted the customs of the Dutch people. The teachings of the Christian humanist Desiderius Erasmus held particular significance for the young heir and later played a large part in the religious toleration for which William was renowned.

William gained favor with Charles, and he was soon named to

 Henry IV Assassinated

In 1609 King Henry IV was preparing to enter the war against the Habsburg empire, which soon developed into the Thirty Years' War. In Germany, Protestant princes had united against Catholic princes, who were allied with Holy Roman Emperor Rudolf II. A dispute over Habsburg control of Bohemia threatened the balance of power in Europe. On May 14 Henry set out for a meeting with his adviser, Maximilien de Béthune, the duke of Sully. Henry's carriage wound its way through the streets of Paris and was caught in a traffic jam. As the coachmen dealt with the situation, a lone assassin approached, lunged at the king through a window, and stabbed him three times. With the carriage rushing back to the palace dripping with blood, the end came for Henry IV. His policy of waging war against the major Catholic powers had not been universally accepted in France. Several theories immediately arose about great conspiracies and the motives of the killer, François Ravaillac, who suffered a grisly public execution. Although nothing of note came from his military preparations, Henry IV has achieved legendary status, and today he is considered a national hero in France.

important court positions. In 1561 Charles's son and successor, King Philip II of Spain, appointed William as the stadholder (governor and captain-general) in Holland, Zeeland, Utrecht, and Franche-Comté. Soon after this appointment, serious dissension arose in the Netherlands over Philip's rule. Two main issues were religion and the king's rigid absolutism, or concentration of all power in his own hands. Philip limited the rights of noblemen, who had enjoyed relative independence under Charles V. He also took measures to drive out the Calvinists. Opposition arose among both noblemen and defenders of religious freedom. William himself openly criticized the king during a speech in the Council of State (group of advisers to the king), in which he challenged the right of any ruler to control the religious conscience of his subjects.

Calvinists gain power

By 1565 leadership of the Dutch opposition to Philip's policies was taken over by a group of low-ranking nobles, called the Gueux (pronounced GOH), or Beggars, who were mainly Calvinists. They advocated violence as a possible solution for their grievances. While most high-ranking nobles quickly broke away from the Gueux, William retained his ties to them. His brother, Louis of Nassau (1538–1574), was an active leader of the group. Although openly connected to the Gueux, William advised religious toleration and nonviolence. Despite his pleas for moderation, however, open revolt against Spain erupted in August 1566. The first stage of the rebellion featured extreme violence. Frenzied Calvinist mobs sacked Catholic churches throughout the provinces, smashing religious idols and vandalizing church property. King Philip responded by

summoning Fernando Álvarez de Toledo (1507–1582), duke of Alba, to crush the revolt. William himself put down a Calvinist riot in Antwerp, Europe's richest city. He then closed the city's gates and denied access to both the rebels and the king's forces. In 1567 William withdrew to his family's estates at Dillenburg and gained his famous nickname "the Silent" because he maintained a neutral position in the conflict.

Alba created the Council of Troubles to arrest, try, and execute religious "heretics." It came to be known as the Council of Blood after Alba executed as many as twelve thousand people. William himself was summoned before the Council of Troubles, but he refused to appear. Alba then confiscated William's possessions and deported one of William's sons to Spain. This harsh treatment pushed the prince of Orange into becoming a rebel. William organized an army and marched on the Low Countries in 1568. Alba met and crushed William's forces at the Ems River. The prince of Orange then sought refuge in a Huguenot region of France. He despised the strictness of the Calvinist faith, but he came to realize that accepting Calvinism was the only way he could receive support from French, German, and English Protestants. In 1572 he succeeded in convincing Queen Elizabeth I of England to send troops and money to help the Dutch Protestant rebels (see "England" section later in this chapter).

Union of Utrecht

In 1572 Calvinist Holland and Zeeland joined the rebellion and called for the prince of Orange to lead them. In accepting leadership, William insisted upon equal protection for both the Catholic and the Calvinist faiths. William formally became a Calvinist, but he would not go along with the Calvinist provinces in declaring Catholicism illegal. In 1576 he took control of the States-General and arranged for acceptance of the Pacification of Ghent. This agreement united the seventeen provinces of the Netherlands and supported religious moderation. King Philip then installed his half brother, Don John of Austria (1547–1578; ruled 1576–78), as the new ruler in the Low Countries. Don John was not overly concerned with suppressing the revolt because he was preoccupied with planning an invasion of England to restore Catholicism in that country. Upon Don John's death in 1578, Alessandro Farnese (1545–1592), the duke of Parma, became governor-general of the Netherlands and began subduing the southern provinces. In 1579 the Treaty of Arras united the southern provinces under Spanish rule and Catholicism. William then agreed to the Union of Utrecht, which united the northern provinces and led the way for the creation of the United Provinces in the Treaty of Westphalia (see "Thirty Years' War" section later in this chapter). William still wanted to unite all of the Dutch provinces, so he sought help from Francis, duke of Alençon and Anjou. Francis was the leader of the Huguenots, a Protestant party that was waging war against Catholics in France (see "France" section previously in this chapter).

In 1580 Farnese captured more than thirty rebel towns along with the city of Antwerp, bringing Holland and Zeeland to the brink of defeat. In 1583 Francis and his French troops attempted to seize Antwerp in a coup d'état (overthrow of the government). The Dutch rose to crush this "French Fury" by killing two thousand Frenchmen and taking fifteen hundred as prisoners. On July 10, 1584, a Catholic extremist shot and killed the prince of Orange at his home in Delft (a community in South Holland). William's son Maurice (1567–1625; ruled 1584–1625), became governor of the republic. During the early phase of the Thirty Years' War he carried on a successful campaign against Spain. Final recognition of Dutch independence by the Spanish government was not obtained until the end of the war in the Peace of Westphalia. The northern provinces were officially declared Protestant, while the southern provinces remained loyal to Spain and to the Roman Catholic Church.

England

The Protestant Reformation reached its height in England during the reigns of the last Tudor monarchs (kings and queens who were members of the Tudor family)—Henry VIII (1491–1547; ruled 1509–47), Edward VI (1537–1553; ruled 1547–53), Mary I (1516–1558; ruled 1553–58), and Elizabeth I (1533–1603; ruled 1558–1603). Whereas most countries on the European continent adopted reforms before breaking with the Roman Catholic Church, England first broke with Rome and then made changes in religious practices. In other European countries, reform began as a reaction to corruption in the Catholic Church, but the establishment of the Church of England, or Anglican Church, resulted from a direct confrontation between the king and the pope.

Henry VIII opens door to Reformation

King Henry VIII took the throne of England at the age of eighteen. Like Europe's other monarchs, he was closely allied with the Catholic Church. In 1511 he formed a triumvirate (three-party association) of power called the Holy League with Pope Julius II and King Ferdinand II of Aragon. The major crisis in Henry's relationship with the church came when his first wife, Catherine of Aragon (1485–1536), failed to produce a male heir to the throne. He sought a divorce from Catherine on the grounds that, since she was the widow of his dead brother, Arthur, he was therefore living in sin. After long and fruitless negotiations with all parties involved, Henry became the first monarch to challenge the doctrines of the Catholic Church, which prohibited divorce. At first he had condemned the German reformer Martin Luther as a poisonous snake who was undermining the church. By 1529, however, Henry was ready to confront the pope and assert his right to marry whomever he pleased. At this time he wanted to marry Anne Boleyn (c. 1507–1536), an attendant in the court of Queen Claude of France. Henry was

having a secret affair with Boleyn, and he hoped she might bear him a son. Infuriated by Pope Clement VII's refusal to grant him a divorce, Henry set out to start his own church. Thus the Church of England was formed, and his divorce was granted in 1533.

Henry's reign opened the door to the Protestant Reformation in England in several ways. Thomas Cromwell (c. 1485–1540), a Protestant lawyer and Henry's chief minister until 1540, proceeded to weaken the Catholic presence in England by taxing papal lands, including monasteries, and burning shrines. During a four-year period Cromwell expelled more than eleven thousand Catholic monks and nuns from England. In 1534 Henry's Parliament (the main law-making body of England) passed the Act of Treason, a law stating that anyone, including church officials, who called the king a heretic would be tried for treason, or betrayal of one's country. This law placed the king above the church and the pope. The act also prohibited either the clergy or the laity (unordained members of a church) from sending money to the pope in Rome. In addition, Parliament passed the Act of Supremacy, which declared Henry to be head of the Church of England.

Closes monasteries One of the most important events of Henry VIII's reign was the closing of monasteries. At the beginning of the Tudor era the Catholic religious houses owned as much as one-fourth of all land in England. These estates had been given or bequeathed (granted in wills) to monks by religiously devout men and women in exchange for prayers for their souls after they died. Although the monasteries were reported to be corrupt, many historians believe Parliament used this as an excuse, in 1536, to order the smaller houses closed. Residents were allowed to either transfer to larger houses that remained open or renounce their vows. Most chose to renounce their vows. The great abbeys, the churches connected with monasteries, were suppressed one by one in the next few years. A second statute, passed in 1540, legalized these closures and mandated the seizing of all remaining Catholic property. Former monastic possessions were managed by a new financial bureau, the Court of Augmentations. The court paid small pensions (financial allowances for retired people) to former monks and nuns, and larger ones to former abbots and priors (heads of monasteries) who had cooperated in the closing of their houses. By the time of Henry VIII's death in 1547, most of the monastic land had been sold to noblemen and members of the gentry. These people would thus profit from the continuation of the Reformation.

The loss of the monasteries was felt in various ways. Earlier they had been centers of learning and the arts, but now the great monastic libraries were divided and sent to other locations. Some collections remained in cathedrals that had earlier been associated with monasteries, like Canterbury and Dudiam, and others were acquired by the universities of Oxford and Cambridge or by private collectors. Much of the wealth seized from the religious houses was spent on warfare.

Edward VI continues reforms

When Henry died, his ten-year-old son Edward VI took the throne. Henry had named a large council of regents to rule England until Edward was old enough to be king. Nevertheless, Edward's uncle, Edward Seymour (c. 1550–1552), duke of Somerset, took control of the government. He was unable to deal with several rebellions that broke out in 1549, so he lost power to John Dudley (1502–1553), earl of Warwick, who became Edward's new adviser. Edward was king for only six years, yet the power of the English church was increased during his reign. Thomas Cranmer (1489–1556), the Archbishop of Canterbury, was a major force in reform efforts.

Somerset , Warwick, and Cranmer approved of further reform in the church. Young Edward was enthusiastic about reform as well. He was raised by Protestants and Renaissance ideas had dominated his education. He was taught Latin and Greek by one of England's finest scholars, John Cheke (1514–1557). He was instructed in religion by Richard Cox (c. 1500–1592), later the bishop of Ely. Protestantism now reached its highest point in English history. Although Edward's Parliament revoked Henry's Act of Treason, it did pass the Dissolution Act of 1547, which ended yearly payments to Catholic priests for saying prayers for the dead. The following year all Catholic icons, or symbols, and images were removed from churches. In 1549 Parliament adopted Cranmer's *Book of Common Prayer* for use in Church of England worship services. It was moderate in tone—that is, it did not reflect drastic changes from Roman Catholic worship services—but a revision issued in 1552 was radically different. For instance, the revision regarded communion as simply a re-enactment of the Last Supper (the final meal that Christ shared with his disciples, or followers), whereas Catholic faith taught that the bread and wine consumed during communion were the actual body and blood of Christ. Edward and Cranmer also persuaded Parliament to issue the Forty-Two Articles, which eliminated most of the remaining Catholic doctrines of faith.

Edward died of a lung disease in 1553. During his last days some of his advisers attempted to give the throne to Lady Jane Grey (1537–1554), the king's distant relative and a supporter of Protestant causes. They knew that Edward's half sister, Mary Tudor, would restore the Catholic faith because she was raised as a Catholic. Lady Jane was proclaimed queen in 1553, but after only nine days she was imprisoned for high treason as a result of an ambitious plot to make her queen. She was beheaded, along with her husband, Lord Guildford Dudley, in 1554.

Mary I restores Catholicism

Mary Tudor took the throne as Queen Mary I in 1553, after Lady Jane Grey's nine-day reign. Soon after being crowned, she married Philip of Spain (soon to be King Philip II), but Parliament prevented him from taking the English throne along with his wife. Mary had widespread popular support, and she immediately began undoing the Reformation in two stages. In 1553 she restored the Latin Mass and the following year she recognized the jurisdiction of the pope in England. Cranmer was dismissed from office and placed under house arrest, while Reginald Pole (1500–1558) was brought back to England to take the archbishop's place. Pole was an English aristocrat who had lived in Italy since Henry VIII's break with the papacy. Many people supported Mary's restoration of the Catholic faith, believing that Edward's reign had gone too far in abolishing cherished ceremonies and beliefs.

Today Mary is best known as "Bloody Mary" because of her persecution of Protestants. During her brief five-year reign nearly three hundred people were burned at the stake. This method of punishment, which was introduced by the Inquisition (an official Catholic Church court charged with finding heretics), supposedly drove evil spirits out of sinners (see "Inquisition" in Chapters 1 and 7). Many who refused to reject Protestant beliefs continued to worship in underground churches or fled to countries on the European continent. Others became involved in a series of plots against Mary's government. Protestant leaders looked to the queen's half sister, Elizabeth, as a possible Protestant replacement. Mary then had Elizabeth arrested and sent to the Tower of London , a prison for members of royalty and the nobility, and later to Woodstock. Five years later Mary, who was now near death, named Elizabeth to be her successor. Thus, on March 17, 1558, the last Tudor monarch of England ascended the throne.

Elizabeth I seeks moderation

Elizabeth set about restoring the Church of England. Although she was raised a Protestant, she had expressed a commitment to Roman Catholicism while she was imprisoned. This position enabled her to gain limited freedom. Now, as queen, she vowed to continue Henry's moderate policies in the Church of England. She could not, however, resist the new Puritanism that was sweeping the Parliament and the land. ("Puritanism" was the name given to the views of strict reformers such as John Calvin; see "Switzerland" section previously in this chapter). In 1563 she approved rules of worship and stated religious beliefs that leaned heavily toward stricter Protestant views. She was then excommunicated from the Roman Catholic Church. During the 1580s, Jesuits came to England and tried to convince the queen to accept Catholicism. (The Jesuits were a Catholic Reformation brotherhood known as the pope's "shock troops"; see "Jesuits" in Chapter 7.) In 1585 Elizabeth retaliated by expelling Catholic priests from the country, telling them that if they did not leave they would be charged with treason. Two hundred priests

Queen Mary I earned the nickname "Bloody Mary" because she ordered the deaths of nearly three hundred Protestants after she took the English throne and restored Catholicism as the country's official religion. *Reproduced by permission of Hulton Archive.*

who defied the queen's order were drawn and quartered (a method of execution that involved hanging a person by the neck, and then cutting his or her body into four parts). Elizabeth also sent six thousand troops to France to aid the Huguenots in their civil war against the Catholic government of Francis II (see "France" section previously in this chapter). Later she waged a naval war against Louis XIV, another French Catholic king.

John Knox, the "Thundering Scot"

The Scottish reformer John Knox was one of the most celebrated followers of John Calvin. Nicknamed the "thundering Scot," he became the chief force in the introduction and establishment of the Presbyterian form of Calvinism in Scotland.

In preparation for the Catholic priesthood, Knox attended a university in Scotland, either Glasgow or Saint Andrews, but did not earn a degree. After ordination in 1532 he returned to Haddington, the region of his birth. Knox's conversion to Protestantism apparently occurred between 1543 and 1546. In 1543 he was loyally serving the Catholic Church under the archbishop of Saint Andrews. By 1546 he was vigorously defending the reformer

George Wishart (c. 1513–1546), who had introduced Swiss Protestantism into Scotland. Wishart gained many followers before being executed for heresy in 1546. The following year David Beaton (c. 1494–1546), the cardinal responsible for Wishart's execution, was murdered. Upon hearing of the deed, Knox eagerly joined the murderers in the castle of Saint Andrews and became their preacher. French Catholic troops attacked the castle, capturing the occupants and making them galley slaves (men who were forced to work on ships). Knox and his comrades were released in 1549, after nineteen months of captivity.

Knox then took a paid position as preacher in England. His popularity grew

Meanwhile, Calvinists and Lutherans had been returning to England since the death of Mary I. They pressed for even more radical reforms. Many insisted that the church be run by "presbyteries," which consisted of unordained clergymen and members of church congregations. Founded by Scottish religious reformer John Knox (c. 1505–1572), this system of church organization was the beginning the modern movement known as Presbyterianism. Puritan leader Thomas Cartwright (1535–1603) asked Parliament to discontinue use of the *Book of Common Prayer*, which he considered too Catholic. He later wrote the *Book*

of Discipline, which outlined a "new order" for the Church of England. Furthermore, the issue of "free speech" was now being debated in Parliament. Elizabeth was frustrated by all this clamoring for power and reform. In exasperation, she sent a message to Parliament warning that even though she was a woman, she would not let any of the factions pressure her into taking action. She ended by saying that the members of Parliament were being ridiculously quarrelsome.

Confronts Catholic threat from abroad
Elizabeth was also confronted with the threat of invasion by Catholic coun-

rapidly. In 1551 he was appointed chaplain to King Edward VI. He worked to rid English religious services of all traces of Catholic ritual and to promote Protestantism. This work made his life precarious when the Catholic queen, Mary I, took the throne in 1553. The following year Knox left England, wandered for a time, and finally moved to Geneva, Switzerland, where he joined Calvin. Knox enthusiastically embraced Calvin's strict version of Protestantism. While he was at Geneva he wrote *History of the Reformation of Religion within the Realm of Scotland,* his best-known work.

Knox returned to Scotland in 1559. Since preaching in the Reformed manner was forbidden, he was considered a criminal. He managed to remain free and become the architect of a new Scottish church. In 1560, under his guidance, Scotland adopted a democratic structure in which congregations elected their ministers and elders (unordained leaders). Under these conditions it is not surprising that Mary, Queen of Scots, a Catholic reared in France, found Scotland uncongenial soon after her arrival in 1561. Since Catholic worship was forbidden, Mary's private masses had to be defended with the sword. In 1568 she was driven from Scotland, and Knox was in the forefront of her pursuers. Knox died in 1572, leaving an independent Scotland under a severe but democratically elected church.

tries. Following the death of Mary I, King Philip II of Spain wanted to marry Elizabeth in order to form a Catholic alliance between Spain and England. When Elizabeth refused his proposal, he realized that England could never be a Catholic country. For the rest of the century England and other Protestant states were involved in conflict with Spain and the papacy. In the Revolt of the Netherlands, Protestants in the Low Countries fought to throw off Spanish rule and Catholic persecution (see "The Netherlands" section previously in this chapter). Initially reluctant to become involved, Elizabeth finally accepted the argument that England, as the chief Protestant power in Europe, had an obligation to aid Protestants elsewhere.

A major threat to Elizabeth's security were various plots associated with Mary Stuart (also known as Mary, Queen of Scots; 1542–1587; ruled 1542–67). Mary was a Catholic who had been driven from Scotland by Protestants. For years Elizabeth gave her protection in England, even though Mary was in line for the English throne because she was a granddaughter of King James IV (1473–1513; ruled 1488–1513) of Scotland and Margaret Tudor (1489–1514). But the discovery of a conspiracy to assassinate Elizabeth in 1586 led to Mary's execution at Fotheringhay castle in 1587. The execution of the Catholic queen was a signal to Philip that he must seize the throne of England. He began organizing the famous "Invincible Armada," a fleet of 130 heavily armored ships that carried 30,000 men, for an invasion of England. The English defeated the Armada during a spectacular battle in the English Channel (the body of water between England and France) in August 1588 (see "Spain" in Chapter 3). This victory positioned England to become a major sea power. Although the final years of Elizabeth's reign were marked by many problems, she managed to maintain control over the church. She was still popular with her subjects when she died in 1603. Since she had no heirs, the Tudor dynasty came to an end.

James I sponsors new Bible

Elizabeth was followed by James VI of Scotland, a member of the house of Stuart, who became King James I of England (ruled 1603–25). James also had to contend with religious unrest. As he rode from Edinburgh to London in 1603, shortly after becoming king, he was met by a group of Puritans (members of the Church of England who advocated strict reforms). They were especially critical of "popish," or Catholic, features of the church. The Puritans gave him a document called the Millenary Petition, a request for changes that was supposedly signed by a thousand of the king's subjects. Among the reforms

they demanded were simplified services, less elaborate church music, simpler vestments (robes worn by clergymen), and more preaching. They also wanted to end the use of wedding rings, which were believed to be popish because Catholics wore them. Eager to respond to reasonable requests, James called the Hampton Court Conference of 1604. Here Puritan leaders met with the king and some of the officers of the Church of England. Hopes of cooperation and compromise were dashed when the Puritans demanded that the church get rid of bishops (heads of church districts), whom they regarded as popish obstacles to true reform. James felt that bishops were necessary, so he adjourned the conference. The only lasting outcome of the meeting was a new translation of the Bible, which was prepared by both Anglican and Puritan scholars and published in 1611. Although it was called the King James Bible, James himself had little to do with the translation. Known for its elegant prose style, the King James Bible is still accepted as the "authorized version" by many Protestant faiths.

Charles I executed by Puritans

After James died in 1625, his second son, Charles I (1600–1649; ruled 1625–49), became king. By this time the Puritans controlled Parliament. Charles lacked the diplomatic skills and mental agility to deal with stern Puritans who wanted to establish the "kingdom of God" or "New Jerusalem" in England. To make matters worse, Charles was married to a

Catholic, Henrietta Maria (1606–1669) of France. She tried to convince Charles to aid Catholic monarchs on the continent in their fight against Protestants, which only caused more ill will against the king in Parliament. Charles lost so much control that his Parliament was dissolved in 1629. Political and religious anarchy (state of lawlessness) then engulfed England as the government sank into bankruptcy and bureaucratic chaos.

Waiting in the wings were the radical Puritans, who gained great popular support under the guidance of Oliver Cromwell (1599–1658). The successes of Elizabeth's moderate policies quickly vanished as dissent spread and the church, headed by Archbishop William Laud (1573–1645), became increasingly more Catholic-oriented. As head of the Church of England (the official religion of the country) and a staunch opponent of Puritanism, Laud aggressively moved to stamp out popular support of the Puritans. At the same time he gave increased emphasis to the Catholic aspects of the Church of England. Charles chose to side with Laud, even though only 1.5 percent of English churchgoers favored a Catholic church. By 1644 the largely Presbyterian Parliament and the monarchy were involved in a civil war. The Parliament was financing its own New Model Army under the leadership of Cromwell. These forces were joined by the radical Protestant groups called Levellers and Diggers. They sought to establish a perfect Christian society based on equality before the law and religious tolerance. After a brief war Charles was taken into custody, tried and convicted of war crimes and tyranny, and finally beheaded on January 30, 1649.

Cromwell ruled England as Lord Protector until 1660, when Charles's son, Charles II (1630–1685; ruled 1660–85), took the throne. His reign was called the Restoration because the monarchy was restored. Charles II had no success, however, in unifying the various religious elements which, once united in war, now fell to squabbling about the nature of the "true church" and the "true state." Nevertheless, England was transformed into the strongest Protestant nation in the world under the rule of Protestant monarchs.

Thirty Years' War (1618–48)

The Protestant Reformation and the Catholic Reformation were brought to an end by the Thirty Years' War. Now considered the first worldwide conflict, the Thirty Years' War began with a seemingly isolated struggle between Catholics and Protestants in Bohemia. Religious differences soon spread to other countries and then escalated into confrontations over social and political issues involving all of the major world powers.

The Habsburg monarchs of the sixteenth century regarded themselves as apostles of the Catholic Reformation. By 1600 they had, to a large extent, eliminated Protestantism from Austria. Bohemia was the next target for their reforming zeal, but the country had become increasingly Protestant, and most of the influential nobility were anti-Catholic. Habsburg efforts at reform fell apart, however, in 1607 when the incompetent Holy Roman Emperor Rudolf II (1552–1612; ruled 1576–1612) quarreled with his brother Matthias (1557–1619), governor of Austria, over control of Habsburg lands. The following year Protestants formed the Evangelical Union, a defensive alliance of princes and cities. When Roman Catholics formed a similar organization in 1609, violence became the most likely solution to the tensions between the religious groups. The Bohemian section of the Evangelical Union triggered the first act of violence, which eventually led to the Thirty Years' War.

Dispute leads to revolt

The incident began when Rudolf found he needed the support of the Bohemians against his brother. In order to buy this support, he granted the Bohemian Estates (representative assembly) a Letter of Majesty, or royal order, in 1609. Under the decree, religious freedom was granted to all Bohemians, along with the right to construct churches and schools on royal lands. But these concessions did little to strengthen Rudolf's position, and in 1611 Matthias won control of Bohemia. When Rudolf died in 1612, Matthias succeeded him as Holy Roman Emperor (ruled 1612–19). The reign of Matthias brought the religious issue in Bohemia to the forefront, but now it was coupled with a political issue, the search for a successor to the childless emperor. Although Matthias lost little time in supporting the Letter of Majesty, the Bohemian Estates soon had cause to wonder if his support meant anything. The emperor quickly removed Protestant officials from key offices in Bohemia and replaced them with Catholics. A more serious threat to Bohemian religious liberty came when Matthias named his cousin, Archduke Ferdinand of Inner Austria (1578–1637; later Emperor Ferdinand II, 1619–37)—the most fanatical Habsburg promoter of the Catholic Reformation—as his successor. The Bohemian Estates were divided and had no candidate of their own. On June 17, 1617, they reluctantly agreed to "accept" Ferdinand as their king. He was to share the title with Matthias. On the following day, Ferdinand announced support of the Letter of Majesty.

Within a few months a dispute developed over the interpretation of the Letter of Majesty. The quarrel resulted in a Bohemian revolt against the Habsburgs and ultimately led to the Thirty Years' War. Two Protestant churches, one in Hrob (Klostergrab) and the other in Broumov (Braunau), had been built on land owned by the Catholic Church. In Bohemia this was customarily regarded as royal property. The Protestants therefore felt that they were within their rights as set forth in the Letter of Majesty. The Habsburg authorities rejected this argument. In 1617 the churches were ordered to close, and the one at Hrob was even torn down. The matter caused such an uproar that a radical wing of the Bohemian Estates, led by Count Matthias Thurn, Baron Colona Fels, and Wenceslaus Ruppa, called for a revolt against the Habsburgs in 1618.

Protestant assemblies were forbidden by law, but in defiance of this ban the Protestants met on May 21, 1618. They were in session for two days. On May 22, they demanded a redress of grievances arising out of the religious dispute, but the Habsburg government rejected their demands. The Protestant leaders, Thurn, Ruppa, and Fels, then plotted the murder of the deputy governors of Bohemia, Count Jaroslav Martinitz and Count Wilhelm Slavata. The deputy governors were leaders of the Catholic, pro-Habsburg group in the Bohemian Estates. An armed band of more than one hundred men marched to Hradcany Castle in Prague, the capital of Bohemia, for a formal confrontation with Martinitz and Slavata. Both officials denied any personal involvement in the rejection of Protestant demands. Heated words were exchanged. Suddenly, Thurn and others stepped forward, seized the two deputy governors, and hurled them through a castle window into the trash-filled moat forty feet below. Miraculously the victims survived the fall and managed to escape.

Revolt leads to war

This confrontation is known in history as the "Defenestration of Prague." It triggered widespread revolt against the Habsburg regime beyond the religious issue, and beyond Bohemia, for the next thirty years. Thurn

and Ruppa became leaders of a revolutionary government in Bohemia. They mobilized fighting forces that fought on the side of Habsburg troops between 1618 and 1620, though the outcome was indecisive. In August 1619 Bohemia formed a confederation with Moravia, Silesia, and Lusatia. This confederation proceeded to arrange a pact of mutual assistance with the Protestant states of Upper and Lower Austria. The revolt was completed when the confederation removed Ferdinand from the Bohemian throne and elected Frederick V (1596–1632), elector of the Rhenish Palatinate (a region on the Rhine River in Germany), to take his place.

Frederick's rule is known as "the reign of the Winter King." It was brief because Matthias died in March 1619 and Ferdinand was elected to succeed him as Holy Roman Emperor in August. As emperor, Ferdinand was determined to suppress Protestantism in Bohemia and regain the Bohemian crown. On November 8, 1620, the Bohemian army was defeated by the Catholic League army at the Battle of White Mountain near Prague. The Catholic League army was under the command of the Flemish (inhabitant of Flanders) general Johann Tserclaes (pronounced TSER-klahs; 1559–1632), count of Tilly. The Catholic victory ended Bohemia's bid for self-rule. Protestantism was outlawed and the Evangelical Union soon disintegrated. Frederick and a few allies continued the Protestant struggle in the Palatinate in Germany. Although they won against Tilly's army at Wiesloch in April 1622, they met numerous defeats during the next two years. By late 1624 the Palatinate, which was now ruled by Maximilian I (1573–1651), duke of Bavaria, was forced to return to Catholicism.

Christian IV aids Protestants

The scope of the war expanded in 1625 when Christian IV (1577–1648; ruled 1588–1648), the king of Denmark and Norway, came to the aid of the German Protestants. Although Denmark was a Lutheran country (see "Denmark" section previously in this chapter), Christian was not motivated by religion. Instead, he wanted to end Habsburg control of the Danish duchy (province) of Holstein, Germany. Allied with Lutheran and Calvinist German princes, Christian organized a large army and invaded Saxony. The Protestants met little resistance until 1625. By this time Ferdinand II had realized that he could not rely solely on Tilly's Catholic League forces to combat the German Protestants and the Danes. The emperor brought in Albrecht von Wallenstein, duke of Friedland (1583–1634), who assembled a powerful army of mercenaries, or hired soldiers. In April 1626 Wallenstein's troops won their first victory at Dessau, Germany. The following August, Tilly completely defeated Christian's army at Lutter am Barenberge, Germany. Ferdinand's combined forces then took all of northern Germany. In 1627 Wallenstein forced Christian to retreat to the Jutland Peninsula (a landmass projecting into the North Sea in western Germany).

Sweden enters war

Ferdinand achieved total victory on March 6, 1629, when he issued the Edict of Restitution. This order provided for the return of some land in Germany to the Roman Catholic Church. It also outlawed all Protestant sects (religious groups) except Lutheranism. Wallenstein was largely responsible for Ferdinand's success. Wallenstein was unpopular with many German princes, however, because of his misuse of power. He had also aroused Swedish fears that the Habsburgs might soon control the Baltic Sea, the lifeline of Swedish commerce and defense. Thus, in 1629, King Gustav II Adolf (1594–1632; ruled 1611–32) of Sweden was able to convince the Swedish *Riksdag* (representative assembly) that the Swedes must take the offensive in northern Germany to meet the threat. Sweden was at war with Poland at the time, but a six-year truce was arranged with the help of Cardinal Richelieu (also known as Armand-Jean du Plessis; 1585–1642), chief minister of France. The Swedish king was now free to give his undivided attention to Germany.

In the mind of Gustav II, politics and religion were closely connected. For this reason he looked upon Swedish intervention in German affairs as necessary. If the Habsburgs were not stopped in Germany, he reasoned, the strong position of Sweden would be jeopardized. The collapse of Protestantism in Germany would also be inevitable. In the interest of Swedish security, he had to gain a permanent hold on the southern coast of the

Mercenaries Used to Fight Wars

In the early sixteenth century European monarchs and princes began relying on mercenaries, or professional soldiers, to fight in wars. This practice arose because military leaders had problems maintaining armies that were recruited from the peasantry. The mercenary system began in Italy in the 1300s and 1400s with condottieri, or contractors who hired soldiers. It then spread beyond the Alps into Germany and Switzerland.

Before mercenaries replaced traditional soldiers, all fit males between the ages of sixteen and sixty were legally eligible to serve in the army. When soldiers were needed the state sent captains to recruit in certain areas. This practice was common in Spain, for example, and gave the government control over the process. Men usually joined the army voluntarily, but military service was often required. Recruiting from the peasantry was not enough, however, because the system did not work properly. Perhaps one-fifth of eligible men avoided service by evasion, bribery, or legal challenge. As many as one-third of new recruits deserted before joining the main army. The situation was even worse once a campaign

had started because 25 percent of soldiers usually deserted. At the end of a campaign, most soldiers were sent home. These dismissed soldiers, now unemployed and often penniless, were hated by the peasantry through whose land they had to pass. Some were unwilling to return home because they were not welcome. Overnight the former soldiers could become bandits who added to the already high level of violence in the countryside.

For these reasons military leaders preferred professional soldiers, who were more disciplined than untrained men. Some states placed permanent agents in certain regions to hire mercenaries. For example, Venice had agents who sought cavalry soldiers in Bosnia and pikemen (soldiers who carried spears with sharp points) in Switzerland. By the sixteenth century mercenaries were the mainstay of all armies. Although a hired soldier's pay was often lower than that of a civilian job, mercenaries could become quite wealthy from looting enemy supply trains and conquered cities. In a society in which violence was common, an occupation that rewarded violence was probably appealing.

Baltic Sea. Gustav spent nine months in 1629 and 1630 organizing and equipping his forces for an invasion of Germany. He also made plans to recruit additional soldiers in Germany and bring in reinforcements from as far

away as Scotland. Late in June 1630, the Swedish army appeared off the coast of Pomerania (then under Polish rule) with an armada, a fleet of ships, consisting of twenty-eight troop carriers and an equal number of warships.

Gustav II Adolf of Sweden is credited as creating the first modern army. *Photograph courtesy of The Library of Congress.*

Numbering only thirteen thousand men, the army was equipped with new flintlock muskets (handheld pistols) and a new type of light artillery, or weapons. In addition, the discipline and morale of Swedish forces was far above the standards then prevailing in Germany. The king led his army into every battle and was idolized by officers and soldiers. Gustav is credited with creating the first modern army (see "Sweden" in Chapter 4).

Conflict now a "foreign" war

Meanwhile the position of both sides, Catholic and Protestant, in Germany had deteriorated. At the Electoral Assembly held at Regensburg in 1630, Emperor Ferdinand II was persuaded to dismiss Wallenstein and a large part of his army. Ferdinand had already realized that Wallenstein's usefulness had come to an end. Wallenstein had enforced the Edict Resolution too strictly, producing disastrous results. His harsh measures had created thousands more Protestant refugees in Germany and had further weakened the emperor's cause. Ferdinand replaced Wallenstein with Tilly. Sweden's entry into the conflict now made this a "foreign war," and not primarily a German struggle. In 1631 Gustav formed an alliance with France and with certain German princes. The French provided only financial aid and moral support. Relying on revenue from Sweden's Baltic ports and the French aid, Gustav built up his forces with mercenaries before opening his German campaign.

Military operations got off to an unpromising start. After moving through eastern Pomerania and Mecklenburg, the Swedes advanced rapidly up the Oder River to Frankfurt. The Swedish monarch hoped to prevent Tilly's troops from taking the German city of Magdeburg, Sweden's ally. Magdeburg fell on May 10, 1631, and 80 percent of its population died in the violence. The defeat of Magdeburg dealt a serious blow to Protestant morale and Gustav's prestige. On August 25 Tilly crossed into Saxony, and on September 7 he met the Saxons at Breitenfeld, five miles north of

Leipzig. The Saxon army disintegrated under Tilly's assault, but by nightfall Gustav had won the Battle of Breitenfeld. He then led his forces in victories at Frankfurt-am-Main, Worms, and Mainz. Hailed as the savior of Protestantism, Gustav controlled most of Germany, and Sweden was now a great world power.

Gustav spent the winter creating an administrative structure to extract "contributions" to his campaign from the regions under Swedish control. He expected to raise an army of more than two hundred thousand men, which required huge sums of money and an effective organization. The closest thing Germany had ever had to a central government took shape during the winter of 1631 and 1632 as Gustav took charge. He planned to launch attacks on Bavaria, Bohemia, and Austria with seven armies. The offensive got off to a brilliant beginning when he staged a surprise crossing of the River Lech on April 5, 1632. The Swedes inflicted a devastating defeat on Tilly's forces, and Tilly himself was killed. The whole of Bavaria and the road to Vienna, the seat of the Habsburg empire, now lay open to Gustav.

Wallenstein was recalled to service by Ferdinand. Moving the emperor's armies through Germany, Wallenstein met Gustav at Lützen in November. The Swedish king took personal command of a cavalry regiment and prepared for the assault. The battle had only begun when Gustav was shot and killed. As news of the king's death spread through the

Stripped of Dignity

King Gustav II Adolf was a fearless military commander who joined soldiers in battle. During his military career, he had countless brushes with death. Twice horses fell through ice beneath him. Another was shot from under him. A legend grew that the Swedish king was an instrument of God and therefore immortal. His luck ran out at the Battle of Lützen in Germany. Almost before the attack got under way, Gustav was wounded by a musket ball. His horse bolted, carrying him into the midst of the fighting, where he died. In spite of his royal status, Gustav was not allowed to preserve any dignity in death: his body, stripped by looters, lay face down in the mud.

Swedish lines, the psychological damage proved greater than any physical losses. A regiment wavered until one of its chaplains started to sing a Lutheran hymn. Soon the Swedish soldiers and their Finnish allies solemnly sang along. Inspired by anguish and the thirst for revenge, they surged forward. The Battle of Lützen ended in another Swedish victory but at a high cost. Sweden's military supremacy ended soon after: in September 1634, at the battle of Nördlingen, Swedish forces were defeated by Wallenstein's armies. To preserve the military balance, France directly entered the war in Germany, supporting Sweden against the Habsburgs.

The Treaty of Prague (1635)

By 1635 the Thirty Years' War had reached a critical stage. With the defeat of the Swedish army and its allies at Nördlingen, the way seemed to be open for peace. Cardinal Richelieu, chief minister of France, and Count Axel Oxenstierna (1583–1654), the chancellor, or chief secretary, of Sweden, signed a treaty at Compiègne in April 1635. This arrangement did not receive much sympathy among the German princes, and a peace movement began to grow in Germany itself. From their point of view it was far better to arrange a German peace and permit the German people to reconstruct their devastated society.

John George I of Saxony (1595–1656) took the lead in arranging such a peace. In 1635 he and Emperor Ferdinand II signed an agreement called the Treaty of Prague. Under the terms of the treaty, John George received Lusatia on the middle Elbe, while his second son was guaranteed the Archbishopric of Magdeburg. The difficult problem of church lands was resolved by a compromise that allowed some property to remain for forty years in the hands of those who possessed them in 1627. During this period attempts at satisfactory settlements were to be made. Other lands that were not currently held by the emperor were to remain permanently in the hands of their holders. Amnesty (freedom from punishment for crimes against the state) was given to Protestants who complied with the Treaty of Prague. John George agreed to put his forces at the disposal of Ferdinand, so that the emperor could regain his former lands, which were now held by Sweden. The emperor would allow Lutherans freedom of worship within the Holy Roman Empire. The Treaty of Prague was proclaimed in Vienna. It was accepted in the Brandenburg and Württemberg districts of Germany and by most of the Protestant rulers.

Nine days earlier, at Brussels (a city in present-day Belgium), Spanish officials learned that Louis XIII of France (1601–1643; ruled 1610–43) had declared war on their king, Philip IV (1605–1665; ruled 1621–65). It soon became obvious to German rulers that peace was not possible. Instead, Germany was being drawn into an expanded struggle between the Habsburgs and France. The German states realized that, under the terms of the Treaty of Prague, they were obligated to fight all the battles of both the Austrian and the Spanish Habsburgs. The Treaty of Prague, far from bringing peace, actually prolonged the war in Germany and elsewhere for another thirteen years.

The Peace of Westphalia (1643–48)

On December 25, 1641, the new emperor, Ferdinand III (1608–1657; ruled 1637–57), agreed to begin peace negotiations the following year in the German region of Westphalia. His negotiators would meet with Swedish representatives at the city of Osnabrück and with French representatives at the city of Münster. Military and political events delayed the formal opening of the peace conference at Osnabrück until July 1643, and the Münster conference did not open until April 1644. Then it took the emperor's negotiators almost three years to hammer out peace treaties with the Swedes and the French. The Treaties of Münster and Osnabrück were both signed on October 24, 1648, and a separate agreement was signed earlier between Spain and the United Provinces of the Netherlands (see "Netherlands" in Chapter 4).

A turning point in European history

All of these agreements are considered parts of a single settlement, known as the Peace of Westphalia. It was designed to bring Protestants and Catholics together within the empire. Calvinism was given equal legal status with Catholicism and Lutheranism, so the Catholic and Protestant states of the empire were now considered to have equal status. Equality was limited to the free exercise of religion by individuals, however, and the princes in several states still had the right to determine the religion of their territories. Finally, territories formerly owned by the Catholic Church were to remain under the religion that was in effect on January 1, 1624. In addition, some lands in the Holy Roman Empire were given to Sweden and France. Sweden obtained Western Pomerania (a region on the Baltic Sea), Bremen (a province in northwest Germany), and Verden (a province in Saxony). France received Metz, Toul, and Verdun, cities in northeast France, as well as Alsace, a province in northeast France. The German district of Brandenburg-Prussia received Eastern Pomerania and several former bishoprics (church districts). The settlement gave the United Provinces of the Netherlands independence from Spain and declared Switzerland independent from the Holy Roman Empire. Each of the German states was also given sovereignty, or the right of self-rule, within the Holy Roman Empire.

The Peace of Westphalia was a landmark in European history. The Protestant Reformation and the Catholic Reformation had ended, so religion no longer played an important role in issues that divided European states. Sweden emerged as a great power in northern Europe for at least the following sixty years. Likewise, the position of Brandenburg-Prussia was greatly strengthened. The Holy Roman Empire, however, became more loosely organized than before. Spain's decline, which had already begun by 1648, was more evident when peace was finally made with France in 1659. In the second half of the seventeenth century, France, which was under the rule of King Louis XIV, emerged as the leading power on the European continent.

7

The Catholic Reformation

The Catholic Reformation was a reform movement that took place within the Roman Catholic Church during the sixteenth and seventeenth centuries. The movement is also known as the Counter Reformation, but many historians prefer not to use this term because it suggests that changes within the church were simply a reaction to Protestantism. In fact, many Catholics were already aware that reform was needed as early as the fifteenth century, one hundred years before the Protestant Reformation. By that time popes, cardinals (church officials ranking directly below the pope), bishops (heads of church districts), and priests had become corrupt and greedy. Neglecting their responsibilities as religious leaders, they pursued their own personal advancement. The church had accumulated more property and wealth than kings and princes. Many Catholics, both inside and outside the church, were troubled by this situation.

During the fourteenth century the church faced a serious crisis that hastened the need for reform. In 1307, following a power struggle among cardinals, the papacy (office of the pope) was moved to Avignon, France, where it remained for seventy years. This period was known as the Babylonian captivity (see "Crisis in the papacy" in Chapter 1). The papacy was briefly returned to Rome in 1378. Then the cardinals had another confrontation that caused a deep split in the church, and soon there were two popes—one in Avignon and one in Rome. At one point there were even three popes vying for control. This period was called the Great Schism. It ended in 1417 with the Council of Constance, a meeting of church officials and heads of European states. There was now only one pope, who was based in Rome.

Once the papacy was permanently returned to Rome, deep corruption and abuse of power became even more obvious. Popes, cardinals, and bishops were members of ruthless Italian families such as the Medicis in Florence and the Sforzas in Milan, who profited from controlling the papacy. They operated complex schemes and appointed family members to high church positions. Cardinals had luxurious homes, bishops did not reside in their districts, and priests were poorly educated. Another crisis occurred in May 1527, when soldiers in the army of Holy Roman Emperor Charles V (1500–1558; reigned 1519–56) sacked, or attacked, the city of Rome. For several months they terrorized citizens and looted and burned buildings. Pope Clement VII (1478–1534; reigned 1523–34) fled to a castle, where he was a virtual prisoner until he paid for his own release the following December. The siege has often been called the "German Fury" because the majority of the marauding soldiers were German Lutherans. Charles's spokesmen claimed the troops had moved on Rome against the emperor's wishes. According to an official report, when the soldiers reached the city they were so upset by the corruption of the Roman clergy that they committed atrocities. Even the pope's supporters agreed that the moral failings of the clergy helped to bring on the catastrophe. Clement himself later preached a sermon on the subject in 1528. Soon pamphlets were circulating around Rome, proclaiming that prophesies of punishment and doom were being fulfilled. One such prophesy was a blade-shaped comet, which was supposedly a sign that disaster would take place. The sack of Rome also gave renewed life to reforming preachers, who warned that Rome would someday have to pay for the sins and corruption of the church.

Reform movements take shape

Many Catholics had already been seeking change for years. Although they did not directly call for reform, they tried to improve the spiritual aspects of the church's mission. For instance, the Devotio Moderna (Modern Devotion) movement stressed a greater commitment to the religious life. Italian activists Catherine of Siena (1347–1380) and Catherine of Genoa (1447–1510), both of whom were later declared saints, worked among the sick and the poor. They left documents that testified to their mystical, or intensely spiritual, experiences and their devotion to spiritual renewal. Humanist scholars also promoted an upright and devout life. Previously, humanists were considered pagans (those who have no religion) because they emphasized the unlimited capabilities of human beings and rejected the Christian ideal of devoting one's life to the glory of God. Now, English humanists such as John Colet (c. 1466–1519) and Thomas More (1478–1535) were studying Scripture (the text of the Bible), and they advocated reform of the church and the education of clergymen. The Dutch humanist Desiderius Erasmus (c. 1466–1536) formed friendships with Colet, More, and others. In 1503 he published *Enchiridion militis Christiani* (Handbook of the militant Christian), in which he stressed the ethical behavior and piety, or holiness, found in the "philosophy of Christ." Within the church, Benedictine monks formed groups of monasteries committed to Christian teachings. The most important were located in Santa Giustina, Italy; Valladolid, Spain; Chézal-Benoît, France; and in the unions of Melk, Austria, and Bursfeld, Germany.

Savonarola is early leader

Several Catholic priests called for reform and achieved fame as inspiring preachers. Among them was Girolamo Savonarola (1452–1498), a Dominican monk who was executed for challenging the church. Savonarola began his career in 1482 as a lecturer at the convent of San Marco in Florence, Italy, the center of the Italian Renaissance (see "Florence" in Chapter 2). Within a few years he became a harsh critic of church practices. He was angered by the corrupt behavior of popes, cardinals, and bishops. He demanded stricter adherence to the spiritual values of Christianity and greater social awareness of the poor. Earning the title of the "Preacher of the Despairing," he gave immensely popular sermons. Around 1491 Savonarola was named prior (second in rank to the abbot, or head, of a monastery) of San Marco. He became famous for having visions that enabled him to predict future events. His first vision was about the "Scourge [whip] of the Church," which would come to banish the evil materialism of the Catholic clergy. He also correctly predicted the deaths of Lorenzo de' Medici (1449–1492), the powerful duke of Florence, and Pope Innocent VIII (1432–1492; reigned 1484–92), who both died in 1492.

Savonarola's sermons reached a peak during Advent (the forty days preceding Christmas) in 1492, when he prophesied the coming of the "Scourge of Italy." This vision may have been prompted by the election of Pope Alexander VI (formerly Cardinal Rodrigo Borgia; 1431–1503; reigned 1492–1503), after the death of Innocent VIII. The behavior of the new pope—taking mistresses, advancing members of his own family to prominent church positions, and squandering money on clothes and horses—was outrageous even in a time known for its corruption and decadence. Savonarola set out to reform the church in Florence. His first step was to withdraw the monastery of San Marco from the Congregation of Lombardy, the ruling organization of monasteries in the region. He then formed a new, stricter congregation, which was approved by the pope in 1493. Savonarola saw the separation as the beginning of the reform of the Roman Catholic Church. Expanding his movement, he convinced other convents to join his congregation. In his own monastery, he demanded that monks give up all possessions, which were then sold to raise money for the poor.

Savonarola had also been criticizing the city government and was a bitter enemy to Lorenzo de' Medici before the duke's death. In 1494 Savonarola's prophecy of the "Scourge of Italy" was fulfilled when King Charles VIII (1470–1498; ruled 1483–98) of France invaded Italy in the first phase of the Italian Wars (a conflict between France and Spain over control of territory in Italy; see "Italian Wars dominate Renaissance" in Chapter 2). Lorenzo's son and the new duke of Florence, Piero de' Medici (1471–1503), fled from Italy and threw himself upon the mercy of the French king. The leading political body of Florence, the Signoria, elected Savonarola to ask Charles to insure Florence's security and safety. Savonarola then turned to the problem of a new government without the Medicis. In his sermons he suggested new policies that became law. For instance, he demanded an increase in jobs for the lower classes and relief for the poor. He also urged the churches to melt down their gold and silver ornaments to buy bread for the hungry. In 1495 he met resistance when a group called the *Tiepidi* (the lukewarm) was formed by priests, nuns, and monks who were opposed to strict observance of the vows of poverty and obedience. The Tiepidi received support from Pope Alexander, Duke Ludovico Sforza (1452–1508) of Milan, and Holy Roman Emperor Maximilian I (1459–1519; reigned 1493–1519), who had formed an alliance called the Holy League to oppose Charles VIII. The League needed backing from Florence, but first they had to remove Savonarola from power.

Challenged by pope In 1495 Savonarola became ill with dysentery (an intestinal disease caused by an infection). Although his doctors told him to rest, he returned to the pulpit and delivered stinging sermons against his opponents, especially the Tiepidi. In response, Pope Alexander sent an official letter stating that certain people had accused Savonarola of committing heresy (violations of the laws of God and the church) and false prophecy and troubling the peace of the church. Although he praised Savonarola's work, Alexander insisted that he come to Rome to defend himself. Since Savonarola was still weak from his illness, he asked permission to stay in Florence. The pope agreed, but told him to stop preaching until the accusations could be proven false. During the next few months, however, the pope became more hostile toward Savonarola and ordered him to stand trial. When an investigation found no evidence against Savonarola, Alexander canceled plans for a trial but would not lift the ban on preaching.

In 1496 the people of Florence persuaded the pope to allow Savonarola to preach the Lenten sermons. Once again Savonarola lashed out at the church, charging that abuses had gone beyond all bounds and that the church no longer observed its own rules. He met opposition, however, when he demanded that the government pass stricter laws regulating the dress and ornamentation of Florentine women. By refusing to pass such a statute, city leaders took their first step away from Savonarola's reform platform. In 1497 new members of the Signoria who supported the Holy League began passing laws that limited Savonarola's preaching. On May 4, a group of rowdies known as the *Compagnacci* started a riot while he was giving a sermon, apparently hoping to kill him. Although loyal monks saved his life, Florentine leaders identified him as the source of discontent in the city, and many demanded his exile. Alexander then excommunicated (forced to leave the church) Savonarola and his followers for heresy. This event brought a deeper split among the Florentine factions, or opposing groups. In July the pope and his cardinals decided Savonarola must either come to Rome to defend his criticism of the church or abandon his reforms.

The final showdown between Savonarola and the pope began on February 11, 1498, when Alexander ordered the Signoria to silence the disobedient monk. In April, Florentine officials conducted two three-day trials. During both trials they tortured and questioned Savonarola for evidence against him and two companions, Fra (Brother) Domenico da Pescia and Fra Silvestro Maruffi. Although Savonarola signed a confession, lack of sufficient evidence led to the second trial. With the verdict already decided, a two-day church trial then took place in May. The church court passed a death sentence for all three clergyman. On May 23, 1498, Savonarola and his two companions were hanged and their bodies were cremated. Government officials scattered the ashes in the Arno River to prevent the veneration, or declaration of holiness, of the remains. Savonarola's attempt to reform the church had failed.

Church starts reforms

Within thirty years after Savonarola's death, the rapid rise of Protestantism brought more demands for reform of the Catholic Church. In keeping with a practice dating back to early times, many religious and political leaders wanted to hold a general council of bishops to discuss problems. A general council met at Rome from 1515 until 1517. This gathering, called the Fifth Lateran Council, agreed to make various reforms. It adjourned shortly before the German reformer Martin Luther (1483–1546) posted his Ninety-Five Theses, a list of grievances with the church, at Wittenberg, Germany, in 1517.

Popes showed no serious interest in reform until 1537, when Pope Paul III (1468–1549; reigned 1534–49) appointed a committee of cardinals to study problems in the church. Their report, *A Council ... for Reforming the Church,* denounced evils and abuses at all levels. Most of these abuses were laid at the door of the papacy itself. For the next few years Pope Paul tried to convene a council, but it had to be postponed several times. In the meantime he initiated his own reforms. He encouraged many new religious communities and approved the Society of Jesus (Jesuits) in 1540 and the Order of Saint Ursula in 1544. In 1542 he founded the Congregation of the Roman Inquisition as the final court of appeal in trials of heresy (see "The Inquisitions" section later in this chapter).

Council of Trent

The first session of a council of bishops finally met at Trent in northern Italy in 1545. Attendance was sparse, with an overwhelming number of Italian bishops. Although no Protestants were mentioned by name in council documents, Protestant teachings were discussed. The bishops agreed to accept the Latin Vulgate as the official Bible of the Catholic Church, including the books of Judith and Maccabees and the Epistle of James. The worth of these books had been questioned by Luther. The delegates at Trent also decided that ancient traditions of the church were equal to the religious truth of the Bible. Luther had asserted that the Bible, not the opinions or practices of

Pope Paul III was the first pope to show serious interest in reforming the Catholic Church. *Photograph courtesy of The Library of Congress.*

church officials, should be "the sole rule of faith."

The most important decree pertained to the Protestant concept that humans are basically sinful and lack free will (the ability to make independent choices). Protestants believed that salvation (forgiveness of sins) is a gift called grace from God and that people are incapable of fulfilling God's law without this gift. Furthermore, they are not free to accept or reject it. The Council of Trent, on the other hand, decreed that people are capable of performing some naturally good works on their own. However, they must be open to God's offer of grace, which enables them to fulfill his law. If they reject grace, they will not gain salvation. The first session also officially declared that there are seven sacraments, or holy rites, established by Jesus Christ—communion, baptism (use of water in admitting a person into the Christian community), confirmation (conferring the gift of the Holy Spirit), penance (confession of sins), anointing (applying oil as a sacred rite) of the sick, marriage, and holy orders (ordination of priests). The church had taught this doctrine since the twelfth century, but most Protestants had rejected all sacraments except baptism and communion. The council was suspended in 1547 because of poor attendance, an outbreak of typhus (bacterial disease), and a bad climate.

The second session met at Trent in 1551 and 1552 under Pope Julius III (1487–1555; reigned 1550–55). It declared that Christ is really and physically present in communion. In contrast, most Protestants, except for Martin Luther, believed that the presence of Christ in the ritual is merely symbolic. The next pope, Paul IV (1476–1559; reigned 1555–59), opposed the council as a threat to papal authority, so he started his own reform measures. In 1555 he strengthened the Roman Inquisition, which Paul III established in 1542. At that time the Roman Catholic Church wrongly suspected Jews of influencing the Protestant Reformation, so the pope established the Jewish ghetto (a part of the city in which a minority group is forced to live) at Rome. He required all Jews to wear an identifying badge, thus separating them from Christians. In 1559 Paul IV issued the first edition of his Index of Prohibited Books.

Borromeo sets example

Toward the end of the sixteenth century, partly under the influence of the Council of Trent, a number of bishops emerged as reformers in northern Italy. Among them was Carlo Borromeo (1538–1584), who served as a model for others and was later declared a saint. Borromeo was born into a prosperous family in the town of Rocca d'Arona. After studying with tutors, he enrolled at the University of Padua, where in 1559 he received the degree of doctor of laws. That same year his uncle was elected Pope Pius IV (1499–1565; reigned 1559–65). Within a few months the new pope had called twenty-one-year-old Borromeo to Rome to help in administering the affairs of the church. Borromeo was given the rank of cardinal to go with his position as personal assistant to the pope. Pius IV then made Borromeo secretary of state and relied heavily on him in directing the third session of the Council of Trent. In 1563 Borromeo was ordained a priest and consecrated archbishop (a supervisor of other bishops) of Milan, but he continued to live in Rome and work with his uncle. He was given responsibility for making reforms required by the Council of Trent in Rome. Borromeo improved religious instruction in the parishes, toned down elaborate wor-

Catholic Church officials meeting at the Council of Trent. *©Archivo Iconografico, S.A./Corbis. Reproduced by permission of the Corbis Corporation.*

ship rituals, and built a new seminary for training priests.

In 1565 Borromeo's services in Rome came to an end with his uncle's death. The following year he moved to Milan, where he directed the church. The diocese of Milan was split into five districts, which he had to operate simultaneously. Over the years he was a highly effective bishop. Almost all of the people of Milan respected him, but his popularity with the people disturbed the senate. His disciplinary measures also antagonized several religious groups. At one point an assassin was hired to kill Borromeo, but the attempt on his life failed. When the plague (a widespread outbreak of disease epidemic; see "Black Death" in Chapter 1) struck Milan in 1576, Borromeo spent much of his time nursing the sick. The centers for religious instruction that he established were so effective that Protestantism made no headway in Milan. He died in 1584, and he was canonized, or declared a saint, in 1610.

Religious orders and congregations formed

During the Catholic Reformation several new religious orders and congregations for men and women were founded throughout Europe, but mainly in Italy and France. Many of them were a new kind of order called clerics regular. They were given this name because members lived according to a *regula* (the Latin term for rule) within a community. They took the traditional vows of poverty, chastity (refraining from sexual intercourse), and obedience. They were officially connected with the Catholic Church, yet they did not live in isolation behind the walls of monasteries and convents. Instead, they devoted themselves to active ministries, mainly in parishes (local church communities) and schools.

Other groups, called congregations, had the same mission as religious orders, but members did not take formal vows. Although they were headed by bishops and priests and worked in parishes, they were not officially connected with the church.

Orders and congregations for men

The prominent new orders for men were the Theatines, the Barnabites, the Piarists, and the Jesuits. The largest was the Jesuits. Although the Jesuits were founded in Italy, most of their original leaders were Spanish, and most Jesuits worked outside of Italy. The Theatines, Barnabites, Piarists were smaller and predominantly Italian orders. The Oratorians, based in Italy, were technically a congregation, but their branches in France closely resembled a religious order.

Theatines The Theatines were founded in 1524 by four members of a Roman confraternity (a society devoted to a charitable or religious cause), the Order of Divine Love. Their leaders were Cajetan of Thiene, Gian Pietro Carafa (later Pope Paul IV), Benefic de' Coli, and Paolo Consiglieri. Thiene worked as a priest in the papal curia (administrative branch of the office of the pope) and founded confraternities and hospitals in several northern Italian cities. Carafa came from a noble family in Naples. As a young humanist he corresponded with the Dutch humanist Desiderio Erasmus, who praised his friendliness and learning. Alarmed by the rising tide of Protestantism, Carafa soon became Italy's most ardent supporter of repression. He resigned as bishop of Chieti when he established the Theatines (from *Theate,* the Latin name for Chieti).

The founders saw a need for communities of morally strict and devout, or religiously faithful, priests. Members of the new order would be dedicated to preaching, hearing confessions, encouraging the frequent receipt of communion, giving spiritual guidance, and working with the sick in hospitals. Like earlier orders of monks and friars, the Theatines took permanent vows of poverty, chastity, and obedience, but two practices set them apart from the others. They refused to beg, which meant that they would live on stipends (grants of money) from their ministries and from free-will gifts. Also, unlike other orders, they recited their religious ritual together, but without singing. They did not wear a distinctive religious habit (garment), but only the usual cassock (ankle-length garment) and biretta (a square cap with ridges on the top) of priests. For their first eighty years Theatines had no official constitution, or set of rules, but depended on a long letter written by Carafa in 1526 that described their lifestyle. Each year the Theatines elected a superior—the head of a religious order—who looked to Carafa's letter for guidance. In 1603, at a general meeting, the order finally proposed official constitutions that were approved by Pope Clement VII the following year.

The Theatines set up their first community at Rome, but they fled to Venice when Emperor Charles V's army sacked Rome in 1527. They set up a second community at Naples in 1533 and returned to Rome in 1557. In 1550 the Theatines had only twenty-seven members, but between 1565 and 1600 new houses were started throughout Italy. A total of 744 men had joined them by 1600. Most were already priests when they entered, though the order had some lay brothers, or unordained priests. During the next century the Theatines slowly moved into Austria, Germany, Spain, Portugal, and Poland. Probably their greatest contribution to Catholic reform originated from the forty-five bishops who came from their ranks between 1524 and 1624.

Barnabites The Barnabite order was founded by Antonio Maria Zaccaria (1502–1539), who studied at the University of Padua. Returning to his home in Cremona in 1524, he briefly practiced medicine but gradually became involved in helping the poor and sick. In 1528 he was ordained and worked briefly in a local parish. Around 1530 he came into contact with Battista Carioni da Cremona (c. 1460–1534), an aging Dominican priest (member of a religious order founded by Saint Dominic). Carioni had been preaching religious reform in Milan and Venice. He condemned humanism for what he viewed as excessive concern with literary matters. Carioni helped to draw up the Barnabite constitutions, but this brought him under the suspicion of the Inquisition.

In 1531 Zaccaria wrote to two friends and proposed a community of clerics that would combine the responsibilities of priests with monastic living. Two years later the three men started such a community. Six others joined them the following year; they all lived in a community, but without taking formal vows. Zaccaria served as the superior until 1536. He was the confessor (priest who hears confessions) to Countess Ludovica Torelli (1500–1569). She was a wealthy widow who organized a related order for women, the Angelic Sisters of the Converted (known as the Angelics). Married people among Zaccaria's friends joined a new confraternity, the Devoted Married Laity of Saint Paul, founded about 1531. The three organizations—one for priests, one for nuns (women who devote their lives to the church), and one for married couples—were closely linked.

Jesuit founder Ignatius of Loyola. His Jesuit order eventually became the single most powerful weapon of the Catholic Reformation. *Painting by Peter Paul Rubens. Reproduced by permission of the Corbis Corporation.*

The early years of the Barnabites were turbulent. In 1534 their public penances (acts of sorrow or repentance for sins) at Milan resulted in their being accused of heresy and public disorder. Carioni's books were put on the Venetian Index of Prohibited Books in 1554 and on the Roman Indexes starting in 1557. They remained there for more than three centuries. What provoked this hostility toward the writings and practices of the Barnabites? At Milan the priests and nuns mixed together to perform public acts of penance—painting fools' masks on their faces, whipping themselves, carrying heavy crosses (the cross is the symbol of Christ's suffering for the sins of all people), and openly confessing their sins. These public displays of penance were considered unseemly because the act of penance was considered a private matter. The Barnabites also went into marketplaces to beg donations for pregnant unwed mothers; such begging on the part of the Barnabites was shocking because so many of them came from the nobility, a class of people generally unaccustomed to such behavior. Zaccaria defended his followers before the Inquisition in Milan. Such attacks could be expected, he said, because the Barnabites were trying to devote their lives to Christ. They were proud of being "fools" for Christ. Although the Inquisition found no real evidence against them, Zaccaria and his followers were not formally declared innocent.

Zaccaria turned to Pope Clement VII for approval. In 1533 Clement placed the Barnabites under church jurisdiction, and in 1543 Pope Paul III put them under the jurisdiction of the office of the pope. Still, new accusations of heresy kept cropping up, so the order grew only to forty members during its first twenty years. In 1551 the Barnabites drafted new constitutions, which were approved by Pope Julius III in 1553. The Angelics received approval from the pope in 1535, but in 1552 they were forced to become cloistered—that is, to live in a convent—rather than living among the general population. Their new constitutions were approved by Pope Urban VIII (1568–1644; reigned 1623–44) in 1625.

Jesuits The Jesuit order, also called Society of Jesus, was led by Ignatius Loyola (1491–1556). Ignatius was born into a noble family in the Basque region of northern Spain. Baptized Iñigo de Oñaz y Loyola, he adopted the name Ignatius in about 1537, in honor of Saint Ignatius of Antioch, an early Church martyr—one who sacrifices his or her life for a cause. After receiving a limited education, he became a soldier. His brief military career ended in 1521 when he was wounded in battle at Pamplona, Spain, during the Italian Wars. While he was recuperating at his home, the castle of Loyola, he had a series of religious experiences that changed the course of his life. Ignatius began a program of asceticism, or strict self-denial, for which his Jesuit followers later honored him. He sometimes went days at a time without food, walked barefoot in winter, and deliberately neglected his long hair, of which he had earlier been proud, until it was matted and filthy. He wore a hair shirt—a garment made of rough animal hair worn next to the skin—and sometimes a nail-studded belt turned inward to his body. The effect of these torments was to weaken him and give him a pale and haggard appearance, which terrified both strangers and acquaintances. It also caused him lifelong stomach problems.

After a period of time in Manresa, Spain, where he spent six or more hours a day in prayer and a few hours a day begging for alms (money or food), Ignatius worked in hospitals, caring for the poor. He had sold all his property and given away the proceeds to the needy. As a local nobleman, however, Ignatius was still well known in the community. His social status, along with his growing spiritual reputation, led to frequent invitations to other nobles' houses to dine and to give religious instruction. He would not stay with the nobility, however, but retired to humble lodgings to sleep.

Ignatius tried to confess and do penance (an act to show sorrow or repentance) for all the sins of his earlier life. When he found he had committed so many sins that he could not enumerate them, a priest suggested writing them out. Beginning in 1522 he spent a year in seclusion at the small town of Mansera outside Barcelona. During this time he put his ideas on paper, eventually producing his masterpiece, the *Spiritual Exercises,* which was published in 1548. This short but influential book outlines a thirty-day regimen, or systematic plan, of prayer and self-abasement (acts of self-denial and punishment), with the understanding that devotion to God must be central. After a pilgrimage, or religious journey, to Jerusalem in 1524, Ignatius decided he needed a better education if he was to do his work effectively. He began to study Latin at Barcelona, then moved in 1526 to the recently founded university at Alcalá de Henares, where humanist influence was strong. Finally he spent a short time at the University of Salamanca.

Ignatius targeted by Inquisition
While Ignatius was at Alcalá de Henares and Salamanca, Catholic officials suspected him of being involved in Luther's reform movement. Holy Roman Emperor Charles V, who was also the king of Spain, was unable to stop the spread of Protestantism in Germany. He therefore used the Inquisition to stamp it out in Spain (see "The Inquisitions" section later in this chapter). Although Ignatius does not appear to have known about Luther, he was imprisoned without trial or formal charges on several occasions. He always insisted on a judgment, but he was usually found blameless despite his unconventional practices. After these experiences with inquisitors Ignatius concluded that he ought to be a fully educated priest rather than a hermit (one who lives in isolation) and preacher. In 1528 he went to the University of Paris, which was then the center of Catholic learning in Europe. Again he lived on alms, begged in Flanders and England between academic sessions, and studied continuously. While in Paris, Loyola met six of the men who were to form the nucleus of the Jesuits. Among them were Diego Lainez (1512–1565), later a theologian at the Council of Trent, and Francis Xavier (1506–1552), who became the first Jesuit missionary to India and Japan.

Ignatius was ordained a priest in 1537. He then requested that Pope Paul III allow his group to make a pilgrimage to Jerusalem, where he hoped they might remain as hospital workers. The pope was delighted by the group's zeal and funded their journey. They planned to take a ship from the port of Venice to Syria, but Turkish pirates in the Mediterranean prevented any pilgrim ships from setting sail that year—contributing to that being the only year in the past half century that pilgrim ships did not leave Venice for Syria. The "Company of Jesus," as the Jesuits now called themselves, took it as an omen, or warning sign, that their future work did not lie in the Holy Land (called Palestine at the time; the territory is now in parts of Israel, Jordan, and Egypt). Apart from taking short trips, Ignatius spent the rest of his life in Italy.

Troubled by serious social and religious problems in Italy, Ignatius saw an opportunity to do his work closer to home. He invited his companions from around Italy to join him in Rome. The time had come, he told them, to establish an order that differed from the older orders of the Church (Benedictines, Carthusians, Franciscans, Dominicans, and others). First, his group would be loyal to the pope. Second, they would not live a monastic life with regular hours of prayer and choral singing. Third, strict obedience to leaders of the order would be the foremost priority. (One of the oldest Jesuit tales is about a mortally ill novice (candidate for the priesthood) on his death bed asking the novice-master for permission to die.) The organization members' task was to act as "trumpeters of Christ." Members of the order were to be made strong and adaptable through prayer, self-surrender, and a very long training period. At first some influential Roman clergymen opposed the new order, but the pope established the Society of Jesus as an order of the Catholic Church in 1540.

Jesuits an influential order In 1541 Ignatius was named the first superior general of the Jesuits. The order eventually grew from the original six followers to more than a thousand. Several Jesuits acted as experts at the Council of Trent. Pierre Favre (Peter Faber; 1506–1546), one of Ignatius's earliest companions, was the first Jesuit to go to Germany. He advocated reconciliation with Protestants rather than conflict. Some Jesuits became missionaries in the New World (the European term for North and South America) and others went to Poland. The Jesuits also moved early into the field of education, founding colleges in Italy, Portugal, the Netherlands, Spain, Germany, and India. These colleges became the basis of the Jesuit educational system that has continued to the present.

By maintaining good relations with the popes, Ignatius was also able to improve conditions nearer to home. In Rome he set up Saint Martha's, a refuge, or safe place, for reforming prostitutes (women who engage in sexual intercourse for money). For most of the last fifteen years of his life he worked a twenty-hour day, resting only to recover from increasingly severe illnesses. He finally died after a day of hard work in 1556. Ignatius was declared a saint in 1622. By that time the Jesuits had become the single most powerful weapon of the Catholic Reformation.

Piarists The Piarist order was founded by José Calasanz (1557–1648). He was a priest from Aragon, Spain, who went to Rome in 1592 to take a position in the papal curia (the body of congregation, tribunals, and office through which the pope governs the Roman Catholic Church). While working with a confraternity that taught catechism (religious doctrines in the form of questions and answers) to poor children, he became aware that these children lacked sufficient schooling. He tried to get city officials and religious orders to provide better education for poor boys, but both agencies claimed they lacked the funds. In 1597 Calasanz and three friends opened a school that did not charge fees for instruction. Students flocked to the doors. Money came from the donations of wealthy church officials. The Jesuits also did not charge fees, but they accepted only students who already knew some Latin, the official language of the church. Therefore poor boys were not usually eligible for Jesuit schools because they rarely knew Latin. The Piarist schools taught catechism along with subjects that would enable the boys to get better jobs. The band of teachers grew to twenty. In 1604 Pope Clement VIII (1536–1605; reigned 1592–1605) authorized them to live as a religious community. Ten years later Pope Paul V (1552–1621; reigned 1605–21) agreed to Calasanz's request that they be merged with the Matritani, a small order founded by Giovanni Leonardi (1541–1609). This association ended three years later, primarily because the Matritani did not focus on education

Peter Canisius, a Jesuit in Central Europe

Peter Canisius (also known as Peter Kanis; 1521–1597), a Jesuit from the Netherlands, was a leading figure of the Catholic Reformation. A prayerful man and tireless worker, he revitalized the Catholic Church in central Europe by preaching, writing, and founding Jesuit colleges.

Peter Canisius was born in the Dutch town of Nijmegen. After studying at the Latin school of Saint Stephen in Nijmegen, he entered the University of Cologne at the age of fifteen. At a monastery in Cologne he was influenced by the Devotio Moderna, a movement stressing a greater commitment to the religious life. In 1540 he earned a master of arts degree and began studying theology. In 1543 he heard about Pierre Favre, one of the first Jesuits, who was then at Mainz. Under Favre's direction he read the *Spiritual Exercises* of Ignatius of Loyola and decided to become a Jesuit. Peter was ordained a priest in 1546.

Peter had a long missionary career in many countries of Europe. In 1546 he participated in the Council of Trent. Two years later he joined nine other Jesuits in opening a school at Messina, and in 1549 he joined the faculty of the University of Ingolstadt. In 1552 he went to Vienna to assist the new Jesuit community there. To meet the challenge of Martin Luther's popular catechism (a book of religious instructions in the form of questions and answers), Peter published his *Summary of Christian Doctrine* in 1555. Designed for boys in the upper classes and clearly written in easy Latin, Peter's catechism was eventually reissued in hundreds of editions. In 1556 he published *Tiny Catechism* for children. His most popular work, *An Abridged Catechism* for students in the middle grades, appeared in 1558. Through the years he embellished this book with engravings, verses, and prayers.

In 1556 Peter became superior (the head of a religious house or order) of the Upper German Province. For the next forty-one years his days were filled with diverse activities. He shared in the establishment of 18 Jesuit colleges, and in the Augsburg Cathedral alone he preached 225 long sermons in 18 months. He also wrote two volumes of church history. In 1557 he traveled about 2,000 miles through Italy, Austria, Bavaria, and the Rhineland. Bishops and abbots constantly sought his advice. Peter's correspondence, which fills eight large volumes, reveals a person of gentle patience and ardent devotion to the Catholic Church. He regarded heresy as "a plague more deadly than other plagues," but he insisted on a spirit of charity in meeting non-Catholics. In 1597, at the age of 76, he died at Fribourg, Switzerland. Pope Pius XI canonized Peter and declared him a doctor of the church (one who defends Roman Catholic teaching) in 1925.

and they were not so devoted to the vow of poverty as the Piarists.

The Piarists were formally approved by Pope Gregory XV (1554–1623; reigned 1621–23) in 1621. Calasanz was elected the first superior of the order and wrote their constitution, which was approved by the pope in 1622. To the traditional three vows—poverty, chastity, and obedience—the Piarists added a fourth vow, teaching. Calasanz did not allow his priests to preach, and he discouraged them from hearing confessions or doing any work that would distract them from teaching.

Growth brings problems The Piarists resorted to begging from door to door when they were low on funds. Their schools filled a need, and the order grew rapidly. New schools were opened in thirteen Italian cities between 1617 and 1634. The first school outside Italy opened in Moravia in 1631. By 1646 the Piarists had five hundred members and thirty-seven houses, almost all with schools. In a few cases the Piarists took over existing town schools and received annual financial support from the town.

Rapid growth caused severe problems for the Piarists. Calasanz seems to have lowered standards to rush teachers into the classroom after only a year of training. The Piarists had a large proportion of lay brothers. The priests taught the more advanced classes, especially those in Latin, and the brothers were restricted to the lower classes. To ease mounting tensions between the priests and the brothers, Calasanz authorized all the brothers to be ordained in 1627. This decision caused even more problems and the order was withdrawn ten years later. Calasanz's authoritarian policies alienated other superiors. The Jesuits resented the Piarists as a rival teaching order, and many nobles saw free education for the poor as a threat to the upper classes. The noblemen feared that peasants would be able to rise above their lowly status once they learned to read and write. Some Piarists were denounced to the Inquisition, and in 1642 Calasanz was arrested briefly. Finally the order was prohibited to take novices, and those who had taken vows as priests were allowed to join other orders. Two hundred members left, but three hundred stayed with the Piarists. In 1656 the pope relented and restored the Piarists as a community. It qualified as a full order in 1669. Once more their ranks swelled, and new schools were opened, notably in eastern Europe and Spain. The Piarists, who were especially devoted to the Virgin Mary (mother of Jesus Christ) and communion, borrowed much of their spiritual teachings from the Jesuits.

Oratorians The Oratorian congregation was founded by the Italian reformer Philip Neri (Filiippo Romolo de' Neri; 1515–1595). He was born in Florence, the son of a lawyer. As a boy, Philip befriended monks at the convent of San Marco. In 1532 or 1533 he went to San Germano to learn business from an uncle, but he decided he wanted a more spiritual life. After a few months he left San Germano and moved to Rome. There he studied philosophy and theology at Sapienza University and Sant' Agostino. He made friends easily and met regularly with some of them at the church of San Girolamo della Carità for discussion, prayer, and communion. San Girolamo became his home for thirty-two years. In 1551, after eighteen years in Rome, Philip was ordained a priest. His room, known as the "Oratory," became the center for meetings. Philip dreaded formality and loved spontaneity. He gave his little groups a definite character with Scripture readings, short commentaries, brief prayers, and hymns. The Italian composer Giovanni Palestrina (c. 1525–1594) set many of the scriptural texts to music, creating the "oratorio"—named for Philip's room—a form of musical presentation that is still popular today.

Popes Paul IV and Pius V (1504–1572; reigned 1566–72) did not approve of Philip's group. But among Philip's friends were some of the great religious figures of the age: Carlo Borromeo, Francis de Sales, and Ignatius of Loyola. As more priests became his followers, Philip rejected the traditional, tightly organized group united by religious vows. Instead, he created a congregation of lay priests living in a community. In 1575 Pope Gregory XIII (1502–1585; reigned 1572–85) approved the Congregation of the Oratory, which was called the Oratorians.

Philip's famous walks through Rome contributed to his earning the title Apostle of Rome. (In the Catholic Church an apostle is the principal missionary sent to a city or country.) Surrounded by a laughing and joking group of followers, he went into all corners of the city, radiating gaiety by his simple friendship and playful wit. Beneath his external life were the deep foundations of an intense spirit of prayer and love for the priestly responsibilities of hearing confessions and holding mass. In 1575 Santa Maria in Vallicella became the Oratorians' church. Eight years later Philip moved to the church, and he died there in 1595. Philip Neri was declared a saint in 1622.

Congregation of Missions The Congregation of Missions was started by the French priest Vincent de Paul (1581–1660) for the purpose of helping the poor. Vincent came from a peasant family in the village of Pouy in southwestern France. He studied theology at the University of Toulouse, was ordained a priest at age nineteen, and completed his theological studies four years later. Using his status as a priest to escape the dull village life of southern France, Vincent went to Paris in 1608. He wrote a curious letter to some friends at this time, telling in detail how he had been captured by Barbary pirates and taken as a slave to Tunisia. This story is not supported by any other evidence, and Vincent never referred to it later in his life.

In Paris, Vincent came under the influence of a spiritual guide who gradually led him to realize that helping others was more important than helping himself. For a few years he worked as a parish priest in Clichy near Paris. In 1613 he tutored the children of the general of the French galleys (ships or boats propelled by oars) and in 1617 became chaplain, or religious adviser, to the galley slaves, people who were forced to operate the oars on galleys. He was concerned for all the peasants on the general's properties because of their terrible living conditions. By 1625 he had influenced a number of young men, some of them priests, to join him in forming a religious group to be called the Congregation of the Mission. Vincent and his friends worked with the poor people of the countryside near Paris, helping them obtain food and clothing and teaching them about Jesus Christ.

Vincent formed associations of wealthy people in Paris, persuading them to dedicate some of their time and money to helping the poor. He started several hospitals, including one in Marseilles, France, for convicts sentenced to the galleys. Several times he was asked to act as a mediator in the wars of religion that were tearing France apart (see "France" in Chapter 6). With Louise de Marillac, one of his followers, Vincent started the Sisters of Charity, the first religious group of women dedicated entirely to works of charity outside the cloister (see "Sisters of Charity" section later in this chapter). He died in 1660 and was canonized a saint in the Roman Catholic Church in 1737. The religious groups he founded continue to carrying on his work.

Orders and congregations for women

Between the mid-fifteenth and mid-seventeenth centuries the church's involvement in the lives of women changed profoundly. Previously, women who were devoted to religious work lived in cloisters, secluded convents. Under the influence of humanism and new thinking in the church in the fifteenth century, women were encouraged to become involved in charitable activities aimed at helping the poor, the sick, and orphans. During the Catholic Reformation these activities expanded to include teaching catechism and performing welfare services. Religious institutions for females provided women with an alternative lifestyle or a substitute for the family. Under these new conditions women were free to remain unmarried, whereas in earlier times being unmarried was considered dishonorable.

Although the Council of Trent required women's communities to be cloistered, many worked within their local communities, principally as teachers. Throughout the seventeenth century, however, the church increasingly brought pressure on communities to become cloistered.

Company of Saint Ursula The Company of Saint Ursula was founded in 1535 by Angela Merici (c. 1474–1540). It was the original model for several communities and congregations bearing the name "Ursuline." The best known is the Order of Saint Ursula, the oldest and most influential Roman Catholic women's teaching order.

Angela Merici was born to peasant parents in Desenzano, on Lake Garda in northern Italy. She was orphaned in early childhood and later became a Franciscan tertiary (member of the third, or lay, order of Saint Francis). She taught poor girls the essentials of the Catholic faith and instructed them in caring for sick women in her native town. In 1516 she was invited to undertake similar tasks in Brescia. In 1524 and 1525 she made pilgrimages to the Holy Land and to Rome. In 1535 she established a more formal group, composed of twenty-eight young women, called the Company of Saint Ursula. As a society of virgins dedicated to the teaching of girls, Angela and her companions bound themselves to the service of their patron saint, Ursula.

Taking no religious vows and wearing simple clothing rather than habits (the garments worn by nuns), these women lived in their own homes or in suitable private households. Although they were not an organized community, they formed a sisterhood, each serving an apostolate, or mission, among her family, friends, and neighbors. Full-fledged members of the Company of Saint Ursula were young virgins, age twelve or older, of lower social status. They were protected and governed by upper-class widows. The organization was approved by the local bishop in 1536 and by the pope in 1544. The bishop of Milan, Carlo Borromeo promoted the Company of Saint Ursula in his diocese.

Angela Merici composed her *Regola* (1535–40) in which she advised her first followers that "if according to times and needs you should be obliged to make fresh rules and change certain things, do it with prudence [sound judgment] and good advice." Without binding her group to rigid rules, she formed a "new company" that took different forms, including communities of sisters taking simple vows. A cloistered order of teachers, the Ursulines of France, was founded in the early seventeenth century and later established in Canada, where it became the first training school for nuns. Some were communities of sisters who took simple vows. Among others was a cloistered order of teachers, the Ursulines of France, which was founded in the early seventeenth century. It was later established in Canada, where it became the first female missionary order. Angela Merici was beatified (declared holy) in 1768 and canonized in 1807.

Visitation of Holy Mary The Visitation of Holy Mary (Visitation Nuns) order was cofounded by the activist reformer Francis of Sales (1567–1622) and his follower Jane Frances of Chantal (1572–1641). Francis of Sales grew up in Thorens-Glières, Savoy, and was educated at the Jesuit college of Clermont in Paris (1580–88). He attended the university in Padua, Italy, where he received a doctorate of law degree in 1591. After briefly practicing law he turned to religion and was ordained in 1593 at Annecy, the chief town of his native Savoy. Francis began intense missionary work in Chablais, a district that had broken away from Savoy and had converted to Calvinism (a strict form of Protestantism; see "John Calvin" in Chapter 6). Chablais was later regained by the duke of Savoy, Charles Emmanuel I (1562–1630), an ardent Catholic. Under Charles's protection, Francis returned the majority of the people of Chablais to Catholicism. Francis was consecrated bishop of Geneva in 1602. In 1610, he and Jane Frances of Chantal founded the Visitation of Holy Mary, called the Visitation Nuns, which became principally a teaching order for women.

Francis wrote the devotional classic *Introduction to a Devout Life* (1609). In the book he emphasized that spiritual perfection is possible for people who are busy with the affairs of the world. Contrary to what many believed at the time, Francis stressed that spirituality was not reserved only for those who withdraw from society. In addition to his spiritual works, his writings include controversies against Calvinists, letters, sermons, and documents on diocesan administration. Francis was the first to receive a solemn beatification at Saint Peter's Basilica in Rome (1661). In 1877 he became the first writer in French to be named doctor of the church, and in 1923 Pope Pius XI named him the patron saint of writers.

Institute of the Blessed Virgin Mary

The Institute of the Blessed Virgin Mary was a network of schools for girls founded by an English lay apostle, or missionary, named Mary Ward (1586–1645). Ward was born into a wealthy recusant family (Roman

Jane Frances of Chantal

Jane Frances of Chantal was the cofounder, with Francis of Sales, of the Visitation of Holy Mary (Visitation Nuns). Born in Dijon, France, she married Baron de Chantal in 1592. Her husband was killed in a hunting accident in 1601, leaving her with four children. Three years later she heard Francis of Sales preach at Dijon and she became his follower. By 1610 Jane Frances's oldest daughter had married and her fourteen-year-old son was provided for. With her two remaining children, she went to Annecy and joined Francis of Sales. Together she and Francis founded the Visitation of Holy Mary, which was primarily a teaching order for women. During the next two decades Jane Frances coped with tragedy. Francis of Sales died in 1622, and five years later her son was killed in battle. Then in 1628 the plague struck France and she turned her convent at Annecy into a hospital. She died in 1641 at a Visitation convent in Moulins; at the time she was returning home from a trip to Paris, where she had been a guest of Queen Anne of Austria. In the year of Jane Frances's death, the Visitation Order had eighty-six houses. Jane Frances of Chantal was canonized in 1767.

Catholics who refused to attend Church of England services) from Yorkshire during a time when Catholicism was outlawed in England and Catholics were legally penalized for their faith. Ward dedicated herself to a religious life at a nearly age. Soon she was one of a wave of women who traveled to the European continent to pursue vocations in the Poor Clare teaching community in Saint-Omer in France. After an unsatisfying one-year novitiate (probationary membership) as a Clarist sister, Ward left Saint-Omer. Inspired by the Jesuits, in 1616 Ward established an English community for ladies, who would follow the spirit of Ignatius of Loyola and live uncloistered.

Pope Paul V approved the institute, and during the next fifteen years Ward started three hundred schools throughout Europe. Her goal was to provide an opportunity to young girls for life in either the secular (nonreligious) world or the religious world. Ward pursued her ambitions as a "jesuitess" by traveling and writing works on education and spirituality. The Jesuits themselves, however, resisted Ward and her fellow "galloping girls," the nickname given to the uncloistered religious women. The church eventually began pressuring women's congregations to become cloistered, so Ward met with hostility and suspicion. Ward's schools were suppressed by Pope Urban VIII in 1631, and Ward was imprisoned for refusing to make her organization a cloistered community. Eventually released from prison, she returned to England, where she died and was buried in her native Yorkshire. In 1701 the Institute of the Blessed Virgin Mary was revived. Ward's influence on lay missions was recognized by Pope Pius XII (1876–1958; reigned 1939–58) in 1951.

Sisters of Charity With the French priest Vincent de Paul, Louise de Marillac (1591–1660) cofounded the Sisters of Charity. It is a congregation dedicated to teaching and hospital work. Born in Ferrières-en-Brie, France, Louise was a member of the powerful de Marillac family and was well educated. She was orphaned by the age of fifteen, but poor health prevented her from joining the strict order of Poor Clares. In 1613 she married Antoine Le Gras (secretary to Queen Marie de Médicis of France), with whom she had a son, Michel. Widowed in 1625, she had already chosen Vincent de Paul as her spiritual guide, and he encouraged her to undertake charitable works.

In 1633 Marillac and Vincent started the Sisters of Charity with four girls who worked in Marillac's Paris home. As the superior of the group, Marillac trained the girls in the spiritual life and taught them to assist in visiting, feeding, and nursing the needy. Community members did not live in a cloister and they were not called nuns. They began taking religious vows in 1642, and then only for a year at a time. This practice continues today. By the late twentieth century the Sisters of Charity was the Roman Catholic Church's largest congregation of women. Louise de Marillac was canonized in 1934 and named the patron saint of Christian social work in 1960.

Carmelite mystics

During the Catholic Reformation men and women in religious communities were encouraged to become active in the world beyond monastery and convent walls. At the same time, however, a renewed emphasis on spirituality produced two of the greatest mystics in the history of Christianity, Teresa of Ávila and John of the Cross. Both were from Spain and both were members of Carmelite orders.

Teresa de Ávila Teresa de Ávila (1515–1582) was the founder of the Reformed Discalced (Barefoot) Carmelite Convent of San Jose. She is most famous today for her experiences as a mystic; she described these experiences in her autobiography, *Life* (1611), and numerous other books. She was born Teresa de Ahumada on a farm near Ávila, Spain. Her father was Alonso (Pina) de Cepeda, son of a wealthy Jewish businessman, and her mother was Beatriz de Ahumada, a farmer's daughter. When Teresa was fourteen, her mother died in childbirth. In her autobiography Teresa recalled that when she was sixteen she would sneak out of the house to meet with a man she loved. When gossip about the relationship reached her father, he took her to Our Lady of Grace, an enclosed Augustinian convent nearby.

Teresa stayed at Our Lady of Grace until 1532, when she became ill with a weak heart. She suffered poor health for the rest of her life. After recuperating for nearly three years at her sister's farmhouse, she decided to become a nun. One of her greatest fears was going to hell when she died, and she claimed that she wanted to be a nun because of that fear. When she told her father about her decision, he was determined not to give her to the church. Teresa then ran away to the Carmelite Convent of the Encarnacion (Incarnation), where she became a nun in 1537 and took the name of Teresa de Jesus. The convent, which was uncloistered, offered great freedom to Carmelites. They wore perfume, jewelry, and colorful sashes. Later, Teresa called it "an inn just off the road of hell." While she was there, she met a nobleman and fell in love, which was a disturbing experience for her.

About a year later she became ill again and left the convent to recuperate at her sister's house. The doctors said she was fatally ill with consumption, a disease that causes the body to waste away. One of her uncles had given her religious books to read the previous time she was ill. This time, he had discovered "mystical theology" and gave her *The Third Spiritual Alphabet* by Francisco de Osuna, a Franciscan monk. Teresa began collecting books on the new theology and entered the mystical stage of her life. When she became strong enough, she decided to go to a healer in Becedas for a "cure." She became so ill that her father had to take her home to die. Teresa went into a coma for four days. She slowly recovered and insisted on going back to the Carmelite convent, where she spent the next three years in the infirmary. After her recovery, she left the infirmary and returned to the convent.

Experiences conversion In 1543 Teresa's father died and she went through a long struggle with inner conflict. She agonized over her feelings for men, especially a nobleman and priest named Garcia de Toledo. In 1554 she experienced a conversion, or spiritual change, when she saw a statue of the wounded Christ. Then someone gave her a copy of *Confessions* by Saint Augustine (354–430), one of the early church leaders. She identified with the spiritual suffering described by Augustine and realized that she was not damned (destined for hell or eternal suffering). In 1556 Teresa asked for permission to leave the convent. Her practices in penance and prayer were considered extreme, compared to the casual lifestyle at the convent. The Carmelites therefore allowed her to leave.

For the next three years Teresa lived with a friend, Dona Guiomar de Ulloa (Yomar). With the help of Juan de Pradanos, her Jesuit confessor and the vice-rector, or assistant head, of the College of Saint Gil, Teresa found more depth in her spiritual experience. Following his instructions she had her first rapture, a spiritual experience in which one achieves knowledge of the divine. As a result, she gave up some of her friendships with men, especially Garcia de Toledo. When de Pradanos became ill, he was moved into Yomar's home so that Teresa and Yomar could nurse him. This situation caused a scandal in the community.

After de Pradanos recovered, he, Teresa, and Yomare left Ávila. Teresa went to her sister's home in Alba for a while. Yomar went to visit her mother and de Pradanos was transferred to Valladolid. After two months, Teresa was ordered to return to the Carmelite convent in Ávila. A young Jesuit priest became her new confessor, but because of the scandal he would not talk to her about spiritual matters. She spent much of her time reading, until 1557, when Pope Paul IV banned many "mystical" books. (At that time the church did not recognize mysticism as a valid religious practice.) In 1559 Teresa's own book collection was burned by inquisitors.

Becomes famous for visions When Teresa finished *Life,* the inquisitors ordered her to expand it, filling in omitted events. They wanted to know more about her visions. Many times she fell into seizures, or trancelike states, and did not remember what had happened. Witnesses described these events, and gossip soon spread throughout the community. Teresa heard voices and saw visions of both the devil and Jesus Christ. Many people thought she was possessed by the devil and should be exorcised, an act in which a priest drives out evil spirits. According to some accounts, Teresa also experienced levitation, or lifting of the body by supernatural forces. She ordered the other nuns not to tell anyone because the inquisitors were searching for heretics and burning them at the stake. She was afraid church officials would think she was making a pact with the devil through these visions and they would convict her of heresy. She completed her expanded version of *Life* in 1559.

By 1560 Teresa had made a decision to reform the Carmelites. She had long been troubled by the lax standards at her convent, and she wanted to return the Carmelites to strict observance of the original rules of the order. After much opposition and struggle, in 1562 Pope Pius IV granted her permission to start the San Jose convent for the Reformed Discalced Carmelite Order. Four nuns were transferred from the Convent of the Encarnacion to her reformed convent. Next, four novices joined the order against opposition from members of the church and the city. But Teresa was determined to achieve her goal, and she continued to write. Before her death she produced numerous books, which are now considered classics in mystical literature. Teresa was instrumental in reforming not only the Carmelite convents for women but also the Carmelite monasteries for men. She is credited with reviving Catholicism at a time when Protestantism threatened to bring down the church. She spent the remainder of her life traveling for the Reformed Discalced Carmelite Order.

Teresa's death considered a miracle
There were several accounts of Teresa's last days before her death on October 4, 1582. One account said that she was kidnapped by Friar Antonio de Jesus Heredia and taken to Alba so she could be present at the birth of an heir of the duke and duchess of Alba. Another account said that Heredia ordered Teresa to go to Alba and even though she was ill, she went willingly. After arriving in Alba, she went to the convent, where she suffered a hemor-rhage, or uncontrolled bleeding, and was taken to the infirmary. Teresa knew she was dying, but she was joyful at the end. Witnesses said that a sweet fragrance filled the room at the time of her death. Teresa was buried at the convent chapel in Alba, though many friends protested that she should be buried in Ávila. Her tomb emitted the mysterious sweet fragrance and miracles were reported.

Nine months later, Gracian, a Reformed Carmelite superior, had Teresa's body exhumed, or removed from the grave. Although her robes were rotting, her body was well-preserved. Gracian cut off Teresa's left hand and took it back to Ávila. He cut off one finger to use as a talisman, or good luck charm, then reburied her in the tomb. Three years later, Gracian convinced the Chapter of the Discalced to exhume her body and take it to Ávila. Teresa's body was still preserved. The Discalced considered this a supernatural occurrence since she had not been embalmed, or preserved with special fluids after death. They agreed to leave one arm in Alba to console the nuns there. The duchess was outraged and the duke convinced the pope to order Teresa's body to be returned to Alba. By the eighteenth century, her body had been exhumed many times for examination and little by little body parts, bones, and pieces of flesh were missing. When Teresa's heart was removed, it appeared to have a knife wound that was burned around the edges. Teresa was canonized in 1622 by Pope Gregory XV. She was declared a doctor of the church in 1970.

Carmelite monk Saint John of the Cross was one of the most important mystical writers in the Catholic tradition.

John of the Cross The Spanish Carmelite John of the Cross (1542–1591) was one of the most important mystical writers in the Catholic tradition. He also played a leading role in the sixteenth-century reform of the Carmelites. John of the Cross was born Juan de Yepes at Fontiveros, Spain. When John was two years old his father died and left the family penniless. After John's mother moved with him and his two siblings to Medina del Campo, he tried several trades without success. He excelled in school and continued his studies at the Jesuit college

in Medina. In 1563 he became a novice at the monastery of Saint Ana in Medina. His superiors sent him to the University of Salamanca, where he was ordained a priest in 1567.

In 1568 the reformer and mystic Teresa de Ávila (see "Teresa de Ávila" section previously in this chapter) visited the Medina monastery to discuss the possibility of including male monasteries in her Reformed Discalced (Barefoot) Carmelite order. Both John and the prior of the house joined Teresa's order, and John was the first friar accepted into the new monastery, Duruelo. After some short stays in Pastrana and Alcalá, John joined Teresa as confessor in the unreformed Carmelite convent of Ávila, of which she had become prioress. During this period they stayed in constant spiritual contact.

Meanwhile, the opposition between Reformed Discalced Carmelites and Calced Carmelites, which had existed from the beginning, took on alarming proportions. In 1575 John was abducted and imprisoned by the Calced friars. He was set free at the request of the papal nuncio (pope's representative in the government). But he was imprisoned again in 1577, and this time he had to escape. For safety he stayed in remote places in Andalusia (a region in southern Spain). During those years of obscurity he wrote most of his mystical works.

After the two branches of the Carmelites were finally split, John remained in the south but regained status as vicar provincial (the deputy district head of a religious order). It was only toward the end of his life, in

1588, that he returned to Castile as prior of the house of Segovia and as councilor (adviser) to the provincial (district head of the order). Because of his disagreement with the radical, innovative provincial, he was soon removed from office and sent back to Andalusia. He became ill in 1591 and died that same year. John of the Cross was canonized in 1726 and pronounced a doctor of the church in 1926. The work of Saint John consists of poetry and mystical commentaries that he wrote on some of his poems. Best known are *The Spiritual Canticle, The Living Flame of Love, The Dark Night of the Soul,* and *Ascent of Mount Carmel.*

A prisoner undergoing torture at the hands of the Spanish Inquisition. He is trapped to a revolving wheel below which a fire is being fanned with bellows while monks in the background wait for his confession.
Reproduced by permission of Hulton/Archive.

The Inquisitions

The most infamous aspect of the Catholic Reformation was the Inquisition. Today the Inquisition is perceived as a single church court that used terrifying tactics to discover and punish heretics throughout Europe. Actually, it consisted of three separate courts—the Roman Inquisition, the Spanish Inquisition, and the Portuguese Inquisition—which were all extensions of the medieval Inquisition that came into being during the thirteenth century (see "Inquisition" in Chapter 1). Although these courts did unleash a reign of terror in the sixteenth and seventeenth centuries, historians have found that many stories about the Inquisitions are exaggerations. For instance, fewer people were executed and torture was used less frequently than is generally believed, especially in Italy and Portugal. The most

horrible methods were used by Tomás de Torquemada (1420–1498), head of the Spanish Inquisition, yet the mass executions that took place under his direction were apparently not duplicated elsewhere, even in Spain. Nevertheless, the Inquisition remains a troubling chapter in European history because the power of the church was used to persecute thousands of people, non-Christian and Christian alike.

Popes implement Roman Inquisition

The Catholic Reformation gained momentum in 1542 when

Index of Prohibited Books

In 1559 Pope Paul IV issued the first edition of his Index of Prohibited Books, a list of works that the Roman Catholic Church considered to be heretical. Paul's Index was not the first such list. In fact, certain books were prohibited in ancient times. The church had been following this practice since the early days of Christianity and throughout the Middle Ages.

During the Catholic Reformation church and government authorities saw an urgent need for an Index. They wanted to prevent the printing, sale, possession, and reading of works by Martin Luther and his Protestant followers. The first printed Index of Prohibited Books was issued by the theology faculty at the University of Paris, the center of Catholic learning, in 1544. The first Index printed in Italy appeared at Venice in 1549 as a cooperative effort of the Roman Inquisition and the Venetian government. The Spanish Inquisition and the Portuguese Inquisition both issued an Index in 1551.

The Index released by Paul IV included titles of more than 1,000 works divided into three classes. The first contained authors whose complete writings were prohibited. The second, with 126 titles, listed individual works under the names of their

Pope Paul III established the Roman Inquisition to prevent the spread of Protestantism in Italy. By that time, however, the Spanish Inquisition, which started in 1478, had already been underway for more than sixty years (see "Inquisition reaches Spain" in Chapter 3). Some historians note that the Roman Inquisition was an attempt to combat the brutality of the Spanish Inquisition. At that time a great part of Italy was under the rule of Spain. Holy Roman Emperor Charles V, who was also the king of Spain, was using the Spanish Inquisition to gain even more control in Italy.

Although Paul III set up the Roman Inquisition, he did not actively enforce it. His successor, Julius III, limited the Inquisition to Italy, but he took no other significant steps. Popes Paul IV and Pius V, however, gave inquisitors more power. In 1555 Paul IV introduced such extreme measures that he alienated nearly everyone. He believed false charges that Jews were influencing the Protestant Reformation, and he established the Jewish ghetto at Rome. He required all Jews to wear a badge, thus separating them from Christians. In 1559 Paul IV issued the first edition of his Index of Prohibited Books, which was used in conjunction with the Inquisition to stop the flow of heretical ideas. Although Pius V was not as brutal as Paul IV, he was determined to suppress heresy and authors. The third, with 332 titles, was reserved for books considered to be anonymous. This section was followed by a list of 45 editions of the Bible and the New Testament (the second part of the Bible), along with the names of 61 printers known to have published heretical books. Many considered Paul's Index too severe, so it was modified later in 1559 and again in 1561. The church continued to publish Indexes. In 1571 Pope Pius V created the Congregation of the Index, which became a permanent part of church government and was charged with keeping the Index up to date. Although the Congregation was to have jurisdiction over the entire Catholic world,

Spain and Portugal published their own Indexes in conjunction with their national Inquisitions. The sixteenth-century Indexes of Prohibited Books hit about 2,000 authors with at least one condemnation. Three-fourths of these writers had all of their works banned. Among the authors were the Dutch humanist Desiderius Erasmus, the French humorist and satirist François Rabelais, and the Spanish mystic Teresa de Ávila.

The Index of Prohibited Books was published until 1948, when the twentieth and final edition appeared. In 1966 the Catholic Church abolished the Index and classified it as an historical document.

all other violations of church laws. In fact, Pius V himself took part in many Inquisition proceedings. During his reign, Protestantism was completely eliminated in Italy.

Roman and Spanish Inquisitions

The Roman and Spanish Inquisitions followed similar procedures. Although both were headed by the pope, the Spanish court was actually controlled by the monarchs of Spain. Each inquisition was administered through a supreme council that consisted of cardinals who acted as inquisitors and judges. Local tribunals were set up to try cases in large areas. Inquisitors in these tribunals did not

necessarily have to be priests or theologians; the only requirement was that they have a law degree. The local tribunals had two or three inquisitors and a small administrative staff of assistants, familiars (clerical workers), and priests.

All Inquisition proceedings were kept secret. Charges were brought to the tribunal by members of the public who suspected people of heresy. In Italy, inquisitors concentrated on people who seemed to be embracing Protestantism. In Spain, insincere Marranos (also called Conversos; Jews who had converted to Christianity) and Moriscos (Muslims who had converted to Christianity) were the targets. The

Spanish Inquisition was therefore most successful in areas where there were conflicts between Christians and non-Christians. Protestants were later sought out by the Spanish court, especially in the Netherlands, which was then ruled by Spain. The Roman Inquisition handled some witchcraft cases (see "Witchcraft trials" section later in this chapter), but the rights of the accused were protected. The Spanish Inquisition was allowed to go beyond finding and punishing heretics. The tribunals often took cases that were usually tried in local courts, putting people on trial for such offenses as smuggling horses out of the country or committing bigamy (being married to more than one person). The Spanish Inquisition sometimes became involved in cases of witchcraft, which were usually tried by local courts. In 1526 the Suprema (supreme council) decided to treat witchcraft as an imaginary offense, which was not considered a crime. Some tribunals exceeded their authority and allowed witches to be executed, but after a famous case in Navarre in 1610 no accused witches suffered the death penalty at the hands of the Inquisition.

Before a person was arrested by the tribunal, the evidence against him or her was examined by theologians to see if heresy was involved. If so, the person was taken into custody and his or her property was seized to pay court and prison costs. The accused was held in the inquisitorial prison and periodically questioned by inquisitors in sessions that were considered the "trial." Torture was rarely used to extract information, and then only in cases involving heresy. During a trial, representatives of the inquisitors and the accused person stated their cases. Sentences were announced in the presence of judges and representatives of the local bishop. The most infamous method used by the Inquisitions, both in Spain and in Italy, was the auto-da-fé ("act of faith"; pronounced awh-toh deh FAY). Introduced by Torquemada in 1481, the auto-da-fé was a public ceremony in which sentences were announced. Executions, usually burning at the stake, were carried out in a different location. They were usually conducted by local authorities because church officials were not allowed to shed blood. In times of great activity, such as the prosecution of Protestants in 1559, autos-da-fé could be held annually. Otherwise they were seldom held more than once every ten years. Between 1480 and 1530, about two thousand people were executed in Spain. After that time, executions, for whatever offense, were few. Records for the Roman Inquisition show that only a small number of trials ended with the death penalty. According to one account, ninety-five people were put to death between 1542 and 1761.

Everyone is a target

Both the Roman and Spanish Inquisitions promoted anti-Semitism, or prejudice against Jews. In Italy and Spain, Jews were segregated and forced to wear an identifying badge. In 1492 about 100,000 Jews were driven out of Spain, and during the next two cen-

Portuguese Inquisition

The Inquisition was founded in Portugal during the reign of King John III the Pious (1502–1557; ruled 1521–57). He wanted to enforce Catholicism in his kingdom and block the circulation of heretical works. In 1531 Pope Clement VII issued a bull, or decree, establishing a Portuguese Inquisition, but it was revoked two years later. Representatives of Portuguese New Christians (also called Conversos; Jews who converted to Christianity) had pressured Rome to prevent the creation of an Inquisition. In 1536, however, Pope Paul III authorized a tribunal in Portugal. It was organized like the Roman and Spanish Inquisitions, with an inquisitor general overseeing local tribunals. The Inquisition extended to Portuguese possessions in Asia, east Africa, and Brazil. After Spain took over Portugal in 1580, the Portuguese and Spanish Inquisitions remained separate.

The list of offenses to be tried by Portuguese inquisitors included practicing the Jewish, Islam, and Protestant religions; witchcraft; sacrilege (violation of anything considered sacred to God); and bigamy. From 1536 to 1674, 32,675 people were put on trial and 1,515 were executed in Portugal. Other punishments included exile, terms as galley slaves, floggings, and property confiscations. The inquisitors also played a role in book censorship. Agents of the Inquisition searched foreign ships for prohibited books. The Portuguese Inquisition issued its own list of prohibited books in 1551 and added titles to several editions of the Roman Index.

---

turies Jews were regularly harassed by inquisitors. Muslims were also targeted by the Spanish Inquisition. In 1609 King Philip III signed a decree of expulsion. From 1609 until 1614, between 300,000 and 350,000 Muslims were forced to leave Spain. Charges were also brought against Catholics who appeared to be guilty of heresy. In Spain, Ignatius Loyola and Teresa of Ávila, founders of religious orders, were sought out by inquisitors. During the Roman Inquisition, Italian astronomer Galileo (Galileo Galilei; 1564–1642) was convicted of heresy for supporting the theory that the Earth moves around the Sun (see "Astronomy" in Chapter 10). During the mid-1500s Catholics suspected of embracing Lutheranism were increasingly targeted by both Inquisitions. Methods of the Spanish Inquisition were especially brutal. In 1567 King Philip II introduced the Spanish Inquisition in the Netherlands. He sent Fernando Álvarez de Toledo, duke of Alba (c. 1507–1582) to crush a revolt staged by Protestants. Álvarez established the Council of Troubles (known as the "Council of Blood") and executed perhaps 12,000 people (see "Netherlands" in Chapter 6). Even King Philip was

Spanish flagellants and soldiers often used torture to obtain "confessions" from accused heretics during the Spanish Inquisition. ©Gianni Dagli Orti/Corbis. Reproduced by permission of the Corbis Corporation.

repulsed by Alba's methods and he recalled the duke to Spain, thus ending the siege of terror.

It is a commonly held opinion that the Inquisition prevented Spain from becoming a Protestant nation, but many historians believe this is inaccurate. The tribunal did not begin to act against suspected Protestants until after 1558. Historians suggest that the real reason Spain remained Catholic was that it was culturally isolated from the rest of Europe. When Protestants were identified, they were eliminated in a number of trials from 1558 until 1562. About seventy were executed, and the rest were imprisoned or penanced (persuaded to confess their error). After 1562 the greatest number of arrests for so-called Lutheranism were of people from foreign countries, such as sailors, who strayed into tribunal districts. In the late 1500s and throughout the 1600s the Spanish Inquisition focused mainly on immorality or other social issues instead of heresy. It was inactive after the 1730s and finally abolished in 1834.

After Protestantism had been eliminated in Italy during the 1570s, the Roman Inquisition became part of the papal government. During the next three centuries the Congregation of the Roman Inquisition focused on maintaining social order and enforcing pure religious observation among Catholics. In 1908 Pope Pius X reorganized the Congregation of the Roman Inquisition and officially named it the Holy Office. In 1965 Pope Paul VI (1897–1978; reigned 1963–78) reorganized the congregation along more democratic lines and renamed it the Congregation for the Doctrine of the Faith.

Witchcraft trials

During the Reformation period witchcraft trials were held throughout Europe by both Catholics and Protestants. The purpose of the trials was to discover and punish people who committed heresy by practicing harmful magic or worshiping the devil. Harmful magic was the use of a supernatural or mysterious power that caused death, bodily injury, illness, or some other misfortune. This type of magic, often called sorcery, was feared because it could harm an entire community, such as when a witch brought down a hail storm that destroyed crops. Worship of the devil involved not only the making of a face-to-face pact with the evil spirit but also group worship of him in secret ceremonies at night. During these ceremonies, known as sabbaths, witches supposedly ate children, danced naked, and had sexual intercourse with demons. The word for witchcraft in most European languages could also mean white (beneficial)

magic, but most judges considered this type of witchcraft to be a lesser offense and punished it less harshly.

The concept of witchcraft was gradually developed over three centuries by theologians and inquisitors. At its root was the Christian belief, first expressed by church fathers in the thirteenth and fourteenth centuries, that the power of all magic came from the devil. Since magic came from the devil, it was therefore a form of heresy. By the fifteenth century the charge of heresy was directed against people who were suspected of casting spells and committing evil deeds, such as killing children. Theologians and judges began to think of witches as members of a new and dangerous heretical sect (small group). Their crimes included rejection of religion and morality, conspiracy (plots against the government), and magical destruction of life and property. Soon learned men were saying that witches could fly. This notion came from the popular belief that some women could turn themselves into cannibalistic screech owls and that other women joined nighttime processions to the Moon with Diana. (Diana was the Roman goddess of the Moon, forests, animals, and women in childbirth.) Scholars proclaimed that the devil had given these women the power to fly.

Malleus Maleficarum triggers witch-hunts

Witchcraft had been added to the list of official punishable heresies in 1320, but it did not become a primary

Stereotypes Fuel Witch Craze

Before the onset of the witch trials in the Reformation period, Jews were especially vulnerable to charges of heresy, as were Muslims, homosexuals, and Gypsies (wandering people who originated in India). Members of these targeted groups were driven to resettle in eastern and southern Europe. Many of the same accusations that later fueled the witch-hunts were initially aimed at these peoples. Charged with making pacts with the devil, eating children, and murdering Christians, these groups were often tortured to the point of confessing to crimes they did not commit. The word *synagogue* (a Jewish place of worship) was actually redefined to describe a time and place of devil worship. The word *sabbath*, traditionally associated with the Jewish day of rest, came to symbolize large group meetings between witches and the devil. Even the stereotype of a witch was borrowed from the racist caricature (distorted representation of certain physical features) of Jews and Arabs as having extremely large, crooked noses.

Although Jews, Muslims, homosexuals, and Gypsies were not actually a political threat, they were used by church and government officials to stir up suspicion and violence during the Inquisition. Thus Christian leaders gained supremacy through growing bigotry and intolerance toward "outsiders" or anyone else who might threaten the status quo (existing state of affairs). This campaign caused great fear among the common people, preparing the way for the persecution of witches.

---

target until more than a century later. Then, in 1484, Pope Innocent VIII issued an edict called a papal bull that ordered the eradication, or complete extermination, of witches and other heathens (people who do not believe in God). Although many such edicts had previously been issued, the Papal Bull of 1484 had the advantage of a recent invention, the printing press, which rapidly spread information about so-called witches throughout Europe.

The printing press also aided the mass publication of more than thirty scholarly works on witchcraft that were written during the fifteenth century. They were the basis of the most famous witchcraft study, *Malleus malificarum* (The hammer of witches; 1487), which became the second-best-selling book in Europe for more than two centuries. This work was the official handbook for detecting, capturing, trying, and executing witches. It was written in 1486 by Austrian priest Heinrich Kramer (also Kraemer) and German priest Jakob Sprenger, at the request of Innocent VIII. As the main justification for persecution of witches, the authors relied on a brief passage in the Bible, which states: "Thou shalt not suffer a witch to live" (Exodus 22:18). According to the *Malleus*, "it has never yet been known that an innocent person has been punished on suspicion of witch-craft and there is no doubt that god would never permit such a thing to happen...."

The *Malleus* was a three-part work that described witchcraft in elaborate detail. The first part acknowledged the existence of witches and condemned them as demons and heretics. Much power was given to an accuser, regardless of his or her status in the community, and anyone accused of witchcraft was immediately discredited. The *Malleus* specified that even criminals, the insane, or children could testify against an accused witch once the person was brought to trial. The second part of the book preyed upon the imaginations and fears of the people by giving evidence of satanic activities of witches. The *Malleus* placed special emphasis on the relationship between female witches and the devil. Witches were accused of eating children, having sex with the devil, going to sabbaths with other witches and demons, and having evil connections with animals known as "familiars." Witches became the human agents of the devil and were held responsible for any number of imagined or real catastrophes.

The conclusion of the *Malleus* outlined the legal procedures required for finding, trying, and executing witches. This section gave free license to lawyers and clergymen, enabling them to take any means necessary to obtain a signed or verbal confession.

To absolve lawyers and clergymen themselves from charges of murder, all accused witches were presumed guilty and innocence did not have to be proven. Any accused person could be taken from his or her home to the courts and subjected to various methods of extreme torture. The book prescribed these methods in detail, noting various markings that could prove a person was a witch. Such evidence included warts, excessive body hair, or extra nipples—all of which gave reason for intense punishment.

Torture brings confessions

The *Malleus* became the guide for civil and church law, going through twenty-eight editions between 1486 and 1600. It was accepted by Roman Catholics and Protestants alike as the authority on ridding Europe of satanism and witchcraft, which were now considered inseparable. The most important impact of *Malleus* was that it united the church and the state, making torture a legal means of obtaining confessions from accused witches. One of the most common means of torture was the stretching rack, a device that would slowly tear a person limb from limb as he or she was repeatedly commanded to confess to specific crimes. A similar tool was the strapado, which involved attaching weights to a victim's legs, then slowly lifting the person off the ground so that the legs would begin to tear away from the body. Another method involved the victim being stripped naked and slowly cut in half by being dragged along a very tight rope. Some people were tied to stakes and placed near a fire that would slowly "cook" them. Many others had their eyes gouged out or were beaten, raped, disemboweled (internal organs cut out), dropped from high above the ground, or subjected to numerous torturing devices. Also popular were "Spanish boots," devices that were put on a victim's legs and could work in either of two ways. One used internal vices that would slowly crush the victim's legs, while the other involved pouring boiling water or oil into the "boots."

These methods were extremely efficient. People were brought close to death and promised relief if they confessed to the charges against them. Thousands gave in, no matter how false or ridiculous the charges might have been, to save themselves from additional torture. In turn, the confessions fanned mass hysteria, proving that the initial suspicions had been correct and creating an enemy out of innocent people. Officials in some regions used so-called tests that pointed to the guilt of an accused person in various ways. A popular method in England (where torture was considered a crime) was the water test. The results were supposed to determine whether or not a person was indeed a witch—yet nobody could actually pass the test. It involved tying the accused person's arms and legs together, then throwing him or her into a body of water. If the victim sank (enduring death by drowning), he or she was not a witch. A person that floated was considered a witch. Since multilayered clothing was worn at the time, people quite often ended up floating because their clothes created pockets of air that forced them to remain at the surface of the water. Many accused witches were declared guilty by this method, then publicly burned at a stake in the center of town. Burning was considered another test, as well as the most severe form of punishment: it was thought that witches could survive fire because of their association with the devil. Those who did not survive the fire were pronounced innocent. The prevalence of the fire test led to this era being called "The Burning Times."

The relatives of the accused were charged money for all manner of details involved in the trial. Not only did they pay the salary of the judge, they also bore the costs of food and lodging for the accused in prison. In addition, relatives were charged for the wood and straw used for kindling the execution fire, and they were billed for the lavish banquets typically held for officials before mass executions. In the case of accused people who had no relatives in the region, personal property was confiscated to pay the bills. The result was that many people lost their land, money, and lives while a few witch-hunters and judges accumulated wealth with every successful trial.

Witch-hunts reach peak

Witchcraft prosecutions reached a peak between 1580 and 1660, and officially ended on June 17, 1782, when the last execution was held in Switzerland. Trials took place mainly in France, Germany, and Switzerland,

An illustration of three accused witches being burned at the stake in Germany in 1555.
Reproduced by permission of Archive Photos, Inc.

but also extended throughout western Europe, into pockets of northern and eastern Europe, and eventually to the American colonies in New England. Spain was one of the few countries not associated with the witch hunts because Spanish officials did not believe in witchcraft as defined by the *Malleus*. In Spain suspected witches were locked up in convents. It is difficult to establish the number of people who were killed in the anti-witch campaign because many died in jails from torture and starvation and were not recorded in official execution counts. Most estimates state

that one hundred thousand trials were held and that about half of the trials resulted in executions. On average, 80 percent of the accused were women and 85 percent of those actually executed were women. Most men who were accused were either related to women who had been tried, or they had criminal records implicating them in other crimes against the church and state. Nearly all of the accused were poor or came from the lower classes.

The most severe measures were taken in Germany. At the start of the seventeenth century the ruling prince of western Germany established a team of prosecutors and torturers equipped with special buildings and devices made specifically for torture. In the city of Bamberg, for instance, officials burned nine hundred witches in the first half of the century alone. Three hundred of the victims were under the age of four. In the village of Langendorf all but two women were arrested as witches. Two other German villages were left with only one female inhabitant each. Records show that in nearby Alsace, a province in France, a total of five thousand people were burned during the witch-hunts. England had its moments of severity as well, particularly after 1604, when King James I (1566–1625) passed a law that officially prohibited pacts with the devil. James stated publicly that out of every twenty-one witches, twenty were women, thus contributing to a focus on women as targets.

Approximately 80 percent of all accused witches throughout Europe were female, mainly because women engaged in types of activities that brought them under suspicion of practicing harmful magic. Midwives (women who assist in childbirth) and lying-in maids (women who assist mothers after delivery of a baby) frequently became targets of accusations from mothers who feared for the well-being of their newborn infants. Female healers (women who treated illnesses and diseases with herbs and other remedies) were often accused of being witches, especially when they did not cure their patients. Suspected witches were described as being outspoken or quarrelsome, and they usually failed to conform to the ruling-class's notion that most witches were women. But most charges of witchcraft came from peasant-class neighbors of the accused, not form the judges who questioned and charged them.

Witch craze ends

Although there were some vocal opponents of the witchcraft trials, very few survived their own outspokenness. Most were considered guilty by association and were virtually powerless against the campaign. By the end of the seventeenth century, however, two factors brought the persecutions to a halt. First, officials were running out of victims: so many people had been killed that entire regional populations had been altered. The high number of executions began raising concerns. In response to the atrocities in Bamberg and other areas of Germany, Holy Roman Emperor Ferdinand II (1578–1637; ruled 1619–37) issued a decree to stop the killings. Other officials slowed down the witch-hunt as they began to realize it was no longer necessary. Another factor that helped grind the machine to a halt was a new European ideology, which envisioned a more rational and ordered universe. This shift in thinking eventually led to the era called the Enlightenment that began in the eighteenth century. By then, past history was dismissed as having been the result of irrational ancient superstitions.

Where to Learn More

The following list focuses on works written for readers of middle school and high school age. Books aimed at adult readers have been included when they are especially important in providing information or analysis that would otherwise be unavailable, or because they have become classics.

Books

Ackerman, James S. *Palladio's Villas*. Locust Valley, N.Y.: Institute of Fine Arts, New York University, 1967.

Ackroyd, Peter. *The Life of Thomas More*. New York: Nan A. Talese, 1998.

Anthony, Arthur. *The Tailor-King: The Rise and Fall of the Anabaptist Kingdom of Münster*. New York: St. Martin's Press, 1989.

Atil, Esin. *Suleymanname: The Illustrated History of Suleyman the Magnificent*. New York: H. N. Abrams, 1986.

Banville, John. *Kepler, A Novel*. New York: Vintage, 1993. (Fiction)

Barstow, Anne Llewellyn. *Witchcraze: A New History of the European Witch Hunts*. San Francisco: Harper, 1999.

Bellonci, Maria. *The Life and Times of Lucrezia Borgia*. Translated by Bernard and

Barbara Wall. London: Phoenix Press, 2000.

Brimacombe, Peter. *All the Queen's Men: The World of Elizabeth I.* New York: St. Martin's Press, 2000.

Brophy, James, and Henry Paolucci, eds. *The Achievement of Galileo.* New York: Twayne, 1962.

Burch, Joann Johansen. *Fine Print: A Story About Johann Gutenberg.* Minneapolis: Carolrhoda Books, 1991.

Canavaggio, Jean. *Cervantes.* Translated by J. R. Jones. New York: Norton, 1990.

Castiglione, Baldassare. *Book of the Courtier; An Authoritative Text, Criticism.* Edited by Daniel Javitch. New York: Norton, 2002.

Cavendish, Margaret. *The Blazing World and Other Writings.* Edited by Kate Lilley. New York: Penguin Classics, 1994.

Cervantes, Miguel de. *Don Quijote.* Edited Diana de Armas Wilson, and translated by Burton Raffel. New York: Norton, 1999.

Christianson, John Robert. *On Tycho's Island: Tycho Brahe and His Assistants, 1570–1601.* New York: Cambridge University Press, 1999.

Copernicus, Nicholas. *Nicholas Copernicus on the Revolutions.* Edited and translated by Edward Rosen. Baltimore, Md.: Johns Hopkins University Press, 1978.

Cox-Rearick, Janet. *The Collection of Francis I: Royal Treasures.* New York: Harry N. Abrams, Inc., 1996.

De La Bedoyere, Michael. *The Meddlesome Friar and the Wayward Pope; The Story of the Conflict between Savonarola and Alexander VI.* Garden City, N.Y.: Hanover House, 1958.

Dobson, Michael, and Stanley Wells, eds. *The Oxford Companion to Shakespeare.* Oxford: Oxford University Press, 2001.

Dommermuth-Costa, Carol. *William Shakespeare.* Minneapolis: Lerner, 2002.

Dwyer, Frank. *James I.* New York: Chelsea House, 1988.

Erlanger, Rachel. *The Unarmed Prophet: Savonarola in Florence.* New York: McGraw-Hill, 1988.

Evans, G. Blakemore, and others, eds. *The Riverside Shakespeare.* New York: Houghton Mifflin, 1997.

Farber, Joseph C. *Palladio's Architecture and its Influence: A Photographic Guide.* New York: Dover, 1980.

Fearon, Mike. *Martin Luther.* Minneapolis: Bethany House Publishers, 1986.

Ferino-Pagden, Sylvia, and Maria Kusche. *Sofonisba Anguissola: a Renaissance Woman.* Washington, D.C.: National Museum of Women in the Arts, 1995.

Finger, Stanley. *Minds Behind the Brain: The Pioneers and Their Discoveries.* New York: Oxford University Press, 2000.

Fisher, Leonard Everett. *Galileo.* New York: Macmillan, 1992.

Fisher, Leonard Everett. *Gutenberg.* New York: Macmillan, 1993.

Fletcher, Jennifer. *Peter Paul Rubens; With Fifty Plates in Full Colour.* New York, Phaidon, 1968.

Fontbrune, Jean-Charles de. *Nostradamus 2: Into the Twenty-*

first Century. Translated by Alexis Lykiard. New York: Holt, Rinehart, and Winston, 1985.

Friedman, Meyer. *Medicine's 10 greatest Discoveries.* New Haven, Conn.: Yale University Press, 1998.

Gäbler, Ulrich. *Huldrych Zwingli: His Life and Work.* Translated by Ruth C. L. Gritsch. Philadelphia: Fortress Press, 1986.

Garfield, Leon. *Shakespeare Stories II.* Boston: Houghton Mifflin Co., 1995.

Garrard, Mary D. *Artemisia Gentileschi Around 1622 : The Shaping and Reshaping of an Artistic Identity.* Berkeley: University of California Press, 2001.

Gelb, Michael. *How to Think Like Leonardo Da Vinci: Seven Steps to Genius Every Day.* New York: Delacorte Press, 1998.

Goldsmith, Mike. *Galileo Galilei.* Austin, Tex.: Raintree Steck-Vaughn, 2001.

Greef, Wulfert de. *The Writings of John Calvin: An Introductory Guide.* Translated by Lyle D. Bierma. Grand Rapids, Mich.: Baker Books, 1993.

Harp, Richard, and Stanley Stewart, eds. *The Cambridge Companion to Ben Jonson.* New York: Cambridge University Press, 2000.

Hillerbrand, Hans J., ed. *The Protestant Reformation.* New York: Harper Torchbooks, 1968.

Hutchison, Jane Campbell. *Albrecht Dürer: A Biography.* Princeton, N.J.: Princeton University Press, 1990.

Hyma, Albert. *The Youth of Erasmus.* New York: Russell & Russell, 1968.

Ibn Khaldûn, 'Adb al-Rahman. *The Muqaddimah: An Introduction to History.* Edited by N. J. Dawood, and translated by Franz Rosenthal. Princeton, N.J.: Princeton University Press, 1989.

Ignatius of Loyola. *The Spiritual Exercises of St. Ignatius.* Translated by Louis J. Puhl. New York: Vintage Books, 2000.

Kamen, Henry. *Philip of Spain.* New Haven Conn.: Yale University Press, 1997.

Kepler, Johannes. *The Harmony of the World.* Translated by E .J. Aiton, A. M. Duncan, and J.V. Field. Philadelphia, Pa.: American Philosophical Society, 1997.

King, Ethel M. *Palestrina: The Prince of Music.* Brooklyn, N.Y.: Theo. Gaus' Sons, 1965.

King, Margaret L., and Albert Rabil, eds., and trans. *Her Immaculate Hand: Selected Works By and About the Women Humanists of Quattrocento Italy.* Binghamton, N.Y.: Medieval and Renaissance Texts and Studies, 1983.

Knecht, R. J. *Renaissance Warrior and Patron: The Reign of Francis I.* New York: Cambridge University Press, 1994.

Krensky, Stephen. *Breaking into Print: Before and After the Invention of the Printing Press.* Boston: Little, Brown, 1996.

Lafferty, Peter. *Leonardo da Vinci.* New York: Bookwright, 1990.

Lapierre, Alexandra. *Artemisia: A Novel.* Translated by Liz Heron. New York: Grove Press, 2000. (Fiction)

Loewen, Harry, and Steven M. Nolt. *Through Fire & Water: An Overview of Mennonite His-*

tory. Scottdale, Pa.: Herald Press, 1996.

MacDonald, Alan. *Henry VIII and His Chopping Block.* New York: Scholastic, 1999.

Marguerite de Navarre. *Heptameron.* Translated by P.A. Chilton. New York: Penguin Books, 1984.

Maurier, Daphne du. *The Winding Stair: Francis Bacon, His Rise and Fall.* Garden City, N.Y.: Doubleday, 1977.

McGuigan, Dorothy Gies. *The Habsburgs.* Garden City, N.Y. Doubleday, 1966.

McLanathan, Richard. *Peter Paul Rubens.* New York: H.N. Abrams, 1995.

Medwick, Cathleen. *Teresa of Avila: the Progress of a Soul.* New York: Alfred A. Knopf, 1999.

Merriman, Roger Bigelow. *Suleiman the Magnificent.* New York: Cooper Square Publishers, 1966.

Michelangelo. *The Complete Poems of Michelangelo.* Translated by John Frederick Nims. Chicago, Ill.: University of Chicago Press, 1998.

Milton, Jacqueline. *Galileo: Scientist and Stargazer.* New York: Oxford University Press, 2000.

Montaigne, Michel de. *Selected Essays.* Translated by Donald M. Frame. New York: Van Nostrand, 1941.

More, Thomas. *Utopia.* Edited by Paul Turner. New York: Penguin Books, 1965.

Netanyahu, B. *Don Isaac Abrabanel: Statesman and Philosopher.* 5th ed. Ithaca, N.Y.: Cornell University Press, 1999.

Noll, Mark A. *Confessions and Catechisms of the Reformation.* Vancouver, B.C.: Regent College Publishing, 1997.

Nuland, Sherwin B. *Leonardo da Vinci.* New York: Viking, 2000.

Olin, John C., ed. *The Autobiography of St. Ignatius Loyola.* Translated by Joseph F. O'Callaghan. New York: Fordham University Press, 1993.

Oliver, Isaac. *Art at the Courts of Elizabeth I and James I.* New York: Garland, 1981.

O'Malley, John W. *The First Jesuits.* Cambridge, Mass.: Harvard University Press, 1993.

Parker, T. H. L. *John Calvin, a Biography.* Philadelphia: Westminster Press, 1975.

Perlingieri, Ilya Sandra. *Sofonisba Anguissola: The First Great Woman Artist of the Renaissance.* New York: Rizzoli, 1992.

Petrarca, Francesco. *Selections from "Canzoniere" and Other Works.* Edited by Mark Musa. New York: Oxford University Press, 1999.

Pieter Bruegel the Elder: Drawings and Prints. New Haven, Conn.: Yale University Press, 2001.

Plowden, Alison. *The Young Elizabeth: The First Twenty-Five Years of Elizabeth I.* Stroud, Gloucestershire: Sutton, 1999.

Purcell, Mary. *The First Jesuit, St. Ignatius Loyola (1491–1556).* Chicago: Loyola University Press, 1981.

Puzo, Mario. *The Family: A Novel.* Completed by Carol Gino. New York: Regan Books, 2001. (Fiction)

Rabelais, François. *Gargantua and Pantagruel.* Translated by J. M. Cohen. New York: Viking Penguin, 1976.

Raboff, Ernest. *Albrecht Dürer.* New York: Harper & Row, 1988.

Rady, Martyn. *The Emperor Charles V.* New York: Longman, 1988.

Richter, Irma A. *Selections from the Notebooks of Leonardo da Vinci.* New York: Oxford University Press, 1977.

Riley, Judith Merkle. *The Master of All Desires.* New York: Viking, 1999. (Fiction)

Ripley, Alexandra. *The Time Returns.* Garden City, N.Y.: Doubleday, 1985. (Fiction)

Roessner, Michaela. *The Stars Dispose.* New York: Tor, 1997. (Fiction)

Saint-Saëns, Alain, ed. *Young Charles V, 1500–1531.* New Orleans: University Press of the South, 2000.

Scheib, Asta. *Children of Disobedience: The Love Story of Martin Luther and Katharina von Bora: A Novel.* Translated by David Ward. New York: Crossroad, 2000. (Fiction)

Seward, Desmond. *Prince of the Renaissance; the Golden Life of François I.* New York: Macmillan, 1973.

Sharpe, James. *The Bewitching of Anne Gunter: A Horrible and True Story of Deception, Witchcraft, Murder, and the King of England.* New York: Routledge, 2000.

Shulman, Sandra. *The Florentine.* New York: Morrow, 1973. (Fiction)

Skinner, Quentin. *Great Political Thinkers.* New York: Oxford University Press, 1992.

Stanley, Diane. *Michelangelo.* New York: HarperCollins, 2000.

Starkey, David. *Elizabeth: The Struggle for the Throne.* New York: HarperCollins, 2001.

Stepanek, Sally. *Martin Luther.* New York: Chelsea House, 1986.

Summers, Montague, ed. *The Malleus Maleficarum Malleus Maleficarum of Heinrich Kramer and James Sprenger.* New York: Dover Publications, 1971.

Teresa de Ávila. *The Life of Saint Teresa.* Translated by J. M. Cohen. New York: Penguin Books, 1957.

Thomas. Jane Resh. *Behind the Mask: The Life of Queen Elizabeth I.* New York: Clarion Books, 1998.

Thrasher, Thomas. *William Shakespeare.* San Diego, Calif.: Lucent Books, 1999.

Veglahn, Nancy. *Dance of the Planets: The Universe of Nicolaus Copernicus.* New York: Coward, McCann & Geohegan, 1979. (Fiction)

Vergani, Luis. *"The Prince," Notes; Including Machiavelli's Life and Works.* Lincoln, Nebr.: Cliff's Notes, 1967.

Vernon, Louise A. *The Man Who Laid the Egg.* Scottdale, Pa.: Herald Press, 1977.

Viroli, Maurizio. *Niccolò's Smile: A Biography of Machiavelli.* Translated by Antony Shugaar. New York: Farrar, Straus and Giroux, 2000.

Voelkel, James R. *Johannes Kepler: And the New Astronomy.* New York: Oxford University Press Children's Books, 2001.

Vreeland, Susan. *The Passion of Artemesia.* New York: Viking, 2002. (Fiction)

Wedgwood, C. V. and the editors of Time-Life Books. *The World of Rubens, 1577-1640.* New York: Time, Inc., 1967.

Weir, Allison. *Henry VIII: The King and His Court.* New York: Ballantine Books, 2001.

Westman, Robert S., ed. *The Copernican Achievement.* Berkeley: University of California Press, 1975.

Zophy, Jonathan W. *A Short History of Renaissance and Reformation Europe.* 2nd ed. Upper Saddle River, N.J.: Prentice Hall, 1999.

Web Sites

"Alexander VI." *Catholic Encyclopedia.* [Online] Available http://www.newadvent.org/cathen/01289a.htm, May 20, 2002.

"Alexander VI." *Encyclopedia.com.* [Online] Available http://www.encyclopedia.com/html/a/alexand6.asp, May 20, 2002.

Ancient Medicine, from Homer to Vesalius. [Online] Available http://www.med.virginia.edu/hs-library/historical/antiqua/anthome.html, May 20, 2002.

"Anguissola, Sofonisba." *A Guide to the Collection of European Art to 1900.* [Online] Available http://www.mfa.org/handbook/portrait.asp?id=195.5&s=6, May 20, 2002.

"Anguissola, Sofonisba." *Art Cyclopedia.* [Online] Available http://www.artcyclopedia.com/artists/anguissola_sofonisba.html, May 20, 2002.

Artemisia's Letter. [Online] Available http://rubens.anu.edu.au/student.projects/artemisia/Artemisia%27s_Letter.html, May 20, 2002.

Artist Profiles: Lavinia Fontana. [Online] Available http://www.nmwa.org/legacy/bios/bfontana.htm, May 20, 2002.

Art of Renaissance Science: Galileo and Perspective. [Online] Available http://www.crs4.it/Ars/arshtml/arstoc.html, May 20, 2002.

"Bacon, Francis." *The Internet Encyclopedia of Philosophy.* [Online] Available http://www.utm.edu/research/iep/b/bacon.htm, May 20, 2002.

Baldassare Castiglione [portrait] by Raphael. [Online] Available http://www.theartgallery.com.au/ArtEducation/greatartists/Raphael/baldassare/, May 20, 2002.

"Bruegel, Pieter the Elder." *Britannica.com.* [Online] Available http://www.britannica.com/eb/article?eu=17000&tocid=869&query=bruegel%2C%20pieter%20the%20elder, May 20, 2002.

"Bruegel, Pieter the Elder." *Web Gallery of Art.* [Online] Available http://www.kfki.hu/~arthp/html/b/bruegel/pieter_e/index.html, May 20, 2002.

A Celebration of Women Writers: 1401–1500. [Online] Available http://digital.library.upenn.edu/women/_generate/1401-1500.html, May 20, 2002.

"Charles V, Holy Roman Emperor." *The Columbia Encyclopedia.* [Online] Available http://www.bartleby.com/65/ch/Charles5HRE.html, May 20, 2002.

Chu, Luthy. *Erasmus, Desiderius.* [Online] Available http://campus.northpark.edu/history/WebChron/WestEurope/Erasmus.html, May 20, 2002.

"Council of Trent." *Infoplease. com.* [Online] Available http:// www.infoplease.com/ce6/ society/A0849364.html, May 20, 2002.

Debus, Allen G. *Paracelsus, Theophrastus—Medical Revolution.* [Online] Available http://www.nlm.nih.gov/ exhibition/paracelsus/paracel sus_2.html, May 20, 2002.

"Don Isaac Abrabanel." *Catholic Encyclopedia.* [Online] Available http://www.newadvent. org/cathen/01050b.htm, May 20 2002.

The Don Quixote Exhibit. [Online] Available http://milton.mse. jhu.edu:8006/, May 20, 2002.

"Dürer, Albrecht." *MSN Encarta.* [Online] Available http:// encarta.msn.com/find/ Concise.asp?ti=038AD000, May 20, 2002.

Early Modern Europe: The Witch Hunts. [Online] Available http://history.hanover.edu/ early/wh.html, May 20, 2002.

"Elizabeth I." *Luminarium.* [Online] Available http://www. luminarium.org/renlit/eliza. htm, May 20, 2002.

"Erasmus, Desiderius." *MSN Encarta.* [Online] Available http://encarta.msn.com/index/ conciseindex/5A/05A6E000. htm?z=1&pg=2&br=1, May 20, 2002.

Erasumus, Desiderius. *Praise of Folly.* [Online] Available http:// www.stupidity.com/erasmus/ eracont.htm, May 20, 2002.

The Essays of Francis Bacon. [Online] Available http://our- world.compuserve.com/home pages/mike_donnelly/bacon. htm, May 20, 2002.

"Francis I." *Infoplease.com.* [Online] Available http://www. infoplease.com/ce6/people/ A0819430.html, May 20, 2002.

Galilei, Galileo—Portrait. [Online] Available http://galileo.imss. firenze.it/museo/b/egalilg. html, May 20, 2002.

"Galileo." *MSN Encarta.* [Online] Available http://encarta.msn. com/find/Concise.asp?z=1&p g=2&ti=017E5000, May 20, 2002.

"Gentileschi, Artemisia." *Web Galleries.* [Online] Available http://www.webgalleries.com /pm/colors/gentile.html, May 20, 2002.

Gournay, Marie de (1565–1645). [Online] Available http:// www.pinn.net/~sunshine/ march99/gournay2.html, May 20, 2002.

"Gournay, Marie de." *Early French Women Writers.* [Online] Available http://erc.lib.umn. edu/dynaweb/french/@Gener ic__CollectionView, May 20, 2002.

"Gustav I Vasa." *Britannica.com.* [Online] Available http:// www.britannica.com/eb/ article?eu=39368&tocid=0&q uery=gustaf%20i%20vasa, May 20, 2002.

"Gustavus I." *Learning Network.* [Online] Available http:// www.factmonster.com/ce6/ people/A0822195.html, May 20, 2002.

The Gutenberg Bible. [Online] Available http://prodigi.bl. uk/gutenbg/, May 20, 2002.

"Gutenberg, Johannes." *Famous People in Printing History.* [Online] Available http://www. ssc.cc.il.us/acad/career/depts/ technology/ppt/whatsup/trivia/ gutenbrg.htm, May 20, 2002.

Gutenberg Museum. [Online] Available http://www.gutenberg.de/, May 20, 2002.

Hagen, J. G. "Copernicus, Nicholas." *Catholic Encyclopedia.* [Online] Available http://www.newadvent.org/cathen/04352b.htm, May 20, 2002.

Halsall, Paul. *Council of Trent—Rules on Prohibited Books.* [Online] Available http://www.fordham.edu/halsall/mod/trent-booksrules.html, May 20, 2002.

Halsall, Paul. "Elizabeth I." *Modern History Sourcebook.* [Online] Available http://www.fordham.edu/halsall/mod/elizabeth1.html, May 20, 2002.

Halsall, Paul. "Luther, Martin." *Letter to the Archbishop of Mainz.* [Online] Available http://www.fordham.edu/halsall/source/lutherltr-indulgences.html, May 20, 2002.

Halsall, Paul. "Petrarch, Francesco." *Letters—circa 1372.* [Online] Available http://www.fordham.edu/halsall/source/petrarch1.html, May 20, 2002.

"Henry VIII." *Britannica.com.* [Online] Available http://www.britannica.com/eb/article?eu=40871&tocid=0&query=henry%20viii, May 20, 2002.

"Henry VIII." *History Channel.* [Online] Available http://www.thehistorychannel.co.uk/classroom/alevel/henry1.htm, May 20, 2002.

"Henry VIII." *Image Gallery.* [Online] Available http://www.tudorhistory.org/henry8/gallery.html, May 20, 2002.

The Heptameron of Margaret, Queen of Navarre. [Online] Available http://digital.library.upenn.edu/women/navarre/heptameron/heptameron.html, May 20, 2002.

"How Nostradamus Works." *How Stuff Works.* [Online] Available http://www.howstuffworks.com/nostradamus.htm, May 20, 2002.

Hudleston, G. Roger. "More, Thomas." *Catholic Encyclopedia.* [Online] Available http://www.newadvent.org/cathen/14689c.htm, May 20, 2002.

Ibn Khaldûn—Iranian Muslim Philosopher. [Online] Available http://www.trincoll.edu/depts/phil/philo/phils/muslim/khaldun.html, May 20, 2002.

"Ignatius of Loyola, Saint." *Britannica.com.* [Online] Available http://www.britannica.com/eb/article?eu=50361&tocid=0&query=ignatius%20loyola, May 20, 2002.

Intelmann, Arthur. "Monteverdi, Claudio." *Unitel—"L'Orfeo."* [Online] Available http://www.unitel.classicalmusic.com/classica/112200.htm, May 20, 2002.

"James I." *Britannia.* [Online] Available http://www.britannia.com/history/monarchs/mon46.html, May 20, 2002.

"Jonson, Ben." *Luminarium Profile.* [Online] Available http://www.luminarium.org/sevenlit/jonson/, May 20, 2002.

"Jonson, Ben." *TheatreHistory.com.* [Online] Available http://www.theatrehistory.com/british/jonson001.html, May 20, 2002.

Kepler, Johannes—Kepler's Laws of Planetary Motion. [Online] Available http://zebu.uoregon.edu/textbook/planets.html, May 20, 2002.

"Kepler, Johannesi" *MSN Encarta.* [Online] Available http://encarta.msn.com/find/Concise.asp?ti=02F84000, May 20, 2002.

"Kepler, Johannes." *NASA Kepler Musem.* [Online] Available http://www.kepler.arc.nasa.gov/johannes.html, May 20, 2002.

Kirsch, J.P. "Savonarola, Girolamo." *Catholic Encyclopedia.* [Online] Available http://www.newadvent.org/cathen/13490a.htm, May 20, 2002.

Kurth, Godefroid. "Philip II (King of Spain)." *Catholic Encyclopedia.* [Online] Available http://www.newadvent.org/cathen/12002a.htm, May 20, 2002.

"Leonardo da Vinci." *Artcyclopedia.* [Online] Available http://artcyclopedia.com/artists/leonardo_da_vinci.html, May 20, 2002.

"Leonardo da Vinci." *MSN Encarta.* [Online] Available http://encarta.msn.com/find/Concise.asp?z=1&pg=2&ti=761561520, May 20, 2002.

"Leonardo da Vinci." *National Museum of Science and Technology.* [Online] Available http://www.museoscienza.org/english/leonardo/leonardo.html, May 20, 2002.

Letters of Philip II, King of Spain, 1592–1597. [Online] Available http://library.byu.edu/~rdh/phil2/, May 20, 2002.

Lipman, David E. "Abraham Senior." *Gates of Jewish Heritage.* [Online] Available http://www.jewishgates.org/personalities/2senior.stm, May 20, 2002.

Lipman, David E. "Isaac ben Judah Abrabanel." *Gates of Jewish Heritage.* [Online] Available http://www.jewishgates.org/personalities/2abrav.stm, May 20, 2002.

"Luther, Martin." *MSN Encarta.* [Online] Available http://encarta.msn.com/find/concise.asp?z=1&pg=2&ti=04875000, May 20, 2002.

"Machiavelli, Nicolo." *Internet Philosophy Encyclopedia.* [Online] Available http://www.utm.edu/research/iep/m/machiave.htm, May 20, 2002.

"Machiavelli, Nicolo." *MSN Encarta.* [Online] Available http://encarta.msn.com/find/Concise.asp?ti=05DD9000, May 20, 2002.

"Margaret of Navarre." *Infoplease.com.* [Online] Available http://www.infoplease.com/ce6/people/A0831778.html, May 20, 2002.

"Marlowe, Christopher." *Luminarium.* [Online] Available http://www.luminarium.org/renlit/marlowe.htm, May 20, 2002.

Martin Luther and the Reformation. [Online] Available http://mars.acnet.wnec.edu/~grempel/courses/wc2/lectures/luther.html, May 20, 2002.

The Medici Family. [Online] Available http://es.rice.edu/ES/humsoc/Galileo/People/medici.html, May 20, 2002.

"Medici, Lorenzo de', 1492–1519—Italian Merchant Prince." *Infoplease.com.* [Online] Available http://www.infoplease.com/ce6/people/A0832477.html, May 20, 2002.

"Michelangelo." *MSN Encarta.* [Online] Available http://encarta.msn.com/find/Concise.asp?z=1&pg=2&ti=761560125, May 20, 2002.

Michelangelo—Sistine Chapel Ceiling. [Online] Available http://www.science.wayne.edu/~mcogan/Humanities/Sistine/index.html, May 20, 2002.

"Michelangelo." *Web Gallery of Art.* [Online] Available http://www.kfki.hu/~arthp/html/m/michelan/, May 20, 2002.

Montaigne, Michel de. *Essays.* [Online] Available http://www.orst.edu/instruct/phl302/texts/montaigne/m-essays_contents.html, May 20, 2002.

Montaigne, Michel de. *On Cannibals.* [Online] Available http://www.wsu.edu:8080/~wldciv/world_civ_reader/world_civ_reader_2/montaigne.html, May 20, 2002.

"Monteverdi, Claudio." *Essentials of Music.* [Online] Available http://www.essentialsofmusic.com/composer/monteverdi.html, May 20, 2002.

Monteverdi, Claudio—Innovator and Madrigalist. [Online] Available http://web.azstarnet.com/public/packages/reelbook/153-4028.htm, May 20, 2002.

"Monteverdi, Claudio." *Milestones of the Millenium.* [Online] Available http://npr.org/programs/specials/milestones/990519.motm.monteverdi.html, May 20, 2002.

"More, Thomas." *The Lumninarium.* [Online] Available http://www.luminarium.org/renlit/tmore.htm, May 20, 2002.

"More, Thomas." *Redefining the Sacred.* [Online] Available http://www.folger.edu/institute/sacred/image8.html, May 20, 2002.

"Nogarola, Isotta." *Sunshine for Women.* [Online] Available http://www.pinn.net/~sunshine/march99/nogarla2.html, May 20, 2002.

Norton Topics Online: Van Schuppen, Engraving [portrait] of Margaret Cavendish. [Online] Available http://www.wwnorton.com/nael/NTO/18thC/worlds/imcavendish.htm, May 20, 2002.

"Nostradamus." *MSN Encarta.* [Online] Available http://encarta.msn.com/find/Concise.asp?z=1&pg=2&ti=761568156, May 20, 2002.

"Palladio, Andrea." *Palladian Buildings in Vicenza.* [Online] Available http://www.ashmm.com/cultura/palladio/copertuk.htm, May 20, 2002.

Palladio, Andrea—Palladio and Pattern Books. [Online] Available http://mondrian.princeton.edu/Campus/text_pattern.html, May 20, 2002.

"Paracelsus, Theophrastus." *Coelum Philosophorum.* [Online] Available http://www. levity.com/alchemy/coelum.html, May 20, 2002.

"Paracelsus, Theophrastus." *Infoplease.com.* [Online] Available http://www.infoplease.com/ce5/CE039437.html, May 20, 2002.

"Paul III." *Infoplease.com.* [Online] Available http://www.infoplease.com/ce6/people/A0837895.html, May 20, 2002.

Petrarch, Francesco—Petrarch's House. [Online] Available http://freia.dei.unipd.it/civici/civici/petra%24.html, May 20, 2002.

"Philip II." *Infoplease.com.* [Online] Available http://www.infoplease.com/ce5/CE040637.html, May 20, 2002.

Pioch, Nicolas. "Bruegel, Pieter the Elder." *WebMuseum.* [Online] Available http://sunsite.unc.edu/wm/paint/auth/bruegel/, May 20 2002.

Pioch, Nicolas. "Dürer, Albrecht." *Webmuseum.* [Online] Available http://metalab.unc.edu/wm/paint/auth/durer/, May 20, 2002.

Pioch, Nicolas. "Leonardo da Vinci." *WebMuseum.* [Online] Available http://mexplaza.udg.mx/wm/paint/auth/vinci/, May 20, 2002.

Pioch, Nicolas. "Michelangelo Merisi da Caravaggio." *Webmuseum.* [Online] Available http://sunsite.unc.edu/wm/paint/auth/caravaggio, May 20, 2002.

Plant, David. *Kepler, Johannes—Kepler and the Music of the Spheres.* [Online] Available http://www.astrology-world.com/kepler.html, May 20, 2002.

Pollen, J. H. "Ignatius Loyola, St." *Catholic Encyclopedia.* [Online] Available http://www.newadvent.org/cathen/07639c.htm, May 20, 2002.

Portrait of Girolamo Savonarola by Bartolomeo, Fra. [Online] Available http://www.kfki.hu/~arthp/html/b/bartolom/fra/savonaro.html, May 20, 2002.

Protestant Reformation. [Online] Available http://www.mun.ca/rels/hrollmann/reform/reform.html, May 20, 2002.

"Rabelais, François." *Infoplease.com.* [Online] Available http://www.infoplease.com/ce6/people/A0840877.html, May 20, 2002.

"Savonarola, Girolamo." *MSN Encarta.* [Online] Available http://en-carta.msn.com/index/conciseindex/4B/04BA3000.htm?z=1&pg=2&br=1, May 20, 2002.

The Schlietheim Confession. [Online] Available http://www.anabaptists.org/history/schleith.html, May 20, 2002.

Senfelder, Leopold. "Vesalius, Andreas." *Catholic Encyclopedia.* [Online] Available http://www.knight.org/advent/cathen/15378c.htm, May 20, 2002.

"Shakespeare, William." *Internet Editions.* [Online] Available http://web.uvic.ca/shakespeare/Annex, May 20, 2002.

"Shakespeare, William." *Shakespearean Homework Helper.* [Online] Available http://hometown.aol.com/liadona2/shakespeare.html, May 20, 2002.

"Shakespeare, William." *MSN Encarta.* [Online] Available http://encarta.msn.com/find/Concise.asp?z=1&pg=2&ti=761562101, May 20, 2002.

The Six Wives of Henry VIII. [Online] Available http://www.larmouth.demon.co.uk/sarah-jayne/wives/wives.html, May 20, 2002.

The Spiritual Exercises of St. Ignatius of Loyola. [Online] Available http://www.ccel.org/i/ignatius/exercises/exercises.html, May 20, 2002.

Suleyman the Magnificent. [Online] Available http://www.wsu.edu:8001/~dee/OTTOMAN/SULEYMAN.HTM, May 20, 2002.

Teresa de Ávila, *Way of Perfection.* [Online] Available http://www.ccel.org/t/teresa/way/main.html, May 20, 2002.

"Vesalius, Andreas." *Infoplease.com.* [Online] Available http://

www.infoplease.com/ce5/CE 054107.html, May 20, 2002.

Women and European Witch Hunts. [Online] Available http://www.kings.edu/womens_history/witch.html, May 20, 2002.

Zimmerman, Benedict. "Teresa of Jesus (Teresa de Ávila)." *Catholic Encyclopedia.* [Online] Available http://www.newadvent.org/cathen/14515b.htm, May 20, 2002.

"Zwingli, Ulrich." *Zwingli and Luther.* [Online] Available http://www.bible.org/docs/history/schaff/vol7/schaf176.htm, May 20, 2002.

Sound Recordings

Don Quixote. St. Paul, Minn.: HighBridge,1997.

Man of La Mancha. New York: Sony Classical, 1996.

Starry Messenger. Prince Frederick, Md.: Recorded Books, 1997.

Video Recordings and DVDs

The Agony and the Ecstasy. Livonia, Mich.: CBS/Fox Video, 1988. (Videorecording)

Artemisia. Burbank, Calif.: Miramax Home Entertainment, 2001. (DVD)

Don Quixote. Los Angeles: TNT Original: Hallmark Entertainment Production, 2000. (Video recording)

Galileo: On the Shoulders of Giants. Toronto: Devine Entertainment, 1997. (Video recording)

A Man for All Seasons. Burbank, Calif.: RCA/Columbia Pictures Home Video, 1985. (Videorecording)

Man of La Mancha. Farmington Hills, Mich.: CBS/FOX Video, 1984. (Video recording)

Martin Luther. Worcester, Pa.: Vision Video, 1990. (Video recording)

Masterpieces of Italian Art, Volume: Da Vinci, Michelangelo, Raphael and Titian. New York: VPI-AC Video Inc., 1990. (Video recording)

The Private Life of Henry VIII. Los Angeles: Embassy Home Entertainment, 1986. (Video recording)

The Radicals [Anabaptists]. Worcester, Pa.: Gateway Films-Vision Video, 1989. (Video recording)

Suleyman the Magnificent. New York: National Gallery of Art and Metropolitan Museum of Art; Home Vision, 1987. (Video recording)

Index

Italic type indicates volume
numbers. Illustrations are
marked by (ill.)

"Epithalamion" *2:* 398

Erasmus, Desiderius *1:* 8, 101, 174, 228–29, 249; *2:* 376–77, 377 (ill.), 379–80, 520, 524, 547

Erik V *1:* 178

Erik XIV *1:* 181

Escobedo, Juan de *1:* 131

Esmā'īl I *1:* 41

Essais 2: 389

Este, Alfonso I d' *1:* 85

Este, Beatrice d' *1:* 67, 78

Este, Isabella d' *1:* 67, 77, 79, 79 (ill.); *2:* 319, 489–90, 537, 555

Eugenius IV, Pope *1:* 88

Europe, Idea of *1:* 43

Evangelical Union *1:* 260–61

Exsurge Domine 1: 204

Eyck, Hubert van *1:* 8

Eyck, Jan van *1:* 8; *2:* 404

F

The Faerie Queene 2: 396, 561

Fairs *2:* 610–11

Farel, Guillaume *1:* 236

Farnese, Alessandro *1:* 131, 177, 251

Favre, Pierre *1:* 281

Fedele, Cassandra *2:* 322, 527

Federal Ordinance *1:* 212–13

Fels, Colona *1:* 167, 261

Felton, Geoffrey *1:* 133

Feltre, Bernardino da *2:* 497

Feltre, Vittorino da *1:* 77; *2:* 517, 521, 527

Feminists *2:* 558–59, 561

Ferdinand V, King of Spain *1:* 75

Ferdinand I, Holy Roman Emperor *1:* 153–54, 167–68, 210–19

Ferdinand I, King of Naples *1:* 88

Ferdinand I, King of Spain *1:* 66–67

Ferdinand II, Holy Roman Emperor *1:* 116, 125, 129, 151, 156, 260, 264, 266

Ferdinand II, King of Aragon *1:* 96–97, 119–20, 122, 124–25, 252; *2:* 403, 479, 496, 553

Ferdinand II, King of Spain *1:* 89

Ferdinand III, Holy Roman Emperor *1:* 266

Fernández de Córdoba, Gonzalo *1:* 120–21

Ferrante I *1:* 59

Ferro, Scipione del *2:* 445

Festivals *2:* 603–05, 607

Feudalism *1:* 12–13, 15–16, 46, 89, 92, 143

Feudalism, map of *1:* 11 (ill.)

Ficino, Marsilio, Philosopher *1:* 57

Field of the Cloth of Gold *2:* 486

Fifth Lateran Council *1:* 272

Fiorentino, Rosso *2:* 417

First Blast of the Trumpet 2: 560

First Northern War *1:* 181

Florence *1:* 49, 53–54, 56, 58, 60, 65, 89

Florensz, Adrian *1:* 125–26

Fludd, Robert *2:* 469

Fontainebleau *2:* 417

Fontana, Lavinia *2:* 565

Fonte, Moderata *2:* 559, 562

Foscari, Fracesco *1:* 74

Foscarini, Ludovico *2:* 321

Four Apostles 2: 408

Four Articles of Prague *1:* 30, 167

Four Books on Architecture 2: 359

The Four Books on Proportion 2: 408

Four humors *2:* 448–49

Fourth Lateran Council *1:* 22

Francesca, Piero della *2:* 446

Franciscans *1:* 24

Francis of Sales *1:* 286–87

Francis I, King of France *1:* 50–51, 53, 68, 75, 77, 84, 97–98, 97 (ill.), 100–01, 106–07, 126–27, 152–53, 184, 229; *2:* 373, 417, 479, 486–87, 489, 520

Francis I, King of Loraine *1:* 18

Francis II, Holy Roman Emperor *1:* 144

Francis II, King of France *1:* 243, 246, 255

François of Lorraine *1:* 243, 245

Franco, Veronica *2:* 326, 562

Frederick V, Elector *1:* 261

Frederick V, Holy Roman Emperor *1:* 168

Frederick V, King of Bohemia *1:* 116

Frederick I, King of Denmark *1:* 178, 238

M

P

Pacioli, Luca *2:* 444
Padilla, Juan de *1:* 126
Painting, Italian *2:* 330, 331 (ill.),
      332, 334–46, 348
Palestrina, Giovanni Pierluigi da
      1: 284; *2:* 364–66, 537
Palladio, Andrea *1:* 69, 82, 117; *2:*
      358–59, 420
Papal States *1:* 21, 27, 192
Paracelsus *2:* 452–53
Paré, Ambroise *2:* 450
Parr, Katherine *1:* 109; *2:* 554
Pascal, Blaise *2:* 446
Passi, Giuseppe *2:* 559
Paul IV, Pope *1:* 274; *2:* 500
Paul II, Pope *1:* 58
Paul III and His Grandsons 2: 341
Paul III, Pope *1:* 128, 273, 273
      (ill.), 294
Peace of Augsburg *1:* 147, 155,
      226
Peace of Barcelona *1:* 86
Peace of Lodi *1:* 66, 74
Peace of Oliva *1:* 182
Peace of Saint Germain *1:* 245
Peace of the Pyrenees *1:* 103
Peace of Westphalia *1:* 20, 103,
      144, 173, 177, 181, 251,
      266–67
Peasant Dance 2: 411
Peasant Wedding 2: 411
Pepin the Short *1:* 81
Pépin III *1:* 13
Perotti, Niccolò *2:* 519
Pesaro Madonna 2: 341
Peter of Aragon *1:* 96
Peter III, King of Aragon *1:* 48, 87
Petrarch *1:* 8–9, 45, 80; *2:* 306–07,
      324, 488, 516
Petri, Laurentius *1:* 238, 241–42
Petri, Olaus *1:* 238, 241–42
Pfefferkorn, Johannes *2:* 378
Phaedrus 2: 431
Philip Augustus, King of France *1:*
      93
Philip of Hesse *1:* 209, 218, 221,
      223–24
Philip I, King of Austria *1:* 124
Philip IV, King of France *1:* 25–26,
      93, 191–92
Philip IV, King of Spain *1:* 134,
      266

Philip II, King of Spain *1:* 111–13,
      123, 129–32, 153, 174–77,
      244, 249, 251, 254, 257–58,
      297; *2:* 412
Philip VI, King of France *1:* 93
Philip III, Duke of Burgundy *1:*
      104
Philip III, King of Spain *1:* 116,
      133; *2:* 496
Piarists *1:* 281, 283
Pico della Mirandola, Giovanni *2:*
      313–14, 380
Pietà (Michelangelo) *2:* 351, 353
      (ill.)
Pirkheimer, Caritas *2:* 527
Pisan, Christine de *2:* 318, 320,
      320 (ill.)
Pisanello, Antonio *1:* 77
Pisano, Nicola *2:* 351, 357
Pius V, Pope *1:* 294; *2:* 500
Pius IV, Pope *1:* 274
Pius II, Pope *1:* 43 (ill.), 44, 82
Pizzaro, Francisco *1:* 127
Plantagenets *1:* 43, 104
Plato *2:* 428
Pliny the Elder *2:* 536
Plutarch *1:* 9
Poggio Bracciolini *2:* 516
Pole, Reginald *1:* 111, 254
Poliziano, Angelo, Philologist *1:*
      57
Polo, Marco *1:* 134
Porta, Giacomo della *1:* 82; *2:* 357
Portrait of a Nun 2: 346
Poverty *2:* 504–08
Pradanos, Juan de *1:* 290
Praise of Folly 2: 376
Prez, Josquin de *2:* 423
Primaticcio, Francesco *2:* 415, 417
Primavera 1: 7
The Prince 1: 8; *2:* 315
Printing press *1:* 6, 7 (ill.)
Procession to Calvary 2: 410
Prodigal Son 2: 406
Professional training *2:* 532,
      534–35, 534 (ill.)
Professions *2:* 495 (ill.)
Protestant Reformation (See: Re-
      formation, Protestant)
Ptolemy *2:* 429–30, 457
Punishment *2:* 512 (ill.)
Puritans *1:* 114, 117, 258

Q

Queen's Chapel *2:* 421
Querelle des femmes 2: 559-561
Quintilian *2:* 516, 526

R

Rabelais, François *1:* 10; *2:* 386–87
Rákóczi, George I *1:* 186
Ramusio, Giovanni Battista *2:* 458
Ramus, Petrus *2:* 432
Rape of Europa 2: 341
Rape of the Sabines 2: 353
Raphael *1:* 6, 54, 82, 101; *2:* 338–40, 454
Ravaillac, François *1:* 249
Recorde, Robert *2:* 445
Reformation, Catholic *1:* 268, 270–73, 275–76, 278–80, 282–90, 292–94, 296–97, 299
Reformation, Protestant *1:* 31, 84, 166, 190–92, 194–96, 198–99, 201–02, 204, 206–11, 213–15, 217–18, 220, 222–24
Reformed Carmelite Order *1:* 291
Reformed Discalced Carmelite Convent *1:* 289, 291; *2:* 549
Reinhart, Anna *1:* 230
Requesens, Luis de *1:* 130
Resurrection of Lazarus 2: 345
Reuchlin, Johann *2:* 378–79
Revolt of the Netherlands *1:* 112, 130, 257
Rheticus, Georg Joachim *2:* 435
Riario, Gerolamo *1:* 66
Richard III, King of England *1:* 105
Richelieu, Cardinal *1:* 103, 262, 266
Riemenschneider, Tilman *2:* 415
Robert Guiscard *1:* 72
Robert the Wise *1:* 87
Roches, Catherine des *2:* 558
Roches, Madeleine des *2:* 558
Roman Catholic Church *1:* 11, 20–27, 29, 31, 165–66, 192–95
Romano, Giulio *1:* 77
Roman ruins *1:* 3 (ill.)
Rosslin, Eucharius *2:* 584

Rudolff, Cristoph *2:* 445
Rudolf I, Holy Roman Emperor *1:* 151
Rudolf I, King of Germany *1:* 32
Rudolf II, Holy Roman Emperor *1:* 154–55, 167, 249, 260; *2:* 438
Rupert, King of Germany *1:* 63
Ruppa, Wenceslaus *1:* 167, 261
Rural Life *2:* 482, 492, 494–95
Rye, Marguerite van *2:* 565

S

Sacchi, Bartolomneo *2:* 597
Safavid Empire *1:* 41
Saint Bartholomew's Day *1:* 102
Saint Bartholomew's Day Massacre *1:* 148, 246, 246 (ill.)
Saint Peter's Basilica *2:* 357, 358 (ill.)
Salons *2:* 319, 555–57
Salutati, Coluccio *2:* 308–09
Sangallo, Antonio da *2:* 357
Sangallo, Giuliano da *1:* 57
Sansovino, Jacopo *1:* 69; *2:* 353, 359
Santorio, Santorio *2:* 466
Sarto, Andrea del *1:* 101
Savonarola, Girolama *1:* 49, 60, 53, 270–72
Scappi, Bartolomeo *2:* 597
Scheppers, Marguerite *2:* 565
Schmalkaldic League *1:* 102, 128, 153–54, 221, 224
Schmalkaldic War *1:* 102; *2:* 341
Scholasticism *1:* 33
The School of Athens 2: 338
Schurman, Anna Maria van *2:* 527, 561
Scientific Instruments *2:* 460, 462–64
Scudéry, Madeleine de *2:* 557–58
Sculpture, Italian *2:* 349–52
Second Helvetic Confession *1:* 235
Sedzimir, Michael *2:* 469
Seignorialism *1:* 12
Selim I *1:* 41
Senior, Abraham *1:* 121
Serlio, Sebastiano *2:* 418
Servetus, Michael *1:* 237; *2:* 457